The United Nations High Commissioner for Human Rights

Nottingham Studies on Human Rights

Published under the auspices of the Human Rights Law Centre of the University of Nottingham

Edited by

Michael O'Flaherty
David Harris

VOLUME 3

The titles published in this series are listed at brill.com/nshr

The United Nations High Commissioner for Human Rights

Conscience for the World

Edited by

Felice D. Gaer
Christen L. Broecker

MARTINUS NIJHOFF PUBLISHERS

LEIDEN · BOSTON
2014

Library of Congress Cataloging-in-Publication Data

The United Nations High Commissioner for Human Rights : conscience for the world / edited by Felice D. Gaer, Christen L. Broecker.
pages cm. -- (Nottingham studies on human rights ; v. 2)
"This endeavor began with a conference entitled: The UN High Commissioner for Human Rights: -- Conscience for the World, which was convened on February 7–8, 2012."--Acknowledgments.
Includes bibliographical references and index.
ISBN 978-90-04-25424-4 (hardback : alk. paper) -- ISBN 978-90-04-25425-1 (e-book) 1. United Nations. Office of the High Commissioner for Human Rights--Congresses. 2. Human rights advocacy--Congresses. 3. Human rights monitoring--Congresses. 4. International agencies--Congresses. I. Gaer, Felice D., editor of compilation. II. Broecker, Christen, editor of compilation. III. Jacob Blaustein Institute for the Advancement of Human Rights.
K3241.U549 2013
341.4'8--dc23

2013028311

This publication has been typeset in the multilingual "Brill" typeface. With over 5,100 characters covering Latin, IPA, Greek, and Cyrillic, this typeface is especially suitable for use in the humanities. For more information, please see www.brill.com/brill-typeface.

ISSN 2211-7342
ISBN 978-90-04-25424-4 (hardback)
ISBN 978-90-04-25425-1 (e-book)

CONTENTS

PART TWO

PROMOTING UNIVERSALITY OF RIGHTS: GLOBAL LEADERSHIP IN AN ERA OF GROWING PARTICULARISM AND RELATIVISM

PART THREE

PREVENTING HUMAN RIGHTS VIOLATIONS AND EFFECTIVE RESPONSE

PART FOUR

INFLUENCING OTHER BODIES TO ACT

PART FIVE

HARD CASES: CAN THE HIGH COMMISSIONER MAKE A DIFFERENCE?

PREFACE

Individuals around the world have long sought to find a way to bridge the gap between the lofty guarantees in the Universal Declaration of Human Rights and reality. Such hopes have spurred advocates to propose the creation of numerous human rights bodies, envoys, courts, and commissions, as well as a United Nations High Commissioner for Human Rights.

While those who advocated the creation of this latter institution – the post of UN High Commissioner for Human Rights – frequently describe this individual's role as that of 'conscience for the world,' in truth, what they sought was far more than a 'global conscience.' Rather, they shared a vision of a leader who could act to protect individuals from abuse, promote dignity, equality and freedom for all, and in so doing, change the world.

To some, this vision sounded like a fantasy: the idea that a single individual could act and bring about seemingly miraculous change. But to many advocates in the late twentieth century, the proposal to create a High Commissioner for Human Rights was a practical plan to breathe life into protecting oft-affirmed but inconsistently-observed universal standards of human rights. To the community of jurists and activists who had suffered through two world wars, the Holocaust, and the Cold War, it seemed time for concrete results. They had participated in the extensive verbal battles involved in the adoption of aspirational human rights instruments like the Universal Declaration and were ready to take action that would lead to the implementation, rather than the mere articulation, of human rights.

For more than 40 years, the Jacob Blaustein Institute for the Advancement of Human Rights (JBI), of which I have served as Chair since 2007, has been at the vanguard of efforts to strengthen human rights protection through the creation and strengthening of effective international institutions. Since JBI's inception, one of its primary concerns has been establishing and advancing successful human rights leadership by a High Commissioner for Human Rights. In 1963, in his Dag Hammarskjold Memorial Lecture at Columbia University, Jacob Blaustein, an industrialist and a former president of the American Jewish Committee (AJC), in whose memory JBI was established, publicly called on the UN to appoint a High

Commissioner for Human Rights. Blaustein, who had previously served as one of the officially appointed non-governmental Consultants to the American delegation at the 1945 founding conference of the United Nations in San Francisco, was convinced of the need for a high-level UN official who could investigate alleged violations of human rights, assist in the development of national human rights institutions, and advise the political organs of the United Nations on human rights.

JBI was particularly instrumental in coalescing NGO advocacy around the creation of the High Commissioner post in the months prior to and following the 1993 World Conference on Human Rights in Vienna, which recommended that the UN General Assembly consider the establishment of the High Commissioner post as a matter of priority. Following the UN General Assembly's December 1993 decision to establish the position of UN High Commissioner for Human Rights, JBI convened seminars with the first two High Commissioners that explored current challenges and charted a future course of action. Thereafter, JBI continued to assess needs and achievements and publish its own analyses aimed at fulfilling the promise of the High Commissioner as 'conscience for the world.'

In February 2012, JBI marked its fortieth anniversary by convening a two-day expert conference in collaboration with the Roosevelt House Public Policy Institute at Hunter College. Participants included the current High Commissioner, Ms. Navi Pillay, and the former Acting High Commissioner for Human Rights, Mr. Bertrand Ramcharan, and renowned experts, human rights defenders, and representatives of human rights organizations. Meeting at the former home of U.S. President Franklin Roosevelt and his wife Eleanor, who served as the first chair of the UN's Commission on Human Rights, the expert participants examined the accomplishments of the several High Commissioners to date. They recommended strategies to enhance the High Commissioner's ability to prevent human rights violations in the future.

This volume, a collection of essays produced by the participants in that JBI conference, is a signal achievement reflecting JBI's longstanding concern with the High Commissioner post. It identifies key challenges that the High Commissioners have faced, including defending the universality of human rights in the face of arguments in favor of 'cultural relativism,' and seeking to improve human rights conditions in some of the most intractable violator states. It examines their performance and recommends ways in which they should modify their approaches in the future.

Authors examine the toolkit used by the High Commissioner in a variety of specific countries and cases—and the results. The accounts are at times favorable, at times quite critical, but uniformly constructive. They point to the need for the High Commissioner, as the leading voice for human rights in the UN system, to defend the content of human rights norms from erosion as well as inflation; to ensure that serious allegations of abuse are investigated and that the UN's protective capacity is deployed to assist victims; and to challenge the governments of the world to acknowledge and fulfill their human rights responsibilities. In all these areas, the High Commissioner must serve as a leader, acting consistently, making strategic choices as to the issues on which to engage vigorously, and ensuring that the UN and its human rights mechanisms remain accountable both to the governments of the world and to individual rights-holders.

By necessity, the institutional, political, and policy issues addressed in this volume are complex and context-dependent. There are no easy answers to the challenge of effective human rights protection. Yet each chapter in this volume undertakes the necessary work of grappling with an issue or set of issues that has challenged past High Commissioners and will continue to challenge those to hold the post in the future.

It is my hope that on the occasion of the 20th anniversary of the establishment of the High Commissioner post, this volume will provoke and facilitate renewed deliberations among policymakers, human rights advocates, academics, and the public at large about how in the coming years, the individuals to serve as High Commissioner can best undertake their vital responsibility to lead the UN in advancing respect for and protection of human rights.

Finally, the volume also reflects the unique role that the Jacob Blaustein Institute has played in strengthening international human rights institutions. Much of this has occurred under the direction of the editors of this volume – JBI's Director Felice Gaer, whose strategic vision and compelling engagement with international human rights bodies has significantly enhanced both human rights protections for countless individuals and the Institute's role during the past twenty years, and JBI's Associate Director Christen Broecker, whose fine-tuned legal professionalism and brilliance have brought exemplary research and in-depth analysis of international human rights issues to this volume and many other JBI projects. The Institute salutes them for this book which offers so much insight into the UN's distinctive role – past and present – in promoting and protecting human rights globally. I hope each reader will reflect deeply, as I am doing, about how much more we all still have to do to bring the promises of human rights for all men and women into reality.

E. Robert Goodkind
Chair
Jacob Blaustein Institute for the Advancement of Human Rights

EDITORIAL ACKNOWLEDGEMENTS

Published to coincide with the 20th anniversary of the creation of the post of UN High Commissioner for Human Rights, this volume highlights the United Nations institutions and leaders that have given life and direction to human rights norms and concepts over the past seven decades. Its publication would not have been possible without the assistance of many people, whom we acknowledge here.

This endeavor began with a conference, entitled *The UN High Commissioner for Human Rights: Conscience for the World*, which was convened on February 7–8, 2012. Enthusiasm for the idea of convening a conference that would examine the roles and accomplishments of the High Commissioners for Human Rights emerged in conversations with editor Felice Gaer during her term as Regents Professor at UCLA in 2010. UCLA Professors Kal Raustiala of the Burkle Center for International Relations, David Kaye, formerly head of the School of Law's International Human Rights Program, and Ellen DuBois, of the Department of History, each offered encouragement and invaluable advice during this conceptual period.

We are grateful to Jonathan Fanton, Interim Director of Roosevelt House Public Policy Institute at Hunter College, who delivered opening remarks at the conference and to his colleagues Joanne Mariner, Fay Rosenfeld, and Jane Brody, for collaborating on the conference and for their enthusiasm during the planning process. The conference facilitated a very insightful discussion on the High Commissioner for Human Rights, and set a very high bar for future such endeavors.

In addition to the authors of the essays in this volume, several individuals made valuable contributions at the conference that contributed substantially to the expert discussion and have informed the content of the book: Roger Clark, Ellen DuBois, Lori Damrosch, Ryan Goodman, Peggy Hicks, Michael Hirschhorn, Zdislaw Kedzia, Joanne Mariner, Vitit Muntarbhorn, Gabor Rona, and Ambassador Richard Williamson. We also appreciated the assistance of Shahrzad Tadjbakhsh, Chief of Staff of the Office of the High Commissioner for Human Rights (OHCHR) and Jane Connors, Chief of the Special Procedures Branch of OHCHR, and the encouragement of Professor Bert Lockwood at the University of Cincinnati College of Law.

AJC's Jacob Blaustein Institute for the Advancement of Human Rights (JBI) spurred us on both substantively and by allocating funding for the conference and essays in this volume. We wish to thank the members of the JBI Administrative Council who supported our suggestion to consolidate thinking about the past and future of the High Commissioner, a concept directly associated with Jacob Blaustein. We particularly appreciate the unflagging encouragement of E. Robert Goodkind, Chair of the Administrative Council, and the guidance provided by the other members of the Administrative Council's Steering Committee: Michael Hirschhorn, Robert S. Rifkind, and David F. Squire. We want to thank past and current Council members Rene-Pierre Azria, Marion Bergman, Jerry H. Biederman, Susan Morton Blaustein, Thomas Buergenthal, Roberta Cohen, Irwin Cotler, Lori F. Damrosch, Edith B. Everett, Lois Frank, David A. Harris, Barbara Blaustein Hirschhorn, Charlotte G. Holstein, Suzanne Denbo Jaffe, Harris L. Kempner, Jr., Edward C. Luck, Jesse Margolin, Louis Perlmutter, Arthur E. Roswell, Elizabeth Blaustein Roswell, Bruce Rubin, Stephen M. Schwebel, Jane Silverman, and Daniel Terris. JBI, founded 42 years ago under the aegis of the American Jewish Committee, has been a steadfast supporter of strengthening international human rights norms and institutions, including the creation and subsequent achievements of a High Commissioner for Human Rights.

This volume would not have been possible without the extensive and meticulous logistical and administrative assistance provided by Marra Guttenplan, JBI Advocacy/Editorial Officer, and Jennifer Izelle, former JBI Administrative Assistant, who worked effectively under many constraints to ensure the conference's success. Many thanks also to Linda Krieg and Sharon Schwartz at AJC for designing and producing the conference materials.

We are grateful to CucHuong Do, JBI's current Administrative Assistant, who provided skilled and timely aid in preparing this manuscript for publication. Aretha Chakraborti, Mariel Fernandez, Jason Schnier, and Ami Shah provided valuable assistance in the form of citation research and formatting.

We want to express our appreciation to Professors David Harris and Michael O'Flaherty, editors of the Nottingham Series on Human Rights, for accepting the volume into the series. Their enthusiasm and professionalism were particularly encouraging as we entered the latter stages of the writing and publication process. Also, our thanks to Bea Timmer, Lindy Melman, and Tessel Jonquière at Martinus Nijhoff Publishers/Brill for their assistance in bringing the volume to print.

Finally, we offer a special word of thanks to High Commissioner for Human Rights Navi Pillay for her participation in the conference and her contribution to the volume, which includes an overview of her work and that of her Office and the record of a question-and-answer session she held with conference participants. Similarly, Dr. Bertrand Ramcharan, former Acting High Commissioner and before that Deputy High Commissioner, offered guidance during the planning of the conference, and we are grateful to him for his participation and remarks at the event itself.

That said, the conclusions and recommendations in this volume are those of the authors, and the authors alone. We hope that everyone concerned will examine them and strive to implement them in ways that will improve human rights protection worldwide.

Felice D. Gaer
Director
Jacob Blaustein Institute for the
Advancement of Human Rights

Christen L. Broecker
Associate Director
Jacob Blaustein Institute for the
Advancement of Human Rights

LIST OF ABBREVIATIONS

AIHRC	Afghanistan Independent Human Rights Commission
ASEAN	Association of Southeast Asian Nations
AU	African Union
CCA-UNDAF	Common Country Assessment and UN Development Assistance Framework
CEDAW	Committee on the Elimination of Discrimination against Women
CoI	Commission of Inquiry
DPA	Department of Political Affairs
DPKO	Department for Peacekeeping Operations
DPRK	Democratic People's Republic of Korea
DRC	Democratic Republic of the Congo
ECOSOC	Economic and Social Council
ECOWAS	Economic Community of West African States
ESCRs	Economic, Social, and Cultural Rights
EU	European Union
GA	General Assembly
HRC	Human Rights Committee or Human Rights Council
ICC	International Coordinating Committee of National Institutions for the Promotion and Protection of Human Rights or International Criminal Court
ICCPR	International Covenant on Civil and Political Rights
ICESCR	International Covenant on Economic and Social Rights
ICRC	International Committee of the Red Cross
ICTR	International Criminal Tribunal for Rwanda
ICTY	International Criminal Tribunal for the Former Yugoslavia
IDPs	Internally Displaced Persons
ILO	International Labour Organization
LGBT	Lesbian, Gay, Bisexual, and Transgender
MDGs	Millennium Development Goals
NATO	North Atlantic Treaty Organization
NGO	Non-Governmental Organization
NHRI	National Human Rights Institution
OAS	Organization of American States
OHCHR	Office of the High Commissioner for Human Rights

OIC	Organization of Islamic Cooperation
OPCAT	Optional Protocol to the Convention against Torture
OSCE	Organization for Security and Co-operation in Europe
R2P	Responsibility to Protect
SADC	Southern African Development Community
SOGI	Sexual Orientation and Gender Identity
SRSG	Special Representative of the Secretary-General
UN	United Nations
UNCT	United Nations Country Team
UNDG	United Nations Development Group
UNDP	United Nations Development Programme
UNESCO	United Nations Educational, Scientific and Cultural Organization
UNHCR	Office of the United Nations High Commissioner for Refugees
UNICEF	United Nations Children's Fund
UPR	Universal Periodic Review

LIST OF CONTRIBUTORS

Sunila Abeysekera, recipient of the 1998 UN Human Rights Prize, is the Director of INFORM Human Rights Documentation Centre, Sri Lanka and a member of the Executive Committee of the Women Human Rights Defenders International Coalition.

Christen L. Broecker is Associate Director at the Jacob Blaustein Institute for the Advancement of Human Rights. She was previously the NYU School of Law Fellow at Human Rights Watch responsible for researching and reporting on human rights abuses in Indonesia.

Roberta Cohen is a Non-Resident Senior Fellow at the Brookings Institution, specializing in humanitarian and human rights issues, and Co-Chair of the Committee for Human Rights in North Korea. She has served on United States delegations to the Human Rights Commission and General Assembly and has authored numerous articles and several books on human rights and humanitarian questions. She is a member of the Committee on Conscience at the United States Holocaust Memorial Museum and the JBI Administrative Council.

Catherine A. Fitzpatrick is a writer, human rights advocate, and Russian translator. She has worked for news agencies and non-profits in the Eurasian field, including Radio Free Europe/Radio Liberty, and Eurasianet.org and is currently at interpretermag.org. She also served as the Executive Director of the International League for Human Rights.

Felice D. Gaer is Director of the Jacob Blaustein Institute for the Advancement of Human Rights (JBI) and Vice Chair of the UN Committee against Torture. She served five terms beginning in 2001 on the bipartisan federal U.S. Commission on International Religious Freedom, including three terms as Chair. Gaer was Regents Professor at UCLA in 2010 and is the author of more than 40 articles on international human rights.

Jared Genser is Managing Director of Perseus Strategies, LLC and Founder of Freedom Now, a non-governmental organization that works to free prisoners of conscience. Among his clients have been former Czech President Václav Havel and Nobel Peace Laureate Aung San Suu Kyi.

Maria Goldman is a paralegal at the Centre de la Protection Internationale, a Russian legal NGO that litigates cases at the European Court for Human Rights on behalf of victims of human rights violations from the countries of the Commonwealth of Independent States.

Michael Ignatieff is a Professor at the Harvard Kennedy School and the Munk School of Global Affairs at the University of Toronto. He was previously head of the Carr Center for Human Rights at Harvard University. A former leader of the Liberal Party of Canada, he also holds eleven honorary degrees and is author of 14 books including *American Exceptionalism* and *The Lesser Evil*, both by Princeton University Press.

David Kaye is an Assistant Clinical Professor of Law at the University of California at Irvine School of Law and was previously Executive Director of the International Human Rights Program at UCLA School of Law. From 1999 to 2002 he was the US State Department's principal staff attorney on humanitarian law. He also served as a legal adviser to the American Embassy in The Hague, where he worked with the international criminal tribunals for the Former Yugoslavia and Rwanda.

Stephanie T. Kleine-Ahlbrandt is the Director of the Asia-Pacific Program at the US Institute of Peace. Previously she was North East Asia Project Director and China Adviser of the International Crisis Group and an International Affairs Fellow at the Council on Foreign Relations. Prior to that she managed the China program at the UN Office of the High Commissioner for Human Rights for five years.

Harold Hongju Koh was the Legal Adviser to the US Department of State from 2009 to 2013. He is presently Sterling Professor of International Law at Yale Law School and previously served as Assistant Secretary of State for Democracy, Human Rights and Labor at the US Department of State from 1998 to 2001.

Karinna Moskalenko is the founder of the Centre de la Protection Internationale, which has filed hundreds of cases raising Russian human rights issues before the European Court for Human Rights. She is a Commissioner of the International Commission of Jurists and in 2000 was presented Russia's highest award in jurisprudence, Femida.

Suzanne Nossel was Deputy Assistant Secretary of State for International Organizations in the Obama Administration. Previously she was deputy to the Ambassador for UN Management and Reform at the US Mission to the UN.

Michael O'Flaherty is Chief Commissioner of the Northern Ireland Human Rights Commission and Professor of Human Rights Law and Co-director of the Irish Centre for Human Rights, NUI Galway. He previously held the Chair in Applied Human Rights and was Co-Chair of the Human Rights Law Centre at the University of Nottingham. He was a member of the UN Human Rights Committee from 2004 to 2012 and established the UN human rights field missions in Bosnia and Herzegovina (1994) and Sierra Leone (1998).

William G. O'Neill is Director of the Conflict Prevention and Peace Forum of the Social Science Research Council. He was Senior Advisor on Human Rights in the UN Mission in Kosovo; Chief of the UN Human Rights Field Operation in Rwanda; led the Legal Department of the UN/OAS Mission in Haiti; investigated mass killings in Afghanistan for the High Commissioner for Human Rights; and worked on judicial, police, and prison reform in Burundi, Liberia, Sierra Leone, South Sudan, Timor Leste, Nepal, and Bosnia-Herzegovina.

Navi Pillay was appointed High Commissioner for Human Rights by UN Secretary-General Ban Ki-moon in 2008. Previously, she was a judge on the International Criminal Court, a judge and President of the International Criminal Tribunal for Rwanda and a judge on the High Court of South Africa.

Bertrand G. Ramcharan has been Professor at the Geneva Graduate Institute of International Studies and Chancellor of the University of Guyana. He served as Deputy UN High Commissioner for Human Rights from 1998 to 2003 and Acting High Commissioner from 2003 to 2004. He is a Commissioner of the International Commission of Jurists.

Victor Rodriguez-Rescia is a member of the UN Human Rights Committee and former President of the UN Subcommittee on Prevention of Torture. He is a Principal Consultant of the Inter-American Institute of Human Rights for the Administration of Justice and Human Rights Program and is the former Deputy Secretary of the Inter-American Court of Human Rights.

Sima Samar was the inaugural chair of the Afghanistan Independent Human Rights Commission. Earlier, she was elected as vice chair of the Emergency Loya Jirga and served as deputy chair and Minister of Women's Affairs in the post-Taliban Interim Administration of Afghanistan.

Tseliso Thipanyane is a South African human rights lawyer and former Chief Executive Officer of the South African Human Rights Commission. He is currently an Adjunct Lecturer in Law at Columbia University Law School.

INTRODUCTION

Felice D. Gaer and Christen L. Broecker

The United Nations General Assembly created the post of UN High Commissioner for Human Rights in December 1993 in response to a recommendation made a few months earlier at the Vienna World Conference on Human Rights.[1] The idea of such a position had emerged early in the UN's history but was too controversial to be realized until the end of the Cold War. In recent years the High Commissioner for Human Rights has been at the vanguard of international efforts to address egregious human rights abuses and demand accountability. Yet this has come about only after many years of effort by those serving in the post and as the importance of human rights in international relations has expanded. Each High Commissioner has brought a different background, style, and strategy to the common aim of finding practical ways to protect oft-affirmed but inconsistently observed universal standards of human rights.

This volume had its genesis in the presentations made at an international conference that marked the fortieth anniversary of the Jacob Blaustein Institute for the Advancement of Human Rights (JBI) on February 7–8, 2012 in New York City and was convened by JBI at the Roosevelt House Public Policy Institute at Hunter College.[2] Meeting in the former home of President Franklin D. Roosevelt and Eleanor Roosevelt, experts explored and critiqued the visions, actions, and achievements of the men and women who have held the post of UN High Commissioner for Human Rights since 1994. Recognizing the upcoming 20th anniversary of the creation of the High Commissioner's position, participants examined aspects of the High Commissioners' work and discussed how each High Commissioner has addressed them and with what results.

The authors include legal scholars, human rights practitioners, and present and former UN policymakers. They examine how the High

[1] UN General Assembly, Resolution 48/141, "High Commissioner for the Promotion and Protection of All Human Rights," UN Doc. A/RES/48/141, December 20, 1993.

[2] Jacob Blaustein Institute for the Advancement of Human Rights, "UN High Commissioner Celebrates 40 Years of Jacob Blaustein Institute at the Vanguard of Human Rights," February 22, 2012, http://www.jbi-humanrights.org/jacob-blaustein-institute/2012/02/un-high-commissioner-celebrates-40-years-of-jacob-blaustein-institute-at-the-vanguard-of-human-right.html.

Commissioners have preserved human rights norms by defending the universality of rights (Abeysekera) and strengthening human rights treaty monitoring bodies that uphold those rights (O'Flaherty). They explore the High Commissioners' differing approaches to support for human rights special procedures (Gaer), managing field-based operations (Broecker, O'Neill), and encouraging the development of national human rights institutions worldwide (Thipanyane). Two chapters assess how High Commissioners have influenced other international bodies – particularly the Human Rights Council, Security Council and International Criminal Court – to act to protect human rights (Kaye, Nossel and Broecker). Key issues that arise in each of these studies are the need for the High Commissioners to balance their public role as spokesperson for universal standards with their diplomatic role as an international executive dealing directly with leaders of 193 UN Member States, as well as the High Commissioners' struggle to preserve their independence of action in that context.

Several authors examine the challenges the High Commissioners have faced in seeking to protect individuals from human rights abuses in more than a half dozen case studies. The case studies address countries that have presented the High Commissioners with very different kinds of challenges: China (Kleine-Ahlbrandt), North Korea (Cohen), Afghanistan and Sudan (Samar), Russia (Moskalenko et al), Burma (Genser), and Colombia (Rodriguez). The authors identify problems within key countries, describe how the High Commissioners handled them, and recommend strategies that might enable the current and future High Commissioners to improve the protection of human rights in the particular country and throughout the world.

This volume begins with the remarks of four distinguished keynote speakers: Michael Ignatieff, Harold Koh, Navi Pillay, the current High Commissioner for Human Rights, and Bertrand Ramcharan, the former Acting High Commissioner and Deputy High Commissioner. Their remarks reflect on the promise of the High Commissioner, the roles taken on and avoided, strategies for success, and proposals for the future.

Many of the chapters in this volume presume the reader's familiarity with the post and mandate of the High Commissioner for Human Rights and the Office of the High Commissioner for Human Rights (OHCHR). For those new to the subject, this introduction provides a conceptual and practical primer. Following an overview of the mandate of the High Commissioner, the introduction discusses the individuals who have served as and developed the post of High Commissioner;

considers questions that have seized the authors about establishing leadership, credibility, and accountability; and summarizes the authors' recommendations.

Evolution of the Concept of the High Commissioner

The first proposals for the post of UN High Commissioner for Human Rights drew upon the models of prosecutor, attorney general, advocate, and ombudsman in envisaging an international figure that would expose abuses and press to end them.[3] During the decades that followed, governmental and non-governmental advocates would continue to call for the creation of an international official who could expose and react to rights violations, offering legal advice and focusing international attention on the need for changes. Yet their suggestions were deferred or defeated at the UN.[4]

As the June 1993 Vienna World Conference on Human Rights approached, many advocates renewed earlier calls to create a High Commissioner, emphasizing that the office-holder should have a high degree of independence to develop strategies for responding to human rights violations, including the ability to speak out against human rights violations wherever they occurred, and to ensure protection of human rights throughout the UN system.[5] Some urged the High Commissioner to

[3] See Roger Stenson Clark, *A United Nations High Commissioner for Human Rights* (The Hague: Martinus Nijhoff, 1972), 39–40. Others called for "an international executive who [could] influence government action through fact-finding, publicity and persuasion." See Richard Gardner, "Foreword," in Clark, *A United Nations High Commissioner,* xi.

[4] For example, in 1963, Jacob Blaustein, industrialist and former president of the American Jewish Committee proposed the appointment of a United Nations High Commissioner for Human Rights who could investigate situations involving alleged violations of human rights, assist in the development of human rights institutions, advise the political organs of the UN on human rights, and review reports from governments on their human rights practices, stressing, above all, the need for the UN to develop greater capacity to deal with specific violations of human rights. Jacob Blaustein, "Human Rights: A Challenge to the United Nations and to Our Generation, Dag Hammarskjold Memorial Lecture," (lecture, Columbia University, New York, NY, December 4, 1963), reprinted in A. Cordier and W. Foote, eds., *The Quest for Peace: The Dag Hammaskjold Memorial Lectures* 315, 318–319 (1965) With support from the U.S. State Department, at the United Nations in 1965 Costa Rica had proposed the appointment of a top human rights official who would conduct investigations and offer advice and assistance to states. However, the proposal faltered in the Cold-War deadlock at the UN.

[5] See Andrew Clapham, "Creating the High Commissioner for Human Rights: The Outside Story," *European Journal of International Law* 5 (1994): 558–559; Felice D. Gaer, "Book Review: The United Nations High Commissioner for Human Rights: The Challenges of International Protection," *The American Journal of International Law* 98 (April 2004): 391.

initiate in-country monitoring and assistance projects such as those developed by the UN after conflicts in El Salvador, Cambodia and elsewhere. After much tension in Vienna, states approved a formal recommendation calling on the General Assembly to begin "consideration of the question of the establishment of a High Commissioner for Human Rights."[6] Despite the lack of enthusiasm of then-Secretary-General Boutros Boutros-Ghali,[7] and the considerable opposition of such states as Cuba, China, and Indonesia,[8] public appeals and determined diplomacy by several key states[9] led the UN General Assembly in December 1993 to adopt by consensus Resolution 48/141 creating the High Commissioner post.[10]

The Mandate of the High Commissioner

The High Commissioner for Human Rights is described in Resolution 48/141 as the "United Nations official with principal authority for United Nations human rights activities," and holds the rank of Under-Secretary-General. He or she is appointed by the Secretary-General, with the approval of the General Assembly, for a fixed term of four years, with one renewal permitted.

The mandate of the UN High Commissioner for Human Rights is multifaceted, broadly formulated and ambitious. Despite the expectations from advocates for the High Commissioner's post, the four-page resolution establishes a mandate in which the word 'violations' appears only once, and noticeably not in the context of emergency response but rather as something to be prevented. It calls for the High Commissioner "to play an active role in removing the current obstacles and in meeting the challenges to the full realization of all human rights and in preventing the continuation of human rights violations throughout the world …" Other elements of the mandate address promotion and protection of

---

6 World Conference on Human Rights, "Vienna Declaration and Programme of Action," UN Doc. A/CONF.157/23, section II.A., paras 17–18, July 12, 1993.

7 Boutros-Ghali argued that the establishment of such a post would "only arouse discontent and resistance" at a time in which quiet diplomacy on human rights was more appropriate. Boutros Boutros-Ghali, "Democracy is the Guarantor of Human Rights," *The Washington Post*, June 9, 1993.

8 Julia Preston, "U.N. Acts to Establish Commissioner for Human Rights," *The Washington Post*, December 17, 1993.

9 These included Canada, Costa Rica, France, Gambia, Germany, Hungary, the Russian Federation, Slovenia, Sweden, and the United States.

10 See *supra* note 1.

rights, engaging in dialogue, coordination and reform of UN bodies, and providing advisory and technical services and aid. The roles of the High Commissioner thus encompass diplomatic engagement, implementing "tasks" assigned by UN bodies, and coordination and management of human rights throughout the UN. There is little in resolution 48/141 that encourages independent initiative.[11]

While early proposals would have made the High Commissioner an entirely independent official, Resolution 48/141 assigns the High Commissioner to function "under the direction and authority of the Secretary-General." Further, the High Commissioner's mandate is placed "within the framework" of the General Assembly, the Economic and Social Council (ECOSOC), and the Commission on Human Rights. Resolution 48/141 instructs the High Commissioner to "carry out the tasks assigned to him/her by the competent bodies of the UN system," and "make recommendations to them." However, the resolution simultaneously suggests that the High Commissioner should enjoy a degree of independence, first, by requiring that the General Assembly endorse the High Commissioner, unlike other Under-Secretaries General, who are merely appointed by and report to the Secretary-General, and second, by mandating the High Commissioner to "promote and protect the *effective* enjoyment" of all human rights and to "play an *active* role" in "preventing the continuation of human rights violations throughout the world."

---

[11] UN General Assembly, Resolution 48/141, para. 4. The resolution provides this detailed list of responsibilities to the HCHR: (a) To promote and protect the effective enjoyment by all of all civil, cultural, economic, political and social rights; (b) To carry out the tasks assigned to him/her by the competent bodies of the United Nations system in the field of human rights and to make recommendations to them ...; (c) To promote and protect the realization of the right to development and to enhance support from relevant bodies of the United Nations system for this purpose; (d) To provide ... advisory services and technical and financial assistance, at the request of the State concerned and, where appropriate, the regional human rights organizations, with a view to supporting actions and programmes in the field of human rights; (e) To coordinate relevant United Nations education and public information programmes in the field of human rights; (f) To play an active role in removing the current obstacles and in meeting the challenges to the full realization of all human rights and in preventing the continuation of human rights violations throughout the world ... ; (g) To engage in a dialogue with all Governments in the implementation of his/her mandate with a view to securing respect for all human rights; (h) To enhance international cooperation for the promotion and protection of all human rights; (i) To coordinate the human rights promotion and protection activities throughout the United Nations system; (j) To rationalize, adapt, strengthen and streamline the United Nations machinery in the field of human rights with a view to improving its efficiency and effectiveness; (k) To carry out overall supervision of the Centre for Human Rights.

One aspect of the High Commissioner's mandate that has tended to significantly affect his or her perception by external audiences such as the media, human rights activists, UN officials, and diplomats is speaking out about human rights violations. Advocates have emphasized that the High Commissioner should take a principled vocal stance against violations of human rights. Yet they also expect the High Commissioner to motivate governments to refrain from engaging in violations, often through negotiation and dialogue. These dual objectives are often in tension with one another. The several High Commissioners have demonstrated differing approaches to speaking out publicly against human rights violations. The choice of whether to speak out or to engage behind-the-scenes may depend on the particular circumstances surrounding the violations, whether speaking out may put individual victims at greater risk, the High Commissioner's long- and short-term view of the prospects for changing the human rights situation in the country in question, or whether the High Commissioner has competing priorities, such as establishing a field office in the country or trying to obtain voluntary financial contributions from the government.

The High Commissioner is also tasked to serve as an administrator, coordinator and manager of a staff dispersed around the world. Initially, the Office of the High Commissioner for Human Rights (OHCHR) was intended to be a small separate office, with the rest of the UN's human rights staff remaining within the UN Centre for Human Rights, directed by an Assistant Secretary-General for Human Rights. This changed in 1998, when Kofi Annan ended the rivalry between the two officials by merging the Centre into OHCHR and placing it under the direction of the High Commissioner.

Today, OHCHR carries out activities under the High Commissioner's direct control and advises programs within peacekeeping missions and UN country teams (UNCTs). It also continues to service the human rights special procedures and treaty bodies. OHCHR's Geneva headquarters contains several different branches, the shape and functions of which have changed over time, with an overall objective to lessen the staff's emphasis on servicing UN bodies and to allow them to focus more on analytical and field-based work. OHCHR also has a New York office at UN Headquarters, which since 2010 has been headed by an Assistant Secretary-General for Human Rights who represents the High Commissioner. Additionally, OHCHR operates field presences, which at the end of 2012 consisted of 13 regional offices and 13 country or stand-alone offices.[12]

---

[12] OHCHR, *2012 Annual Report*, 182.

Over time, the number of OHCHR staff members has increased significantly – from 106 staff members in Geneva in 1993,[13] to 1,069 staff (587 in Geneva, 460 in the field, and 22 in New York) in 2012.[14] As of year-end 2012, OHCHR also supported and provided guidance to approximately 820 human rights field officers serving in 15 UN peace missions or political offices.[15]

A final responsibility of the High Commissioner is obtaining adequate funding for the functioning of OHCHR and the human rights mechanisms it supports. Since the establishment of the High Commissioner post, the amount of UN funding dedicated to human rights has grown significantly, both as a percentage of the total UN budget and in absolute terms. In 1993, prior to the establishment of the High Commissioner post, the Centre for Human Rights received $25 million, representing 0.7 per cent of the entire UN budget, for the biennium 1992–1993.[16] By 2012–2013, OHCHR received a biennial allocation of $168.5 million, representing just under three percent of the UN budget (a fourfold increase from 1993).[17] The High Commissioners also began soliciting voluntary funding, and in 2012 received $111.1 million in such funding. In 2012, OHCHR expended approximately $196.5 million, $82 million from the regular UN budget and $114.5 million from voluntary donations.[18]

Persons Who have Held the Post of High Commissioner

Since its establishment, five persons have held the post of High Commissioner, and one has served for over a year in the capacity of Acting High Commissioner. Each has brought his or her own perspective to the position and has attempted to shape the post in different ways.

José Ayala Lasso (1994–1997)

Ambassador José Ayala Lasso, the first UN High Commissioner for Human Rights, began his term on April 5, 1994, only one day prior to a plane crash that caused the deaths of the presidents of Rwanda and Burundi and

---

[13] See Navi Pillay "Address by the High Commissioner at the Jacob Blaustein Institute for the Advancement of Human Rights," in this volume, page 64.

[14] OHCHR, *2012 Annual Report*, 9.

[15] Ibid.

[16] See Tom J. Farer and Felice Gaer, "The UN and Human Rights," in *United Nations, Divided World*, ed. Adam Roberts and Benedict Kingsbury (Oxford: Clarendon Press, 1993); UN General Assembly, Resolution 47/220, "Programme budget for the biennium 1992–1993," U.N. Doc. A/47/49, December 23, 1992.

[17] OHCHR, *Report 2012*, 116.

[18] See OHCHR, *2012 Annual Report*, 131.

sparked genocidal violence in Rwanda. He had been Ecuador's foreign minister, ambassador to several countries, permanent representative to the UN, and representative on the Security Council. He had also chaired the General Assembly working group that drafted the mandate of the High Commissioner post. Ayala Lasso resigned in March 1997, after serving nearly three years as High Commissioner, to return to Ecuador as foreign minister to broker peace negotiations between Ecuador and Peru over a border dispute.

Representatives of human rights advocacy organizations initially criticized Secretary-General Boutros-Ghali's appointment of Ayala Lasso as High Commissioner, noting that the latter had never conducted a human rights investigation or written a scholarly article on the subject of human rights. During the three years that he served as High Commissioner, he indeed developed a reputation for refraining from criticism of governments in the face of serious human rights violations.[19] Human Rights Watch described its disappointment, noting, "His voice was not heard on the major human rights questions of the day... By pointedly refraining from public criticism, the High Commissioner squandered his unique capacity to stigmatize abusive conduct and abandoned his most powerful weapon to defend human rights."[20]

Ayala Lasso initiated numerous country visits in an attempt to assess support and influence the behavior of states, but his first two trips as High Commissioner were to Austria and Switzerland, reportedly to signal that his dialogues with countries were not tinged with the stigma of looking into human rights violations. During later visits to countries with poor human rights records, Ayala Lasso's preference for exploring possibilities for cooperation with governments garnered significant criticism. His 1994 visit to Cuba was noted for his failure to consult with the Special Rapporteur on Cuba, whom the government had refused to allow into the country, and for his decision not to make public comments about the human rights situation in Cuba during or after his trip.[21] Reports from

---

19 Addressing the Third Committee of the UN General Assembly in November 1994, he asserted, "I will not report to you the tragedies that afflict individuals and groups throughout the world..." José Ayala-Lasso, "Statement of the High Commissioner for Human Rights to the 49th session of the General Assembly," November 21, 1994.

20 Human Rights Watch, *1995 World Report*.

21 See William Korey, "The 'Diplomatic Approach' vs. the 'Human Rights Approach': The High Commissioner for Human Rights, and the Blaustein Institute," in *NGOs and the Universal Declaration of Human Rights, 'A Curious Grapevine'* (New York City: Palgrave, 1998), 370.

envoys sent by Ayala Lasso to Russia and to Colombia in 1995 also were not made public.

However, Ayala Lasso made important efforts to secure the agreement of governments that initiated the first UN human rights field presences – a strategy that would be embraced by his successors. In one example, although Ayala Lasso traveled to Colombia and did not raise the recommendations of two rapporteurs who had just visited the country, he did successfully negotiate with the government to establish a permanent stand-alone field office for OHCHR, which continues today and which is the subject of Victor Rodriguez-Rescia's chapter in this volume.

Mary Robinson (1997–2002)

Mary Robinson, who began her term in September 1997, had previously been President of Ireland, a Senator, a professor of law, and a barrister. As President of Ireland, she visited Rwanda after the 1994 genocide and was the rapporteur for the European preparatory meeting for the 1993 Vienna World Conference. Human rights activists praised Secretary-General Kofi Annan for nominating Robinson, who promised to be a 'moral voice' favoring human rights at the UN.[22]

Robinson significantly raised the profile and visibility of human rights at the UN and called the world's attention to human rights violations in a number of countries. However, her outspokenness and mismanagement of certain key challenges ultimately brought her into conflict with the US government, among others, and even the Secretary-General himself. Citing constraints on her and her staff such as a lack of resources, Robinson announced in late March 2001 that she would not seek reappointment to the High Commissioner post for a second term. Some commentators suggested her departure was a result of political pressure from countries such as China, and particularly Russia, which had expressed dissatisfaction with her vocal stance on human rights violations in Chechnya.[23]

Following her announcement, Robinson agreed to serve as High Commissioner for an additional year. It would prove to be tumultuous, as Robinson came into conflict with the United States both over her criticism

---

[22] Craig Turner, "U.N. Chief Picks Irish President as Top Rights Official," *Los Angeles Times*, June 13, 1997.

[23] Peter Capella, Owen Bowcott, and Rosie Cowan, "Leaders United to Get Robinson to Stay," *The Guardian*, April 4, 2001; Barbara Crossette, "U.N. Chief On Rights Decides to Leave Office / 'Constraints' prompt surprise resignation," *The New York Times*, March 20, 2001.

of its conduct in the wake of the September 11, 2001 terrorist attacks and regarding her management of the 2001 World Conference Against Racism in Durban, South Africa.[24] Robinson left the High Commissioner post in August 2002, and her term formally ended on September 11, 2002.

In stark contrast to her predecessor, Mary Robinson spoke out forcefully on human rights violations in numerous countries. During six trips to China, she engaged the government in technical assistance programs and signing a 'cooperation pact,' but she publicly criticized the country for its policies in Tibet; said it had "a long way to go" in meeting international standards of freedom of association, expression, and religious belief; and echoed a recommendation of the UN Committee Against Torture, appealing for an end to the 're-education through labor' detention system.

Robinson publicly criticized the Russian Federation for its policies in Chechnya,[25] Burma for its repression of political opposition,[26] Ethiopia for its expulsion of Eritrean nationals,[27] and Algeria for human rights abuses,[28] and called for accountability for serious human rights violations against civilians in Sierra Leone.[29] She named Cuba, Libya, and Iraq as countries that were "very hostile" to human rights.[30] Robinson also reported on violations of human rights perpetrated by Western countries. She criticized not only Serb and KLA forces in Kosovo, but also NATO for bombing civilian targets.[31] Following the September 11, 2001 terrorist attacks against the United States, Robinson expressed concern about disproportionate infringements of human rights by the US and other governments undertaken in the name of national security, US detention policies, and the bombing campaign in Afghanistan.[32]

---

24 Gustavo Capdevila, "UN's Robinson Departs Repeating Criticisms against US," *Inter Press Service: News Agency*, September 10, 2002.

25 "Statement by High Commissioner for Human Rights on the Situation in Chechnya, Russian Federation," UN press release HR/99/104, November 16, 1999.

26 "High Commissioner for Human Rights Concerned Over Intensification of Repression in Myanmar," UN press release HR/98/73, October 6, 1998.

27 "High Commissioner for Human Rights Expresses Deep Concern at Continuing Expulsion of Eritrearn Nationals from Ethiopia," UN press release HR/98/44, July 1, 1998.

28 Melinda Deslatte, "Robinson Consults on Rights in Algeria: Eyes Intervention to Stop Violence," *The Washington Times*, October 25, 2007.

29 "High Commissioner for Human Rights Condemns Ongoing Abuses in Sierra Leone," OHCHR press release, April 29, 1999.

30 "We Have Not Heard the Last of Mary Robinson," *Irish Times*, March 20, 2001.

31 Steven Boggan, "War in the Balkans: NATO Warned on War Crimes," *The Independent*, May 5, 1999.

32 Zeinab Badawi, "Mary Robinson, UN Human Rights chief," *BBC Talking Point* (interview with Mary Robinson), November 21, 2002.

Despite – or because of – her outspokenness, Robinson was criticized for her selective silence in the context of the 2001 World Conference against Racism, in Durban, South Africa. At three preparatory regional meetings in Strasbourg, Santiago, and Dakar leading up to the Durban event, Robinson appealed to governments to acknowledge and take steps to address discrimination within their own societies. However, at the fourth such conference, held in Tehran in February 2001, she failed to make a similarly strong appeal for Iran and other countries in the Asian and Middle East region to address discrimination within their countries.[33] The document resulting from the Tehran preparatory conference contained politically charged language equating Zionist practices with racism – language which the UN itself had rejected and the Secretary-General had called "a low point" for the UN.[34] The Tehran PrepCom report explicitly condemned actions by Israel, when no other country had been criticized in any of the other regional conference documents.[35] Some observers criticized Robinson's reluctance to condemn this language in the preparatory document from Tehran and her congratulations to the participants for "a productive dialogue," alleging that it encouraged certain delegates and NGO representatives to engage in hateful and anti-Semitic rhetoric at the Durban Conference itself.[36]

Powerful states such as the US and other permanent members of the Security Council reacted negatively to aspects of Robinson's approach to speaking out on human rights, which led to her departure at the completion of her fifth year in the post. While many human rights advocates saw Robinson's outspokenness as key to the UN's credibility on human rights, some questioned whether she might have been more effective had she taken a more diplomatic approach or engaged more skillfully in the politics of the post.

---

33 As congressman Tom Lantos wrote, "There was no appeal to focus on the proliferation of anti-Semitic textbooks and curricula in Arab schools; no appeal for tolerance of religious practice by non-Muslims; no appeal to improve the horrendous treatment of imported domestic workers…; and no demand for the elevation of the status of women…" Tom Lantos, "The Durban Debacle: An Insider's View of the UN World Conference against Racism," *The Fletcher Forum of World Affairs* 26, no. I (Winter/Spring 2002), 35–6.

34 Ibid., 37. See also UN Press Release SG/SM/6504/Rev.1, March 25, 1998 ("This brings me to the lamentable resolution… equating Zionism with racism and racial discrimination. That was perhaps the low point in our relations…").

35 Note by the Secretary-General, "Report of the Asian Preparatory Meeting," UN Doc. A/CONF.189/PC.2/9, para. 21, April 10, 2001.

36 Lantos, "The Durban Debacle," 36, 31–52 *passim*.

Sergio Vieira de Mello (2002–2003)

Sergio Vieira de Mello became High Commissioner on September 12, 2002 after serving in high-level UN positions such as head of the UN's Office of Coordination of Humanitarian Affairs (OCHA) and Transitional Administrator of East Timor. Some human rights activists saw Vieira de Mello's appointment as a signal that Secretary-General Annan would henceforth take a more cautious approach to human rights. Others welcomed Vieira de Mello's ability to work within the UN and directly with states, believing it would improve the UN's human rights protection efforts.[37] Vieira de Mello was killed on August 19, 2003 in a suicide bomb attack on the Baghdad headquarters of the UN Mission in Iraq, which he headed during a four-month leave from his post as High Commissioner.

In July 2002, Vieira de Mello had emphasized his intention "to transform human rights into a source of unity, not of division,"[38] and many viewed his appointment as an attempt to mollify states hostile to his predecessor. However, as High Commissioner, Vieira de Mello publicly called on the United States to curtail human rights abuses committed in the context of domestic and international counter-terrorism efforts, particularly regarding suspects at Guantanamo Bay, Cuba.[39] On a visit to the Democratic Republic of Congo, Vieira de Mello echoed concerns raised by two UN special rapporteurs regarding troubling death sentences; in Pakistan, he held a news conference in which he raised the issue of discriminatory laws and 'honor' crimes against women, urging authorities to prosecute the perpetrators.[40]

Bertrand Ramcharan (2003–2004)

Bertrand Ramcharan, who had been Deputy High Commissioner for Human Rights since 1998, was named Acting High Commissioner for Human Rights in late May 2003 when Vieira de Mello accepted a temporary position heading the UN Mission in Iraq. Following Vieira de Mello's

[37] See Felice Gaer, "Forward," in *Subcontracting Peace: The Challenges of NGO Peacebuilding*, ed. Oliver P. Richmond and Henry F. Carey (Hampshire: Ashgate Publishing Limited, 2005), xv-xx.

[38] "Transcript of Press Conference by Secretary-General Kofi Annan at UN Headquarters," UN press release SG/SM/8318, July 29, 2002.

[39] "Top UN Rights Official Raises Concerns About US Treatment of Terror Detainees," *UN News Centre*, March 6, 2003.

[40] Tahir Ilkram, "U.N. Asks Pakistan to Review Laws Against Women," *Washington Post*, February 26, 2003.

death, Ramcharan remained Acting High Commissioner until July 2004, when Louise Arbour began her term. Ramcharan's lengthy UN service included appointments as director for Africa in the UN Department of Political Affairs, director of the International Conference for the Former Yugoslavia, and special assistant to the Assistant Secretary-General on human rights. A UN insider, Ramcharan was recognized as having played a key role behind the scenes in encouraging the establishment of special rapporteurs and other UN human rights mechanisms.

Ramcharan was an outspoken defender of human rights despite the constraints associated with his status as 'Acting' High Commissioner. Significantly, he carried out investigations on his own initiative and reported back to UN bodies on a number of human rights situations of importance, without waiting for specific authorization to do so. In 2003, Ramcharan ordered and submitted the first emergency report to the Commission on Human Rights by the Office of the High Commissioner on the situation in Liberia.[41] In 2004, following revelations of abuse of Iraqi prisoners at Abu Ghraib, Ramcharan prepared a report on the human rights abuses in Iraq for the Commission, again on his own initiative.[42] He also acted on his own initiative in deploying a fact-finding team to investigate allegations of gross violations of human rights in Darfur, though when Sudan offered long-sought access to its territory on the eve of a special session of the Commission on Human Rights on the subject, Ramcharan received criticism for declining to submit the fact-finding team's report for its consideration.[43]

Louise Arbour (2004–2008)

Louise Arbour, who began her term on June 30, 2004, was previously a justice of the Canadian Supreme Court and the prosecutor of the International Criminal Tribunals for the Former Yugoslavia and Rwanda, where she issued the first indictment against a sitting head of state on charges of crimes against humanity by an international court. Human rights activists largely welcomed Arbour's appointment as High

41 UN Commission on Human Rights, *Situation of human rights and fundamental freedoms in Liberia*, UN Doc. E/CN.4/2004/5, August 12, 2003.

42 UN Commission on Human Rights, *The Present Situation of Human Rights in Iraq*, UN Doc. E/CN.4/2005/4, June 9, 2004.

43 UN Commission on Human Rights, *Situation of human rights in the Darfur region of the Sudan*, UN Doc. E/CN.4/2005/3, May 7, 2004. See also "Accusations fly at UN rights forum over leak of report on Darfur," *Agence-France Presse*, April 22, 2004.

Commissioner, noting her combination of diplomatic skills, political courage, and outspokenness at the tribunals.[44] Arbour stepped down in July 2008, ostensibly for personal reasons. Her refusal to seek a second term came at a time of intense challenge to the independence of the High Commissioner and as her influence diminished following the appointment of Secretary-General Annan's successor, Ban Ki-moon. It followed conflict with the US government regarding her criticism of US counter-terrorism policies and at a time when the potential for further controversy was very high, as the High Commissioner had been tasked to organize a 2009 high level review of the controversial 2001 Durban Conference.

As High Commissioner, Arbour secured a major expansion of OHCHR's resources, coinciding with the reform of the UN Commission on Human Rights, the UN political organ dedicated to human rights, and supported Kofi Annan's proposal to replace the Commission with the Human Rights Council in 2006. Human rights advocates generally praised her performance and regretted her departure.[45]

Arbour initially expressed an intention to engage in quiet diplomacy to a greater degree than Mary Robinson. At the same time, she was outspoken in her criticism of US counter-terrorism policies and use of the death penalty.[46] She also criticized human rights violations in abusive situations. During her term, OHCHR produced several extensive reports on human rights violations in Darfur and carried out a fact-finding mission at the request of the UN Security Council that led to a report recommending referral of the situation in Darfur to the International Criminal Court.[47] Arbour also criticized the governments of Burma and Zimbabwe for repressing political opposition[48] and the Democratic Republic of the Congo for stymieing an investigation ordered by the

---

[44] See Amnesty International, "UN: High Commissioner for Human Rights resigns; replacement must preserve independence of post," press release, March 7, 2008; Amnesty International, "UN High Commissioner for Human Rights Resigns," March 10, 2008.

[45] Ibid.

[46] Louise Arbour, interview by George Negus, *Dateline*, March 19, 2008, http://www.sbs.com.au/dateline/story/transcript/id/543024/n/Interview-with-Louise-Arbour.

[47] The Security Council endorsed the report, adopted the recommendation, and for the first time exercised its authority to refer to the Prosecutor of the ICC a situation in a State not party to the Rome Statute.

[48] "UN Human Rights Council calls on Myanmar to Release Detainees, Political Prisoners," *UN News Centre*, October 2, 2007; "Alarmed by violence in Zimbabwe, Arbour Urges Restraint," OHCHR press release, April 27, 2008.

Security Council into the deaths of a large number of refugees and others in 1997.[49]

While human rights organizations complimented Arbour on her willingness to challenge powerful and persistent human rights violators, some questioned her consistency in doing so. Indeed, Arbour championed the value of 'quiet diplomacy' and in 2008, expressed her view that "naming and shaming is a loser's game" when dealing with Russia, China, and the 130-nation 'Group of 77.'[50] For them, she chose a strategy of private engagement "that is likely to yield some positive results."[51] Some commentators questioned whether this strategy was effective in practice, noting that North Korea refused to allow her to visit and that China refused to allow her to visit Tibet despite the fact that she largely refrained from condemning their human rights performance.[52]

Navi Pillay (2008-Present)

Navanethem 'Navi' Pillay began her first term on September 1, 2008, and in June 2012 was asked to continue in the post for an additional two years. She previously served as a judge on the Appeals Division of the International Criminal Court and as the President of the International Criminal Tribunal for Rwanda. Prior to that, she was the first female judge on the High Court of South Africa and for nearly 30 years worked as a lawyer defending clients including anti-Apartheid activists. As a judge, Pillay had not had occasion to take bold public positions on human rights issues. However, activists who had worked with her during her years as a defense attorney recalled her substantial first-hand experience defending human rights.[53]

During her first term as High Commissioner, Navi Pillay spoke out against human rights violations by states, powerful as well as weak. She spoke out on a number of occasions about the conduct of both the government and rebels in 2009 in the conflict in Sri Lanka and reiterated her call for the establishment of an international commission of inquiry

---

[49] Colum Lynch, "U.N. Human Rights Chief to Leave Post," *Washington Post*, March 3, 2008.

[50] Ibid.

[51] Ibid.

[52] Marlise Simons, "Departing Rights Official Raised Volume on Issues," *New York Times*, July 6, 2008.

[53] "New United Nations High Commissioner for Human Rights Takes Up Her Post," UN press release, September 1, 2008.

on the end of the conflict for more than a year after its conclusion.[54] In 2010, Pillay oversaw OHCHR's public release of a 550-page report documenting 617 serious violations of human rights and humanitarian law by several African states and non-state actors in the Democratic Republic of the Congo between March 1993 and June 2003 (known as the 'Congo Mapping Report'), despite reported Rwandan government threats to withdraw peacekeepers from UN peacekeeping missions in retaliation.[55] As the outbreak of protests in the Arab world in early 2011 led to crackdowns by a number of governments, Pillay issued statements condemning violence against peaceful protesters, arbitrary arrests, abuses in detention, and unjustified restrictions of freedom of expression.[56] She called for international inquiries into human rights abuse in Libya and Syria in 2011 and North Korea in 2013.[57]

Some advocates criticized Pillay for muting discussion of human rights problems in public while visiting the six Gulf Cooperation Council countries in April 2010. Yet in Jeddah, she publicly criticized "prolonged detention and lack of judicial remedies" for workers who escaped abusive employers, as well as the male guardianship system.[58] Yet Pillay at times proved willing to provoke tension with countries under scrutiny. On a visit to the Maldives in November 2011, Pillay condemned the practice of flogging women convicted of extra-marital sex and said that a constitutional provision prohibiting citizens from practicing any faith other than Sunni Islam was discriminatory and out of line with international standards.[59]

---

[54] "Serious Violations of International Law Committed in Sri Lanka Conflict: UN Human Rights Chief," OHCHR press release, March 13, 2009; "Urgent International Scrutiny Needed in Sri Lanka, Say UN Rights Experts," UN News Centre, May 8, 2009.

[55] Jeffrey Gettleman, "Rwanda Threatens to Pull Peacekeepers From Darfur," *New York Times*, August 31, 2010; Office of the High Commissioner for Human Rights, "Statement by the High Commissioner for Human Rights Navi Pillay," statement, October 1, 2010.

[56] See "Statement by UN High Commissioner for Human Rights Navi Pillay at the Human Rights Council 18th Special Session to Examine the Situation of Human Rights in the Syrian Arab Republic," OHCHR, December 2, 2011; "Bahrain Square is New Center for Arab Protest," *USA Today*, February 15, 2011; "Arab Nations Need to Ensure Sustainable Transition to Democracy – UN Rights Chief," *UN News Centre*, May 30, 2011.

[57] "Pillay Calls for International Inquiry into Libyan Violence and Justice for Victims," OHCHR press release, February 22, 2011; "UN Launches International Inquiry Into Syria's Crackdown on Protesters," *Haaretz*, August 23, 2011; "Pillay urges more attention to human rights abuses in North Korea, calls for international inquiry," OHCHR press release, January 14, 2013.

[58] "NGO: UN Renewal of Rights Chief Pillay Should Be Preceded by Public Discussion of Her Record," Canada Free Press, May 15, 2012; "UN Rights Chief Calls for End to Sponsor System, Seeks Improvement in Position of Gulf Women," Arab News, April 19, 2010.

[59] Pillay said the practice "constitutes one of the most inhumane and degrading forms of violence against women and should have no place in the legal framework of a

In late 2012, Pillay provoked condemnation from China when she issued a statement criticizing human rights abuses against Tibetans and urging China to allow independent monitors to visit Tibet and to implement relevant recommendations of UN human rights mechanisms.[60]

Reflections and Recommendations

As Bertrand Ramcharan has commented, "there is no magic wand in human rights work—it is a work of constant endeavor."[61] In the nearly twenty years that have elapsed since the establishment of the post, observers have expected the High Commissioners to be all things to all who seek to realize all kinds of human rights.[62] From the outset, advocates have urged the High Commissioner to be a champion who opposes all human rights abuses wherever found and a critic of states large and small and governments powerful and weak. The High Commissioner has been called on to engage with victims of abuse yet at the same time speak truth to power. The High Commissioner is asked to reach the world's top diplomats

democratic country." "UN rights official urges Maldives to stop flogging," *CNS News.com*, http://cnsnews.com/un-rights-official-urges-maldives-stop-flogging.

[60] "China Must Urgently Address Rights Violations in Tibet – UN Senior Official," *UN News Centre*, November 2, 2012.

[61] "Bertrand Ramcharan, Acting High Commissioner," Front Line Defenders, http://www.frontlinedefenders.org/es/node/12027.

[62] At a June 1995 event, human rights practitioners and other observers encouraged the High Commissioner to see his mandate as requiring the following: "speaking out on human rights violations and pressing for change; providing emergency response to gross violations of human rights; affirming the universality, indivisibility and irreducibility of international human rights norms, addressing challenges to the universality of human rights, and preventing any regression from the Vienna and Beijing Declarations and Programs of Action; promoting normative development of human rights law at the UN; promoting the effective operation of OHCHR, including in the field, and specifically ensuring its capacity to conduct information-gathering and monitoring, provide early warning of grave human rights abuses, engage in preventive action, assist peacemaking and peacekeeping missions, and provide technical advice and assistance to help countries establish, maintain, and enhance national human rights systems; preserving the independence of the OHCHR; providing support to and ensuring the effective operation of the human rights treaty bodies, special rapporteurs, and other experts; coordinating the High Commissioner's and OHCHR's activities with those of other fact-finding and protection instruments; mainstreaming human rights throughout the UN, including in work concerned with development and issues affecting international peace and security; coordinating and cooperating with other aspects of the UN system…; managing the OHCHR and its staff; ensuring that the OHCHR has sufficient resources to carry out its work; supporting national human rights mechanisms and human rights defenders; [and] engaging non-governmental organizations fully…" "The Promise of the United Nations High Commissioner for Human Rights," outcome document from the event *The UN and Human Rights*, convened by the Human Rights Program of the Carter Center and the Jacob Blaustein Institute for the Advancement of Human Rights, June 4–6, 1995.

and prime ministers and to be a consensus-builder with the power to convince even the cruelest among them to change their abusive practices. At the same time, the High Commissioner is instructed to respond to human rights crises, as well as to take preventive action to avert future emergencies. As if this were not enough, the High Commissioner is also mandated to carry out the instructions of governments acting through the Human Rights Council and to be an administrator, coordinator and manager for OHCHR. These expectations are extraordinary and perhaps unachievable, and the individuals nominated and selected for the post of High Commissioner have felt the pressure of trying to satisfy them.

A review of the chapters that follow illuminates a number of overarching themes which the authors in this volume have used to assess the performance of the High Commissioners for Human Rights, particularly in terms of leadership, credibility, and managing accountability. The following section explores these issues and tensions that the High Commissioners have faced in pursuing them when faced with real world crises and summarizes initial conclusions drawn from the authors' analyses.

Leadership

A key point of discussion among our authors concerns the leadership role of the High Commissioner as the UN official with 'primary responsibility' for the world organization's human rights work. While some contributors highlight personal qualities and personality attributes of the High Commissioners that have facilitated their ability to exercise leadership and engage effectively with states, others focus on how their achievements may be hindered by the limited resources provided to enable them to carry out those functions. The High Commissioner's mandate also contains its own contradictions, giving the High Commissioner vast authority and responsibility to promote and protect all human rights, yet simultaneously making the High Commissioner into a lowly bureaucrat who is instructed by political bodies to carry out assigned 'tasks.'

To manage these tensions, Michael Ignatieff recommends that the High Commissioner be at once a UN insider with experience navigating the system and also an outsider, ideally a 'global politician' with the status and standing necessary to challenge the system and confront Member States. Harold Koh and Stephanie Kleine-Ahlbrandt both highlight the advantages conferred on Mary Robinson by her prior role as president of a country, which enabled her to command respect and attention at high levels of government. Yet Kleine-Ahlbrandt argues that Louise Arbour overcame any disadvantage resulting from her lower political standing by proving herself personable and knowledgeable on the issues when engaging China.

Throughout the volume, three core leadership priorities repeatedly emerge: establishing and maintaining the High Commissioner's independence; monitoring and publicly presenting accurate facts about egregious human rights abuses; and enhancing the national protection of human rights on the ground by developing effective field presences and national institutions.

Identifying Leadership Priorities

As Ignatieff reminds us, the task of leadership necessarily requires the High Commissioner to make political choices as to which human rights 'battles' she will fight with her very limited resources. This choice is a high-stakes decision that can have repercussions for the High Commissioner's credibility with stakeholders and ability to solicit resources from states, and can even affect the length of her tenure.

Several contributors emphasize that the High Commissioner must prioritize the defense of the independence of the UN's human rights mechanisms against challenges from states. These mechanisms include not only the High Commissioner and OHCHR, but also the special rapporteurs and treaty bodies. Sunila Abeysekera argues that the High Commissioners have been successful in this regard, while Suzanne Nossel and Christen Broecker urge the High Commissioner to be vigilant in anticipating and pushing back against such challenges in the future, noting that the High Commissioner is the guardian for her role not just for herself but in perpetuity.

The need to promote and defend the universality of human rights should guide the High Commissioner in identifying priorities, as several of the authors stress. Abeysekera asserts that universality of human rights is more contested today than in the past, and concludes that it will be incumbent on the High Commissioner to defend women, migrants and refugees, LGBT individuals, and members of minority ethnic, religious, and racial communities in the face of growing attempts to restrict their rights. Sima Samar, drawing on her experiences in both Sudan and Afghanistan, calls on the High Commissioner to remain vigilant in opposing those who seek to deny the universality of human rights through calls for respect for cultural and religious particularities. High Commissioner Navi Pillay responds to these concerns by affirming her commitment to fighting back against challenges to universality, and providing as an example her support for the human rights of all persons regardless of their sexual orientation or gender identity.

Much is already presented above about the importance High Commissioners and observers have given to 'speaking out' and presenting accurate information about violations of international human rights law. Ignatieff advises the High Commissioner to focus on battles that can be won and that impact the core of the High Commissioner's mandate, particularly 'fighting cruelty.' He also mentions two other priorities, with the objective to increase human rights observance on the ground: building the capacity of human rights defenders and enhancing the capacity within states to protect human rights. Ignatieff cautions against the High Commissioner succumbing to 'role inflation,' noting that her role and that of OHCHR must be distinguished from that of development agencies, international criminal justice institutions, or entities with a security mandate like the Security Council.

Several contributors call on the High Commissioner to take early action to bring human rights crises that have not been taken up by the political bodies of the UN to their attention in order to catalyze a response. Ramcharan credits past High Commissioners with having spoken out clearly in emergency situations. He argues that the High Commissioner should develop a 'thinking role' so as to become the figure that the international community looks to for guidance on emerging human rights situations. An early advocate for developing national protection systems, he places particular emphasis on the need for the High Commissioner to craft an overarching strategy to lead OHCHR, and the UN more broadly, to more concerted action on *prevention* of violations. Koh similarly urges the High Commissioner to use proactive power to serve as a catalyst on human rights issues or crises that have been neglected by international or regional rights systems and to lead in addressing new human rights challenges likely to arise in the coming decades.

Koh also suggests that the High Commissioner should adopt a 'smart power' approach in determining which issues to take on, identifying potential partners and areas for cooperation. He suggests that the High Commissioner is more likely to win battles that have the support of indispensable governments within the human rights system. He thus advocates for the High Commissioner to establish points of contact at high levels within major governments to ensure that she is aware of opportunities for cooperation, as well as to encourage political actors to take political risks in support of human rights objectives that the High Commissioner has championed.

Leadership in Carrying Out Fact-Finding and Advancing Protection

Contributors to this volume have also proposed strategies that can advance particularly significant priorities of the High Commissioner. Several authors highlight the necessity for the High Commissioner to be aware of and to strategically employ the uniquely independent power which has been called 'the self-activating mandate.' Several essays point to Ramcharan's independent action to gather facts about the critical human rights situation in Darfur and to spur action by other parts of the UN system.

The High Commissioner can seize opportunities to leverage the capacity of other UN institutions and simultaneously bolster her status as the recognized expert on human rights violations worldwide by publicly bringing information to the attention of other bodies. With regard to the Human Rights Council, Nossel and Broecker describe how the High Commissioner was able to use special sessions on the crises in Côte d'Ivoire, Libya, and Syria to present her analysis of facts on the ground, attract greater media attention to the scale and severity of crises, and propose directions for future action; and then to lead OHCHR as it supported the fact-finding mandate or commission of inquiry the Council subsequently created on the crisis situation. Nossel and Broecker suggest that the High Commissioner could play an even greater role in the future in driving the Council to address situations of concern and recommending appropriate responses to violations.

David Kaye highlights the important role the High Commissioner can play in driving action in pursuit of accountability for abuses by the Security Council and the International Criminal Court (ICC). As an example, he points to the report of the OHCHR fact-finding commission on Darfur, which motivated the Security Council to refer that situation to the ICC, and also created a file on alleged perpetrators that the High Commissioner then shared with the ICC. Kaye recommends that in the future, the High Commissioner and the ICC enter into information-sharing agreements to ensure that such transfer of knowledge and expertise becomes routine.

Pillay reminds us that in a matter of only a few years, the Security Council has progressed from questioning the propriety of Arbour's mere presence as an observer at one of its sessions to actively requesting the High Commissioner to brief it on situations of concern. As of February 2012, Pillay had already addressed the Security Council 11 times – more than all her predecessors combined (eight times). Nossel and Broecker suggest that the High Commissioner could make even greater use of the recently-created Assistant Secretary-General for Human Rights position in New York to raise the profile of human rights issues at the Security Council and create more opportunities for public presentation of facts about ongoing abuses.

Strategic enlargement of OHCHR field presences has been emphasized as a core priority by a number of our contributors. Indeed, Pillay has acknowledged this as a key objective, noting that she seeks to play a catalytic role ensuring that states implement Universal Periodic Review (UPR) recommendations on the ground, including through the placement of human rights advisers in UN country teams and regional organizations. Koh and Ignatieff argue that engagement through field presences and technical cooperation activities allows the High Commissioner to make a greater connection both with governments and civil society and communities on the ground and to make human rights and international institutions meaningful to their intended beneficiaries. Kaye calls on the High Commissioner to deploy the Office in conflict zones to build domestic constituencies that will seek to promote accountability in its aftermath. As Broecker notes, the High Commissioner must also exert leadership in securing governments' agreement for OHCHR to carry out activities on the most important human rights issues in the country and in a manner that is likely to accomplish results, both through technical cooperation programs conducted from Geneva and through one of a variety of forms of field presences.

Another area in which the High Commissioners have endeavored to promote greater human rights protection on the ground is through the establishment of national human rights institutions (NHRIs). As Tseliso Thipanyane describes, successive High Commissioners have encouraged states to establish strong, independent NHRIs. A dedicated unit of OHCHR helps coordinate and support their activities. Whereas in 1993 there were 20 NHRIs, there are more than 70 today. Thipanyane identifies areas where the High Commissioner could improve support for NHRIs, including by providing greater resources to the coordinating body of NHRIs, for which OHCHR serves as secretariat, and encouraging the coordinating body to assess thoroughly the quality and independence of NHRIs. He also urges a reevaluation of how the High Commissioner engages with government officials to ensure that NHRIs are independent, effective, and well-resourced. Samar also calls on the High Commissioner to champion the work of strong NHRIs and directly call on governments, UN bodies, and others to act on their reports.

Leadership in Advancing Human Rights in Challenging Country Situations

Several of the authors focus their remarks on the efforts of the High Commissioners to increase protection for human rights on the ground in particularly challenging country situations. They note the critical need for the High Commissioner to exercise leadership and develop a strategy for obtaining and defending mandates for OHCHR to carry out its in-country work while not sacrificing the ability to speak out independently on key issues of concern in those countries. Kleine-Ahlbrandt reflects on Mary Robinson's personal commitment to pursue a technical cooperation agreement with China. Regular travel of the High Commissioner to the country, dialogue between the High Commissioner and senior government officials, and a carefully-tailored diplomatic approach helped bring about such an agreement. She notes the importance of building trust through engagement and capacity-building work, but cautions that technical cooperation projects must be designed to make a measurable impact and frequently assessed to ensure that they are having their intended results.

Along the same lines, Samar emphasizes the importance of visits by the High Commissioner to Afghanistan and Sudan in drawing global attention to serious human rights issues there. In the case of Afghanistan, such visits motivated the government to adopt a more receptive attitude to the findings of the Independent National Human Rights Commission on the need for transitional justice measures. She calls on the current and future High Commissioners to visit both countries on an annual basis and to use their visits as an opportunity to engage in high-level advocacy on key human rights issues. Victor Rodriguez-Rescia describes how the complex set of activities carried out by the OHCHR stand-alone office in Colombia, paired with a tailored diplomatic approach, has enabled OHCHR to make significant progress on certain endemic human rights issues.

The authors uniformly advocate that future High Commissioners develop concerted strategies for engagement on these challenging countries in the future. Roberta Cohen applauds Navi Pillay for issuing the first ever press release of a High Commissioner devoted solely to abuses in North Korea, and calls on Pillay to follow up on her groundbreaking statement by developing and implementing a comprehensive strategy, involving the entire UN system, to investigate, publicly condemn, and put an end to human rights violations in North Korea. Jared Genser similarly calls on the High Commissioner to increase her personal engagement on Burma. Finally, Moskalenko and colleagues challenge the High Commissioner to undertake an objective analysis of the progress realized by the OHCHR field presence in Russia, which they argue has been unable to achieve progress on the most pressing human rights issues facing the country as a result of its very limited mandate. They call upon the High Commissioner either to encourage the field presence to interpret its mandate more creatively or to consider withdrawing it from the country completely.

Credibility

Another key issue addressed by contributors to this volume is the need to ensure that both the High Commissioner and OHCHR establish and maintain credibility as authoritative sources of information on human rights issues worldwide. This requires first, that the High Commissioner be able to gather accurate information and to convey this information to relevant parties in an effective manner. Yet it also requires that the High Commissioner make use of various UN mechanisms, institutions, and field presences so that they respond to new facts by taking action to end abuses and enforce international human rights law. In order for the High Commissioner to maintain credibility, he or she must strategically manage OHCHR staff as well.

Consistency Through Universality

Several contributors stress that it is particularly critical that High Commissioners base their legal conclusions on an accurate assessment of facts on the ground, and many see a positive overall trend in the High Commissioners' performance in this area. Ignatieff notes that the facts in human rights cases are often complex and ambiguous but finds that the High Commissioner's credibility has grown as Navi Pillay made herself 'the gold standard' on the facts of the evolving human rights crisis in Syria.

Several contributors note that the High Commissioner can bolster her own credibility and create greater authority to challenge governments by applying international human rights law consistently. Pillay concurs, asserting that her office derives its strength from invoking obligations under international law and emphasizing her "commitment to truth, impartiality, and integrity, with no tolerance for double-standards or selectivity." As Abeysekera reminds us, the concept of universality involves ensuring that human rights obligations are applied not only to protect all persons but also to place obligations on all states. Ignatieff similarly calls on the High Commissioner to safeguard respect for human rights in the capitals of the global North as much as in the capitals of the global South. Michael O'Flaherty recommends that the treaty bodies have a more central place in the High Commissioner's interactions with governments, as their work is key to maintaining universality.

However, Koh asserts that to gain and maintain credibility, the High Commissioner must do even more than gather facts and identify violations consistently. Koh suggests that the High Commissioner should be not merely accurate and consistent, but that she should also be a "comparative evaluator of human rights abuses," clarifying the relative severity of abuses in conflict situations and identifying the parties who bear greater or lesser responsibility for them.

Strategic Management

In order for the High Commissioner to obtain accurate facts, and to ensure that other human rights mechanisms of the UN also operate on the basis of accurate information, she must have a managerial strategy that ensures that the OHCHR is structured, staffed, sufficiently resourced and internally coordinated so as to quickly and accurately transmit information to headquarters and to assist the UN human rights mechanisms in interpreting it. Koh emphasizes the importance of the High Commissioner's role as 'point person' for the human rights bureaucracy and stresses that the High Commissioner should serve as primary coordinator for its working groups, special rapporteurs, and treaty bodies, ensuring that bodies are aware of one another's' findings and produce a coherent, consistent body of work. Koh also calls on the High Commissioner to provide these entities with a 'home base' of resources and publicity, as well as protection from attacks by states.

Several contributors elaborate on the importance of the High Commissioner's support for the work of the special procedure mandate-holders: the special rapporteurs, independent experts, and other mechanisms created by the Human Rights Council to monitor and report on human rights violations, including through country visits. Samar, reflecting on her time as Special Rapporteur on Sudan, applauds the support provided to her by OHCHR's field presence in Sudan and by staff based in Geneva. Genser calls on the High Commissioner to ensure greater resources to assist the Special Rapporteur on human rights in Myanmar (Burma) as the country experiences an unprecedented transition. While the mandates of the High Commissioner and the special procedures both involve fact-finding and reporting, and the High Commissioner convenes an annual meeting of Special Rapporteurs, Felice Gaer concludes that High Commissioners have demonstrated little appetite for strategic interaction to promote these mechanisms. This may be partly to protect the independence of both the High Commissioner and the mandate holders, who are both colleagues and competitors. Yet, Gaer continues, such an emphasis on independence has led the High Commissioners to underestimate the value of timely consultation and more strategic deployment and management of the special procedures.

O'Flaherty, discussing the relationship of the High Commissioner and OHCHR to the treaty bodies, notes significant improvement over time: whereas OHCHR once simply delivered secretariat support to the treaties, there is far more interaction today. He commends the High Commissioners for calling for changes to meet new challenges facing the expanding treaty body system. He welcomes greater cross-committee coordination and efforts to ensure that the OHCHR's field presences use the treaty bodies' recommendations. O'Flaherty calls for the High Commissioner to ensure that OHCHR increases its engagement with and provision of information to the treaty bodies. He also urges the High Commissioner to engage in diplomatic efforts to strengthen the treaty bodies, including at the General Assembly.

The High Commissioner also plays an important role in managing OHCHR as it carries out its field activities. Broecker notes that the success or failure of OHCHR's field activities has often depended on the High Commissioner's provision of sufficient political backing, direction, resources, staff, and training. Commending the High Commissioners for convening an annual meeting of heads of field presences and creating a rapid response capacity within OHCHR to deploy personnel for field-based technical assistance, she recommends greater support of field-based staff as a future priority of the High Commissioner and OHCHR. William G. O'Neill reviews the challenges that arise in the context of human rights components of peacekeeping missions, in which the majority of field-based human rights officers are deployed. He emphasizes the need to build capacity at the local level as well as to leverage the greater resources of UN military, police, humanitarian and development agencies. He particularly encourages the High Commissioner to embrace the Guiding Principles for Human Rights Field Officers Working in Conflict and Post-Conflict Environments and to incorporate them into training, doctrine, and evaluations of field work.

Samar, drawing on her experiences in Afghanistan and Sudan, highlights challenges resulting from the limited independence of human rights officers attached to peacekeeping operations. She notes that human rights officers occasionally appear to view local NHRI's, NGOs, and human rights defenders as competitors rather than partners and calls on the High Commissioner to develop operational practices that will prevent this.

Samar applauds the cooperative relationship between OHCHR and the Afghanistan Independent Human Rights Commission (AIHRC) and OHCHR's work to ensure that the AIHRC's findings were reflected in the High Commissioner's own reports on Afghanistan. Discussing China, Kleine-Ahlbrandt notes that technical cooperation programs must be tailored realistically to fit to the resources – staffing and monetary – available to carry them out, noting that the High Commissioner's projects were designed with a view to the aspiration to establish a permanent field presence in China and not the reality that the programs were directed from OHCHR's Geneva headquarters.

Many authors note the significant role that OHCHR has played in carrying out fact-finding mandates including commissions of inquiry established by the Human Rights Council. However, Nossel and Broecker point out that OHCHR could better carry out this work if key operational shortcomings were more effectively addressed. They recommend that OHCHR develop a better assessment system for anticipated operations; an ability to deploy staff on a rapid basis on more than 90-day contracts; and a strengthened recruitment capacity. Several authors emphatically agree with this assessment, lamenting the bureaucratic obstacles that impede efficient program administration and staffing.

Koh notes that the Office also plays an important role in supporting the UPR process, which Gaer reminds us has substantially expanded attention to the findings and recommendations of the special procedures system. Koh sees great potential in the UPR exercise as a source of sustained, long-term monitoring and reporting on human rights conditions in every country and credits OHCHR with a key role in compiling the human rights reports that inform the process and in working with states to digest and follow up on the recommendations made.

It is in the context of her role as manager of the human rights system that the High Commissioner confronts what many authors have identified as a significant obstacle to her effectiveness and that of her Office: a lack of sufficient resources from states to carry out the myriad responsibilities placed upon her. Nossel and Broecker, addressing this issue, propose the creation of a private funding arm for OHCHR akin to what has been done by other UN agencies such as UNICEF and UNHCR.

Credibility Beyond Fact-Gathering

There are other factors that can increase or decrease a High Commissioner's credibility, some of which may be beyond the High Commissioner's personal control. Ignatieff argues that the failings of the broader UN system "eat[ ] away at the legitimacy of the High Commissioner herself." He particularly cites the singular treatment of Israel by the UN's human rights bodies and at the Durban Conference and the election of states with very poor human rights records to the UN's political bodies on human rights in this regard. Ignatieff laments that Pillay's role requires her to justify these legitimacy gaps even when she has no power to correct them. Pillay's comments in a discussion at the JBI conference, the transcript of which is included in this volume, reflect this challenge. In one example, she points to her public condemnation of Iranian President Ahmadinejad's inflammatory address at the Durban Review Conference as proof of her willingness to "steadfastly raise our voice when it needs to be raised," and "point the finger where it needs to be pointed."

Nossel and Broecker argue that the High Commissioner must endeavor to help the Human Rights Council establish and maintain its credibility, just as the Secretary-General must endeavor to do with respect to the UN Security Council. They suggest that the High Commissioner do this by playing a more active behind-the-scenes role at the Council, calling for issues to be placed on its agenda and highlighting reporting on human rights violations in cases where the Council seems poised to make a decision that may vindicate an abuser and hurt its credibility. Gaer points out that the credibility of the High Commissioners – and indeed, of the entire UN – has been affected by cases in which senior UN officials have been reluctant to criticize mandate-holders when their actions call into serious question their impartiality and objectivity. She calls for High Commissioners to ensure that mandate holders can be reasonably be held accountable to their diverse stakeholders but at the same time to maintain and protect the independence of the special procedures, a balance which requires a well-informed, well-reasoned, and politically courageous High Commissioner.

Accountability

A final and critical issue addressed in this volume is to whom – and for whom – the High Commissioner should consider herself accountable, and how this accountability should shape the High Commissioner's work. Ignatieff notes that the High Commissioner faces a fundamental conflict, as she is responsible both to the people of the world – and particularly to victims of human rights abuse – but also to the UN system and to the Member States that perpetrate those abuses. Several contributors highlight this conflict between being a UN politician expected to engage in diplomacy and a global voice of conscience expected to publicly champion victims.

Ignatieff concludes that since the creation of the post, the High Commissioners have gradually "chosen to privilege defense of victims over deference to states" and that while this has been welcomed by victims and advocates, it has in some cases made it more difficult for the High Commissioners to maintain their access and leverage with governments. In her remarks, High Commissioner Pillay asserts that her task "is to be squarely and unequivocally on the side of victims," and points to her early call for Libyan President Muammar Qaddafi to be charged with war crimes and crimes against humanity for abuses committed against his own population as an example of speaking out on behalf of victims of gross human rights abuses. As several contributors note, Pillay has also spoken out clearly and unequivocally in defense of victims of human rights abuse in Syria. But Pillay also asserted in the discussion at the JBI conference that she communicates with governments through private written appeals far more than through public press releases, explaining that in many cases, a different approach is required in order to actually convince states to change their behavior.

Many of our contributors reflect upon how the High Commissioner has handled this identity conflict when directing OHCHR's work in the field. Rodriguez-Rescia describes the experience of the OHCHR Office in Colombia, noting that the High Commissioner came under serious pressure from the Colombian government, which threatened to severely curtail the office's mandate in the country and perhaps to close the office entirely in response to public criticism by certain heads of the OHCHR Colombia office. While the Colombian government ultimately allowed the OHCHR office to remain open with its mandate intact, a similar confrontation between OHCHR and the government of Nepal was not resolved so amicably. As Broecker relates, at the insistence of the government of Nepal, OHCHR agreed to significant revisions to its previously robust monitoring mandate, giving rise to an outcry from advocates. However, when these concessions failed to appease the government, and the OHCHR office was forced to close entirely, the High Commissioner reacted by boldly publishing a groundbreaking report on violations of human rights and humanitarian law and database of materials that OHCHR had prepared for the purpose of delivery to transitional justice mechanisms that the government of Nepal ultimately failed to create. This move was met with intense criticism by the government but with applause by victims' advocates and many other governments.

It is certainly true that the High Commissioner must speak out against the commission of gross abuses as a function of accountability to victims, but several of our commentators suggest that even more may be required, echoing Abeysekera's conclusion that in every country where the High Commissioner and OHCHR are active – and perhaps in every country in the world – the High Commissioner has a responsibility not only to act, but also *to be seen to act*, in a way that provides protection for the work of human rights defenders and that affirms the principle of 'all human rights for all.' Abeysekera calls on High Commissioners to increase the accessibility and usefulness of UN human rights mechanisms to human rights defenders. Samar concurs, calling on the High Commissioner to ensure that her field presences in Afghanistan and Sudan cooperate with local human rights defenders and facilitate cooperation between those defenders and the government.

Some of the contributors paint a dismal picture of human rights defenders' perception of the High Commissioner's performance in countries with particularly challenging human rights situations. Moskalenko, Goldman, and Fitzpatrick lament the fact that the OHCHR field presence in Russia is limited to human rights advisers authorized only to carry out technical cooperation in the area of 'human rights education,' and blocked from engaging on the human rights issues of greatest concern to local human rights defenders. They note that the High Commissioner engages meaningfully on key human rights issues with civil society in places with worse human rights records than Russia and raise credibility questions as they demand that the High Commissioner attempt to do more inside Russia.

Other authors express a more optimistic, albeit cautious, view of the High Commissioner's performance. Cohen applauds Navi Pillay for breaking with her predecessors, who from 1994 to 2011 declined to publicly criticize North Korea for human rights abuses pending attempts at behind-the-scenes negotiations with the government for cooperation and access. By issuing in early 2013 a statement roundly condemning the government's human rights record, Pillay focused particular attention on North Korea's extensive political prison camp system, repeating allegations relayed to her in personal interviews with two former prisoners. Pillay called for an international commission of inquiry to investigate and promote accountability for abuse. Cohen calls on her to do more, independently and as a catalyst for the rest of the UN system, to shed light on human rights abuses in North Korea, reminding the High Commissioner of her responsibility to bring UN scrutiny to bear on one of the world's worst human rights abusers, despite its government's vigorous efforts to block these attempts.

Conclusion

The UN General Assembly's creation of the post of UN High Commissioner for Human Rights in 1993 advanced a longstanding aim of establishing a leader who could act to protect individuals from abuse and promote dignity, equality, and freedom for all. The scholars, policymakers, and advocates who have examined the achievements of the High Commissioner for Human Rights to date suggest that the post has evolved and grown substantially since its creation. They recognize how individual High Commissioners, both alone and together with a growing staff and relatively modest resources (in UN terms), have worked to breathe life into universal standards of human rights.

Though the mandate of the High Commissioner was meandering, creating neither a judge nor an enforcer, it authorized the appointee to "play an active role" to protect and implement human rights. Creative occupants of the position have helped make the post active and effective. The authors of this volume characterize José Ayala Lasso as a weak and even timid first High Commissioner; Mary Robinson as an advocate, bearing witness to violations, who raised the public profile of the High Commissioner; and Sergio Vieira de Mello as a UN veteran eager to achieve human rights protection on the ground. They appreciate Bertrand Ramcharan as a long-serving UN official who deeply understood the complex mandate and potential of the High Commissioner post and invoked the independent authority in the High Commissioner's mandate at key moments; and Louise Arbour as the promoter of a strategic vision of OHCHR as a UN agency with worldwide presence who pursued the increased resources necessary to realize this vision. Both she and her successor Navi Pillay are noted for placing increased focus on accountability for human rights violations, and Pillay is praised for implementing the strategic vision and for her work on Syria and with the Security Council, even as she is encouraged to obtain additional resources to build all aspects of the UN's human rights apparatus.

The High Commissioners for Human Rights are seen in these essays as confronting many dilemmas as they seek to deliver on the promise of the Universal Declaration of Human Rights and the post they hold. The authors bring to light contradictions in the role of the High Commissioner and challenges in their choices of methods. They chronicle and analyze the difficult decisions and results of many of the initiatives taken and offer recommendations that reflect a realistic sense of what can reasonably be expected from the High Commissioners to advance human rights protection worldwide. They encourage the individuals who currently and in the future will hold the post of High Commissioner for Human Rights to maintain the independence of the office, to speak out with authoritative information on human rights so it can be brought to bear on public policy, and to act firmly and rapidly to advance the protection of individuals within countries worldwide.

We hope that this volume will prove useful in ensuring that in the future the post of High Commissioner for Human Rights continues to be strengthened in ways that will fulfill the post's ambitious mandate.

PART ONE

THE PROMISE OF THE HIGH COMMISSIONER: REFLECTIONS ON THE PAST AND PROPOSALS FOR THE FUTURE

RIGHTS INFLATION AND ROLE CONFLICT IN THE OFFICE OF THE HIGH COMMISSIONER FOR HUMAN RIGHTS

Michael Ignatieff

The scholars, activists and UN civil servants taking part in this collection are all asking the same question: has the UN human rights system as a whole gained legitimacy and effectiveness since the creation of the Office of the High Commissioner for Human Rights? This is a question worth asking. International institutions can't improve unless they subject themselves to a process of adversarial justification at the hands of governments, activists and academics. By 'justification,' I mean UN agencies need to account for their record within the UN, but also beyond it, to critical audiences outside the system. By 'adversarial,' I mean, they need to be ready to answer tough questions when their justifications seem to fail.

The last 20 years have been a testing time for the UN human rights system. The first UN High Commissioner for Human Rights took office within days of the genocide in Rwanda.[1] The times since then include Kosovo plus 9/11, followed by the war in Iraq, the operation in Afghanistan, the bloody conclusion of the Sri Lankan civil war, Libya, and now Syria. The UN High Commissioner for Human Rights has affirmed that there are massive human rights violations in Syria.[2] We could say that she did her job and the Security Council didn't. So Syria is a framing context for our discussion.

An obvious role conflict is built into the office of the High Commissioner for Human Rights. On the one hand, she is a senior UN human rights official accountable to the UN system and Member States.[3] On the other hand, she is accountable to 'we the peoples of the United Nations' and is often described, with some exaggeration, as 'the conscience of the world.'

---

[1] José Ayala Lasso arrived in Geneva on April 5, 1994 to begin a four-year term as the first United Nations High Commissioner for Human Rights. On April 6, 1994, Rwandan President Juvénal Habyarimana was assassinated when his plane was shot down above the Rwandan capital of Kigali, marking the beginning of the genocide there.

[2] "Top UN Human Rights Official Says Member States 'Must Act Now' to Protect Syrian People, as Violent Crackdown Continues, in briefing to General Assembly," UN Department of Public Information, news release GA/11206, February 13, 2012.

[3] UN General Assembly. Resolution 48/141, "High Commissioner for the promotion and protection of all human rights," UN Doc. A/RES/48/141, December 20, 1993.

Accountability pulls her in two different ways. She is accountable to the world's victims and she is accountable to a Human Rights Council made up of states responsible for the abuses. She has to be both a master of quiet diplomacy with rights violating states and a public champion of the abused. She has to extract resources from wealthy states for her UN field presences while criticizing their often faulty human rights records, especially in the fight against global terrorism. She is mandated to provide assistance to the treaty bodies and the special rapporteurs and she has to be accountable to the press, and through them to global public opinion, when the UN human rights system fails victims, as it often does.

This conflict in roles is intrinsic to the office, and all of the personalities who have held the office have handled the conflict differently: José Ayala Lasso; Mary Robinson; Sergio Vieira de Mello; Bertie Ramcharan; Louise Arbour; and Navi Pillay, the current High Commissioner.

If you look at the men and women who have held the post, with one exception, all of them were UN insiders. They got the job in part because they knew the UN system from the inside. They had been UN ambassadors, UN officials, prosecutors, or judges in the emerging system of international justice.[4] The one High Commissioner who wasn't a UN insider was Mary Robinson, but she had an independent political base as a head of state and human rights lawyer in her native land. To be successful, a High Commissioner has to be an insider with experience navigating the UN system and an outsider, a global politician with the status and standing to challenge the system and confront Member States. No wonder it is a tough job.

When Sergio Vieira de Mello was transitioning into the High Commissioner's job, Harold Koh, then a professor at the Yale Law School, gave him a good piece of advice. "Well the test, Sergio, for success is when you get in a cab in Mumbai, Beijing, London, or Paris, the cabbie will turn around and say 'oh, you're the human rights guy!'"[5] Koh went on to say, "you will then have the independent political base that will make you the global conscience, the global spokesman."[6] The story captures the global expectations that go with the role, but it also captures the conflict between being a UN politician and a global voice of conscience.

---

[4] See biographies of the High Commissioners at UN Office of the High Commissioner for Human Rights, "High Commissioner," http://www.ohchr.org/EN/AboutUs/Pages/HighCommissioner.aspx.

[5] Harold Hongju Koh, *A Job Description for the U.N. High Commissioner for Human Rights*, 35 Colum. Hum. Rts. L. Rev. 493, 495 (2004).

[6] Ibid., 495.

There is a further conflict between legacy roles and emergent ones. The legacy roles include serving as the secretariat for the overburdened and often ineffective treaty bodies that monitor state compliance with UN human rights conventions and treaties. Another legacy role is supporting the work of the voluntary special rapporteurs who produce themed or country-specific reports on human rights abuses. These legacy roles are built into the UN system long-term, but they draw staff and resources away from emerging roles. The chief of these are being a norm entrepreneur for emerging human rights issues like gay, lesbian, and transgender rights and being a global spokesman for the human rights crises, like Syria, that draw global media attention. Over the last twenty years, the High Commissioner has had to transition from quiet diplomacy in the corridors of power to public diplomacy through the global media. Feeding the ravenous beast of the media can take any manager away from core business, and for the High Commissioner the core business has to be building the capability, resources, and competence of the UN human rights system itself.

Sometimes these role conflicts have been excruciatingly difficult. Sergio Vieira de Mello's struggle with these roles ended in tragedy. In 2003 he left his job as High Commissioner for Human Rights, in part out of frustration at the paralysis and legalism in the UN human rights machinery. While High Commissioner he was ferociously criticized for being a willing accomplice to American imperialism in Iraq. When he told an interviewer in 2003 that "It's not for me to uphold or to applaud," American conduct in Iraq, his attempt to balance relations with America and its critics did the authority of the High Commissioner real damage.[7] He then went to Iraq as the Secretary-General's Special Representative to put the UN back into the center of the global power game. Vieira de Mello's story could be read as a parable of the role conflicts in senior UN posts. Faced with the choice between low profile quiet diplomacy as High Commissioner and a high-risk role as a global politician in Iraq, he chose the latter and paid for the choice with his life.

Over the last twenty years, the potential for role conflict has grown as High Commissioners have chosen to privilege defense of victims over deference to states. If you read the first High Commissioner's reports there is no occasion in which he mentions a Member State negatively under any

---

[7] Tim Sebastian, "War: what price human rights?" *BBC HARDtalk* (interview with Sergio Vieira de Mello), April 14, 2003, http://news.bbc.co.uk/2/hi/programmes/hardtalk/2946949.stm.

circumstances.[8] Periphrastic generality ruled. If you look at the current High Commissioner's reports, Member States are named, one after another: Libya, Syria, Russia, Sri Lanka, and so on.[9] The contrast is an important sign, I think, that the High Commissioner is acquiring the authority to privilege her role as global conscience, accountable to victims, over her political responsibility to Member States.

The increasing outspokenness of the High Commissioner is an excellent thing, as far as activists and victims are concerned, but it comes with a price. In response, states are shutting the High Commissioner out, refusing to co-operate with special rapporteurs or comply with recommendations from UN treaty bodies.[10] Criticizing states while maintaining access and leverage has not proven easy for the High Commissioner, but on balance, most activists would recommend that a High Commissioner should never pull her punches in order to gain access to some rights-offending politician.

Another important evolution in the High Commissioner's role has been more authoritative human rights reporting. The current High Commissioner made herself the gold standard on the human rights situation in Syria.[11] Her count of the victims and her blunt reporting to the Security Council have consolidated the authority of her office at a time when the UN itself has lost credibility because of the Security Council impasse on Syria.[12] A vital function of a High Commissioner and a key lever for acquiring greater authority is to become the gold standard on the facts. In this role, she faces strong competition. Human Rights Watch and Amnesty International have led a revolution in human rights research, marked by a professionalization of standards, improved access on the ground and

---

[8] See, e.g., UN General Assembly, *Report of the United Nations High Commissioner for Human Rights*, UN Doc. A/50/36 (1996), Official Records of the General Assembly, Fiftieth Session, Supplement No. 36.

[9] See, e.g., the annual OHCHR reports since 2000: http://www.ohchr.org/EN/PUBLICATIONSRESOURCES/Pages/AnnualReportAppeal.aspx.

[10] For example, under President Alexander Lukashenko, the government of Belarus has engaged in an increasingly harsh campaign to suppress political opposition and has refused to cooperate with the OHCHR or comply with UN recommendations. See Navi Pillay, "Oral report by the United Nations High Commissioner for Human Rights on The Human Rights Situation in the Republic of Belarus to the 18th session of the Human Rights Council," (statement delivered in Geneva, September 20, 2011), http://www2.ohchr.org/english/bodies/hrcouncil/docs/18session/Oral_report-on_Belarus 20Sep2011.pdf.

[11] See e.g. UN Human Rights Council, 18th Session, *Report of the United Nations High Commissioner for Human Rights on the situation of human rights in the Syrian Arab Republic*, UN Doc. A/HR/18/53, September 15, 2011.

[12] Ibid.

adept use of the internet and social media to publicize results. Competition with aggressive, well-funded, multi-million dollar human rights organizations like Amnesty and Human Rights Watch has forced successive High Commissioners to raise their game.

In this competition for voice and influence in the human rights world, the High Commissioner and the NGOs both have had to keep on the right side of the line between propaganda and information. Strong feelings are not a substitute for the facts and the facts in human rights cases are often complex and ambiguous. A High Commissioner is not in the business of awarding gold stars or conferring moral immunity to the weaker side in a conflict. Of all the role conflicts a High Commissioner has to struggle with, one of the most acute must be inside her own head, struggling to maintain impartiality, discipline, and professionalism in the midst of human rights crises that test every observer to the limit.

As she confronts these conflicts of role, and the struggle to maintain impartiality, she has to do so without the resources she needs. There is a ludicrous gap between the UN's human rights rhetoric and the actual resources that Member States commit to the Office of the High Commissioner. Louise Arbour was vocal in her complaints on this score, pointing out that less than two percent of the UN budget was allocated to human rights defense.[13] This makes the High Commissioner a larger player than Human Rights Watch, but not by much, and successive High Commissioners now compete with private NGO rivals that are nearly as well resourced and have none of the constraints she faces within the UN system. Mary Robinson was voicing a certain institutional resignation when she said, at one point in her mandate, "The tools at my disposal are modest, the tools being mainly advocacy and persuasion."[14] This is putting the best possible face on it, but advocacy and persuasion are no substitute for a robust field presence in rights offending countries and vigorous support for national human rights commissions, independent commissions of inquiry, and special rapporteurs. All of these vital functions are drastically underfunded.[15]

---

[13] Louise Arbour, "Plan of action drawn up by the United Nations High Commissioner for Human Rights," in Report of the Secretary-General, *In larger freedom: towards development, security and human rights for all,"* Addendum 3, UN Doc. A/59/2005/Add.3, May 26, 2005.

[14] Mary Robinson, "Realizing Human Rights: 'Take hold of it boldly and duly…,'" Romanes Lecture, Oxford University, November 11, 1997, http://www.un.org/rights/50/dpi1938.htm.

[15] See OHCHR, *Management Plan 2012–2013*, Part II, http://www2.ohchr.org/english/ohchrreport2011/web_version/media/pdf/13_OHCHR_OMP_2012-13-Budget.pdf; See also

The resource deficit is made worse by the fact that successive High Commissioners have struggled to move staff out of headquarters onto the front-lines. You can't protect human rights in Geneva and New York. You have to be in Turkmenistan, Equatorial Guinea, Damascus, Benghazi, and so on. Rather like Western development agencies that can't get their staff out of their nation's capitals, the High Commissioner has had recurrent problems in staffing up robust field presences on the human rights front line.[16]

This issue, the resistance of the UN bureaucracy itself to making the High Commissioner more visible on the front lines, needs to be put in a wider context. I said at the outset that there's a conflict between her UN role and her role as conscience of the world. You could put the point more sharply: the UN system eats away at the legitimacy of the High Commissioner herself. This is a familiar problem to anyone who knows the UN system. The High Commissioner goes to Human Rights Council meetings in Geneva for six weeks, and then has to spend the rest of the year trying to explain why some notorious rights violator was in the chair, why Israel was singled out for sanction and so on.[17] Her role requires her to justify the legitimacy gaps of the UN system itself. You can't get chosen for the job in the first place if you are too obviously hostile either to the UN human rights system or to the dubious human rights conduct of important states. Equally, you can't do the job unless you call a spade a spade. Managing these role conflicts is the core political challenge of the job.

It ought to be obvious that the High Commissioner's role is inescapably political, but many human rights activists and defenders resolutely insist that human rights work cannot be political. Human rights, it is said, is above politics. It's a kind of anti-politics. That's true in the sense that there are no acceptable political justifications for the abuse of human beings. There are no higher causes, no justification on grounds of political expediency or national emergency that justify indefinite detention without trial, torture or denial of voice rights. To that extent, human rights *is* an anti-politics. But getting results in human rights is also an intensely political

---

Navi Pillay, "Statement by Ms. Navi Pillay, United Nations High Commissioner of Human Rights," (statement delivered in New York, October 24, 2012), http://www.ohchr.org/en/NewsEvents/Pages/DisplayNews.aspx?NewsID=12690&LangID=E.

[16] See generally OHCHR Annual Reports, http://www.ohchr.org/EN/PUBLICATIONS RESOURCES/Pages/AnnualReportAppeal.aspx.

[17] See e.g., "Statement by Ms. Navanethem Pillay, UN High Commissioner for Human Rights, on speech by President of Iran at Durban Review Conference," April 20, 2009, http://www.un.org/en/durbanreview2009/statements.shtml.

activity. At least one High Commissioner acknowledged as much. At the end of a particularly hypocritical and tendentious Human Rights Council meeting in Geneva in 2003, when a delegate accused another of 'politicizing' human rights, Sergio Vieira de Mello intervened:

> Give me a break. Let me suggest that the word 'politicization' be retired from active service. Let me be frank, most of the people in this room work for governments or seek to effect the actions of governments; that is politics. For some to accuse others of being political is a bit like fish criticizing one another for being wet.[18]

The current High Commissioner said recently that she doesn't do politics, she does human rights.[19] This seems to ignore the fact that any High Commissioner has to pick her spots and choose which battles to fight. She's a human rights politician. Of course her politics has to be disciplined by commitments to the conventions, the treaty bodies, the reports of the special rapporteurs. Human rights has a legal frame which limits political discretion. There's the ethical frame as well, which should limit moral partiality in her selection of which human rights causes to champion. But let's be honest with ourselves: she picks battles she believes she can win. If she gets the politics wrong, she's accused of partiality or of being a tool of the permanent five members of the Security Council. If she challenges powerful states, she puts her resources at risk. It's politics, politics, politics, all the way down.

In the High Commissioners' discharge of this highly political role, there have been some high points. They have stood up for the indivisibility and universality of human rights in the face of strong counter challenge from the Muslim world,[20] and in 1995, they helped lead the re-affirmation at Beijing that women's rights are human rights.[21]

---

[18] "Commission's Structures Are Sound, Problems Can Be Surmounted, High Commissioner Says As Main Human Rights Body Ends Session," OHCHR press release, April 25, 2003.

[19] See National Museum of Australia, "Mike Gooda joins the conversation," Audio recording transcript, October 28, 2011, http://www.nma.gov.au/audio/transcripts/NMA_Gooda_20111008.html.

[20] For example, on a visit to the Maldives in November 2011, High Commissioner Navi Pillay condemned the practice of flogging women convicted of extra-marital sex and said that a constitutional provision prohibiting citizens from practicing any faith other than Sunni Islam was discriminatory and out of line with international standards. "Opening remarks by UN High Commissioner for Human Rights Navi Pillay at a press conference during her mission to the Maldives," OHCHR, November 24, 2011.

[21] In the months preceding the 1995 Beijing World Conference on Women, as states were negotiating the draft outcome document for the conference, the Vatican, certain states with Catholic governments, and the Organization of the Islamic Conference had allied with one another in an attempt to condition the content of women's rights on

Louise Arbour also stood up against the damage done to the international human rights framework by the counter-terrorism policies of the US, Great Britain and other liberal democracies after 9/11.[22] Safeguarding respect for human rights in the core countries of the common law tradition has turned out to be more difficult than anyone would have supposed in the heady days after the fall of the Berlin Wall and we supposed, for an instant, that human rights would advance in tandem with the spread of democracy. The High Commissioner has to defend human rights in Washington, London, Paris, Ottawa, and Canberra just as much as in the capitals of the Global South, and the High Commissioner cannot afford to back down from that challenge.

If these were some of the high points of the High Commissioner's work in the past twenty years, the low points were a failure to control rights inflation, the tendency to codify aspirations in the economic, social and cultural field into rights language.[23] It's hard to think of a single poor person in the developing world who gained anything from the attempt to turn aspirations for global justice and a fairer international division of labor into a 'right to development.' A rights-based approach to development is a whole other story.[24] Empowering women with voice rights and participation rights is crucial to economic development. The human rights agenda that matters is always simple: protect voice, enhance agency, put cruelty first. Keep it simple. Voice, agency, cruelty: these are the core of the mandate. The right to development effort was the pursuit of a mirage.

It's also obvious that the Durban Conference on racism, however well intended, was a disaster for the UN human rights system, with the

---

religious and cultural values. High Commissioner José Ayala Lasso, at the request of several NGOs, played a helpful role in pressing these issues by writing the Secretary-General to express concern, emphasizing that "language which could be read to indicate that cultural, religious or other particularities should have priority consideration over human rights, would not respect the well-crafted balance achieved" in earlier UN human rights texts such as the Vienna Declaration. Thereafter, Ayala Lasso also made a strong statement to the World Conference itself, reiterating these points. See Jaya Dayal, "U.N. Human Rights Tsar Says Beijing Draft Weakens Rights," *Inter-Press Service*, July 25, 1995.

[22] See Column Lynch, "U.N. Human Rights Chief to Leave Post," *Washington Post*, March 3, 2008.

[23] On "rights inflation," see Stanford Encyclopedia of Philosophy, "Human Rights," http://plato.stanford.edu/entries/rights-human/.

[24] See OHCHR, *Frequently Asked Questions on a Human Rights-Based Approach to Development Cooperation* UN Doc. HR/PUB/06/8 (2006), http://www.ohchr.org/Documents/Publications/FAQen.pdf.

conference deformed by efforts to insert the unseemly and false equivalency of Zionism as racism.[25] Israel has a right to be judged by exactly the same standards as any other state, and the spectacle of flagrant rights-abusing states using a conference to put Israel exclusively in the dock damaged the UN system in the eyes of European and North American opinion. The High Commissioner herself may not be responsible for the conduct of delegations at global conferences, but – and this is how politics works – she has to carry the can when things go wrong.[26]

In managing her always scarce supply of resources and legitimacy against the almost infinite demands on her time, it seems important, in conclusion, for the High Commissioner to fight role inflation, just as she needs to fight rights inflation. Role inflation occurs when you succumb to headline chasing. A reasonable desire to stay relevant can degenerate into a scramble to say something about each and every abuse that occurs in our turbulent and bitter world. This is why she needs to pick her battles. She does so to use scarce resources wisely and to convey the sense that she drives the agenda instead of allowing herself to be driven by civil society, the media, and victim's groups. Maintaining control over your own agenda is how to preserve the political standing of the office.

Finally, doing the job well means knowing what your business is. The High Commissioner is not in the development business: leave that to the development agencies, governments and economists. She is not in the prosecution business: leave that to the prosecutor and the court at the ICC. She is not in the intervention business: leave that to states and the Security Council. She is in the human rights business, and the core of that is to build the capacity of human rights defenders in states around the world; to anchor rights in the constitutions of emerging states; to advance judicial and police training so that ordinary people actually experience that blessed thing, the rule of law; to promote the independence of human rights commissions so that ordinary people have real redress in their own countries; and finally, to use her unique power as the sober, fact-based voice of the global conscience to call states large and small, democratic

25 Tom Lantos, "The Durban Debacle: An Insider's View of the World Racism Conference at Durban," *The Fletcher Forum of World Affairs*, 26 (1) Winter/Spring 2002, Reprint. http://www.eyeontheun.org/assets/attachments/articles/568_durban_debacle.pdf.

26 See ibid. ("To many of us present at the events at Durban, it is clear that much of the responsibility for the debacle rests on the shoulders of UN High Commissioner for Human Rights Mary Robinson, who, in her role as secretary-general of the conference, failed to provide the leadership needed to keep the conference on track.").

and undemocratic, powerful and powerless to account for their conduct towards their citizens. The goals of the office are simple, really: to fight cruelty, enhance voice, and protect agency. Judged by that standard, the Office of the High Commissioner has a challenge ahead: to anchor human rights observance on the ground, where it matters, among the people of the world that she serves.

THE UN HIGH COMMISSIONER FOR HUMAN RIGHTS: FROM THE PERSONAL TO THE INSTITUTIONAL

Harold Hongju Koh*

The subject of my remarks is carefully chosen: 'The Office of the High Commissioner, from the personal to the institutional.' From Max Weber on, there has been a discussion about how one transforms institutions that are led by high-profile individuals into institutions that have a life and energy of their own.[1] Over the last two decades, I have watched this Office from at least four different perspectives: as an international law professor interested in the development of international institutions and regimes; as a human rights advocate; as Assistant Secretary of State for Human Rights in the Clinton Administration; and as Legal Adviser to the State Department in the Obama Administration.

From each of these perspectives, I have seen the importance of the High Commissioner for Human Rights. Six remarkable individuals have held that job and I have had the great honor of knowing them all. It was nine years ago that I came to Columbia Law School to give a talk to an audience that included Sergio Vieira de Mello – someone with whom I had the pleasure of working both in Kosovo and in East Timor – about what the High Commissioner's Office ought to do.[2] I never realized that that would be the last time I would speak to Sergio, because then, as you know, he went to Baghdad and was tragically killed in the line of duty.

What I suggested at the time was that the High Commissioner – the person of the High Commissioner – should do five things:

First, and most important, 'just show up.' The High Commissioner must be the world's 'emergency human rights first-responder,' someone always ready to go into the teeth of the human rights disaster, in a high-profile way, along with the humanitarian relief workers. In many respects, this is

---

* This is a lightly edited and footnoted version of remarks made while I was Legal Adviser to the U.S. Department of State under Secretary of State Hillary Rodham Clinton. It draws heavily upon remarks first given in 2004, see footnote 2 below.

[1] Max Weber, *The Theory of Social and Economic Organization* (New York: The Free Press, 1964), 386–406.

[2] Harold Hongju Koh, "A Job Description for the U.N. High Commissioner for Human Rights," *Columbia Human Rights Law Review*, no. 35 (2004): 493–503.

the most important thing: to 'fly into the flame,' as John Shattuck told me when I took over as Assistant Secretary for Human Rights. You should be 'the second person in,' I was told. The first person in does humanitarian work, the second person in does human rights work. You have to be the equivalent of an emergency first responder. In other words, when everybody else is running away from a disaster, you have to be running toward it. You have to be prepared to go in in a way in which you meet the relevant players and assess the situation. If you're not prepared to do that, you shouldn't take the job. You shouldn't take the job as Assistant Secretary for Human Rights if you're not prepared to do that, and if your first instinct when a human rights conflagration is breaking out is to wait, then you're the wrong person for the job. So the first imperative is 'just showing up.'

Now, obviously, in the process of being present and speaking to these issues, you can make mistakes, and every High Commissioner has made mistakes. On the other hand, if people become comfortable in knowing that a human rights situation is being appraised by the High Commissioner and his or her Office, they feel a lot better that this dimension is being covered. So it should not be just the UN relief workers; it should not be somebody from the Secretary-General's office; it has to be someone whose mandate is human rights to show that the world cares, cares enough to show up.

Showing up also tells you that the person is more than just a diplomat, but also a human rights reporter and appraiser. When I was at the Human Rights Commission during the Kosovo controversy, it was a six-week experience during which the Kosovo issue was going on. So I first arrived in Geneva, gave a speech, and then flew to Kosovo.[3] And then about two weeks later, after I spent a week in Kosovo, I came back to Geneva, and there was a dinner at which many of the diplomats said, "we saw you on TV in Kosovo," and their reaction was intense surprise: they seemed startled that a U.S. official would actually *go* to Kosovo, as opposed to simply *talk* about Kosovo. In my view, Geneva was very close to Kosovo. It seemed crazy to be talking about a human rights crisis, then not actually going to observe the situation on the ground. So the number one element of the job description is 'just show up.' Now, that's easy to say, hard to do. In most of these places, transportation is bad, communication is nonexistent, security is minimal, conditions can be incredibly dangerous. You have

---

[3] Harold Hongju Koh, "Remarks to U.N. Human Rights Commission on Kosovo" (speech, Geneva, April 1, 1999).

a full-time job going on, so the question is how to make this actually part of your job, as opposed to something done by somebody else who reports to you. The most important reason to 'just show up' is also the most obvious: it puts you in the same situation of jeopardy as the people whose human rights you're speaking for, and it helps you then to understand it from their perspective. If you're walking down the same streets that they are, and you could be killed as easily as they could be, it's hard not to empathize with the people who are defenseless in these kinds of circumstances.

There's a second element: The High Commissioner must not just be a human rights monitor and reporter, but a *comparative evaluator* of human rights abuses according to global standards. Amid cycles of violence and counter-violence, the High Commissioner must be willing to catalogue the abuses that are going on and clarify roughly what percentage are being committed by which actors. This helps the world to understand exactly what is happening and which players bear the brunt of human rights explanation.

When the High Commissioner for Human Rights shows up somewhere, there are human rights NGOs on the ground as well as other internationals – reporters, humanitarian workers, International Committee of the Red Cross (ICRC) – and they often have extraordinarily important insights. In the bar of the best hotel in town are the reporters who will actually tell you what's happening on the ground and which refugee camp you should go visit, and you can talk with them without traveling somewhere else, which allows you to synthesize a large amount of information that you can get out to the world. What is the information that you're fundamentally trying to get out? Mainly, to characterize the situation as a particular type or level of human rights abuse. When we were in East Timor, Sergio, who was not the High Commissioner at that time, said to me, "Harold, this is not Kosovo. This is a *scorched earth policy*. There are massacres in which houses are being destroyed, people are being driven out, windows are being broken and houses are being looted by militias, and then they burn those houses to the ground." And he said, "I've seen many kinds of atrocities, but I have never seen this kind of scorched earth before." So when I gave a press conference later that day, I used that phrase, because it helps people in another part of the world understand what's going on.[4]

[4] Harold Hongju Koh, "Koh Special Briefing on Indonesia/Timor Visit" (speech, Washington, D.C., October 12, 1997).

When there is a conflict going on – and this is very often the case – usually, both sides are not equally blameless. Just who are the people who are more responsible and who are the people who are less responsible? The obvious way out is to say there are abuses on all sides, and there often are, but usually, one side is committing more abuses. And it is very important in the initial assessment to give some sense of comparative responsibility to those who are observing from the outside world, so they know who are the people who are basically on a rampage, and who are the people who are caught up in that rampage. Mary Robinson, who was a former barrister, did an extremely good job of appearing on the scene and, in a very concise way, expressing the scale of abuses that were going on – saying who bore the most responsibility, and who bore lesser responsibility.

The third imperative is that the world needs a *human face for human rights.* The High Commissioner has to be the human face. Jacob Blaustein called for a High Commissioner for Human Rights in his Dag Hammarskjold Lecture.[5] Rene Cassin called for an Attorney General for Human Rights.[6] But in the age of CNN, Facebook, and Twitter, the world cannot understand the concept of human rights unless there is a face behind it, a global human face. Just as UN Secretary-General Kofi Annan provided that human face for peace and security; and Mrs. Ogata provided it for refugee affairs, we in the human rights world need someone who can and will be viewed as the conscience of the world, a secular pope for global human rights. Ideally, this person must pass what I call the 'taxi driver test.' When the driver of the average taxi cab that you hail – whether in Delhi, Rio, Nairobi, Cairo, Paris, Beijing, or New York – asks, "Aren't you the High Commissioner?" you will be on your way to having the independent political base that you will need to deal with the many difficult actors you will have to contend with in this job.

There were many who had this idea and pushed it forward, but this has a different kind of meaning in the digital age. You now need someone who is a trusted figure on these issues. Why is this important? Because the High Commissioner doesn't have a political base. In presidential politics, the way that people acquire political bases is by having people who listen to you, and who are excited by you and excited by the issues you represent.

---

[5] Jacob Blaustein, "Human Rights: A Challenge to the United Nations and to Our Generation" in *The Quest for Peace: The Dag Hammarskjold Memorial Lecture Series*, ed. Andrew W. Cordier and Wilder Foote (New York, Columbia University Press, 1965), 315, 318–19.

[6] Roger Stenson Clark, *A United Nations High Commissioner for Human Rights* (The Hague: Martinus Nijhoff, 1972).

So building a personal image is a tremendously important part of having the necessary political base to take on the various establishments that you're going to have to take on.

A fourth requirement is that the UN High Commissioner must be an explicitly hybrid creature: part politician, part bureaucrat, and part human rights expert without tipping too far in any direction. Philip Alston has spoken of the Commissioner's established 'right of independent initiative,' which allows the Commissioner to play a potentially invaluable 'missing link' in the world's human rights arsenal.[7] As Mary Robinson noted, the High Commissioner has a 'self-activating mandate': she is a global point person for human rights who is capable of acting without waiting to be authorized.[8]

Those of you who have headed organizations know that in leadership roles, if you are too much the politician, you may not succeed; if you're too much the bureaucrat, you may not succeed; if you're too much the expert, you may not succeed. You have to play all of these roles at the same time. The key is the 'self-activating mandate,' the self-referral.[9] There are cases, many cases – and this is true of any executive – where issues are presented to you, and you decide what to do. But the test of your accomplishment is not your reactive ability; it is your *proactive* ability. What places the High Commissioner in a unique position is that the High Commissioner has a right of independent initiative in the human rights system, which everybody else lacks. Now, the Secretary-General also has a right of independent initiative, but not specific to human rights per se. He must deal with many other issues. And many of the things that I'm describing are also characteristics of some of the best Secretaries-General. But it seems to me that the High Commissioner has to understand and try to play all the roles well, in the same way that a university dean or CEO does.

Fifth and finally, the High Commissioner must coordinate and play the role of point person for the human rights bureaucracy. This is an under-discussed topic, which ought to be more and more important as

---

[7] Philip Alston, "Hobbling the Monitors: Should U.N. Human Rights Monitors be Accountable?," *Harvard International Law Journal* 52 (2011): 563–648.

[8] Mary Robinson, "Realizing Human Rights: "Take Hold of it Boldly and Duly..."" (Romanes Lecture, Oxford University, Nov 11, 1997), UN Department of Public Education, http://www.un.org/rights/50/dpi1938.htm.

[9] This also has been deemed the High Commissioner's "right of initiative". Bertrand Ramcharan, "The United Nations High Commissioner for Human Rights and International Humanitarian Law," *Harvard University Program on Humanitarian Policy and Conflict Research Occasional Paper Series*, no. 3 (Spring, 2005).

time goes on. Within the UN system, it is relatively easy to create an organization and virtually impossible ever to eliminate one. Therefore, the more organizations, working groups, and special rapporteurs that come into existence, the more the world needs someone whose primary job description is coordination: to take the conclusions of one body and bring it to the attention of another, so that the different groups do not step on each other's toes and reinvent each other's work. The entity that can coordinate among those is an extraordinarily important entity. Today, this is even more important than it was, because so many things flow through the High Commissioner. Not only that, most of the human rights apparatus of the UN consists of people doing part-time jobs, and they need a home base, they need resources, they need someone who will back them up. They need someone who will advertise their conclusions, they need someone who is a screener who assigns people credibility: who says "this person is serious, and this person is not." At the end of the day, in this business, reputation is everything. And people who have big titles and no 'street cred' can give speeches, can hold positions, but if they have no 'corridor reputation,' it is very unlikely that they can achieve their goal.

If these are the five roles that the High Commissioner plays, what then are the *assets* that the Commissioner brings to these positions? The first is what I would call the concept of 'distinctive voice.' Andrew Clapham called it the 'French horn mentality.'[10] The High Commissioner is part of an orchestra – the UN orchestra – but your voice is so distinctive you always hear it. This is a unique role that the High Commissioner plays, which then is enhanced if you play the role of 'insider/outsider' – in other words, someone who's part of the system, but also a little bit outside the system, the 'in-house NGO,' as it were. Therefore, the High Commissioner must be viewed not just as compliant, but as a little bit dangerous. When you go to a meeting with the High Commissioner, people should be not sure what she's going to say, and be a little bit afraid of what she's going to say, because frankly, it may or may not be the party line, but if properly expressed, it will *become* the party line.

Second, the creation of a High Commissioner for Human Rights position has had the effect of creating '*mirror people*': interlocutors in many

---

[10] Andrew Clapham, "The UN High Commissioner for Human Rights: Achievements and Frustrations," Background paper for Columbia Law School Symposium on the United Nations High Commissioner for Human Rights: The First Ten Years of the Office, and the Next, http://www2.law.columbia.edu/hri/symposium/ClaphamPaper.htm.

coordinate organizations. These are mirroring point people for human rights, both within national governments and within intergovernmental organizations, whose job description is to interact with the UN High Commissioner. So we have Assistant Secretary of State for Democracy Human Rights and Labor Michael Posner who plays that role for the Obama Administration. Now almost every major political system has someone who is the point person. It turns out that while part of their job is to connect to the human rights point person in the UN bureaucracy and to share their concerns, sometimes their job is to keep them occupied so they don't seriously interfere in the country they are going to examine. There are countries in Africa where if you go as U.S. Assistant Secretary for Human Rights, someone meets you who is the National Commissioner for Human Rights; you soon understand that their job is to basically take you to dinner, and show you files, and make sure you don't actually use your time doing anything productive. So managing the 'mirror people' is a huge task for the High Commissioner, and one that the High Commissioner needs to do very proactively.

Third, the High Commissioner draws strength from his or her relationship to the major political players in the geopolitical system, the indispensable political forces within the human rights system, particularly the United States and the European Union. These contacts are helpful in the best of times and they are critical in the worst of times. This means that the High Commissioner must have good relations at a very high level with the governments that really matter, even if they disagree with those governments a lot of the time. They have to be people of consequence who people within those governments feel the need to meet at a high level. To succeed, the High Commissioner must find a reliable point of contact at a high place within the major governments, preferably at the National Security Adviser or the Secretary of State level.

One of Mary Robinson's greatest assets was the fact that she was president of a country. When you're a president of a country and you go to another country, protocol dictates that you be met at the presidential level. And if your next job is to be the High Commissioner for Human Rights, and you come to the same country, and they want to have a deputy assistant secretary meet with you, you say, "Excuse me, I want to be met at the proper level! I want to meet the President, the Secretary of State, the National Security Adviser, and all the people who work for them." Now, obviously, this is a tricky business, because you cannot spend all your time worrying about protocol. But establishing these baselines is incredibly important.

Fourth, the High Commissioner can build partnerships with human rights governmental and non-governmental organizations (NGOs) to promote or give heightened visibility to issues which have been relatively under-discussed, e.g., economic, social, and cultural rights; indigenous rights; LGBT rights. Recently, Secretary Clinton gave an extraordinary speech on LGBT rights.[11] She chose to use the forum of the UN Human Rights Council in Geneva on Human Rights Day to bring out an issue that a lot of people didn't want her to talk about. But it's incredibly important, when the Secretary of State of a very powerful country makes such a statement, for the rest of the community to get out there and start pushing the same issue. Hillary Clinton at Beijing famously said "women's rights are human rights" and had a huge impact;[12] it made good sense that she should do so on this issue as well. And by the way, there were plenty of people saying, "you shouldn't do this," yet she did it anyway. So when someone who's in a politically responsible position takes a risk like that, it's very important for other people – NGOs and governments alike – to echo the core of the message, and say something positive, even if you aren't in the habit of saying something positive about the United States or the Secretary of State. Because the fact of the matter is what she did is hard to do, and when someone shows the capacity to do it, they deserve the support of those with whom they would and should partner.

Finally, with all of these mirror people, governmental contacts, and organizational partnerships, only the High Commissioner can play the role of catalyst, particularly in parts of the world where there is no regional human rights system. Perhaps the only other possible catalysts are the indispensable nations of the human rights system – the US and the European Union play this role. I watched directly Mary Robinson's role as a catalyst for a human rights response in East Timor in 1999, and her credibility with African governments from her time in Rwanda and Somalia, when she was President of Ireland and had established her regional credibility for the later human rights crisis in Sierra Leone. She once said to me, "Harold, I think Ireland is a little bit like Africa. I've always said to them, 'we're also a developing nation, so let's work together on

[11] Hilary Clinton, "Remarks In Recognition of International Human Rights Day" (speech, Geneva, Switzerland, December 6, 2011), U.S. Department of State, http://www.state.gov/secretary/rm/2011/12/178368.htm.

[12] Hilary Clinton, "Remarks for the United Nations Fourth World Conference on Women" (speech, Beijing, China, September 5, 1995), http://www.columbia.edu/cu/augustine/arch/hrclinton.txt.

these kinds of things.'" It was strategically very clever. She also used her voice to provoke stronger responses from the European regional regime on such issues as human rights conditions in Chechnya.[13] The ICC's Prosecutor must follow the cases where they go, but the High Commissioner has more freedom to pick an affirmative agenda, to exercise her self-activating mandate.

Which brings me to the High Commissioner's biggest asset, the Office itself. Everything I've spoken of up to now is based on the personal attributes of particular individuals who, as we know, will serve for four or eight years. Therefore, anyone who has served in an institutional leadership role, like dean or president, comes to understand that the institutional development is much more timeless than whatever you accomplish personally. What's interesting about the UN General Assembly resolution that created the Office of the High Commissioner[14] is how broad and general it is. It tasks the High Commissioner, and accordingly her office, with broad and general responsibilities, such as the promotion and protection of all human rights. It says nothing about what the Office ought to do. But over its first eighteen years, the office itself has developed to fill in vacuums in the UN human rights world, integrating the practical with the aspirational. That this development has been ad hoc does not diminish it, and illustrates that the Office's future development is open to creative leadership and future adaptation. In fact, although I've specified what I think are the High Commissioner's job description and the High Commissioner's personal assets, what's become more and more clear to me is that the next generation should focus on strengthening the Office and its possibilities.

Think of this as like the 'panda's thumb.' Stephen J. Gould, the great evolutionary biologist, points out that pandas don't have thumbs.[15] Pandas basically do three things: they eat bamboo, they sleep, and they try (often unsuccessfully) to create new pandas. But if you go to the National Zoo in Washington, where they have a couple of pandas, you will notice that they spend most of their time stripping leaves from bamboo stalks with their 'thumbs.' Now, the oddity is that pandas don't have a thumb – Stephen J. Gould pointed this out. Unlike primates, pandas don't have opposable

13 "Council of Europe considers suspending Russia over Chechnya," *RTE News*, April 4, 2000.

14 UN General Assembly. Resolution 48/141, "High Commissioner for the promotion and protection of all human rights," UN Doc. A/RES/48/141, December 23, 1993.

15 Stephen J. Gould, *The Panda's Thumb: More Reflections on Natural History* (New York: Norton Books, 1980).

thumbs. But what they have evolved over time, adaptively, is a bone which they use in a crude, non-primate-like way, to perform the function that is required for their survival, which is to strip away the leaves from the bamboo stalk.

Why this biology lesson? For the simple reason that there's no Office of the High Commissioner specified, but there's an adaptive, evolutionary process by which various functions have been developed and addressed by a bureaucracy that is largely invisible to the world and of little interest, except to a group like this. And the real question ought to be, how can that adaptive evolution be proactively furthered to make the Office as effective it can be, so the same Office can both survive a weak Commissioner and empower a strong Commissioner to new heights?

Let me suggest how that can be done: by focusing on the five critical functions of (1) field offices, (2) support for the Human Rights Council, (3) the Office's role in the Universal Periodic Review, (4) its work on individual complaints, and (5) the Office's support for other human rights mechanisms, including the treaty bodies, special rapporteurs, and the like.

With regard to the field offices, I think that the High Commissioner's Office has made some very substantial moves. They don't have an embassy in every country in the world like the leading governments, but they do have 13 country or stand-alone offices, 12 regional offices, from Colombia to Cambodia and including, most recently, one in Tunisia to support Arab transitions in North Africa through a variety of functions: civil society capacity-building, training for government officials, assistance in drafting legislation, capacity building for transitional justice.[16]

Some of these offices have been extraordinarily effective. I think, for example, of Anders Kompass, who served brilliantly as the leader of the office in Colombia, and with whom I worked very closely for three years in the late nineties, who is now in the High Commissioner's Office in Geneva, after having been a superb leader of a regional operation. Today, the Tunisia office could not be more important. So even if you've never heard about this office, one thing should be to say, "shouldn't our office in Tunisia have more resources than it did before, because it's going to be the pivot point for the Arab Awakening?" Moreover, the offices, once fully staffed, can play an increasingly important role at the front lines of human rights, through monitoring, assessment, technical assistance, working with host

[16] See "OHCHR in Tunisia," http://www.ohchr.org/EN/Countries/MENARegion/Pages/OHCHRTunisia.aspx.

governments, assisting special rapporteurs working with those countries, and assisting governments with human rights processes, as they seek to ensure that regional UN operations act in ways that are consistent with human rights law.

The development of these offices, I think, is the central challenge for the High Commissioner's Office. Why should it be that the US government has more embassies than the High Commissioner's Office? Why should it be that Human Rights Watch, a private organization, has more field offices than the High Commissioner for Human Rights? That should not be. Until that kind of organizational throw-weight can be achieved, the High Commissioner's Office will be under-resourced.

What has been an interesting side development is that having human rights field offices under the High Commissioner in the field allows the field offices to directly connect, not just to governments, but to civil society, local communities, and to focus in on issues like bringing rights home, complementarity, making sure that it becomes meaningful to its intended beneficiaries. And so we see that the East Africa regional office assisted the Tanzania human rights institutions, the Pacific office helped the Solomon Islands to establish a juvenile court. These did not get a lot of press, but the field offices are going to be incredibly important in the years ahead.

A second function the Office plays is providing support for the Human Rights Council.[17] All in all, the Human Rights Council has had good success, particularly after the United States, having initially not joined, came in several years later. The Human Rights Council's work involves public sessions whose work is then passed along to the Office. In that function, the High Commissioner's Office plays an important role as the Secretariat for the Council, providing the knowhow, support, experience, and continuity that are key to the HRC's successful functioning: e.g., writing reports, writing analyses, focusing on facts on the ground. What is impressive about the Office's work product is the way in which the quality of the Secretariat and the substantial human rights expertise the staff possesses has filled interstitial gaps that currently exist within the UN human rights system.

The OHCHR implements the important initiatives that the US has supported. I've seen this close up because during my time, we've engaged in our first Universal Periodic Review;[18] we supported creating the Special

17 "United Nations Human Rights Council," http://www.ohchr.org/EN/HRBodies/HRC/Pages/HRCIndex.aspx.

18 "Universal Periodic Review," http://www.state.gov/j/drl/upr/index.htm.

Rapporteurs on freedom of association[19] and Iran;[20] working groups on laws that discriminate against women;[21] new commissions of inquiry, particularly on Syria,[22] Libya,[23] and Côte d'Ivoire;[24] and combatting intolerance through means consistent with freedom of speech and expression – resolutions that would bridge the gap between the West and the Muslim world on issues of intolerance and human rights and free expression.[25] On each of these, the Office has been extremely expert, helpful and supportive. The stronger that it can become, the more the Office can address the full range of these initiatives.

Third, in its role as Secretariat for the HRC, the staff of the Commissioner's Office is the essential unsung hero of the UPR process.[26] We are now near the end of the first cycle of UPRs. In each case, civil society and NGO reports are collected, and somebody has to work with the governments in preparing for the UPR and pointing out the best practices, rather than the worst practices. We have been extremely impressed by the way in which the High Commissioner's Office functioned with regard to our UPR report. We did civil society consultations in 12 cities; the High Commissioner's Office sent someone to Chicago to observe one of our consultations; they were never onstage but they spent hours backstage, and we viewed the net results as a far better product because of the staff of High Commissioner Pillay.[27]

A UPR session comprises both the initial presentation and report and a follow-up session to respond to a series of recommendations, which

---

[19] US Department of State, "UNHCR Creation of Special Rapporteur on Freedom of Assembly and Association," http://www.state.gov/secretary/rm/2010/09/148486.htm.

[20] "Human Rights Council creates mandate on Iran, extends mandate on Democratic People's Republic of Korea," OHCHR news release, March 24, 2011.

[21] "Human Rights Council establishes Working Group on Discrimination against Women in Law and Practice," OHCHR news release, October 1, 2010.

[22] "Human Rights Council decides to dispatch a commission of inquiry to investigate human rights violations in the Syrian Arab Republic," OHCHR news release, August 23, 2011.

[23] "Human Rights Council passes resolution on Libya in Special Session," OHCHR news release, February 25, 2011.

[24] "Human Rights Council extends mandates on Myanmar and Torture, decides to dispatch Commission of Inquiry to Côte d'Ivoire," OHCHR news release, March 25, 2011.

[25] UN Human Rights Council. Resolution 16/18, "Combating intolerance, negative stereotyping and stigmatization of, and discrimination, incitement to violence, and violence against persons based on religion or belief," UN Doc. A/HRC/RES/16/18, April 12, 2011.

[26] "Universal Periodic Review," http://www.ohchr.org/EN/HRBodies/UPR/Pages/UPRMain.aspx.

[27] See "Summaries of UPR Civil Society Consultations," http://www.state.gov/j/drl/upr/summaries/index.htm. See also UN Human Rights Council, "Draft Report of the Working Group on the Universal Periodic Review: United States of America," November 1–12, 2010.

requires incredibly close work between the reporting country and the Secretariat to determine exactly what the recommendations are, which ones can be accepted or not accepted, to create a formal record of progress. It is very clear now that if this is done with a high level of diligence over a long period of time, it will create a kind of monitoring and accountability over the long term for every country. And because we hope that every country will appear for its UPR, the more that there's an insistence and focus on countries showing up and defending their human rights records to the world – and not a gullible world, but a world that is expert, informed by human rights reports, informed by national human rights reports, as well as NGO reports – the better off the institution of the UPR is going to be.

Fourth, the Office plays a hugely important role in processing individual complaints, because individual complaints allow ordinary citizens to bring their issues directly to the human rights apparatus. It often raises issues that have escaped the notice of national government officials.

Fifth and finally, the Office has played a lead role in working with the special rapporteurs and treaty bodies in giving what we call 'home-based' institutional support. I get many, many calls from people who have been asked to be special rapporteurs and special experts, and their question is always exactly the same: how do I do this, given the resources I've gotten, which amount to little or nothing. All too frequently, the answer is, "talk to your dean," because many of these are professors, and the only resources available are students, a computer, or other in-kind contributions available to professors. This raises obvious questions about uniformity, training, orientation, best practices, quality control, etc. We are also at the moment engaged in a number of exercises where we're looking back at the *travaux preparatoires* – the legislative history – of a number of major human rights instruments. It's very hard to find some of these documents. It's very hard to do an intelligent treaty interpretation without a carefully kept set of records. So what is essentially a repository function will end up emerging for lawyers and others who care about systems of precedent and primary materials as an incredibly important function of the High Commissioner's Office.

All of these duties require that the Commissioner's staff be first-rank, knowledgeable, professional, hard-working, and most of all, insulated from political interference. Protecting the independence of the High Commissioner's staff against such interference is a task for all of us: the Commissioner herself, UN Member States, NGOs, academics, other human rights advocates, and countries that are members of the Human Rights

Council. Everybody has a tremendously important role to play. If we have a High Commissioner who is viewed as biased in any direction, that is a death-knell for the entire operation. So keeping a staff that holds itself to the highest standards of independence, and the Commissioner himself or herself, is extraordinarily important.

This brings me to my final point: a central challenge for the High Commissioner and the Office going forward will be how to shift to a smart-power approach, which Secretary Clinton has defined[28] as in part responding to opportunities, not just threats, finding the nexus between the domestic and international, figuring out new ways to lead, partnering with different players, adopting soft-power tools that emphasize cooperation over confrontation, preserving shared values, and the like.

Perhaps the central challenge for the High Commissioner and her Office will be to step away from the inbox and step toward more proactive planning with regard to this set of issues. This fits with what the Obama/Clinton doctrine has really been, which is, as much as possible, to engage around principle, to use diplomacy as a critical element of smart power, to strategically use multilateralism when you can and in as many circumstances as possible, and following the rules of domestic and international law. While everyone can point to a particular aspect of the Obama foreign policy that they didn't like, international law as an aspect of a broader smart power approach is an emerging feature of what this Administration has tried to accomplish.

As an international lawyer for the U.S. government, probably the most difficult challenge of all is that the laws are relatively unchanging while the technology is rapidly changing. In the area of national security and international law, the most important treaties were done after World War II, while in the national security area, the most prominent pieces of legislation were enacted after Vietnam and Watergate.

There are two ways to deal with 21st century challenges when you only have 20th century laws. One way is to say that the 20th century laws are 'quaint,' or outmoded, or irrelevant; to claim that they don't address the situation so there must be a black hole. But there is another strategy, which is to try to determine what Montesquieu would call 'the spirit of the laws,' and to try to translate principles from one body of law that's meant to cover a certain kind of situation, to a parallel situation that does not quite

[28] Hilary Rodham Clinton, "Leading Through Civilian Power: Redefining American Diplomacy and Development," *Foreign Affairs*, November/December 2010.

map onto any body of law. As Legal Adviser, much of the work that I've done has been on the question of what rules govern armed conflicts with non-state actors (like al-Qaeda) that are engaged in transnational conflicts with the United States.[29] The Supreme Court called the post-9/11 situation a non-international armed conflict, but not in the same way as the term 'non-international armed conflict' was originally coined. The term originally addressed civil wars within a single country's territory, not conflicts between states and transnational non-state actors who are operating across borders. One way to deal with this phenomenon is to call it a 'global war on terror.' But another way to deal with it, which is the way that the Obama Administration has dealt with it, is to call it an armed conflict with al-Qaeda and associated forces, which is narrower, and to try to translate the spirit of the laws to this new paradigm.

Or take the issue of cyber conflict, which sounds very exciting. But if you actually go and look at what they're doing, it's a bunch of operators sitting in a room changing zeros to Os. And the question is, what do the Geneva Conventions say about that? You can either say that the Geneva Conventions didn't think about that, so there is no law to apply. Or you could say instead that the Geneva Conventions did think in broad strokes about the consequences of these types of actions, and thus the challenge is to decide how do you translate the spirit of the laws to meet these concerns?[30] So in the 21st century, a big challenge is how to leverage soft power resources like diplomacy, development, technology, markets, international law and institutions, into effective global action that's consistent with the laws that are on the books, even though new laws have not yet been adopted.

Our greatest challenge – and it will continue to be so – is to address the Arab Awakening. In the last year, I've seen dramatic developments in Tunisia, Bahrain, Egypt, Libya, Yemen, Syria, changes in the Middle East peace process, of course Iran and Iraq. As Secretary Clinton said, "It's a historic moment of opportunity and change. Millions are pushing their nations to move away from repression, embracing universal human rights. This has discredited the extremist argument that only violence can bring

[29] See e.g. Harold Hongju Koh, "The Obama Administration and International Law," (speech, Washington D.C, March 25, 2010), U.S. Department of State, http://www.state.gov/s/l/releases/remarks/139119.htm.

[30] See e.g. Harold Hongju Koh, "International Law in Cyberspace," (speech, USCYBERCOM Inter-Agency Legal Conference, Ft. Meade, MD, September 18, 2012), Opinio Juris, http://opiniojuris.org/2012/09/19/harold-koh-on-international-law-in-cyberspace/.

about change." That is the last, and I think the most important, point. Whatever you think about the people on the Arab streets, their main impulse doesn't seem to be to join al-Qaeda. They now have other channels and avenues for their energies. And the question is, without using a one-size-fits-all mechanism, how to adapt strategies, national and international, governmental and non-governmental, to address each of these situations?

There are many other human rights challenges facing us in the 21st century: atrocities prevention, the law of cyberspace, balancing security, internet freedom, internet governance, intellectual property. Genetically modified organisms, particularly the possibility of transforming different viruses into ones that can be weaponized and used for attack purposes. And not a day goes by that I don't address the issue of assisted reproductive technology. Take the most important question with regard to nationality: biological link. What do you do when same-sex partners, using surrogates, give birth to children conceived when the sperm and the egg came from different countries? What is birthright citizenship in that circumstance? Or take the most difficult issue of all: clones. There have been pronouncements against the cloning of human beings, but if there is a cloned human being, will that be a person with lesser rights, who is treated as having lesser rights because they are treated as somehow less than human? Or will they be treated as people who, having been born in a test tube, nevertheless hold these truths to be self-evident, that all persons are created equal, in rights and dignity?

How do we prepare for these kinds of radical technological changes? We need a human rights system and a High Commissioner that has the capacity and the resources and the Office to see these things through. The smart-power realities of the 21st century require a High Commissioner and an Office that can adapt 20th century approaches to 21st century realities, staying true to the core principles and tackling emerging issues of human rights and globalization – not yesterday's issues, but tomorrow's issues.

One final thought: the International Committee of the Red Cross has won three Nobel Peace Prizes,[31] and it is hard to find someone who can tell you who was the President of the International Committee of the Red Cross on each of those three occasions. The UN High Commissioner for

[31] See "All Nobel Peace Prizes," http://www.nobelprize.org/nobel_prizes/peace/laureates/.

Refugees has won two Nobel Peace Prizes,[32] and I'm not sure that anyone could tell you who was the High Commissioner each time. My point: the Office made the transition from the personal to the institutional. It was the Office that won the Prize, not any one individual. What this means is that, going forward, it is the Office of the High Commissioner for Human Rights that ought to be the focus of your ongoing work. As friends of that Office, we must all strive in the long-term to support that Office in its critically important, ongoing mission to support the promotion and protection of universal human rights.

[32] Ibid.

ADDRESS BY THE HIGH COMMISSIONER AT THE JACOB BLAUSTEIN INSTITUTE FOR THE ADVANCEMENT OF HUMAN RIGHTS[1]

Navi Pillay

I am very pleased to join you at this conference marking the 40th anniversary of the Jacob Blaustein Institute for the Advancement of Human Rights. I am honored to address you in the house where Franklin and Eleanor Roosevelt lived. They and other founders of the modern human rights movement have left us with a legacy that continues to flourish despite seemingly immutable ideologies.

Indeed, the human rights movement keeps expanding in jurisprudence and action. Much is due to the intuitions and advocacy of visionaries, such as Jacob Blaustein, who believed firmly in the need for a United Nations human rights program. Due also to the efforts of organizations such as the Jacob Blaustein Institute, the General Assembly created the post of High Commissioner for Human Rights in 1993 to spearhead the protection and promotion of human rights globally.

Let me note that each High Commissioner made his or her own mark as the Office evolved.

- The first High Commissioner, José Ayala Lasso, built the foundation of the new Office, expanding the focus of the then Centre for Human Rights from supporting intergovernmental and expert human rights mechanisms, including the Commission on Human Rights, special rapporteurs and human rights treaty bodies, to technical cooperation, as well as education activities in the field.
- The second High Commissioner, Mary Robinson, further institutionalized these avenues for action and strengthened the High Commissioner's advocacy role. To this day, her insistence on one of the central messages of the World Conference on Human Rights that civil and political rights

[1] Adapted from "Address by the High-Commissioner for Human Rights at the Jacob Blaustein Institute for the Advancement of Human Rights," available at http://www.ohchr.org/en/NewsEvents/Pages/DisplayNews.aspx?NewsID=11807&LangID=e. Remarks delivered by Navi Pillay on February 8, 2012. Copyright 2012 Office of the United Nations High Commissioner for Human Rights.

and economic, social and cultural rights constitute an indivisible whole continues to resonate and inform the debate.

- The third High Commissioner, Sergio Vieira de Mello, was instrumental in moving forward the process of engaging the larger UN system on human rights issues, until his work was sadly cut short by a fatal bomb attack. It fell upon the acting High Commissioner, Bertrand Ramcharan, who is with us today, to pursue a wide-ranging agenda, continue to build the capacity of the Office and draw the attention of the Commission on Human Rights to human rights situations warranting its consideration.
- Subsequently, High Commissioner Louise Arbour led the Office through a period of great change. Her exceptional drive and strategic thinking led to a reform of the Office and its expansion into the field. At the same time, she tirelessly advocated the centrality of human rights and accountability including during the delicate period of transition from the Commission to the Human Rights Council.

The combined efforts of its leaders led to the Office growing from the small headquarters-based Centre for Human Rights – with some 106 staff and a biennial budget of $31 million at the end of 1993 – to the current structure with 1,108 employees. Currently, 48 per cent of OHCHR staff is based in the field, 50 per cent in Geneva, and 2 per cent in New York. In 2010–2011, our budget was US$ 408 million. We have established 12 regional offices or centers and 13 country or stand-alone offices. Further, 15 human rights officers serve in UN peace missions and 18 human rights advisers are embedded within UN Country Teams in the field. In all, OHCHR has presences in 58 countries.

The impact of OHCHR advocacy has grown steadily throughout the past 19 years. Let me highlight the celebrations of Human Rights Day last December. We ran a 'Celebrate Human Rights' social media campaign which engaged a rapidly expanding online audience. The campaign, in particular the global social media human rights conversation I hosted and the '30 Days and 30 Rights' multilingual discussion on the 30 articles of the Universal Declaration of Human Rights, helped us reach tens of millions of previously untapped audience. On Twitter alone, our messages and tweets were viewed 27 million times and the hashtag #AskRights my Office created was used six million times, within 48 hours of the event. Some were inspired to take action for human rights. For example, a reputable publisher, using hashtag #AskRights, offered everyone seven days free access to its database for human rights research to celebrate Human

Rights Day. The social media discussion about the Universal Declaration, through '*Weibo*' in Chinese and Facebook pages in English, French and Spanish, were viewed at least nine million times during the 30-day campaign period.

As the popular movements in many countries, including in North Africa and the Middle East have demonstrated, there is a growing demand for advocacy and monitoring of human rights. The High Commissioner's intellectual leadership must be responsive to rights holders of all ages and in all walks of life. It should be directed to help strengthen civil society and human rights activists to claim their human rights.

As High Commissioner, I begin from the premise that human rights norms provide universal obligations that help us ensure that all are held to the same standard. There is no hierarchy of human rights, and I believe that the credibility of human rights work depends on a commitment to truth, impartiality and integrity, with no tolerance for double-standards or selectivity. I strive to ensure that the universality of human rights standards, which speaks to our common humanity and priorities, informs discussions in politically charged environments and instills both substance and objectivity to political discourse.

I am supported by remarkably committed individuals, affected groups and other stakeholders. This is a diffuse approach, encompassing the advocacy-enhancing leadership and consistent calls for accountability that has produced historic humanitarian change, including the creation of the International Criminal Court where I was a judge.

One of the key aspects of such advocacy – and a crucial element of its success – is that many individuals and organizations, as well as different branches of States' institutions, are encouraged to go beyond their immediate scope of intervention or mandates, and embrace an overarching goal that, in part or in all, transcends their specific field of specialization. Thus, they are able to enlarge their basis of support among constituencies that are not necessarily well-versed in all the sophisticated details of a campaign, but who could "buy" into it through clear and immediately resonant messages.

And therein lies the crux of the matter for human rights enforcement and the leadership needed to realize it. Although most States – at least in their pronouncement – pledge to uphold human rights, implementation lags behind.

Another factor is that, beyond the work of specialized or directly affected individuals and organizations, there is inadequate familiarity with those human rights mechanisms that are mandated to exercise vigilance over the implementation of human rights standards, and facilitate access for rights holders. I refer here to the special procedures and the human rights treaty bodies comprised of experts who serve in their independent capacities.

We have a number of such experts with us here today, including of course Felice [Gaer], who was elected to the Committee Against Torture in 2000, and in that capacity, has made a profound contribution, in particular by ensuring that freedom from torture is defined against the singular experiences of women and girls. She also served as co-rapporteur as the Committee developed its ground breaking general comment on article 2 of the Convention against Torture. I also refer to national human rights institutions, independent national bodies, charged with encouraging implementation of human rights on the ground.

One of my priorities as High Commissioner is crafting more intelligible and more compelling messages, as well as making the avenues to redress for victims more accessible, attractive and responsive to spur implementation of human rights. To this end, I will continue to reach out to victims of abuse and like-minded States, thinkers and activists, and all those constituencies whose aspirations and work is contiguous to our advocacy. I actively support and promote the work of the human rights mechanisms and my Office has produced an impressive array of material and tools on how to access them.

I can always count on the work, commitment and passion of OHCHR staff who are eager and ready to confront new challenges. My Office has responded with agility and a deeply felt sense of mission to the growing demands for our work and the increasing activities mandated by the Human Rights Council. While meeting rapidly unfolding crises, we continued to address chronic human rights issues. These concomitant and multiplying pursuits have put a great strain on our human and financial resources.

Let me turn now to another challenge to human rights which our discussion will tackle, that is, *Promoting Universality of Rights: Global Leadership in an Era of Growing Particularism and Relativism.*

Borrowing from the framers of the Universal Declaration of Human Rights, I maintain that human rights law, far from being suitable to some cultures, but irrelevant or even harmful to others, embodies a common standard of achievement for all which would help to secure a 'higher standard of life' and a 'greater enjoyment of freedom.'

There will always be those who, for their own political or personal designs, would deny the universality of our rights, and seek to use arguments of tradition and culture to oppose them. Yet, I do not know of anyone who demanded the right to be tortured, summarily executed, starved or denied medical care, or discriminated against in the name of their culture.

Tradition is a complex notion. No society, regardless of its geographic location or level of economic development, can be said to be represented by a single and comprehensive set of shared values covering all social matters. Traditions and values change over time and are viewed and interpreted differently by various actors in society. Nuances and, in some cases, radical differences in such values depend on the historical period, societal divides, or, at any given moment, the tension between conservatives and progressives. Moreover, the history of all countries comprise, often concomitantly, traditions of hate and traditions of tolerance, traditions of repression and traditions of liberation, and traditions of deprivation and exclusion and traditions of social justice. Our task is to be squarely and unequivocally on the side of the victims who promote and defend human rights in every society.

Indeed, while the Vienna Declaration recognizes that the significance of national and regional particularities and various historical, cultural and religious backgrounds must be borne in mind, it reaffirms that it is the duty of all States, regardless of their political, economic and cultural systems, to promote and protect all human rights and fundamental freedoms.

My Office has not shied away from such issues which, while sensitive, nevertheless are important for a consistent and universal application of human rights standards. For example, I am proud of our work to raise awareness of the range and prevalence of human rights violations perpetrated on grounds of sexual orientation or gender identity. There is ample evidence of the problem: individuals murdered, beaten, raped and tortured, arrested, imprisoned and executed, or simply discriminated against, whether at work, at home, at school or in the hospital.

In our approach to this issue, we have insisted on the consistent application of universal human rights standards to protect all persons, regardless of their sexual orientation or gender identity.

And we are making progress. Last year we saw the human rights machinery start to gain traction on this issue with the first UN resolution specifically addressing human rights violations based on sexual orientation and gender identity, adopted by the Human Rights Council last June. That resolution requested me to provide to the Council a report on violence and discrimination directed at LGBT people – the first official UN report on the issue. Its findings and recommendations will be debated at the Council next month.

And now to the topic of *Preventing Human Rights Violations and Effective Response.*

In any preventive efforts, the human rights community greatly benefits from the work of the special procedures among the most effective conveyors of early warning. Their knowledge and expertise are indispensable to devising or fine-tuning prevention measures against violations, observing situations of concern over time, and addressing the plight of voiceless victims.

I am fully aware that the credibility of my Office, and the United Nations as a whole, depends on being close to victims, helping them and assisting when they are threatened with or exposed to violations. This requires our independence of judgment, responsiveness from headquarters, and – crucially – service on the ground. The mandate of our country and regional offices consists largely in monitoring and reporting on human rights violations, and providing technical cooperation to prompt promotion and protection of human rights. Our public reports serve as diagnostic tools which inform our cooperation and technical assistance to Governments and other partners.

Recent innovations in the human rights field may also help prevent the recurrence of violence and abuses. Transitional justice initiatives following armed conflict are particularly suited to this effect. Our work in this area emphasizes a four pillar approach to the rights of victims of past human rights violations: the right to justice, truth, reparations and guarantees of non-recurrence. To ensure a bottom up approach, we insist on national consultation processes on all transitional justice options. Last year, I sent teams to Tunisia, Egypt, Yemen, and Bahrain to assess the human rights priorities in these countries during their historical transition.

Equally valuable are fact finding missions and Commissions of Inquiry dispatched to identify violations and recommend ways to stop them. OHCHR supported Commissions of Inquiry appointed by the Human Rights Council for Côte d'Ivoire, Libya and Syria, and established OHCHR's own investigative mission for Syria.

The international community has come to regard such investigations among the responses of choice by international community in the face of a crisis. This is because they serve a multiplicity of purposes. They help identify perpetrators and protect victims, help deter violations, and contribute to establishing a chain of accountability and means to deliver justice and redress to the victims once violations subside. Investigations aim at influencing positive change in laws and practice by drawing attention to serious violations and accountability gaps. Their ultimate goal is preventing abuses or, at a minimum, mitigating and stopping violations when they do occur, as well as challenging impunity.

The report and recommendations of an investigation can have far-reaching consequences as was the case when, based on the recommendations of a commission of inquiry, the Security Council issued a referral to the International Criminal Court. Findings and recommendations of such inquiries have contributed to transitional justice mechanisms and helped to set the record straight to pave the way for societal wounds to heal.

Let me now offer some observations on the topic of *Influencing Other UN Bodies to Act.*

We constantly seek to expand and deepen our interaction with UN agencies and other crucial partners in international organizations both at headquarters and on the ground.

We see this cooperation particularly in our interaction with the Human Rights Council which by 2011 had held 19 regular sessions and 18 special sessions. Significant progress has been achieved with the universal periodic review of the Council. The first cycle of the UPR will be completed next month and thousands of recommendations have been issued. The task for the next cycle is to streamline these recommendations, make them more manageable, focused and actionable, so that their implementation will be easier to monitor and evaluate. My Office is defining its catalytic role with regard to supporting UPR follow-up at country level, which includes development of strategic partnerships with the UN system. This also entails the placement of human rights advisers in UN country teams and regional organizations.

We have also played a pivotal role in ensuring the incorporation of human rights into the outcome of the Millennium Development Goals Review Summit in September 2010. On that occasion, Member States recognized that human rights are indispensable for the realization of the MDGs, and committed themselves to a wide range of specific human rights actions.

In the same year, during my term as chair of the Global Migration Group (GMG), we promoted a human-rights based approach within the UN system to address the rising challenge of migration better. A key outcome of this work was a landmark joint statement on the human rights of irregular migrants adopted by the GMG principals.

I have also been increasingly called upon to address the Security Council: 11 addresses in recent times, while before then, my predecessors had been invited to do so only eight times since the creation of this post. Today, we have reached a point where the Council systematically includes human rights, notably monitoring and reporting functions, as a core element of all mandates of multi-dimensional peace missions.

Through my briefings and reports, important human rights material is placed on the record, made public, and used to ensure effective decision-making by the Security-Council. We jointly draw lessons where we need to learn: building on the experience in the DRC and the Security Council's landmark conditionality policy in Resolution 1925, the Secretary-General last year adopted a ground-breaking UN system-wide Human Rights Due Diligence Policy, which applies to all UN support to non-UN security forces. This policy was developed by a UN inter-agency forum which we co-led together with DPKO, and requires all UN actors providing support to non-UN security forces to exercise due diligence by conducting a human rights risk assessment before support is given to such forces.

In effect, UN actors cannot provide support to non-UN security forces where there is a real risk that recipient entities may commit grave violations.

Human rights partners come in many forms. From my perspective, taking rights-based positions is not the exclusive responsibility of human rights advocates. In the most recent meeting of the United Nations Chief Executive Board, I challenged the broader UN system to put the norms and standards of the UN system at the forefront of all UN activities, including in the Organization's dealings with individual member Governments. My call was for a single standard of norm-based, constructive engagement with all governments, rich and poor, north and south, strong and less-strong. I argued that the UN Charter and the many binding international human rights treaties adopted under UN auspices since the Second World War prove that the UN is not intended as a mere forum for diplomatic dialogue, and a rush to the lowest common denominator. We stand for something. And at the centre of that something, is human rights. Clearly, our duty to the intergovernmental system cannot include a requirement to turn a blind eye to injustice and abuse. This, in my view, is a clear lesson of the Arab Spring.

The challenges ahead for the human rights movement are multiple. I am particularly concerned at four main challenges that will continue to engage the human rights community in the future as they have done in the past, namely impunity, discrimination, conflict and poverty.

Because of their scale, deep roots and their effects on the well-being of countless victims everywhere, these are not only challenges, but veritable priorities for the human rights movement. Another priority for my Office is supporting and strengthening those institutions and mechanisms that are crucial to respond both to emergencies and chronic human rights situations, in particular the human rights mechanisms.

Today we look with great concern at the renewed turmoil in the financial markets and the threats to state-solvency. One can readily think of the devastating effects on global welfare and on the most vulnerable that these crises are producing and can produce in the absence of safety nets firmly anchored to human rights.

Climate change, scarcity of food, and crumbling welfare systems pose direct threats to people's enjoyment of a wide range of universally-recognized human rights, including the right to food, to education and health, to an adequate standard of living, and to the right to life itself. No means should be overlooked to mitigate the most negative effects of these crises on the rights of those who live at the margins, particularly the very poor and people eking out a living at subsistence levels.

Some political and economic leaders seem to have forgotten that health care, education, housing and access to justice are not commodities for sale to the few, rather they are rights to which all are entitled without discrimination. An important lesson from the Arab Spring is that human rights should provide the central litmus test for good governance. Not economic growth, not free markets, not sophisticated governmental institutions, but rather the degree to which governments ensure 'freedom from fear and want,' the standards of which Roosevelt spoke.

In my presentation to the World Economic Forum in Davos, I pointed out that an analysis of the assessments provided by our financial institutions and development agencies in the immediate lead-up to the Arab Spring is illuminating. Even as the events were unfolding, we read, for example, that Tunisia showed "remarkable progress on equitable growth, fighting poverty, an achieving good social indicators," that it was "on track to achieve the MDGs," was "far ahead in terms of governance, effectiveness, rule of law, control of corruption and regulatory quality," was "one of the most equitable societies," "a top reformer," and that "the development model that Tunisia has pursued over the past two decades has served the country well."

At the same time, the human rights mechanisms, and voices from civil society, were painting a different picture. We heard of excluded and marginalized communities, imposed indignities, and a denial of economic and social rights. We heard of inequality, discrimination, absence of participation, absence of decent jobs, absence of labour rights, political repression, absence of fundamental freedoms, including free assembly, association, and speech. We heard of censorship, arbitrary detention, and the lack of an independent judiciary. In sum, we heard of fear, and want. The events in Tunis and across the region need not have been such a surprise to so many.

Another lesson that we should draw from transitions in the Arab world and elsewhere is that the sustainability of the democratization processes is very contingent on the existence of independent institutions which should safeguard the separation of power between the executive, the legislative and the judiciary. Equality and non-discrimination, particularly regarding women and minorities, depend on such sustainability.

And the international community must begin to take more seriously its commitment to the free, active and meaningful participation of civil society – including women, minorities, indigenous peoples, and human rights defenders – in decision making at both the national and international levels. The age of public decision-making being reserved to the back rooms of government or the boardrooms of corporations is coming to an end. This is the age of an increasingly informed, interconnected, and mobilized civil society. We should be attentive to the powerful role that the internet and social media can play in mobilizing forces for change and the apparatus of repression, including the bloggers working in their rooms at home, and those who monitor bloggers and advocates' every move with sophisticated surveillance equipment.

The human rights movement has grown and thrived since the Roosevelts lived here. We know that we have much to do until human rights are enjoyed by every woman, man and child everywhere.

A CONVERSATION WITH THE HIGH COMMISSIONER

[*This discussion took place following the address by High Commissioner Navi Pillay on February 8, 2012. Felice Gaer initiated questions with the High Commissioner, which were followed by her responses as presented below.*]

Felice Gaer: Thank you very much, High Commissioner, for this comprehensive presentation and discussion. It's a very important part of our deliberations and discussions here today. You know, the title of the conference is "The UN High Commissioner for Human Rights: Conscience for the World." I'd like to begin by asking if the title of 'conscience for the world' is appropriate for you? Do you feel that that's an apt description of your position?

Navi Pillay: I have heard of the role being described as a 'conscience for the world.' I often say, if there's a single person suffering injustice or abuse somewhere, then all our consciousness is alerted to that, and it does trouble us. But unfortunately, institutions and governments do not have the quality of conscience that individuals have. And so there, I stay strictly to obligations. Obligations under international law – where States have to deliver on their core responsibilities to ensure freedom from fear and freedom from want. Conscience, of course, appeals to everyone, ordinary people, who don't like to see suffering anywhere. That's why there's a huge volume of correspondence addressed to my Office. Because when people see something is wrong, they want some action to be taken, and they write to us. They see this as a very important office that could take the matter to international fora or draw public attention to it.

Felice Gaer: Well, thank you. The keynote speaker yesterday spoke about the fact that you in your position have made yourself 'the gold standard' when it comes to facts and information. He was speaking of the case of Syria, but he was speaking more generally also about the fact-finding role of the High Commissioner's Office. You spoke in your remarks today about the remarkable number of times you have appeared before the Security Council; and that it's more than the number of times of all your predecessors combined. Can you tell us if you feel that those briefings have had specific effects on what the Security Council has then gone on to do, whether in the case of Syria or in any others where you've briefed them?

Navi Pillay: Let me first emphasize how remarkable it is that the High Commissioner has been invited to address the Security Council. When the Secretary-General, Ban Ki-moon, took my predecessor Lousie Arbour in, the Secretary-General told me he had the High Commissioner seated behind him, and yet there were objections – e.g., what was she doing here, that she had to leave the room. Meaning, what are human rights doing in the Security Council, it doesn't belong here. In each of these addresses, I persuaded them that you cannot de-link human rights from peace and security, and I think that that's accepted now. They have said to me that it is very important that the Security Council has reliable information. And if our keynote speaker yesterday spoke about a gold standard, it's the judicial standard to be accurate and truthful and verify your information, because people rely on that information. So I'm very strict about that, and the benefit of it is that the Security Council is now relying on information from my Office and calls it reliable. They have incorporated our recommendations in many of their resolutions. The Security Council has, for the first time, passed resolutions on thematic matters such as sexual violence and children and armed conflict.

Our recommendation has always been to have human rights components within peace missions, because we have a monitoring role. So that's been followed in many cases – at least 17 – and there are one or two where we are not present. There have been resolutions or even statements from the Security Council asking governments to let OHCHR in. So I see these as some of the results of our briefings to the Security Council.

Felice Gaer: Thank you very much. One of the things we've talked about is the fact that as the High Commissioner, you travel to countries. That's an independent role of the High Commissioner. I have a list of the countries – there are more than 40 of them – to which you've traveled during your tenure as High Commissioner. There was some reflection on the fact that the first High Commissioner, for example, went to countries and didn't tell his team, didn't tell the Special Rapporteur beforehand – instead, he simply showed up. Do you leverage your country visits for results; do you set out priorities or issues that you want addressed before you'll go to the countries? Can you give us specific examples of some of the countries you've visited where you've achieved specific results, using your country visits?

Navi Pillay: This is a big list of countries, by the way. This should have killed me, all this travel. It's very interesting that requests from governments for me to visit their countries have increased seven-fold, yet there are others who take years to fix a date. We prepare for these visits very, very carefully. That's very, very important. From the time of the establishment of the Office, where the first High Commissioner clearly had to take bold and courageous steps; I think within months Mr. Ayala Lasso had sent a team down into Rwanda where the genocide was going on, I consider that a courageous step. I am much more reinforced now by the special procedures, treaty body jurisprudence, and the Universal Periodic Review recommendations, so we go well armed and stay within the framework of international human rights law. Particularly the recommendations of special procedures are very useful to me, and the conclusions and recommendations of treaty bodies, so I would raise these. For instance, torture is prevalent in so many countries that even if the particular country has not been reviewed by the Committee against Torture, I would state the principle as the treaty body has stated it. This has been received quite well, because we're sticking with the law, and we're sticking with expert recommendations. The special procedures base their recommendations on thoroughly researched facts, and that's why their opinions are respected.

So, while preparing for a trip, I generally have more or less the same standard for all missions: we must be able to get all the meetings we want. I get to see the heads of state. I went to six or seven Gulf countries at one time and was seen by the head of state, the kings, in each one of those countries. I see ministers, of course, but I also see human rights defenders, civil society organizations, and particularly watch out for human rights defenders against whom action has been taken. On my mission to Colombia, for instance, the government was hostile to human rights activists, just detained them, and there were public statements from the then-president saying what he's going to be doing – real threats against human rights defenders. And after our discourse, he issued a statement that he's going to consult with them. So therefore, very thoroughly prepared visits matter.

Sorry to give you such a long answer. I just think it's very interesting the access the High Commissioner can have.

Felice Gaer: In my capacity as a member of the Committee against Torture, we recently examined Belarus. We were told that there was a whole series of preconditions created by the High Commissioner for Human Rights for the government prior to any trip. They want you to come and visit. Of course, this is a country that has been criticized by the Human Rights Council for gross abuses. In a case like that, do you go, do you in fact set up conditions before you go, and do you send an advance assessment team? How do you decide if you're going to go to a place where conditions are terrible, and where you might be able to make a difference, but they might be able to exploit you being there as the High Commissioner? How do you sort that out?

Navi Pillay: Let me say in respect of Belarus, DPRK, Myanmar; these countries have made it very clear to me, "we have no problem with the High Commissioner, we have problems with the Human Rights Council resolution, which links you to them, we object to those resolutions and we're not going to cooperate." Whatever the situation with the HRC resolutions and mandates might be, I go on mission per my own independent mandate, with the same set of standards and requirements to enable a successful mission. They are not 'conditions' per se, but if need be, I do send an advance assessment team to prepare the mission, including to make sure that we meet with the right counterparts, both inside and importantly outside the government circles.

There is always a risk that certain governments will capitalize on these visits, but since it's such a public visit, extremely well-publicized, civil society are so alert – I found this in Russia, for instance – they find us, and we have huge and long meetings. My longest meetings are always with civil society actors because there are so many of them and they have so much to say. Media and press usually cover these visits, from all perspectives; so government points are covered, as well as mine. At the end of every mission, we issue a public statement. We acknowledge what has been done, and we point out what needs to be done. It's a kind of balance, which gives the High Commissioner credibility. That's why these doors are being opened.

Felice Gaer: High Commissioner, the issue of speaking out about countries is one that we discussed a great deal during the conference yesterday, and we reflected on how this may conflict with other roles of the High Commissioner. We have noted that there are many other countries that you've spoken out about. You've visited 40 countries but you've spoken out about many, many more than that. But there are some countries that have been listed by those who list the worst countries in the world, like Freedom House or others, countries like Eritrea, Equatorial Guinea, Turkmenistan, Cuba, Uzbekistan. We searched your website, and it may be a problem with the search function, but it may not be. We haven't found any critical statements about these countries. We're wondering if you have a system for assuring that you speak out on serious conditions; if there's a way that you set priorities, or do you respond to events as they take place. Could you comment on this?

Navi Pillay: I think because it's so overwhelming, the pattern is that we appear to be responding to situations. I say this is overwhelming because there's always something critical – we do a great deal of letter-writing directly with governments; it's far more done at that level than in public statements. I do have to make a choice sometimes: do I want to get some impact, do I want a detainee to be released, for example, and will I be more successful in private or public? We have to make that call, and at times have to remain engaged privately. You know, the Secretary-General does much more of that, and that's why it's not known publicly – it's a price he has to pay. But I know he's very, very effective, and I draw lessons from him.

I was talking about public statements and the countries that you raised. We don't target countries, because I don't feel there is a country in the world that is free of human rights violations. So we look at the violations. A huge conflict and killings in Eritrea is of course of concern, but I have to also worry about the fact that Roma children in Italy are not getting water to drink or to wash themselves. So that's what I mean. An issue is important in every place. It's not like we rank rights, or we rank violations, but we have been remiss in not addressing those countries. Eritrea we're now looking at, because we, with great diplomacy, got them to participate in the Universal Periodic Review process, otherwise there wouldn't have been a 100% participation record. So that means reaching out to that government just to get them there. Now let's see the recommendations made with regard to Eritrea, and that will be our opening to address issues there. I have not asked to go there, and also I think I've more recently been troubled by Ethiopia. But these are countries we would look at. We have a desk person covering every country, so that's why we're really on top of what is happening there right now. And we do not take a decision not to make a statement – we're just getting there. There's only one High Commissioner.

Felice Gaer: High Commissioner, when you took office, you were faced right away with the political challenge of the planned Durban review conference. I wondered if you could tell us what you learned from this experience about conference diplomacy. We spoke yesterday quite a bit about conference diplomacy, and how the High Commissioners have related them to the universality issue. But I'm wondering if you could tell us what you learned about conference diplomacy, relationships with states and the like, and was last fall's 'Durban Plus 10' review any different?

Navi Pillay: I understood that there will always be political differences, national and regional interests, which play out at these conferences. I'm happy that we played a role in getting a document by consensus. So no matter what the politics and arguments are, and the walkouts that occurred then, and also at the 10th anniversary celebration, where there was also a walkout, the point is that there is a consensus document with recommendations on how to address racism, and we are following up on all those activities. That's what I learned; to keep the focus on the matter at hand, which is addressing racism. And even the countries who withdrew came to me and said very clearly of course they want to undertake activities to address racism in their own countries; Europe has many challenges with regard to racial hatred, they're very mindful of the issue and they will be working together with us.

One lesson I did learn there is that the address of President Ahmadinejad of Iran was quite disruptive, and caused the walkout. So I decided to make a public statement that he shouldn't bring his politics into a conference on racism, he should've addressed the issue of racism in his own country. So the heads of four regional groups came to complain to me that as a public civil servant you should not be criticizing a head of state; it's just not proper. And you see where we are from then, to me calling for Qaddafi, while he was still alive, to be charged for war crimes and crimes against humanity. So we very steadfastly raise our voice when it needs to be raised whether I'm a civil servant or a head of state. All I can say to you now, the lesson of Durban is that it's now accepted that I would point the finger where it needs to be pointed.

Felice Gaer: High Commissioner, you just raised the issue of the independence of the High Commissioner. This is something that some of the governments have been challenging; the question of whether you have to follow the instructions of the Human Rights Council and the Member States, or whether there's some independence to your Office. Could you discuss with us briefly whether you think there are other initiatives you can take to establish greater independence, or do you feel that you need to be more responsive to the states?

Navi Pillay: What is significant is that the General Assembly resolution creating the mandate of the High Commissioner came before the establishment of the Human Rights Council, so as I see it I have to follow that mandate and do our own independent work, which includes the mission travel, the reports we do, and so on. A great deal of our time is taken up by mandated activities of the Human Rights Council and this is where we experience the subtle intrusions into the independence of the High Commissioner. There's a preference that I should only be doing work dictated by members of the Human Rights Council or I should be focusing just on civil and political rights or just on economic and social rights and the right to development. And I understand that states have political interests and this will be played out there. But I get less and less of this now, because the way I've addressed the risk of oversight of our work was to go right before them and say these are our thematic priorities for next year; so I go and report to each regional group and to Member States. What we resist is being obliged to report to a formal session of the Human Rights Council, because then we might invite oversight, resolutions and so on. Louise struggled with that, and we continue with that struggle. More recently we managed to avert one more attempt to have us come with our report and our program of work for approval before the Human Rights Council. So for the March session, it's not going to come up. We get little breathing space before the issue comes up again.

Felice Gaer: High Commissioner, I'm really grateful to you for taking the time to be here today and to engage with us. I have one more question for you before you have to go. The question is simply this: We examined the records of the High Commissioners since the post was created in 1993 and occupied for the first time in 1994, and we noticed that of the six people who have served as High Commissioner or Acting High Commissioner, none has served what the General Assembly resolution permits, which is to say, two four-year terms. No one has served two full four-year terms. I wonder if you have any comments on that, and in that context, if Secretary-General Ban Ki-moon should happen to invite you for a second term, do you have a reaction? Could you tell us how you might respond?

Navi Pillay: I was wondering where Felice was going with this question. That really puts me in a spot. Clearly it's a political appointment, it's a recommendation from the Secretary-General and a vote in the General Assembly. So Member States have a great deal to say on the caliber of the candidate that they want. All I can say is that I am able and willing to serve another term, but it's very much the decision of Member States.

Felice Gaer: Thank you very much.

FUTURE PREVENTIVE STRATEGIES OF THE OFFICE OF THE HIGH COMMISSIONER FOR HUMAN RIGHTS

Bertrand G. Ramcharan

Introduction

Human rights protection is best achieved by preventing violations, to the extent feasible. Preventive human rights strategies are beginning to receive attention these days. Addressing a conference on the responsibility to protect, on 18 January, 2012, Secretary-General Ban Ki-moon declared:

> ...(L)et me speak to an issue that I believe has not received sufficient attention: That is the importance of prevention. Today I ask you to join me in making 2012 the year of prevention. This is going to be one of my five generational opportunities of the United Nations for the coming five years.[1]

Since the establishment of the Office of the High Commissioner for Human Rights (OHCHR) in 1993, the High Commissioners, and under their leadership, OHCHR, have emphasized national capacity building and technical assistance, field operations, justice for victims and prosecutions of perpetrators, use of the voice of the High Commissioner in emergency situations, the mainstreaming of human rights, gender justice, and implementation of the UN Millennium Development Goals. Without doubt, the High Commissioners, and OHCHR, have made valuable contributions to the promotion and protection of human rights world-wide. That said, a review of the experience of the High Commissioners and of the Office over a decade and a half behooves us to ask what new strategies might be pursued in the future. Human rights work can be placed in the categories of seed-planting or promotional, fire-brigade or responding to human rights violations, and preventive. While promotional work contributes to prevention in the long-term, more is entailed in a strategy of prevention. So far, there has been little explicit use of preventive strategies, and they should be accentuated in the future.[2]

---

[1] Ban Ki-moon, "Address to Stanley Foundation Conference on the Responsibility to Protect," *UN News Centre*, January 18, 2012.

[2] See generally B.G. Ramcharan, *Preventive Human Rights Strategies* (Oxon: Taylor & Francis, 2010); B.G. Ramcharan, *Preventive Diplomacy at the UN* (Bloomington: Indiana

The Need for a Modernized Approach to the Role of OHCHR

Since the beginning of the United Nations, its human rights bodies, including the secretariat, have contributed to research and studies; standard-setting; advisory services to governments; fact-finding; the consideration of reports by human rights treaty bodies; the consideration of petitions; visits to prisons in preventive mode; and human rights advocacy by the UN Secretary-General and, since 1994, by the High Commissioner for Human Rights.

The historical journey of OHCHR since the assumption of duty by the first High Commissioner in 1994 has seen it go through a struggle to become established, struggle for resources, provide services to human rights bodies and special procedures mandate holders, establish human rights field offices, develop programs to help countries strengthen their national human rights structures, use the voice of the High Commissioner for protection, and, especially more recently, develop a partnership with the Human Rights Council and the UN Security Council. The High Commissioner is nowadays a highly respected figure on the international scene.

In this journey of OHCHR to date, it may be the case that some historical insights have been overlooked by the human rights movement. When the former Sub-Commission on the Prevention of Discrimination and the Protection of Minorities (later the Sub-Commission on the Promotion and Protection of Human Rights) existed, the former Division/Centre for Human Rights and OHCHR partnered with this body as a thinking arm of the human rights machinery. At the request of the Sub-Commission, for example, the Secretariat did some pioneering studies in the 1970s and 1980s on human rights and scientific developments.[3] This 'thinking function' has been diminished inasmuch as the successor of the

University Press, 2008). The Human Rights Council has, since its establishment, adopted two general resolutions on prevention and a few other resolutions dealing with decreasing maternal mortality. The Council has not yet worked out a clear-cut policy on preventive human rights strategies. See generally B.G. Ramcharan, *The UN Human Rights Council* (Oxon: Routledge, 2011).

[3] See, e.g., Audrey R. Chapman, "A Human Rights Perspective on Intellectual Property, Scientific Progress, and Access to the Benefits of Science," Presented at the World Intellectual Property Organization's Panel Discussion on Intellectual Property and Human Rights, November 9, 1998, http://www.oapi.wipo.net/edocs/mdocs/tk/en/wipo_unhchr_ip_pnl_98/wipo_unhchr_ip_pnl_98_5.pdf; Yo Kubota, "The Institutional Responses," http://archive.unu.edu/unupress/unupbooks/uu06he/uu06he0d.htm.

Sub-Commission, the Advisory Committee, may only consider topics specifically requested by the Human Rights Council.

Since the establishment of OHCHR, it might also be the case that human rights leadership has become somewhat dispersed, with the UN Secretary-General and the High Commissioner occasionally taking the lead on different issues. As OHCHR moves forward it should assert its role as the leading human rights arm of the United Nations and should be the body that the international community looks to for intellectual, policy, normative, preventive and protection guidance in a rapidly evolving world. In short, OHCHR should not only aim for classical activities but should develop its 'thinking role'.[4] This would be a contemporary interpretation of the role of OHCHR. For OHCHR to discharge a thinking function in the cause of prevention, it would need to be attentive to its research and policy functions.

OHCHR as the Human Rights Component of a Global Watch Over Human Security

Like other UN departments such as the Department of Political Affairs (DPA), the Department of Peacekeeping Operations (DPKO), and the Office for the Coordination of Humanitarian Affairs (OCHA), OHCHR does have a history of cooperation in preventive efforts within the UN Secretariat. OHCHR has been a regular participant within the 'Framework Team' that brings different UN departments together to consider situations that might be submitted to the UN Secretary-General for the exercise of his good offices in preventive mode. OHCHR has on occasions submitted country situations to senior policy management groups within the UN for consideration about possible preventive action. OHCHR supports special procedures mandate-holders in their urgent action appeals and in the preparation of their reports drawing attention to grave risks of future violations of human rights. The report of then-Special Rapporteur Bacre Waly NDiaye warning of mass atrocities in Rwanda comes to mind.[5]

---

4 OHCHR has occasionally asserted its leadership role in human rights. See, e.g., Human Rights Council, *Report of the High Commissioner on the Question of the Realization in All Countries of Economic, Social and Cultural Rights*, UN Doc. A/HRC/17/24, March 21, 2011, paras. 3–18.

5 UN Commission on Human Rights, *Extrajudicial, summary or arbitrary executions / Addendum / Report by Mr. B.W. Ndiaye. Special Rapporteur, on his mission to Rwanda from 8 to 17 April 1993*, UN Doc. E/CN.4/1994/7/Add.1, August 11, 1993.

Good offices actions by the High Commissioner have, on occasions, been exercised in preventive mode, as have public statements of the High Commissioner.

However, if OHCHR is to rise to the challenge launched by Secretary-General Ban Ki-moon for greater emphasis to be given to prevention it would need to have a stronger vision when it comes to preventive human rights strategies. The concept of a 'global watch' over human security could help it develop its future role, and it would be well-advised to project itself as the human rights arm of such a global watch.

The concept of a global watch has been around for some three decades now. In his *Perspectives for the 1990s*, which he presented to the General Assembly in 1987, then UN Secretary-General Pérez de Cuéllar made the case for the establishment and maintenance of a global watch over human security. His vision was one in which international security, including disarmament and international law, development and international economic cooperation, social advancement, basic rights and fundamental freedoms, and human well being would be the broad areas for the future programs of the United Nations.[6]

Among the ideas advanced in the report for dealing preventively with economic and social problems were the following:

- The human population, the earth's greatest resource, must live within the earth's supportive capacity.
- The protection of vulnerable groups must be enhanced.
- Health for all must be progressively achieved through preventive action and through fight against diseases.
- The growth of population in the poorer countries, where it was the largest, could well result in the future in massive migratory pressure on relatively more developed countries.
- Enhancement of safety in nuclear energy production, including the disposal of nuclear waste, warranted sustained multilateral attention given its importance for present and future generations that extended beyond any national border.

This was a blueprint for the future of the United Nations that saw the Organization working on problems susceptible to multilateral alleviation and coordinating a comprehensive global watch over issues of peace

---

[6] UN General Assembly, *Preparation of the Next Medium-Term Plan: Notes from the Secretary-General*, UN Doc. A/42/512, September 2, 1987, 2.

and security, protection of the environment, economic and social welfare, and human rights protection. The concept of a global watch remains as valid as ever and requires renewed attention. The United Nations should make intellectual and policy efforts to be a 'reliable source of timely information across the range of human activities' in the future, and OHCHR should consider ways and means through which the international community would look to it as the human rights arm of a comprehensive global watch.

OHCHR's Lack of Explicit Preventive Strategies to Date

Granting that most human rights work has an implicit preventive rationale inasmuch as it strives to advance a universal culture of human rights, it might be considered overdoing it to state that OHCHR has so far had little experience with explicit preventive human rights strategies. OHCHR does service human rights treaties like the Convention against Torture and its Optional Protocol (OPCAT) which have pronounced preventive dimensions. OHCHR also services the urgent action procedures of human rights treaty bodies and of special procedures. Human rights field offices might, on occasion, strive to head off or to contain violations of human rights. So yes, the Office does have experiences in the area of prevention, but as a servicing entity, not in its own right as a spearhead of the human rights movement, a leadership role that the High Commissioner was intended to serve.

Of the High Commissioners to date, only one has tried, fleetingly, to articulate a strategy of prevention. High Commissioner Ayala Lasso announced the establishment of a human rights hot-line[7] which was in fact a telephone number and which never worked. His successor, Mary Robinson, devoted her 2000 annual report to the then Commission on Human Rights to a discussion of preventive strategies.[8] She made important policy pronouncements but the Commission never discussed it and she never sought to activate a discussion of it in the Commission. She never returned to the issue thereafter.

---

[7] UN, "24-Hour 'Hot Line' for Reporting Human Rights Violations," background note, http://www.un.org/rights/dpi1550e.htm.

[8] UN Commission on Human Rights, *Report of the High Commissioner submitted pursuant to Commission resolution 1999/54*, UN Doc. E/CN.4/2000/12, December 28, 1999. Reproduced in B.G. Ramcharan, *A UN High Commissioner in Defence of Human Rights* (Leiden: Brill, 2004): Appendix III.

The report, drafted by specialists in OHCHR and coordinated by this author as the then Deputy High Commissioner contained chapters offering strategies for the prevention of the crime of genocide, prevention of racism and racial discrimination, the right to development and the prevention of human rights violations, prevention of gross violations of civil and political rights, fundamental standards of humanity, prevention of slavery, prevention of trafficking in women and children, prevention of violations through human rights education, and combating impunity as a preventive approach. The report concluded that:

> The quest for the prevention of gross violations of human rights and of conflicts is a defining issue of our time. As we begin the new millennium, it must be a matter of the utmost priority that we seek, at the national, regional and international levels, to develop societies fashioned in the image of international norms of human rights.[9]

The High Commissioner announced her intention to give high priority to the push for prevention but, unfortunately, under pressure of events, including her Secretary-Generalship of the World Conference on Racism and Racial Discrimination held the next year, never returned to the matter. It has not been on the radar screen of any High Commissioner since then, a decade later.

High Commissioner Vieira de Mello served barely a few months before he was deployed to Iraq and did not have time to place his mark in this area. In the fourteen months that this author served in the position of High Commissioner, I was active in fire brigade mode, launching four fact-finding investigations, and I sought to advance the concept of national systems for the protection of human rights – one element of which was prevention. I also proposed and secured the appointment of a special rapporteur against human trafficking.[10] But I did not have room to mount broader initiatives such as on preventive strategies.

High Commissioners Arbour and Pillay, reflecting their experience in the area of international criminal justice, can both be said to have emphasized the justice dimension as their commanding strategy. They have both mounted initiatives on reform of the human rights treaty system.[11]

---

[9] Ibid., para. 92.

[10] "Commission on Human Rights Concludes Sixtieth Session: Appoints Special Rapporteurs on Situations in Belarus, Democratic People's Republic of Korea; Trafficking in Persons," UN press release HR/CN/1099, April 23, 2004.

[11] See Louise Arbour, *Concept Paper on the High Commissioner's Proposal for a Unified Standing Treaty Body*, UN Doc. HRI/MC/2006/CRP.1, March 14, 2006. See also Navi Pillay, *Strengthening the United Nations human Rights Treaty Body System: A Report by the United*

The Arbour initiative met with mixed reception and the Pillay initiative is facing fire from states and even some NGOs at the time of this writing.

While I am reluctant to make this comment, it would probably be fair to say that no High Commissioner to date has had an overarching grand strategy. They have come in as prominent leaders and have served for varying periods: Ayala Lasso for two and a half years; Robinson for four, then an additional year; Vieira de Mello for seven months; yours truly for fourteen months; Arbour for four years; and Pillay, at the time of writing, has entered her fifth year of what will probably be a six-year term. Lasso was a former Foreign Minister, Robinson a former President, Vieira de Mello a former UN civil servant with long experience in the humanitarian area; Arbour had experience as a judge and prosecutor; and Pillay was a practicing advocate and international criminal judge. All have, without doubt, provided courageous leadership. But leadership is not necessarily strategy. And strategy requires the developing of a policy on prevention. The need is compelling.

Developing the Research and Policy Function of OHCHR to Put it in the Service of Prevention

In the world of internet communications, if one wants to tap into leading analyses on a particular issue, one places a search question on the particular issue and may be able to access good thinking on the topic. This raises the question, what can one access from OHCHR when it comes to insights into issues where a preventive approach might be useful? The internet website of OHCHR is full of materials on the activities of the different human rights bodies, some of which touch on prevention. The deliberations of the Human Rights Council, its special procedures, and the Sub-Committee on the Prevention of Torture come to mind.

But there is need to develop considerably on this in the future. OHCHR must become a source of analyses in its own right on issues where a preventive approach is needed. The High Commissioner and OHCHR are uniquely placed to perform this function. As examples of threats on which it would be important to present human rights analyses to the world we discuss some pressing global issues.

Nations High Commissioner for Human Rights, June 2012, http://www2.ohchr.org/english/bodies/HRTD/docs/HCreportonTBstrengthening210612.doc.

In the contemporary world human rights are affected by eight phenomena: environmental changes, migratory movements, poverty, conflicts, terrorism, gross violations, inequality, and poor governance. It will be crucial to develop preventive strategies in respect of all eight of these phenomena if we are to ever hope to achieve the universal realization of human rights.

Environmental Changes

Whether they are due to natural or human causes, environmental changes, global warming, encroaching deserts, and rising oceans can affect the rights to life and livelihood of large numbers of people. To the extent that preventive actions are possible they should certainly be undertaken. But preventive action is also required from a human rights point of view. Environmental mapping and projections and discussion of desirable policy options can help anticipate human rights problems related to mass exoduses, internal displacement and refugee movements. One should not wait until the problem is upon us before scrambling to deal with them.

Migratory Movements

There are some projections that indicate that if the warming trend continues and if oceans rise, millions upon millions of people will seek to move across frontiers in the quest for life. It will be necessary to think through a human rights regime to plan for, and cope with, such massive changes. The present international and normative policy instruments we have are nowhere near being adequate.

Extreme Poverty

Two-thirds of the world population lives in dire poverty. The Millennium Development Goals, which sought to halve world poverty by 2015, are woefully far from being achieved. It would be essential, in the future, to bring into the picture the concept of preventable poverty: every country should be expected to map the situation of its poor people, identify the extremely poor, and act to prevent extreme poverty to the extent that this can be achieved using already available national resources. The concept of preventable poverty can be buttressed by giving courts and national human rights institutions the competence to adjudicate on situations of gross violations of economic, social and cultural rights. Some courts, such as the Indian Supreme Court, have developed social action jurisprudence precisely along these lines.

Conflicts

While recent years have seen a reduction in the number of conflicts, they nevertheless continue to be distressingly frequent in many parts of the world. The prevention of conflicts, especially in multi-ethnic countries, is closely related to the promotion and protection of human rights and cultural rights, especially the rights of composite populations and minorities. Strategies for the prevention of conflicts must be built on the foundations of respect for human rights.

Terrorism

Whatever the doctrinal debates about whether terrorists commit violations of human rights or crimes, for the victims the consequences are the same: deaths, maiming, and fear. The Security Council has called on Member States of the UN to cooperate in fighting against terrorism. It has also called for counter-terrorism efforts to be pursued with respect for human rights. Preventive measures are necessary to safeguard against violations of human rights in the struggle against terrorism. The US 9/11 Commission called for independent monitoring bodies to "safeguard against excesses."[12] That would be a good starting point for preventive measures in the field of human rights.

Gross Violations of Human Rights

Gross violations of human rights are rampant in the world. United Nations human rights special procedures among others, endeavor to document these violations, to take urgent intercessionary action where possible, and to make the case for justice for the victims. But international efforts in the future should place the accent more and more in the future on preventive strategies, beginning with preventive strategies at the national level to guard against the dangers of gross violations of human rights.

Inequality

Inequality on grounds of gender, race, social origin, or economic situation is, alas, widespread in the world. It would be interesting to make an assessment of how strategies pursued to date are contributing, or not contributing, to the prevention of discrimination. Educational efforts could be decisive in preventing gender or racial discrimination.

---

12 Ramcharan, *Preventative Human Rights*, 13.

Poor Governance

Without a doubt, a great part of the miseries of the world have to do with bad governance which, in turn, wreaks havoc on human rights. Efforts for the promotion of democracy and the rule of law are meant to help here but they have so far seen only partial results. The Human Rights Council should establish a special rapporteurship on the promotion of democratic governance, and efforts to promote democracy and the rule of law should increasingly build in a preventive dimension. The responsibility to protect must also come into the picture here.

Through human rights preventive strategies on issues such as the above, future efforts to build the world of the Universal Declaration of Human Rights might help bring us nearer to the mark.

Threats to Humanity that Call for the Articulation of their Human Rights Dimensions

With global threats such as climate change, natural disasters, and global competition for depleting resources, the High Commissioner must be in the lead in articulating the human rights dimensions and calling attention to the need for responses that are anchored in respect for human rights and fundamental freedoms. There are estimates that, depending on the degree of global warming, millions of people could be forced to seek refuge on safer ground. Some have even mentioned the figure of 300 million.[13] The UN High Commissioner for Human Rights must empanel human rights and technical experts to project the human rights needs of such a situation and to come up with recommendations that could be discussed in the international community.

In the response to natural disasters such as Hurricane Katrina in the USA there was clearly inequity. While the USA has thoughtful policies for responding to natural disasters the human rights dimensions were clearly missing. The High Commissioner can help by empanelling experts to come up with recommendations for responding to such situations with due regard to considerations of human rights. These admittedly are not easy issues to deal with, but if the UN High Commissioner is not providing leadership on the human rights dimensions, who will?

---

[13] Global Humanitarian Forum, *Human Impact Report: Climate Change*, (Geneva: Global Humanitarian Forum, May 2009): 48, http://www.ghf-ge.org/human-impact-report.php.

It is in the nature of the Office of High Commissioner that one should expect think pieces from it in which it is trying to present the human rights dimensions of new threats and challenges to the international community. There are threats to humankind that the international community is struggling with, the human rights dimensions of which have hardly been articulated. Climate change is an example. The Human Rights Council has asked the Office of the High Commissioner to do a study on this topic[14] and the International Council on Human Rights Policy has published an exploratory monograph on it.[15]

Climate change threatens the lives of large sections of humanity and possibly of the whole human species unless the warming trends are contained and reversed. Viewed from the perspective of human rights and having regard to the importance of preventive strategies there is a need to consider the duty of care that falls upon governments, regional and international organizations, upon business enterprises, and upon individual human beings. Mindful of the threats posed to the right to life and the importance of a duty of care, one can make the case that people have the right to advance information, to the extent possible, of foreseeable risks as well as the right to advance action nationally, regionally, and internationally wherever feasible.

There is a duty upon governments to cooperate in good faith to deal with the problem of global warming. The duty to cooperate is one of the fundamental principles of international law recognized by the General Assembly in the 1970 Declaration on Principles of International Law Concerning Friendly Relations and Cooperation among Nations.[16] The duty to cooperate in this instance encompasses a responsibility to act for anticipatory mitigation.

Furthermore, one must insist on the principle of accountability on the part of all those in whom is vested a duty of care to watch over the right to life of the human species. The global watch over human welfare and rights must give prominent place to preventive actions to preserve the human environment.

---

[14] UN Human Rights Council. Resolution 7/23, "Human Rights and Climate Change," UN Doc. A/HRC/7/78, March 28, 2008.

[15] International Council on Human Rights Policy, *Climate Change and Human Rights: A Rough Guide* (Geneva: International Council on Human Rights Policy, 2008).

[16] UN General Assembly. Resolution 25/2625, "Declaration on Principles of International Law Concerning Friendly Relations and Co-operation Among States in Accordance with the Charter of the United Nations," A/RES/25/2625 October 24, 1970.

The Protection of Vulnerable Groups

In the contemporary world groups such as minorities, indigenous populations, and migrants face numerous vulnerabilities. There are normative instruments and UN bodies devoted to promoting and protecting their human rights. But the UN High Commissioner has a spearheading and crystallizing role to play. At any one time the world should be on notice through alert statements and studies from OHCHR drawing attention to the dangers to particular communities. Such alerts can be brought to the attention of the General Assembly, the Security Council, and the Human Rights Council, as well as to regional bodies. The aim here should be to head off and prevent violations of human rights. Vulnerable groups facing imminent problems should be able to address the High Commissioner and to seek the articulation of their concerns. This would be prevention in action.

In a recent book on the prevention of genocide, Dr. David Hamburg made a powerful case for prevention in the future.[17] He offered suggestions for the crisis prevention approach and made the case for international cooperation for the prevention of genocide. New research on genocide offers, he thinks, clues to the future of prevention. Every modern case of genocide, he notes, has been preceded by a propaganda campaign directed through the mass media by political leaders who applied to human destruction the latest technological and organizational capabilities available to them.

At a UN seminar in Geneva on 21 January 2009, Ms. Yakin Erktuk, then UN Special Rapporteur on Violence against Women, its Causes and Consequences, made an eloquent presentation on preventive strategies.[18] Based on her experience as Special Rapporteur she focused on three areas that she saw as critical for prevention of human rights violations and ultimately genocide: (i) socio-economic justice; (ii) gender analysis; and (iii) accountability.

She considered that one of the most predictable features of impending violence was the deepening of disparities. An inclusive analysis of the patterns of gendered vulnerabilities before, during, and after conflict,

[17] David A. Hamburg, *Preventing Genocide: Practical Steps toward Early Detection and Effective Action* (London: Paradigm, 2010).

[18] Yakin Erktuk, "Talking Points," Prepared for the UN Seminar on the Prevention of Genocide, January 21, 2009, Geneva, Switzerland, http://www.ohchr.org/Documents/Issues/RuleOfLaw/TalkingPointsYakin.pdf.

factored into the analysis and monitored as warning signs to prevent genocide, could, she felt, contribute to the efforts to stop atrocities from occurring.

The Preventive Dimensions of the Responsibility to Protect

The high-level group of experts who first advocated the doctrine of the responsibility to protect saw it as having three core components: the responsibility to prevent, the responsibility to react, and the responsibility to rebuild.[19] The UN Secretary-General has established the positions of Special Adviser on the Responsibility to Protect and Special Adviser on the Prevention of Genocide. They have both made useful contributions.

But the High Commissioner is the world leader on human rights protection and must be in the vanguard of efforts to discharge the responsibility to prevent. The concept of the responsibility to protect, as approved by the UN General Assembly in 2005 covered genocide, ethnic cleansing, crimes against humanity, and war crimes.[20] As a political choice this was understandable in the circumstances. But the responsibility to prevent, generically, must reach far beyond these four offences to the entire gamut of threats to human rights. The High Commissioner must surely shoulder the responsibility for the responsibility to prevent world-wide, drawing upon the complementary efforts of the Special Advisers of the UN Secretary-General and of regional officials such as the OSCE High Commissioner on National Minorities. To date there has been no evidence whatsoever of High Commissioners seeking to discharge the responsibility to prevent.

The Preventive Roles of National Protection Systems

A national human rights system should consist of constitutional, legislative, judicial, educational, institutional, and preventive pillars. OHCHR has a good program of cooperation with national human rights institutions, regionally and internationally. But the cooperation has been generic

[19] See, e.g., "RtoP and Rebuilding: the Role of the Peacebuilding Commission," International Coalition for the Responsibility to Protect, http://www.responsibilitytoprotect.org/index.php/about-rtop/related-themes/2417-pbc-and-rtop.

[20] UN General Assembly. Resolution 60/1, "2005 World Summit Outcome," UN Doc. A/RES/60/1, paras. 138–140, October 24, 2005.

so far. There has, to date, been little or no highlighting of the preventive pillar of national protection systems.

But this is the key to the future protection of human rights world-wide. Competent national human rights institutions should be expected to take the lead in heading off and preventing gross violations of human rights. OHCHR needs to commission as soon as possible a study of the preventive pillar of national human rights systems and to place this issue under the spotlight. The High Commissioner should take personal charge of efforts to highlight the importance of the preventive dimension of national protection systems and to foster their development in every country of the world. The High Commissioner, in cooperation with national human rights institutions where they exist, should also keep under review the adequacy of national prevention systems designed to head off gross violations of human rights.

Using the Universal Periodic Review Process to Advance Prevention

The Universal Periodic Review (UPR) has valuable features inasmuch as, once every four and a half years, every Member State of the UN prepares a report, supplemented by two reports from OHCHR, on efforts to advance human rights in the country and on problems being encountered. The report is reviewed within the Human Rights Council, with the participation of the country concerned and, at the plenary stage, with the participation of NGOs. The system is now only in its second cycle and one must withhold judgment on its eventual efficacy. There are strong political currents that make this more of a diplomatic than a legal process, in comparison to the consideration of reports by human rights treaty bodies.

OHCHR is still in the process of developing a policy of building on the UPR. So far its efforts have veered in the direction of capacity-building within countries. That is understandable, but OHCHR can make a decisive difference by focusing on the strengthening of national protection systems and on national efforts for the prevention of gross violations of human rights. OHCHR could, for example, commission a global study on national policies, strategies and institutions for the prevention of human rights violations. The study could be cast in terms of the sharing of experiences among countries and the identification of good practices.

At the end of the day, however, the aim should be to assist each country to define and operate a policy of prevention. That would be genuine human rights protection at work. Capacity building sounds good, and can be useful. But it can also be vague and ephemeral. Prevention is concrete, and the real stuff of human rights protection.

INJECTING HUMAN RIGHTS DIMENSIONS INTO REGIONAL PREVENTIVE REGIMES

Regional mechanisms for the prevention of conflict and violence exist today in ASEAN, AU, ECOWAS, SADC, the OAS, OSCE, and other regional and sub-regional organizations.[21] The AU Charter specifically supports AU action in the event of gross violations of human rights. In addition to these conflict and violence-prevention mechanisms, regional institutions for the promotion and protection of human rights exist in ASEAN, AU, the Council of Europe, OAS, and OSCE.

OHCHR and the High Commissioner have spasmodic cooperation with some of these bodies but there is no evidence of spearheading and leadership provided by the High Commissioner. For this to happen there must be policy choices. General cooperation can degenerate into courtesies. We suggest that the policy choice should be for prevention. The High Commissioner should periodically visit each of the regional preventive mechanisms and address them with human rights insights and recommendations. The High Commissioner should also periodically visit regional and sub-regional human rights institutions and beckon them to stronger preventive efforts. The thrust of prevention would define the relationship and help give sharper definition to OHCHR in the process.

---

[21] See generally B.G. Ramcharan, ed., *Conflict Prevention in Practice: Essays in Honour of Jim Sutterlin* (Leiden, Martinus Nijhoff: 2005); International Peace Institute, *Preventive Diplomacy in Focus*, (New York: International Peace Institute, 2011). See also *Report of the Secretary-General: Preventive Diplomacy: Delivering Results*, UN Doc. S2011/552, August 26, 2011. The Secretary-General in the *Report* states, "In the past five years, we have deepened existing or established new conflict prevention and mediation partnerships with the African Union, the European Union, OSCE, OAS, the Caribbean Community (CARICOM), ECOWAS, SADC, ASEAN, OIC and others. Partly through the use of extra-budgetary resources, we have been able to undertake initiatives to help build regional capacities and learn from regional experiences. Joint training programs on a broad range of peace and security issues are now available. Still, synergies take time and hard work to attain and are not rendered easier by the fact that, with very few exceptions, the United Nations, regional organizations and other actors have no shared mechanism or procedure to decide, in real time, who should do what in a given case. As we work to improve our formal institutional channels and protocols in that regard, we are also investing in key personal relationships with regional partners, which form the bedrock of closer cooperation." para. 52. The question that must be posed is: where does OHCHR fit into all of this? So far the answer is: not in many places. This should change in the future. OHCHR should be a key player in all these processes.

Leadership on Preventive Treaties such as OPCAT

Historically, the relationship between the High Commissioner and the human rights treaty bodies has been an ambiguous one. True, OHCHR provides servicing for the human rights treaty bodies. True, High Commissioners have been addressing human rights treaty bodies from time to time. As mentioned earlier, High Commissioners Arbour and Pillay have issued reports on the rationalization of the human rights treaty system.[22]

This chapter will not enter into this broader relationship.[23] We are, rather, making the case that High Commissioners should take a special interest and place their shoulders to the wheel when it comes to treaties with pronounced preventive thrusts. The OPCAT, for example, provides for states parties to establish national preventive mechanisms, regular visits by national bodies, and regular visits by the OPCAT sub-committee. In their contacts with national authorities, High Commissioners should highlight the importance of the OPCAT arrangements and seek to use their influence to strengthen them. There can be no more important human rights work than preventing torture. High Commissioners should be identified with this. This would, again, help sharpen the definition of OHCHR.

Cooperating with Partners to Advance Prevention

This essay has argued for stronger emphasis on preventive strategies by OHCHR and by High Commissioners and we have already made the point that High Commissioners should develop cooperation with regional preventive and human rights mechanisms to help prevent gross violations of human rights world-wide. There are other actors active in the field of prevention with which OHCHR and High Commissioners should also have more pronounced cooperation. These include the major human rights NGOs and organizations with a pronounced preventive focus. OHCHR could invite these organizations to periodic meetings on cooperation for prevention, with a view to drawing insights and suggestions from them and with a view to building up a culture of cooperation for the prevention of human rights violations.

22 See generally UN Secretariat, "Concept Paper."

23 See the chapter in this volume by Michael O'Flaherty on this subject.

Using the Voice of the High Commissioner for Prevention

Finally, whenever the High Commissioners consider that a group or people are in particular danger, they should be ready to use the voice of the High Commissioner by issuing public statements or calling for the attention of the Human Rights Council, the Security Council, the Secretary-General, or the leadership of regional or sub-regional organizations, with a view to heading off dangers of gross violations. Through such a practice over time the High Commissioner and OHCHR would become more sharply defined as a preventive organization.

Opportunities for Putting OHCHR's Fact-Finding Role in the Service of Prevention

One of the readily available ways of drawing attention to a situation or threat is to initiate fact-finding into that situation and presenting the results to the international community. This chapter has already advocated the establishment within OHCHR of a Centre for Human Rights Policy and Research that could offer analyses on emerging global issues from a human rights perspective. In cases or situations where High Commissioners consider this warranted, they could initiate fact-finding processes into the issues and present the results to the international community for its attention. The High Commissioner is ideally placed to do this.

Conclusion: Making Prevention the Decisive Rationale of a Grand Strategy

Human rights work has an inherent preventive rationale. This chapter notes that UN human rights work can be grouped under the categories of seed-planting, fire-brigade, or preventive. It acknowledges that High Commissioners and OHCHR have done much in the areas of seed-planting and fire-brigade reactions. However, it submits that there has so far been little effort for prevention. It has made a call for prevention to become a defining priority of OHCHR and of High Commissioners. Global threats to humanity make this imperative. And it sets out other areas where there is room for the development of preventive policies and strategies.

Secretary-General Ban Ki-moon stated in his 2011 report on prevention:

> We should build on the improvements that have been made in the United Nations and in various regional and sub-regional organizations in developing early warning mechanisms. The establishment of regular and informal early warning dialogues between the United Nations and regional and other partners would allow us to pool information and help us to anticipate 'threshold moments', when key actors might decide to use violence. However, early warning is useful only if it leads to early action, and we need to consider a broader range of options for addressing an emerging threat, including seemingly small steps, such as multi-actor statements of concern or fact-finding missions, which can affect the calculations of parties on the ground early on.[24]

The High Commissioner must be an integral player in these efforts.

[24] *Report of the Secretary-General*, para. 66.

PART TWO

PROMOTING UNIVERSALITY OF RIGHTS: GLOBAL LEADERSHIP IN AN ERA OF GROWING PARTICULARISM AND RELATIVISM

THE HIGH COMMISSIONER AND THE TREATY BODIES

Michael O'Flaherty

Introduction

Writing in 1992, Theo van Boven described the relationship of the then United Nations (UN) Centre for Human Rights with the UN human rights treaty bodies (or 'committees') as no more than that of secretariat to substantive bodies. By way of illustration, he recounted how, when he headed the then UN human rights division, he was sharply criticized by members of one treaty body, the Human Rights Committee (HRC), when he ventured to suggest how it might improve its working methods.[1] Twenty years later, in April 2012, I witnessed the UN Secretary-General and the High Commissioner for Human Rights address a crowded meeting of states parties to the treaties on the topic of the strengthening of the committee system.[2] Not one state objected to this exercise of leadership (albeit there were plenty of dissonant voices as to specific suggestions). Clearly much had changed in those 20 years. It is the purpose of this chapter to explore the process of that change and to assess the current state of the relationship of the High Commissioner and her Office with the treaty bodies.

Before Ever there was a High Commissioner

Each of the human rights treaty bodies (with the exception of the ECOSOC-established Committee on Economic, Social and Cultural Rights) is a *sui-generis* independent body, established by treaty and not answerable to the political organs of the UN. However, the treaties specify that secretariat services be provided by the UN Secretary-General. This secretariat function has always been provided by the UN's human rights program (other than in the case of the Committee on the Elimination of Discrimination Against Women (CEDAW) which, until the early 2000's,

[1] *The United Nations and human rights: a critical appraisal*, ed. Philip Alston, (Oxford: Clarendon Press, 1992).

[2] Informal consultation for States Parties on Treaty Body Strengthening, UN New York, 2–3 April 2012, http://www.ohchr.org/EN/HRBodies/HRTD/Pages/Documents.aspx.

was serviced by the UN Division for the Advancement of Women). At the outset, as recounted by van Boven, the relationship was one solely of administrative support. He does venture that such a role need not be an arid one – since the secretariat, at its best, should reflect and uphold the core values of the UN, as found in the Charter. He also recalled the manner in which the secretariat played an important role in generating the drafts of important treaty body texts. He referred, for example, to the first drafts of the rules of procedure of the HRC and of the Committee on the Elimination of Racial Discrimination (CERD). One might also add reference to the manuals that were developed to assist states with the treaty reporting procedures – tomes that, in the absence of detailed committee guidance, were essential tools for diplomats and civil society.[3] Nevertheless, as van Boven's anecdote acknowledged, such services had always to be discreet and unsung, with credit usually being accorded to the treaty bodies themselves. Thus remained the situation until at least the mid-1990s when the present writer, in my capacity as secretary of CERD, was rebuked by a member of that committee for having the temerity to express an opinion – any opinion – during committee proceedings.

Another dimension of the secretariat support that, over time, would come to be identified as a major impediment to effective functioning of the treaty bodies, the inadequate levels of staffing, was already apparent then. My own situation exemplified the problem – I was the sole full time professional staff member assigned to CERD. Writing in 1997, I described the impact of the under-staffing as follows, "At its present staffing and resource levels, the secretariat is barely able to carry out its task in respect of the regular activities of the treaty bodies....It does not have the resources to identify and gather pertinent documentation, liaise with non-conventional mechanisms, provide useful political advice or professionally to assist in the drafting of decisions and concluding observations."[4]

José Ayala Lasso

By the mid-1990s important changes were afoot that would, over time, radically reform the relationship of the UN secretariat and the treaty

[3] See, e.g., OHCHR, UN Institute for Training and Research, and UN Staff College Project, *Manual on Human Rights Reporting under Six Major International Human Rights Instruments*, UN Doc. HR/PUB/91/1 (Rev.1) (Geneva: UN, 1997).

[4] Michael O'Flaherty. "Treaty bodies responding to states of emergency: The case of Bosnia and Hezegovina," in *The Future of UN Human Rights Treaty Monitoring*, ed, Philip Alston et al. (Cambridge: Cambridge University Press, 2000), 439–460.

bodies. In 1994, the UN General Assembly adopted Resolution 48/141, whereby the post of High Commissioner for Human Rights was established. It is worth recalling elements of the mandate that was entrusted to the High Commissioner. Preliminary paragraphs of the resolution stipulate that the General Assembly was, *inter-alia*:

> Determined to adapt, strengthen and streamline the existing mechanisms to promote and protect all human rights and fundamental freedoms while avoiding unnecessary duplication; recognizing that the activities of the United Nations in the field of human rights should be rationalized and enhanced in order to strengthen the United Nations machinery in this field and to further the objectives of universal respect for observance of international human rights standards; ... [and] re-affirming the necessity for a continued adaptation of the United Nations human rights machinery to the current and future needs in the promotion and protection of human rights and the need to improve its coordination, efficiency and effectiveness...

On the basis of these and other considerations, the resolution stated that the High Commissioner would function within the framework of the Charter of the United Nations, the Universal Declaration of Human Rights, and other international instruments of human rights and international law, to respect the sovereignty, territorial integrity and domestic jurisdiction of states and to promote the universal respect for and observance of all human rights; and that the High Commissioner would be the UN official with principal responsibility for United Nations human rights activities.

Specific responsibilities of the High Commissioner were listed to include:

- Promotion and protection of the effective enjoyment by all of all civil, cultural, economic, political and social rights;
- The playing of an active role in removing the current obstacles and in meeting the challenges to the full realization of all human rights;
- Enhancing international cooperation for the promotion and protection of all human rights;
- Coordination of human rights promotion and protection activities throughout the UN system;
- Rationalization, adaptation, strengthening and streamlining of the UN machinery in the field of human rights with a view to improving its efficiency and effectiveness.

It can be seen from these elements of the resolution that the High Commissioner would need to engage with the treaties and the treaty bodies in at least two ways. In the first place, in seeking to uphold the universality of human rights, the High Commissioner would have to rely on the normative framework provided by the treaties and by the findings of the treaty bodies. Secondly, the resolution offered a platform, if not an explicit instruction, whereby the High Commissioner might work, in the terms employed by the resolution, to rationalize, adapt, strengthen and streamline the treaty body system.

Thus, the first High Commissioner for Human Rights, José Ayala Lasso, took up office in 1994 with a mandate that supported the continuance of the secretariat function but also provided the platform for significant new forms of engagement.[5] In fact, and notwithstanding the promise of the mandate, Ayala Lasso's tenure was not noted for any significant innovations in our area of interest. This is not at all surprising when we recall the dysfunctional arrangements that he inherited – he was located within the UN Centre for Human Rights but without clear oversight responsibility for it. I can however attest, from my experience serving on his staff that he can be credited with the practice whereby senior UN officials would seek and obtain briefing materials based on treaty body findings to assist them in their engagement with governments. In so acting, he acknowledged his responsibility to uphold the universality of human rights on the basis of the normative framework. His office also devoted resources to the building up of national-level capacity to implement the treaties and meet the reporting requirements. For instance, this form of capacity building was a significant component of the 'technical cooperation' delivered to the government of Cambodia by the UN human rights field operation in that country.[6] In another example, he deployed to Bosnia-Herzegovina human rights officers (I was one of them) to support implementation of the UN human rights treaties that had been included in the Dayton/Paris peace agreement (this focus on the treaties as the principal substantive reference point for field work had been missing entirely from my previous deployment to that country by the Centre for Human Rights in 1993).

Ayala Lasso's term of office also coincided (by chance) with a phase of intense reflection by academics and other experts as to how best to improve the work and effectiveness of the treaty bodies. Some years

---

5 UN General Assembly. Resolution 48/141, "High Commissioner for the Promotion and Protection of Human Rights," A/Res/49/141 ¶ 4, December 20, 1993).

6 Report of the Secretary-General, *Role of the United Nations Centre for Human Rights in assisting the Government and people of Cambodia in the promotion and protection of human rights*, addendum to *Situation of human rights in Cambodia*, UN Doc. A/49/635/Add.1, November 3,1994.

previously, the UN Commission on Human Rights had appointed an independent expert on the topic, Philip Alston, who proceeded over a decade to issue a number of thoughtful reports.[7] Another academic, Anne Bayefsky, was generating wide-ranging research findings and recommendations to strengthen what was already then being described as a treaty body 'system.'[8] These two specialists, and their associated projects and consortia of authors, were identifying a range of reform options that would come to inform efforts of future High Commissioners.

Mary Robinson

With the appointment of Ayala's successor, Mary Robinson, her office and the UN Centre for Human Rights were merged to form the Office of the High Commissioner for Human Rights (OHCHR). She was thus empowered to make a significant mark regarding the treaty bodies.

Robinson's tenure is best understood as one of vision and innovation (and related risk). Within this context, the evidence demonstrates that she perceived the treaties and the findings of the treaty bodies to be a core normative framework for all the work of her Office and, more generally, for UN efforts to promote and protect human rights.[9] This is evidenced, for example, in her efforts for the mainstreaming of human rights across the UN system and for the development of rights-based approaches to development.[10] Two culminating moments in this effort were the adoption of the UN Common Understanding of the Human Rights Based Approach to Development[11] and the instigation of the UN-wide 'Action 2' program to mainstream human rights in the work of UN country teams.[12] In both cases there is explicit reference to the central significance of the treaties, the need to promote ratification and withdraw reservations and

[7] UN Commission on Human Rights, *Final report on enhancing the long-term effectiveness of the United Nations human rights treaty system / Note by the Secretary-General*, UN Doc. E/CN.4/1997/74, March 27, 1996.

[8] Anne F. Bayefsky, *The UN human rights treaty system in the 21st century*, (The Hague: Kluwer Academic Publishers, 2003).

[9] Ibid., 1.

[10] *A Voice for Human Rights*, eds. Mary Robinson & Kevin Boyle, (Phildelphia: University of Pennsylvania Press, 2006).

[11] "The Human Rights Based Approach to Development Cooperation: Towards a Common Understanding Among UN Agencies," http://hrbaportal.org/the-human-rights-based-approach-to-development-cooperation-towards-a-common-understanding-among-un-agencies.

[12] "Action 2," Strengthening UN Support for the Promotion and Protection of Human Rights Worldwide, http://www.un.org/events/action2/programme.html.

the programmatic value of the concluding observations adopted by the Committees.

In the same vein, OHCHR significantly expanded its presence in the field, either in the form of independent offices or as a component of peace-keeping operations, and standard operating procedures placed the treaties/treaty body findings at center stage. This emphasis, in a time when such field work was still both new and experimental resulted in some unusual initiatives. For instance, when I was head of the UN human rights team in Sierra Leone we provided considerable assistance to lawyers acting for soldiers who had been sentenced to death to take cases to the HRC under the Optional Protocol to the International Covenant on Civil and Political Rights (ICCPR). This action, which had the full support of headquarters, resulted in the issuance by the Committee of an interim measures request and the ultimate saving of the lives of a small number of the condemned men and women.[13] It was also in Sierra Leone that I had my first opportunity to see the extent to which Robinson relied on treaty body findings in her engagement with government. During a visit by her to that country in 1998 it was notable that she led every meeting with reference to relevant findings of the Committees. This was a practice that she maintained throughout her tenure. She was also assiduous in calling for the ratification of treaties. For instance, her persistent emphasis on the need for China to ratify the two covenants was to become a main plank of her strategy concerning that country (it ratified the Covenant on Economic, Social and Cultural Rights in 2001).[14] These aspects of the working methods of High Commissioners are now commonplace and will not be addressed further in this chapter.

Robinson appreciated that the treaty body system was in need of remedial attention. Addressing the Chairs of the Committees, in June 2001, she spoke of "deficiencies and bottlenecks" and of "the various problems linked to the lack of adequate visibility of the work of treaty bodies – the reporting burden, backlog of reports, and delays in processing individual complaints, as well as the lack of follow-up."[15] She identified the basic problem as "the extremely heavy workload facing the treaty bodies" and also emphasized the inadequacy of the resources made available to the

---

[13] As told to me by an aide to the then Sierra Leone President Kabbah.

[14] Charles Hutzler, "U.N. Urges China on Human Rights," *Associated Press* (September 14, 1998).

[15] Mary Robinson, "Statement by the High Commissioner for Human Rights to the Meeting of Chairpersons of the Treaty Bodies" in Geneva June 18, 2001, in *A Voice for Human Rights*.

system. In that same speech, Robinson referred to a major review of the treaty bodies by Anne Bayefsky, funded by the Ford Foundation, that she had facilitated and that had reported in April of that year.[16] This report was commissioned in order to demonstrate the levels of effectiveness of the treaty body system and the extent of its impact for human rights protection at the country level.[17] It contained an extremely detailed presentation on the plight of the system. The findings were disturbing, with the conclusion drawn that, "the gap between universal right and remedy has become inescapable and inexcusable, threatening the integrity of the international human rights legal regime. There are overwhelming numbers of overdue reports, untenable backlogs, minimal individual complaints from vast numbers of potential victims, and widespread refusal of states to provide remedies when violations of individual rights are found."[18] The report was accompanied by 228 recommendations addressed to states, treaty bodies and OHCHR. Many of these go to practice and procedure and appear eminently reasonable. Re-reading them in 2012 one is struck by the extent to which so many of the proposals have actually been implemented over time and under the watch of various High Commissioners. It is in the Bayefsky report that we find early variants of proposals for such by now well-established practices as the adoption of lists of issues within the report review procedure, the shape and form of concluding observations, the form of the dialogue of committees with delegations and, most significantly, the framework for follow-up by the committees with states. Other recommendations that eventually came to be implemented are the establishment of a petitions unit within OHCHR that would handle individual communications and the transfer of secretariat support for CEDAW from the Division for the Advancement of Women to OHCHR.

Although Robinson did not seek any fundamental re-ordering of the system, the Bayefsky report was oriented towards a future merger whereby, in the first instance, there would be just one consolidated report by states to all treaty bodies and, ultimately, the re-ordering of the committees so that, eventually there would be just two bodies – one to deal with periodic reports and the other to consider individual communications and inquiries.[19] Neither idea was new – both having also been considered by Philip

---

16 Anne Bayefsky, *The UN Human Rights Treaty System: Universality at the Crossroads* (The Hague: Klewer Academic Publishers, 2001).

17 Felice Gaer, in discussion with the author.

18 Bayefsky, *The UN Human Rights Treaty System*, 1.

19 Ibid.

Alston in his expert studies. Variants of these two proposals came to dominate the debate around treaty body reform during the tenures of Bertie Ramcharan and Louise Arbour.

Bertrand Ramcharan

Sergio Vieira de Mello was not in office long enough for any achievements to be observed or other actions noted with regard to the operation of the treaty body system. It was his deputy and subsequent Acting High Commissioner, Bertie Ramcharan, who took the next notable steps. He acted on UN Secretary-General Kofi Annan's UN reform initiatives. In the report, "Strengthening the United Nations: An Agenda for Further Change," Annan called, among other things, for greater cross-committee coordination, involving standardization of reporting requirements and procedures, with a view to an eventual transition to a single state report[20] (thus reducing the reporting burden for states). This proposal from New York caught many of the treaty bodies and states by surprise. Ramcharan was faced with the dilemma; how to support the Secretary-General's proposal and yet ensure that all treaty bodies would be provided with sufficient information to perform their work. As Ramcharan recounts,[21] he conducted extensive consultations, culminating in a meeting in 2003 hosted by the government of Liechtenstein in the tiny mountain hamlet of Malbun. I attended the Malbun meeting and can attest to the vigorous engagement and skillful diplomacy by Ramcharan, who clearly had the responsibility to ensure that if the Secretary-General's proposal were to fail that, nevertheless, some progress might be made to improve the reporting process. The event was also notably positive in tone, reflecting a general desire among all present to strengthen the system in the interest of rights-holders. This was the context for the meeting's conclusion that, while the idea of the single report was flawed and would weaken the impact of the reporting procedure, nevertheless states should submit 'expanded common core documents' to OHCHR that would detail those elements of the general country situation that were of interest for all committees while continuing to submit targeted and shorter treaty-specific reports.[22] In this way,

[20] Report of the Secretary-General, *Strengthening of the United Nations: an agenda for further change*, UN Doc. A/57/387, September 9, 2002.

[21] Bertrand Ramcharan, *A UN High Commissioner in Defense of Human Rights* (Leiden: Brill, 2004), 169–174.

[22] Annex to the letter dated 13 June 2003 from the Permanent Representative of Liechtenstein to the United Nations addressed to the Secretary-General, "Report of a

there would be an effort to avoid duplication, lower costs, and yet encourage adequate scrutiny of states parties' implementation of each specialized treaty that it ratified. This proposal – a common core document supplemented by treaty-specific ones – ultimately came to be agreed upon by the treaty bodies and remains applicable today. The Malbun outcome also emphasized the need for much greater cooperation between the treaty bodies, thus bringing a new attention to the framework in which the committees interact – the annual meetings of several representatives from each treaty committee and, separately, of their chairs. From there on, the so-called 'inter-committee meetings' would become an important focus to advance what has become known as the 'harmonisation of working methods.'

Ramcharan is also to be credited with effecting changes at OHCHR that benefitted the treaty bodies. In 2003, he reorganized OHCHR whereby the treaty bodies, with the Commission on Human Rights, would be serviced by a dedicated secretariat unit or 'branch' with clearly laid out functions. He made clear that this branch would be in 'support' of the treaty bodies, allaying any concern that the committees were becoming subordinated to the High Commissioner or his Office.[23]

Louise Arbour

The period of office of Ramcharan's successor, Louise Arbour, was one of great change – for OHCHR, for the human rights architecture of the UN and, at least in intent, for the treaty bodies themselves.

The first change concerned the nature of Arbour's own Office. She had a vision of OHCHR as the UN's human rights agency, active across all fronts and present across the world, as in the manner of UNICEF, UNHCR and other such bodies.[24] This ambition, which I have critiqued elsewhere,[25] had at least two meeting points with the work of the treaty bodies. The first of these, overwhelmingly positive, concerned the

---

meeting on reform of the human rights treaty body system (Malbun, Liechtenstein, 4–7 May 2003)," UN Doc. A/58/123, July 8, 2003.

23 Ramcharan, *A UN High Commissioner*, 152–53.

24 Louise Arbour, "Plan of action drawn up by the United Nations High Commissioner for Human Rights," in Report of the Secretary-General, *In larger freedom: towards development, security and human rights for all,"* Addendum 3, UN Doc. A/59/2005/Add.3, May 26, 2005.

25 Michael O'Flaherty, "Human Rights Field Operations: An Introductory Analysis," in *The Human Rights Field Operation: Law, Theory and Practice*, ed. Michael O'Flaherty. (London: Ashgate, 2007), 30.

possibilities such expansion opens up for OHCHR to engage with the treaty bodies as a substantive partner – relaying information and analysis to and from headquarters and the national level, championing follow-up, and undertaking capacity-building with governments and civil society. Such work was underway, of course, before the Arbour period; nevertheless her ambitions would bring the possibilities for cooperation to new heights.

Much of this potential did come to be realized, during the Arbour years and subsequently, particularly at the national level, where training related to the treaty bodies and other forms of country support have become an important part of the Office's field work. Curiously though, one potentiality has yet to be fully realized – that of OHCHR and the treaty bodies operating in more direct partnership, such as by means of the Office systematically briefing the committees on country situations or otherwise suggesting courses of action for the committees in their review of states. To this day, while OHCHR does a very good job of ensuring that the committees hear from any number of other UN bodies (the Human Rights Committee, for instance, is briefed on country situations by UNHCR at every session), briefings from staff of OHCHR itself are rare, at least in the practice of the Human Rights Committee. In puzzling over this persistent issue with staff of the Office such reasons are suggested as the result of a 'silo' management attitude within OHCHR within which many field people are disdainful of the treaty body work and, more significantly, an inherent tension in the balancing of the roles of secretariat and active substantive partner.

There is one unwelcome consequence of the expansion into the field of OHCHR – that is its negative impact on the availability of resources for the treaty bodies. The transfer of OHCHR personnel and resources had been a feature already in the Robinson years. It became more pronounced under Arbour, with the relative proportion of OHCHR staff dedicated to treaty body work falling precipitously with a concomitant rise in levels of support to field activities. This slide is demonstrated by the adjustments over time to staffing levels. In 2001, treaty bodies were supported by 35 professional staff[26] when OHCHR had some 226 professional staff in total.[27] By 2011, the respective figures had risen to 62 treaty body staff[28] out of 1,131

---

[26] Bayefsky, *The UN Human Rights Treaty System*.

[27] Report of the High Commissioner, *Composition of the staff of the Office of the United Nations High Commissioner for Human Rights*, UN Doc. E/CN.4/2002/115, December 28, 2002.

[28] OHCHR, "Resources in support of the human rights treaty body system," (paper, Informal Technical Consultation with States parties, Sion, Switzerland), May 11, 2011, 6, http://www2.ohchr.org/english/bodies/HRTD/docs/SionBudgetPaper.pdf.

total staff.[29] In other words, notwithstanding the historic under-staffing and the persistent growth of the treaty bodies, there was a drop from 16% to 5.5% of OHCHR professional staff supporting them.

The second set of changes that occurred in the Arbour period concerned the UN's political human rights architecture, with the demise of the Commission on Human Rights and the establishment of the Human Rights Council. In particular, the Council's peer review procedure – the Universal Period Review (UPR) – gave cause for concern. There were worries, for instance, that UPR would produce findings that were contradictory to those of treaty bodies and that it would still further sap the resources of the treaty body system. On the other hand, it was also recognized that UPR could constitute an important system of protection of human rights that might be complementary to treaty body work, for instance in the context of follow up to committee recommendations. All of these issues were and remain important and I have commented on the topic elsewhere.[30] However, since they do not directly engage the topic of this chapter – the relationship of the High Commissioners and the treaty bodies – they will not be explored further.

The third and final issue of change during the Arbour period concerns her efforts to directly tackle the problems of the treaty body system. Writing in 2006, she identified a litany of concerns, some familiar and others expressed for the first time by a High Commissioner:[31]

- The extent to which states accept the human rights treaty system on a formal level, but do not engage with it, or do so in a superficial way, either as a result of lack of capacity or lack of political will;
- The ad-hoc manner in which the treaty body system has grown, with an overlap of provisions and competencies, resulting in duplication;
- The growth in the number of treaties and ratifications, resulting in a steep increase in the workload of the treaty bodies and their secretariat, backlogs in the consideration of reports and individual complaints, and increasing resource requirements;

---

[29] This total figure does not include the close to 800 human rights officers serving in 15 UN peace missions or political offices and 18 human rights advisers based in UNCTs in the field also supported by OHCHR in 2011. See OHCHR, *Annual Report 2011*, 22.

[30] Michael O'Flaherty and Pei-Lun Tsai, "Periodic Reporting: The Backbone of the UN Treaty Body Review Procedures," in *New Challenges for the UN Human Rights Machinery*, eds. M. Cherif Bassiouni & Willam A. Schabas, (Cambridge: Intersentia 2011), 37.

[31] See Louise Arbour, *Concept Paper on the High Commissioner's Proposal for a Unified Standing Treaty Body*, UN Doc. HRI/MC/2006/CRP.1, March 14, 2006.

- The low levels of public awareness of the treaty body system outside specialist communities and how it is rarely perceived as an accessible and effective mechanism to bring about change;
- The uneven levels of expertise and independence of treaty body members, as well as problems of geographical distribution, representation of the principal legal systems and gender balance;
- A lack of coordination and collaboration among the treaty bodies resulting in a risk of conflicting jurisprudence;
- The variable quality of state party reports submitted to treaty bodies and the frequent failure of the reporting process to achieve its objective of providing regular opportunities for individual states to periodically conduct a comprehensive review of their treaty-compliance;
- The fact that treaty bodies often have insufficient information to enable them to undertake a full analysis of country situations and, as a result, their recommendations may lack the precision, clarity and practical value required to enhance implementation;
- The absence of effective, comprehensive follow-up mechanisms for recommendations at the national level.

Louise Arbour's solution was a bold one – that the treaty body system as we know it be done away with entirely and that it be replaced by a single unified body.[32] As we have seen, this idea was far from new. Nevertheless it was radical in its intent and had never garnered much support. Indeed, just weeks before Arbour published the proposal, all the relevant senior staff of her Office participated in a brainstorming event that I convened at the University of Nottingham. Aware of the High Commissioner's likely proposal, many of the participants were of the view that, in the absence of consensus around any one reform model and without any agreed global master plan for change that was likely to succeed, a modest piecemeal and step by step approach should be considered.[33] Obviously, we were not to sway the High Commissioner!

From the moment of its publication, the Arbour proposal was very badly received. I recall in particular the comprehensive manner in which it was repudiated at a second Malbun meeting.[34] Very few states spoke in

[32] Ibid.

[33] Report of the Expert Workshop on Reform of United Nations Human Rights Treaty Monitoring Bodies (Senate Chamber, University of Nottingham , February 11–12, 2006) March 6, 2006, http://www.nottingham.ac.uk/hrlc/documents/publications/treaty monitoringbodies2006workshopreport.pdf.

[34] "Chairperson"s Summary of a Brainstorming Meeting on Reform of the Human Rights Treaty Body System ("Malbun II")," Annex to the Letter dated 14 September 2006

its support and various stakeholder groups indicated opposition for such reasons as the danger of opening the treaties to revision, the loss of attention to particular groups of rights-holders and, in the minds of some diplomats, the fear that a unified body was an intentional step on the way to an unwelcome world human rights court. There is no doubt, also that many were disconcerted by the manner in which the proposal had been tabled in advance of any process of consultation.

It was unfortunate that the comprehensive rejection of the idea of the single treaty body also brought a close to a more general reflection on how to improve the system. Arbour's report had contained many sensible ideas (such as regarding improvements in the method of election of treaty body members) but they were all considered irrelevant once the concept paper was rejected. Crucially, as she herself said in an impromptu after-dinner speech at Malbun, her prescription may have been rejected but nobody had challenged her diagnosis of a system in crisis.[35]

Navanethem Pillay

I discussed treaty body reform with Navi Pillay soon after she took up office and was struck by her sense of the urgent need to again tackle the problems. As she made clear at a January 2009 Wilton Park meeting, the situation was going from bad to worse with the establishment of three new treaty bodies, the related pressure on resources and the added burden for states and civil society of the UPR procedure.[36]

The High Commissioner moved quickly. Her first target was the cumbersome and inefficient practice whereby the committee chairs, meeting in the inter-committee framework, were unable to adopt decisions and could only propose recommendations that would then need to be considered by each treaty body. This arrangement, while entirely understandable in terms of the respecting of the autonomy of each body, did not lend itself to speedy adoption of harmonized working methods. Pillay's proposal was that the treaty bodies give their respective chairs the power to adopt decisions on their behalf at inter-committee meetings on matters

from the Permanent Representative of Liechtenstein to the United Nations addressed to the Secretary-General, UN Doc. A/61/351, September 18, 2006.

35 Remarks made by the High Commissioner in the presence of the author.

36 Isobelle Jaques, "Contemporary and Future Human Rights Challenges," Report on Wilton Park Conference No. 954 (Thursday 22 – Saturday 24 January 2009), http://www.wiltonpark.org.uk/resources/en/pdf/22290903/22291307/wp954-report.

that had already been considered by the treaty body itself. This suggestion was debated at a December 2008 inter-committee meeting and garnered some support.[37] It then lay fallow for a period, being picked up again in 2010 in a meeting of experts at Poznan, Poland, that I will discuss further below. What had become known by now as the "Poznan Formula" was approved by the annual meeting of chairs and by treaty bodies in 2011.[38] The potency of the formula was demonstrated in 2012 when it provided the basis for the recommendation for the treaty bodies to adopt a draft set of guidelines for the independence and impartiality of treaty body members endorsed by that year's meeting of chairs.[39]

Harmonization of working methods is only one dimension of the necessary action. Pillay appreciated this and, in October 2009, she reported to the General Assembly on the need to address the problems comprehensively and systematically. Crucially, and in an evident bid to distance herself from the diplomatic problems experienced by her immediate predecessor, she invited comment and consultation among all the stakeholder groups.[40]

In response to that invitation I convened a meeting of treaty body experts and other specialists in Dublin, Ireland, in November of that year, for the purpose of charting a road map for such a consultative process. The High Commissioner was supportive of the initiative and attended the meeting in person, offering an address with encouragement of reform proposals. Our conclusions, contained in the 'Dublin Statement,'[41] went to process rather than specific reform outcomes and indicated the goal of a

37 UN General Assembly, "Report of the eighth inter-committee meeting," in *Report of the chairpersons of the human rights treaty bodies on their twenty-first meeting*, UN Doc. A/64/280, August 6, 2009, Annex I, paras. 5 and 49(c).

38 UN General Assembly, *Report of the Chairs of the human rights treaty bodies on their twenty-third meeting*, UN Doc. A/66/175, July 22, 2011, para. 9.

39 UN General Assembly, *Report of the Chairpersons of the human rights treaty bodies on their twenty-fourth meeting*, UN Doc. A/67/28442, July 20, 2012, paras. 13–15 (recommending that the guidelines be promptly adopted by the respective treaty bodies, inter alia through inclusion, in an appropriate manner, in their rules of procedure). Ibid., Annex I (guidelines).

40 "Ms. Navanethem Pillay, United Nations High Commissioner for Human Rights: Statement to the General Assembly Third Committee," October 21, 2009, http://www.ohchr.org/EN/NewsEvents/Pages/DisplayNews.aspx?NewsID=9562&LangID=E ("Human rights treaty bodies have continued to work together to streamline and harmonize their working methods. States parties to human rights treaties and other stakeholders should also reflect on how to strengthen the treaty bodies and promote better coordination and coherence among these mechanisms.").

41 "The Dublin Statement on the Process of Strengthening of the United Nations Human Rights Treaty Body System," November 19, 2009), http://www2.ohchr.org/english/bodies/HRTD/docs/DublinStatement.pdf.

treaty body strengthening process (enhanced protection of human rights), the actors that would need to be consulted and the treaty body functions that must be protected. We also suggested a key role for the High Commissioner as the obvious facilitator of the reform reflection who could then bring proposals forward for adoption by the relevant decision makers.[42]

Following on from the Dublin Statement, during 2009–2011, the High Commissioner invested a considerable degree of OHCHR resources and personnel to supporting a series of consultation events across the world and that engaged states, civil society, treaty body members, national human rights institutions, UN agencies and academics (the Poznan meeting was one of these).[43] The events culminated with a second Dublin meeting that I convened in November 2011. There the treaty body chairs and other treaty body members drew together all the findings of what had by then become known as the 'Dublin Process' in the form of the 'Dublin II Outcome Document.'[44] The High Commissioner was represented at this meeting by the Deputy High Commissioner, Kyung-wha Kang and a team of OHCHR officials.

With the conclusion of the Dublin Process the initiative came to rest with the High Commissioner herself. The moment had come for her to present her own report with specific reform proposals. Before that though she had to contend with a move by a group of states to locate the treaty body debate within the General Assembly.[45] The ploy was entirely political, intended to strengthen the role of states vis-à-vis the committees, and many of the attendant demands made by its originators, who thereafter deemed themselves the "Cross-Regional Group" (CRG) – for instance for

---

42 Michael O'Flaherty, "Reform of the UN Human Rights Treaty Body System: Locating the Dublin Statement," *Human Rights Law Review* 10.2 (2010), 319–335.

43 O'Flaherty and Tsai, "Periodic Reporting," 43–44. See also OHCHR, "The Treaty Body Strengthening Process," http://www2.ohchr.org/english/bodies/HRTD/.

44 "Outcome Document," Strengthening the United Nations Human Rights Treaty Body System, Dublin II Meeting (Dublin, 10–11 November 2011), http://www.ohchr.org/EN/HRBodies/HRTD/Pages/Documents.aspx.

45 UN General Assembly, Resolution 66/254, "Intergovernmental process of the General Assembly on strengthening and enhancing the effective functioning of the human rights treaty body system," UN Doc. A/RES/66/254, May 15, 2012; see also International Service for Human Rights, "66 States abstain on GA resolution creating treaty body strengthening process," February 26, 2012, http://www.ishr.ch/treaty-bodies/1254-66-states-abstain-on-ga-resolution-creating-treaty-body-strengthening-process-66-states-abstain-on. The resolution was tabled by the Russian Federation and co-sponsored by Algeria, Bangladesh, Belarus, Bolivia, China, Cuba, the Democratic People's Republic of Korea, India, Indonesia, Iran, Nicaragua, Pakistan, Syria, Sudan, Tajikistan, Thailand, Venezuela, Viet Nam, and Zimbabwe. The outcome of the vote on the resolution was 85 in favor, 0 against, and 65 abstaining.

the imposition on the treaty bodies of a 'code of conduct' – clearly are outside the powers of either the General Assembly or the respective assemblies of states parties to the treaties.

The General Assembly discussion remains a live and developing issue at time of the writing of this chapter and, while it is not possible to draw any conclusions as to its impact, some preliminary observations may be suggested. In the first place, the very existence of the debate is testimony to the manner in which treaty body reform has come center stage at the UN. Such high visibility brings risks but also shines light on what had until now been so neglected and misunderstood a component of the international human rights framework. Second, the High Commissioner should be credited for having put the conditions in place whereby states have become so engaged – it has been her insistence on repeated consultations that contributed most to the raised levels of awareness. Third, the manner in which she has planned the consultations with states, including those following the CRG initiative, has been effective in promoting reasoned approaches. In particular, the heavy emphasis of the agendas on sequentially discussing the enhancement of specific treaty body functions has encouraged a technical discussion with less polemic than might otherwise be expected. In addition, her initial invitation to have treaty body members participate in such discussions as invited experts did much to challenge misapprehensions that may have crept into the discussions. For instance, in a consultation with states in New York in March 2012, I had the opportunity to correct the contention on the part of a number of government speakers that the committees were intending to develop criteria against which candidates for election to membership must be assessed (the states apparently had misconstrued the work on the guidelines on independence and integrity to have such a purpose).[46]

The High Commissioner finally published her report, "Strengthening the United Nations Human Rights Treaty Body System" in June 2012.[47] It comprises an analysis of the situation and proposes recommendations that range across all treaty body functions as well as with regard to issues of membership. The recipients of the recommendations are states, treaty bodies, NGOs, national human rights institutions, OHCHR itself and UN

---

46 Report of the Third Consultation with States Parties on Treaty Body Strengthening, para. 36, April 2, 2012, http://www2.ohchr.org/english/bodies/HRTD/docs/ReportConsultation2_3April2012.doc.

47 Navi Pillay, *Strengthening the United Nations human rights treaty body system: A report by the United Nations High Commissioner for Human Rights*, June 2012, http://www2.ohchr.org/english/bodies/HRTD/docs/HCreportonTBstrengthening210612.doc.

agencies – this point is worth noting when considering an underlying theme of the post-CRG-initiative consultations to the effect that treaty body reform is predominantly a matter for states alone. All recommendations are costed. There is little that is new in the recommendations as all of them had been anticipated to a greater or lesser extent in the Dublin Outcome Document. What is novel is the heavy emphasis placed on just one recommendation – that for a "comprehensive reporting calendar." This proposal is for the alignment of the reporting schedules of all treaty bodies whereby states would report to no more than two committees per year and the review would proceed in this clearly timetabled fashion regardless of whether a report is actually submitted. If implemented, the recommendation would deliver significant improvements in the transparency, predictability and efficiency of the reporting procedures. That said, many details remain to be worked through regarding the willingness and capacity of states, the treaty bodies and the secretariat to implement the Calendar and to ensure that it does not sacrifice the level of expert detailed scrutiny that should characterize the review of reports. The report also contains a recommendation for the establishment of a working group on communications that looks like a pre-cursor of the communications body that Alston and Bayefsky had called for years before.

Preliminary reactions to the High Commissioner's report are encouraging. As of time of writing this chapter, one treaty body, the Human Rights Committee, has had the opportunity to adopt a statement welcoming it, albeit with some reservations as to detail.[48] Leading NGOs, as well as National Human Rights Institutions have reacted similarly.[49] In the one state consultation that has taken place since its launch, voices in general support of the report outnumbered those of the naysayers.[50] Of course the

---

[48] Human Rights Committee. 105th session, "Preliminary Statement of the Human Rights Committee on the Strengthening of the United Nations Treaty Bodies," July 12, 2012.

[49] Amnesty International, "Strengthening the UN treaty bodies, a preliminary response from non-governmental organizations," AI Index: IOR 40/015/2012 (13 July 2012). Commonwealth Forum of National Human Rights Institutions, "NHRIs Respond to Treaty Body Strengthening Process" October 11, 2012, http://cfnhri.org/nhris-respond-to-treaty-body-strengthening-process/.

[50] No public reports are available on the informal consultations in connection with the Intergovernmental process on the strengthening of the Human Rights Treaty Bodies, July 16–18, 2012. For concerns expressed by non-governmental organizations on the progress of the consultations, see, e.g, Amnesty International, "Inter-governmental process of the General Assembly on Strengthening and Enhancing the Effective Functioning of the United Nations Human Rights Treaty System," AI Index Number IOR 40/017/2012, September 4, 2012.

degree of acceptance of the various recommendations on the part of all stakeholders will only become clear in the light of the further discussions scheduled among states and others through 2012–2013.

The ultimate measure of success – still far too early to consider – will be the extent to which Pillay's recommendations will be implemented and will truly strengthen the system. That, in turn, will require the continued and determined diplomatic efforts of the High Commissioner. Her work did not end with the delivery of her report. On the contrary, we are now embarked on a necessary process of debate and consideration by states that carries high risk – as evidenced by the formation and actions of the CRG. In this context the ongoing and high level engagement by the High Commissioner and her Office is of critical importance. Indeed, taking account of the High Commissioner's role, as stipulated in resolution 48/141, it can be argued that she has a formal mandated duty to maintain her leadership.

Conclusion

As we have seen, the relationship of a High Commissioner and her Office with the treaty bodies has come over time to embrace at least three dimensions: delivery of secretariat support, substantive partnership of human rights actors, and the High Commissioner's facilitatory leadership in confronting the problems of the system. All of these are anticipated in and draw their legitimacy from General Assembly resolution 48/141. With regard to each of the elements there are achievements to be acknowledged and weaknesses to be addressed.

As secretariat, OHCHR has proved itself to be reliable and professional. However, its services have been consistently compromised by the inadequacy of resources. Much of the fault in this regard lies beyond the Office itself – residing instead with UN Member States – and this has been the subject of specific recommendations in the 2012 Pillay report. As we have seen though, consecutive High Commissioners also have overseen a drain of the existing resources from the servicing of the treaty bodies towards such new work areas as the OHCHR field operations. There is the need to halt this process and correct the imbalances in the financial commitment of OHCHR to its various core functions.

The burgeoning of the field operations and the broader human rights diplomacy of the High Commissioners have, of course, also benefited the treaty bodies. They have done much to put the treaty standards at the heart of the UN's advocacy, intervention and capacity-building work. They have also been important instruments of follow-up for treaty body findings. As has been observed, though this too is an area in need of attention, with the existence of so many missed opportunities for OHCHR to engage with the committees as a channel of expert information and analysis. OHCHR, side by side with its role as service provider, should develop a stronger institutional and office-wide self-awareness as partner to the committees.

Finally, with regard to the role of the High Commissioner in championing a strong treaty body system, one must conclude that successive holders of that office have risen to the challenge, albeit with varying degrees of ambition and success. Navi Pillay is but the latest to try – time will tell whether she is also the most successful.

THE HIGH COMMISSIONERS' PROMOTION OF UNIVERSALITY OF HUMAN RIGHTS

Sunila Abeysekera

The Concept of Universality

The principle of universality, as enshrined in all human rights documents generated and created by the world's most comprehensive multilateral institution, the United Nations, focuses on the universality of application as well as on the universality of obligation. The affirmation that human rights are inalienable and interrelated, that the human rights system should operate in a non-discriminatory and inclusive manner, and that violations of human rights should be remedied and perpetrators of violations held accountable forms the bedrock of the system of human rights.

Universality is perhaps one of the most contested terms in contemporary human rights, even more so now than when it first emerged, and is an often divisive and always contentious concept. The growth of identity-based politics in the context of globalization has fuelled the challenge to the principle of universality in more recent years. In the arenas where the terminology of universality was most hotly debated in the 1990s, for example at the World Conference on Human Rights in Vienna in 1993 and at the Fourth World Conference on Women in Beijing in 1995, it became clear that this terminology has the most resonance with groups and communities that are most marginalized and that suffer the greatest and most diverse forms of discrimination.

Those who challenge the concept of universality maintain that since the universe is so different there can be no potential to define the universal. They argue that differences in culture and tradition merit different treatment and recognition of rights. They also argue that the concept of rights should be 'relative' or 'culturally specific.' In reality, these arguments are used to justify the persistent denial of women's equality, or of the equality of a range of communities who are cultural, ethnic or religious minorities as well as communities who live 'beyond the pale' such as indigenous people, migrants, refugees and asylum seekers and lesbian, gay, bisexual, transgender, intersex and queer people.

Arguments that are based on 'relativism' or on 'cultural specificity' also seek to place individuals and groups from marginalized communities outside the protection of international and national human rights protection mechanisms.

Human rights defenders who have observed developments on human rights concepts and practice within the UN system have been a part of these debates since the World Conference on Human Rights in Vienna, where the outcome document affirmed that, "While the significance of national and regional particularities and various historical, cultural and religious backgrounds must be borne in mind, it is the duty of states, regardless of their political, economic and cultural systems, to promote and protect all human rights and fundamental freedoms."[1] The Beijing Platform for Action from the Fourth World Conference on Women reaffirmed the Vienna Declaration and Programme for Action that all human rights – civil, cultural, economic, political and social, including the right to development – are universal, indivisible, interdependent, and interrelated, and also said "the full and equal enjoyment of all human rights and fundamental freedoms by women and girls is a priority for Governments and the United Nations and is essential for the advancement of women."[2] The debates around universality and cultural specificity were even more intense in Beijing than they had been in Vienna because women were so directly affected by the imposition of restrictions on their rights and freedoms on the basis of arguments of culture and tradition. Here, it was agreed that "any harmful aspect of certain traditional, customary or modern practices that violates the rights of women should be prohibited and eliminated."[3]

In the 21st century, the debates around universality and cultural specificity have gained in complexity and in strength as the war against terror has generated modern manifestations of xenophobia, as well as diverse forms of fundamentalisms and extremisms. A common feature of these organizations and institutions is their denial of the equal rights of women and their demonization of the 'Other.' The ways in which women's bodies and lives and choices have fallen prey to patriarchs and demagogues who preach against women's equality and the universality of rights poses ever

1 World Conference on Human Rights, "Vienna Declaration and Programme of Action," UN Doc. A/CONF.157/22, July 12, 1993, Part I, para. 5.

2 Fourth World Conference on Women, "Beijing Declaration and Platform for Action," Annex I, UN Doc. A/CONF.177/20 (1995) and A/CONF.177/20/Add.1 (1995), September 15, 1995, para. 9.

3 Beijing Declaration, para. 224.

greater and more complex threats to the achievement of all human rights protection for all.

This has led to an increasing focus on the nature and form of cultural rights, within the overall rubric of economic, social, and cultural rights in the human rights discourse. Perhaps because of this, in 2009, the UN Human Rights Council created the post of an Independent Expert on Cultural Rights.[4] In her first report to the Council in 2010, Farida Shaheed of Pakistan, who presently holds the position, stated,

> Provided that cultural rights are fully understood as being part of the wider human rights system and therefore grounded in existing norms and principles of international human rights law, they allow for an enriched understanding of the principle of universality of human rights by taking into consideration cultural diversity.[5]

In her work, Shaheed consistently argues that culture can be understood as a product, as a process and as a way of life, and implies that culture includes references beyond ethnicity, language, and religion.[6] This is key to ensuring that the commitment to universality remains strongly and firmly on the agenda of the UN human rights system, the Office of the High Commissioner for Human Rights, and the High Commissioner.

The Role of the High Commissioner

In terms of assessing the role played by various High Commissioners with regard to affirming the principle of universality in terms of women's rights and in terms of economic, social, and cultural rights, first of all one should say that they have all done so. However, two High Commissioners stand out in this regard.

One is the first High Commissioner, Mr. Ayala Lasso, whose contribution to the process of defining the outcomes of the Beijing Conference on Women in 1995 deserves special recognition. The term 'equality' was at risk, and institutions such as the Holy See and the Organization of the Islamic Conference (OIC) were proposing the term 'equity' instead, also calling for the inclusion of terminology such as rights for women that would be 'equitable' with the rights of men. Mr. Ayala Lasso wrote to the

[4] Human Rights Council. Resolution 10/23, "Independent expert in the field of cultural rights," in UN Doc. A/64/53, March 26, 2009.

[5] See, e.g., UN General Assembly, *Report of the Independent Expert in the Field of Cultural Rights, Ms. Farida Shaheed*, UN Doc. A/HRC/14/36, Part II(A)(1) March 22, 2012, para. 3.

[6] Ibid., para. 5.

Secretary-General of the UN to express his concerns regarding this situation pointing out that "language which could be read to indicate that cultural, religious or other particularities should have priority consideration over human rights, would not respect the well-crafted balance achieved" in earlier UN human rights texts such as the Vienna Declaration.[7] He also specifically stated that references to the "dignity of women" would not be adequate substitutes for recognition of the concept of "the dignity and worth of the human person and the equal rights of men and women" enshrined in the Universal Declaration of Human Rights. Mr. Ayala Lasso also made a strong statement to the World Conference itself, reiterating many of these points, and his defense of universality helped bring about a successful conclusion to the Beijing Conference in terms of this issue.[8]

Mary Robinson's strength in terms of the universality of rights discourse within the UN system was to focus on the interrelated and interdependent nature of all rights, and to ensure that her Office gave equal importance to economic and social rights and to civil and political rights.[9] It was during her tenure that the Commission created six rapporteurs focusing on economic and social rights: on the right to education (1998); extreme poverty and human rights (1998); the right to adequate housing (2000); the right to food (2000); on the effects of foreign debt and other related international financial obligations of states on the full enjoyment of human rights, particularly economic, social and cultural rights (2000); the rights of indigenous peoples (2001); and the right to health (2002). It was also Ms. Robinson's initiative to call for universal ratification of the UN's human rights treaties as a part of the Millennium Summit of the UN: speaking in May 2000, in advance of the Millennium Summit, she said: "In championing the cause of universality I should emphasize that universality does not negate cultural diversity; on the contrary, I believe that it reinforces and protects cultural diversity."[10]

---

[7] Jaya Dayal, "WOMEN: U.N. Human Rights Tsar Says Beijing Draft Weakens Rights," *Inter Press Service News Agency*, July 25, 1995.

[8] José Ayala-Lasso, "Statement by the High Commissioner of Human Rights" (statement delivered at the Plenary of the Fourth World Conference on Women, Beijing, China, September, 4–15, 1995) http://www.un.org/esa/gopher-data/conf/fwcw/conf/una/950906124120.txt.

[9] Mary Robinson, "Realizing Human Rights: "Take Hold of it Boldly and Duly...."" (Romanes Lecture, Oxford University, Nov 11, 1997), UN Department of Public Information, http://www.un.org/rights/50/dpi1938.htm.

[10] Mary Robinson, "The Universality of Human Rights" (remarks delivered at Weltachsen 2000, Bonn, Germany, November 11, 1999) http://www.unhchr.ch/huricane/huricane.nsf/view01/2370024D1ECEAC0B8025682A003DE864?opendocument.

Key Ideas for the Future

In reviewing the practice of different High Commissioners for Human Rights over time, there are some key areas that I would like to highlight in general.

I would like to start by affirming that for the community of human rights defenders around the world, the UN High Commissioner for Human Rights is considered to be the 'conscience of the world.' This brings with it a burden of responsibility but also the potential to act, and to be seen to act, in a way that provides protection for the work of human rights defenders and that affirms the principle of 'All human rights for All.' Maintaining the independence of the Office and of the position of the High Commissioner from the political ramifications of the various UN bodies that have the mandate to define and to interpret human rights norms and standards remains a profound challenge. Right from the beginning the lack of resources has placed many obstacles in the paths of successive High Commissioners in implementing their mandate. Ensuring adequate human and financial resources in a time of a shrinking resource pool will also undoubtedly be a key challenge in the future.

The role played by the various High Commissioners in supporting the emergence of a strong network of independent national human rights institutions worldwide remains an area that requires review. Over the years, the emergence of strong parallel institutions, the Asia Pacific Forum on National Human Rights Institutions,[11] for example, that is very active in monitoring the performance of NHRIs in the Asia Pacific region, should indicate to us that a constructive space exists for better and interactive engagement between OHCHR and the various regional and national human rights institutions to improve the enforcement of and respect for human rights in countries and regions where they exist.

Overall, one could say that the universality of human rights is more contested today than it has been in the past. Challenges to universality are primarily located in the geographic and ideological arenas where deep-rooted prejudices against women and against members of other marginalized communities still remain. The challenges to the High Commissioner are huge. For example, in a context in which states propose tactical engagement with the Taliban in order to secure stability in Afghanistan, how can one defend principles of universality and women's human rights?

---

[11] Asia Pacific Forum of National Human Rights Institutions, http://www.asiapacificforum.net.

High Commissioners have all played a role in highlighting human rights abuses in specific countries, and in specific situations. The practice of naming and shaming individual countries has always been highly contested, first within the UN Human Rights Commission, and now in the Council, especially by states that commit and condone human rights abuse. For High Commissioners, there is no rule of thumb by which they can assess the situation and the potential response by the state concerned when brought under external scrutiny. Some cry foul and point to the infringement of national sovereignty; they even berate the High Commissioner at a personal level; others make commitments and promises they have no intention of keeping; of course, there are also those who respond constructively and make changes in laws and policies that can improve the situation. It depends on the political context within which the commentary on human rights violations is presented and received, and on the political will of the state to undertake transformation. The High Commissioner should assess these factors and ensure that OHCHR develops an overarching strategy for dealing with the human rights situation in a particular country including through consultations with members of treaty bodies and special procedures that have considered the situation of human rights in a particular country.

The use of 'human rights diplomacy' by a High Commissioner is also a part of the process of engagement with the diverse nation states that make up the United Nations. Again, such diplomacy succeeds only when it is undertaken in an environment where there is a political will to resolve a human rights crisis and works best when the diplomacy of the High Commissioner reflects other diplomatic initiatives being undertaken by other concerned member states and intergovernmental and multilateral institutions. This again calls for very close monitoring of the situation on the ground in collaboration with partners from the UN Country Team and other UN agencies, as well as with civil society partners.

In all cases, however, as human rights defenders working at local and national levels, we believe that it is key for the High Commissioner to at least inform, if not discuss, anticipated public statements and actions with human rights defenders that live and work in a state that is about to become the focus of attention. This is because states frequently extend angry or hostile reactions to criticism by the High Commissioner to the local organizations and individuals known to be working in collaboration with the UN system.[12]

---

[12] Report of the Secretary-General, *Cooperation with the United Nations, Its Representatives and Mechanisms in the Field of Human Rights*, UN Doc. A/HRC/21/18, August 13, 2012.

The role of the High Commissioner is also critical when it comes to increasing the effectiveness of the UN human rights treaty bodies and special procedures, which often provide the information and analysis that draw attention to violations of human rights in a particular country or situation. Over the past years, various High Commissioners have supported the process of treaty body reform and reforms to reporting procedures of the various mechanisms in the UN human rights system paying attention to the concerns of the various mechanisms as well as the concerns of civil society groups that work closely with these mechanisms.[13] It seems that to date, through consistent advocacy on their behalf, the High Commissioner has been able to ensure the independence of the 'independent experts' from political interference and to refute attempts to limit their role in defining and interpreting evolving human rights norms and standards. However, some of the challenges that have been faced in this regard are likely to recur in the future.[14]

In reviewing the Annual Reports of the Office of the High Commissioner over the years from 2000 onwards, it is clear that there are several areas in which the leadership displayed by High Commissioners in promoting and protecting human rights had had a significant impact on the normative development of international human rights concepts.

The role of successive High Commissioners in supporting the adoption of an Optional Protocol to the International Covenant on Economic Social and Cultural Rights is an example.[15] So are the various documents developed through collaborative processes with other UN agencies, such as the UNDP in particular, which have defined the relationship between human rights and business practices, and the Human Rights Mainstreaming program with the UN Development Group which seeks to strengthen the UN's country teams in using a human-rights based approach to national level planning and policy making regarding development issues.[16]

The present High Commissioner has consistently spoken out on the rights of those facing discrimination and violence because of their sexual

---

[13] See, e.g., OHCHR, "The Treaty Body Strengthening Process," http://www2.ohchr.org/english/bodies/HRTD.

[14] Philip Alston, "Hobbling the Monitors: Should U.N. Human Rights Monitors be Accountable?" *Harvard International Law Journal* 52, no. 2 (Summer 2011): 593. See also Amnesty International, *Strengthening of the United Nations Treaty Bodies: Questions and Answers*, September 2012.

[15] "Human Rights Council Achieves Important Milestone Adopting the Optional Protocol to the International Convenant on Economic, Social, and Cultural Rights," UN press release, June 18, 2008.

[16] "Human Rights Mainstreaming Mechanism," http://hrbaportal.org/human-rights-mainstreaming-mechanism.

orientation and gender identity (SOGI).[17] As we all know, taking a stand on the right of all persons to live without discrimination and violence to communities that challenge hetero-normativity is not a popular one in these times. As the attempts to restrict the rights and freedoms of women, of migrant and refugee communities, of lesbian, gay, bisexual, transgendered and intersex communities, of minority ethnic, religious and ethnic communities continue to grow, it will be incumbent on OHCHR and the High Commissioner to maintain the role as 'voice of the voiceless' especially in international arenas where the future of these communities is often determined.

A major challenge that confronts the present High Commissioner, and which presented a challenge to past High Commissioners as well, is that of actually making the many documents, normative guidelines, and training programs developed in collaboration with UNDP, the UNDG and UN Country Teams on mainstreaming gender and human rights into their on-going work a reality.[18] Despite the engagement of OHCHR and the High Commissioner in a range of high level discussions, task forces, and expert group meetings, much of the UN's development practice still does not take human rights principles and obligations into consideration. In this context, OHCHR's efforts to ensure that corporate social responsibility initiatives and partnership between the UNDP and private corporations reflect human rights and gender equality have been largely confined to rhetoric.[19]

In the context of the Rio+20 Conference, for example, there is a pivotal role to be played by OHCHR in collaboration with UNDP, to implement the thinking of the multi-agency human rights mainstreaming mechanism which is chaired by both agencies.[20] OHCHR and the High Commissioner should deepen their engagement in the discussion on 'common but differentiated responsibilities' that has been supported by

---

[17] See, e.g., "UN Issues First Report on Human Rights of Gay and Lesbian People," *UN News Centre*, December 15, 2011, http://www.un.org/apps/news/story.asp?NewsID=40743#.UM-6Y-S5PTo.

[18] See, e.g., OHCHR, "Gender Mainstreaming and Human Rights of Women: OHCHR Policy Statement," www.unrol.org/files/POL_GENDER_HR_WOMEN.pdf.

[19] Dan Banik, "Implementing Human Rights-Based Developments: Some Preliminary Evidence from Malawi," prepared for Expert Seminar: Extreme Poverty and Human Rights, Geneva, Switzerland, February 23–24, 2007, www2.ohchr.org/english/issues/poverty/expert/docs/Dan_Banik.pdf.

[20] See, e,g., "UN Work in Focus: UNDG – HRM Senior Policy Retreat," UN Practitioners' Portal on Human Rights Based Approaches to Programming, March 2012, http://hrbaportal.org/news.

many civil society organizations working on the environment, climate change, and economic and social justice around the world.[21]

In addition, in the current political and economic environment globally, OHCHR can look forward to being ever more placed in a situation where it becomes a strong advocate for the poor and the dispossessed. The close links between human rights and extreme poverty have been analyzed by the Special Rapporteur on Extreme poverty and human rights, presently Ms. Sepulveda Carmona of Chile. Her report for 2011 addressed the human rights violations arising out of a growing body of laws, regulations and practices that punish, segregate, control and undermine the autonomy of persons living in poverty.[22] She pointed to the fact that such measures have been adopted with increasing frequency over the past three decades, intensifying in recent years owing to the economic and financial crises, and now represent a serious threat to the enjoyment of human rights by persons living in poverty.[23]

Finally, I cannot emphasize more the role of the High Commissioner in advancing the work and safety of human rights defenders at the national and international levels. We hope that OHCHR and the High Commissioner will continue to work towards increasing the accessibility and usefulness of the UN's human rights mechanisms to human rights defenders. The High Commissioner has a critical role to play in ensuring that the principles of equality, non-discrimination and universality of rights are constantly reiterated and reaffirmed in the work of the Office and the human rights mechanisms of the UN system.

---

[21] See OHCHR, *OHCHR Study on the Relationship Between Climate Change and Human Rights*, UN Doc. A/HRC/10/61, January 15, 2009, providing evidence that OHCHR is doing so.

[22] Report by the Secretary-General, *Extreme Poverty and Human Rights*, UN Doc. A/66/265, August 4, 2011.

[23] Ibid. The Rapporteur also pointed out that the ways in which States and social forces penalize those living in poverty are interconnected and multidimensional: laws, regulations and practices which unduly restrict the performance of life-sustaining behaviors in public spaces by persons living in poverty; (b) urban planning regulations and measures related to the gentrification and privatization of public spaces that disproportionately impact persons living in poverty; (c) requirements and conditions imposed on access to public services and social benefits which interfere with the autonomy, privacy and family life of persons living in poverty; and (d) excessive and arbitrary use of detention and incarceration that threatens the liberty and personal security of persons living in poverty.

PART THREE

PREVENTING HUMAN RIGHTS VIOLATIONS AND EFFECTIVE RESPONSE

THE HIGH COMMISSIONERS AND THE SPECIAL PROCEDURES:[1] COLLEAGUES AND COMPETITORS

Felice D. Gaer

Introduction

Finding the political support and the practical means to enforce universal human rights principles has been a controversial matter for governments since the founding of the United Nations and a principal concern of the High Commissioner to the present.

Although the UN Charter proclaims the importance of human rights and setting up a UN Commission on Human Rights, for the first several decades of the UN's existence, norms were debated and treaties drafted, but little practical protection was achieved. By the 1980s and 1990s, however, the Commission (replaced in 2006 by the Human Rights Council) had established a number of independent experts, called 'special rapporteurs,' (and now, 'special procedures') to examine human rights in certain countries and to study cases and concerns, addressing thematic issues such as torture, arbitrary detention, 'disappearances,' and religious intolerance.[2] Their findings were often praised by civil society observers but criticized and scorned by the government under scrutiny. Countries often demanded their elimination, or, in polite terms, their 'rationalization.' Special procedure mandates nonetheless continued to grow in number and range of issues covered, from a handful in the 1980s to 48 special procedures today.

High Commissioners have generally praised the special procedures, calling them "one of the main pillars" of the UN's human rights system (Mary Robinson, 2001),[3] "crucial" (Sergio Vieira de Mello),[4] "first-line

[1] The special procedures system encompasses many individual mandate holders whose designations vary from special rapporteur to independent expert, working group member, and, previously, special representative. Almost all perform monitoring functions. In this essay, the terms 'special procedures' 'special rapporteurs' and 'rapporteurs' are used generically and interchangeably to refer to the individual experts appointed by the UN's principal intergovernmental human rights bodies (the Commission on Human Rights and its successor, the Human Rights Council). See "Special Procedures of the Human Rights Council," http://www.ohchr.org/EN/HRBodies/SP/Pages/Welcomepage.aspx.

[2] Initial thematic special procedure mandates called for study of 'questions' on these topics, which were later called 'incidents' or 'matters,' and eventually, for some mandates, 'investigating cases.'

[3] Mary Robinson, Address to 8th Meeting of Special Rapporteurs, June 18, 2001.

[4] OHCHR, *2002 Annual Report*, 161.

protection actors," (Bertrand Ramcharan),[5] "a unique link" (Louise Arbour),[6] and "active and unique" mechanisms (Navi Pillay).[7] Every High Commissioner has had to contend with complaints and growing government demands to review, reform, and 'rationalize' them, along with other human rights mechanisms – a task assigned to the High Commissioner in General Assembly resolution 48/141.

As the system of special procedures grew, criticism of them also rose. Yet the members of the General Assembly agreed in 2006 to carry over all special procedure mandates into the new Human Rights Council, recognizing that they represented a core UN achievement in human rights – an array of flexible, independent fact-finders who act as first responders when human rights violations are reported. However, the governments also established term limits, a code of conduct for the special procedure mandate holders, and professionalized selection procedures involving a Consultative Group that makes proposals to the Council's President. Nonetheless, governments exercise informal vetoes over selections, and the High Commissioners still encounter complaints about appointees from governments in public and private. The mandate holders routinely urge the High Commissioners to do more to facilitate their work, and to provide them with support – human, analytical, financial, and logistical. They fiercely defend their own status as independent experts.

Beginning with a summary of the development of the mechanisms, this chapter examines differing approaches taken by the High Commissioners towards the special procedures, including serving as their leader, partner, manager, promoter, and/or protector. The essay concludes with a discussion of country visits and with recommendations for strategic management of the special procedures by the High Commissioner to strengthen their common goal: more effective responses to human rights violations.

A Need for Facts

As a result of the initial refusal of the Commission on Human Rights to examine cases, there was no United Nations mechanism that could perform human rights fact-finding for the first several decades of the

---

5 Bertrand Ramcharan, "Opening Statement," 10th Annual Meeting of Special Rapporteurs, June 23, 2003.

6 OHCHR, *2007 Annual Report*, 27.

7 *Report of the Sixteenth meeting of Special Rapporteurs/Representatives, Independent Experts, and Chairpersons of Working Groups of the Special Procedures of the Human Rights Council*, UN Doc. A/HRC/12/47, July 22, 2009, para 14.

organization's existence. At its first session in 1946, Member States declared that the body had no power to take up individual cases of abuse brought to its attention. Opposition to action to stop human rights abuses became more strident during the Cold War. Jacob Blaustein, recognizing this shortcoming, called in 1963 for the establishment of an international official, a High Commissioner, who could investigate situations of human rights abuse.[8]

In 1967, this slowly began to change when the Economic and Social Council adopted Resolution 1235, which allowed the Commission on Human Rights to study gross violations of human rights. In 1980, states created a working group composed of independent experts from each of the UN's five regions to examine "the question" of enforced and involuntary disappearances. This working group became the first thematic special procedure mandated to examine specific abuses on a topic anywhere in the world, and it took up individual cases.[9]

By 1992, a year before the General Assembly created the High Commissioner post, the Commission had established six thematic mechanisms with a worldwide focus and twelve country-specific mandates.[10] In 1993, two more thematic mechanisms were created along with three new country rapporteurs,[11] for a total of 23 special procedures (8 thematic and 15 country-specific). As of December 2012, 48 special procedures (36 thematic, of which 6 are 5-member working groups, and 12 country-specific) involve a total of 72 independent experts.[12]

Each special procedure concentrates on a particular theme or country, offering an independent analysis resulting from thematic assessment, fact-finding missions to countries, and/or communications on specific cases with governments. Thereafter, they report publicly to the Human Rights Council. Most also appear at the General Assembly.[13]

---

[8] See Jacob Blaustein, "Human Rights: A Challenge to the United Nations and to Our Generation" in *The Quest for Peace: The Dag Hammarskjold Memorial Lecture Series*, ed. Andrew W. Cordier and Wilder Foote (New York: Columbia University Press, 1965), 315, 318–19.

[9] UN Commission on Human Rights, Resolution 20 (XXXVI), "Question of Missing and Disappeared Persons," UN Doc. E/CN.4/RES/1980, February 29, 1980, para. 1.

[10] Several other country-specific mechanisms (on Bolivia, Poland, Kuwait, Romania) had already been discontinued.

[11] Thematic rapporteurs on freedom of expression and racial discrimination; country mechanisms on the Occupied Palestinian Territories, Cambodia, and Somalia.

[12] For a list of mandate holders, see *Special Procedures of the Human Rights Council*, http://www.ohchr.org/EN/HRBodies/SP/Pages/Welcomepage.aspx.

[13] For more on special procedures and UN human rights bodies, see Philip Alston, "Hobbling the Monitors: Should UN Human Rights Monitors be Accountable?," *Harvard International Law Journal*, Vol. 52, Number 2, 561–649 (Summer 2011); and Ted Piccone,

The High Commissioners and the Special Procedures

While the High Commissioner was envisioned by some as a top UN official who could be active in response to human rights violations, many governments opposed this, and later proposals for the post turned more bureaucratic, emphasizing management of human rights inside the UN system.[14] In December 1993, the General Assembly assigned the High Commissioner responsibility to carry out "the tasks assigned to her/him" by UN bodies, and to conduct "rationalization, adaptation, strengthening and streamlining" of the UN machinery and other forms of coordination.[15]

When the High Commissioner was created, there was already frequent controversy over the accuracy and credibility of the rapporteurs' reports. Countries never before held up to public scrutiny, from China to Algeria, from Indonesia to the USSR, were now the subject of critical examination.

Official responses to the rapporteurs' reports, delivered orally at the Commission on Human Rights, often revealed an antipathy to scrutiny, rebutted allegations of abuse, and sometimes denied the need for such mechanisms altogether. For example, in 1992, Iran's representative complained that Special Representative Galindo Pohl's report was filled with "unfounded negative remark[s]" and that "there was no longer any justification of the monitoring machinery" as "the myth of a consistent pattern of gross violations of human rights in Iran had been completely dispelled."[16] In 1998, Cuba's Foreign Minister Roberto Robaina insisted that Special Rapporteur Johan Carl Groth's report was "just another slander" as "[N]o one ever was or is tortured or missing."[17] Others spoke similarly.[18]

Catalysts for Change: How the UN's Independent Experts Promote Human Rights (Washington, DC: Brookings Institution Press, 2012).

[14] See Roger S. Clark, *A United Nations High Commissioner for Human Rights* (The Hague: Martinus Nijhoff, 1972), 39–59. See also F. Gaer, *Book review* of *The UN High Commissioner for Human Rights* by B. Ramcharan, *American Journal of International Law*, Vol. 98 (2004), 391–395.

[15] UN General Assembly. Resolution 48/141, "High Commissioner for the promotion and protection of all human rights," UN Doc. A/RES/48/141, December 20, 1993.

[16] UN Commission on Human Rights, *Summary Record of the 44th Meeting*, UN Doc. E/CN.4/1992/SR.44, paras. 41–2, April 10, 1992.

[17] F. Gaer, 'Human Rights', in *A Global Agenda: Issues before the 54th General Assembly of the United Nations*, eds. John Tessitore and Susan Woolfson (Maryland, USA: Rowman & Littlefield, 1999), 186.

[18] Saddam Hussein's representative in 1999 declared that Special Rapporteur Max van der Stoel has "invented lies and fabrications" in all his reports. See F. Gaer, "Human Rights," 181.

José Ayala Lasso

José Ayala Lasso, as the first UN High Commissioner for Human Rights, positioned himself primarily as a coordinator working to streamline the existing special procedures and other mechanisms. As former chair of General Assembly negotiations that crafted the High Commissioner's mandate, he saw himself as neither an investigator nor a report-writer.[19]

Ayala Lasso declared that the reports of the special procedures would be an "important tool" enabling him to "highlight problem areas." In November 1994, he set out limits:[20]

> … I will not report to you the tragedies that afflict individuals and groups throughout the world. … This catalog of horrors will be detailed in the reports of the various rapporteurs and mechanisms of the Commission on Human Rights….[21]

While special rapporteurs would investigate cases, he would be different: "The High Commissioner is … not intended to replace or duplicate the existing mechanisms. Rather it is charged with using the tools of policy and diplomacy to … establish dialogue with Governments."[22]

Ayala Lasso's approach was widely criticized by key human rights advocates after his visits to Colombia and Cuba. No UN human rights official had previously visited Cuba, yet Ayala Lasso failed to consult the special rapporteur, ask to visit prisons or meet with victims of abuse. Although his visit to Colombia followed a visit by two thematic rapporteurs, Ayala Lasso did not reinforce their recommendations.

Ayala Lasso's approach appeared to reward uncooperative human rights-violating states and to undercut the special procedures.[23] NGOs told the High Commissioner that he had to do better. They reminded Ayala Lasso of his mandate to coordinate, and deemed it crucial that the High Commissioner's activities reinforce other fact-finding mechanisms.[24]

---

19 José Ayala Lasso, "Defining the Mandate: New UN Efforts to Protect Human Rights," *Harvard International Review,* (Winter 1994–95), 39–41.

20 José Ayala Lasso, "Statement of the High Commissioner for Human Rights to the 49th session of the General Assembly," November 21, 1994.

21 Ibid.

22 See Ayala Lasso, "Defining the Mandate," fn. 10.

23 F. Gaer, "NGOs and the UN High Commissioner for Human Rights," in *Human Rights, The United Nations and Nongovernmental Organizations*, The Carter Center, 1997, 81–95, 88.

24 "The Promise of the UN High Commissioner for Human Rights," June 6, 1995, Atlanta, Georgia, USA. The message apparently did not get through. When the Cubans tried to limit the mandate of the arbitrary detentions working group in 1996–97 to prevent addressing cases of individuals sentenced by a national court, many governments fought back. High Commissioner Ayala Lasso appeared silent.

Ayala Lasso left the situation no better than when he assumed office. Regrettably, his abrupt departure left no one as High Commissioner precisely when the special procedures were being directly challenged, as governments censored a rapporteur's report for the first time.[25] Ayala Lasso's final speech in 1997 commended the special procedures for "saving lives, preventing violations, and helping to resolve serious situations." Ominously, states tabled three resolutions at the end of the 1997 Commission explicitly calling for review and revitalization – in essence, curtailment – of the special procedures.

Managerially, Ayala Lasso provided neither the coordination nor support that the special procedures sought. At the 1997 annual meeting of all special procedures, mandate holders expressed "disappointment" and "frustration" at not receiving a promised paper on how the High Commissioner would facilitate follow-up of their recommendations. Ironically, after three years of Ayala Lasso's term, it was the special procedures that initiated demands for 'coordination' from a High Commissioner who had stressed that his job was largely just that.[26]

Mary Robinson

In her memoirs, Robinson reflects on how difficult she found the High Commissioner's post when she arrived.[27] She saw her role as inspiring others. She traveled to hot spots – not to enable others to enter, but to witness and investigate situations herself.[28] This would give her added credibility, which she considered "essential."[29]

In her initial UN press conference, Mary Robinson explained that she "intended to use the work of the special rapporteurs as a resource" and "reference point."[30] Two months later, she delivered her "vision" of human rights, stating that "the essence of rights is that they are empowering ..."[31]

---

[25] Because of a Commission decision, the Chair instructed Special Rapporteur on Racism Maurice Glele-Ahanhanzo to remove a reference to the Holy Quran from his report, as some states demanded. There was no comment from the High Commissioner, as the post was vacant.

[26] *Report of the UN High Commissioner for Human Rights*, UN Doc. E/CN.4/1998/122, February 23, 1998, paras. 111–116.

[27] Mary Robinson, *Everybody Matters* (London: Hodder and Stoughton, 2012), 202.

[28] Ibid., 228–235.

[29] Ibid.

[30] Press release, Sept. 30, 1997.

[31] Mary Robinson, "Realizing Human Rights: "Take Hold of it Boldly and Duly..."" (Romanes Lecture, Oxford University, Nov 11, 1997), UN Department of Public Information, http://www.un.org/rights/50/dpi1938.htm.

and must have meaning at ground level. As High Commissioner, she intended to be "a catalyst" stimulating action throughout the UN.[32] Yet, Robinson's 'vision' speech did not refer to any special rapporteur or special procedure.[33] We can only speculate on the reason for this absence and the fact that, three days later, in her first speech to the UN General Assembly, she similarly avoided any reference.[34]

During her term, the special procedures came under repeated attack from those who sought to diminish their visibility and effectiveness. Param Cumaraswamy, Special Rapporteur on the independence of judges and lawyers, was facing civil litigation in his own country over published comments that he made as a special rapporteur. In September 1997, the General Assembly's Third Committee was considering a draft resolution to restrict the work of the special rapporteurs. In this context, Robinson's failure to mention the rapporteurs in her early public remarks seems to suggest that she would concentrate on establishing herself, not the rapporteurs, as the premier defender of human rights.

Greater verbal support of the special procedures followed.[35] In December, Robinson publicly affirmed the independence of special rapporteurs. Citing the "crucial value of these procedures to saving human lives and helping resolve serious situations of violations," she stated that she would give them special attention.[36] Later, she spoke of the lawsuit against Cumaraswamy, citing Malaysia's failure to recognize his immunities as an attack on the entire system of special procedures.[37] Robinson's

---

[32] Ibid.

[33] Ibid.

[34] Yet Robinson's written annual report called for giving special procedures the "highest priority," and recognized them as "one of the cornerstones of the international system…of human rights." *Report of the UN High Commissioner for Human Rights*, UN Doc. A/52/36, October 29, 1997.

[35] In a report to the special procedures meeting, Paulo Sergio Pinheiro noted that he had met the High Commissioner in person five times from September 1997 through May 1998, and also had several telephone conversations. In New York, Pinheiro spoke with the UN Legal Advisor in November about Cumaraswamy's case where he likely also pressed Robinson to publicly defend him. *Report of the Chairperson of the fourth meeting of special rapporteurs/representatives, experts and chairpersons of working groups of the Commission on Human Rights and of the advisory services programme concerning his activities from June 1997 to May 1998*, UN Doc. E/CN.4/1999/3.Add. 2, February 5, 1999, paras. 7, 11.

[36] "Statement by Mary Robinson, United Nations High Commissioner for Human Rights, on the importance of the independence of special rapporteurs and similar mechanisms of the Commission on Human Rights," UN press release HR/97/88, December 16, 1997.

[37] Eventually, the International Court of Justice in an advisory opinion defended his immunity, after which the suits were withdrawn. See International Court of Justice, *Difference Relating to Immunity from Legal Process of a Special Rapporteur of the Commission on Human Rights*, Advisory Opinion of 29 April 1999.

1998 report commended the Commission on Human Rights for authorizing new rapporteurs on the right to education[38] and on extreme poverty and human rights.[39] Three others on the rights to adequate housing, to food, and to health, created during her term, were supported for giving attention to economic and social rights.

At the Commission on Human Rights, Robinson promised "to prioritize" working with the rapporteurs and recalled that the Vienna World Conference had underlined the importance of preserving and strengthening them.[40] She expressed "grave concern" that some states had refused to cooperate with them.[41] But she did not vigorously fight on their behalf as Member States in April 1998 demanded "a review of the mechanisms of the Commission" to assess their effectiveness.[42] Their calls for 'rationalization' were reportedly motivated "more by the prospect of reducing the number of mandates than by assessing any overlaps that might hinder their effectiveness."[43]

There is no public record to suggest that Robinson backed up the special procedures during this review.[44] The review concluded that the special rapporteurs "constitute an essential cornerstone of the UN's efforts to promote and protect human rights" and should be preserved, strengthened, depoliticized, and cooperated with. The Commission's officers requested a new Rapporteurs' manual.[45] They also sought increased regular budget allocations, 'annual work-planning,' and communications systems, and "underline[d] the importance of continuing and enhancing

---

38 *Report of the UN High Commissioner for Human Rights*, UN Doc. A/54/36, September 23, 1999, para. 28.

39 Ibid.

40 Mary Robinson, Statement to the 54th Session of the Commission on Human Rights, March, 19 1998.

41 Ibid. See also "Statement by Mary Robinson, the United Nations High Commissioner for Human Rights," UN press release HR/98/10, February 24, 1998.

42 Commission on Human Rights. Decision 1998/112, "Enhancing the effectiveness of the mechanisms of the Commission on Human Rights," UN Doc. E/CN.4/DEC/1998/112, April 24, 1998.

43 See Tania Baldwin-Pask and Patrizia Scannella, "The unfinished business of a special procedures system," in *New Challenges for the Human Rights Machinery*, eds. M.C. Bassiouni and W.A. Schabas (Portland, OR: Intersentia, 2011), 425.

44 *Report of the UN High Commissioner for Human Rights*, UN GAOR A/56/36 (2001), paras 25–27.

45 Commission on Human Rights, *Rationalization of the Work of the Commission*, UN Doc. E/CN.4/1999/104, 23 December 1998. Some other proposals suggested reducing working groups of five into a single rapporteur, as a cost-savings measure, but this was never carried out.

effective coordination between the special procedures and substantive activities of the High Commissioner..."[46]

Robinson's 1998 and 1999 Annual Reports mentioned improving the human rights machinery.[47] During her term, the annual meeting of special procedures, where logistical and administrative matters were discussed, was extended. There, the special procedures discussed ways the Office of the High Commissioner for Human Rights (OHCHR) could work more effectively with them. They received an OHCHR report outlining procedures to ensure implementation of their recommendations,[48] in which the High Commissioner affirmed her responsibility "to play an integral role in the follow up of recommendations of special rapporteurs." The report, while comprehensive, seemed highly bureaucratic and hierarchical to some rapporteurs, setting out obligations of the rapporteurs and their staffs to inform the High Commissioner, but detailing little for the High Commissioner to do in return.[49]

Some special rapporteurs questioned the hierarchical approach outlined in that report, calling for a free flow of information in both directions. They complained about lack of coordination on country visits by the High Commissioner, emphasizing the need for consultation *before* High Commissioner country visits, and for briefings afterwards. They raised concerns that the High Commissioner's visits to countries that did not cooperate with special procedures could undermine progress. Even follow-up, they insisted, should proceed only *after* consultation with the relevant special rapporteur, and should be described publicly in her annual reports.[50]

---

[46] Ibid., para. 45.

[47] *A Voice for Human Rights*, eds. Mary Robinson & Kevin Boyle, (Philadelphia: University of Pennsylvania Press, 2006).

[48] *Study of the High Commissioner for Human Rights on procedures for ensuring implementation of, and follow-up to recommendations of special rapporteurs/representatives, experts and working groups*, UN Doc. E/CN.4/1999/3/Add.1, July 31, 1998.

[49] For example, the report provided that special procedures should transmit a summary of conclusions and recommendations to the High Commissioner (ibid., para. 7), inform the High Commissioner of any press briefing given or statement issued during the course of a mission, and in "high-profile cases that draw extensive media coverage," inform the High Commissioner of any recommendations made, as she "might choose to join the special rapporteur in the appeal" (ibid., para.10). It states that in certain cases, the High Commissioner "may propose certain action by a particular special rapporteur...." such as being invited to a country, or a joint statement. But as for recommendations of the High Commissioner, "it is the responsibility of the desk officer to inform the special rapporteur of recommendations that may be of relevance to his or her work" (ibid., para.14).

[50] Ibid., paras. 19–24.

During Robinson's term, more than 80 states were cited by one or more of the special procedures.[51] Over 30 states, including some of the world's most powerful nations, received rapporteurs' visits or were the focus of specialized reports. Yet the High Commissioner frequently failed to coordinate with the rapporteurs on country visits and follow-up.[52] OHCHR claimed in a 'Fact Sheet' that overlap between the special procedures and the High Commissioner was "avoided through coordination,"[53] but the rapporteurs' concerns had not been resolved.

Sergio Vieira de Mello

Sergio Vieira de Mello's concept of his role was more pragmatic. In a July 2002 interview, he remarked "It is not enough to blame. It is also necessary to help governments ...emerge from their own mistakes ... ."[54] He looked to the ground – not the conference room, and not Geneva – as the focus of protection efforts. As one special rapporteur remarked: "He was able to navigate within the humanitarian and human rights galaxies . ... He had more proximity to the real world than the other High Commissioners . ..."[55]

Vieira de Mello created a Special Procedures Branch in the Secretariat to "enhance professionalism."[56] He referred to "the impartiality, objectivity and independence" of these mechanisms as "crucial to the effectiveness" of the UN human rights system.[57] He encouraged extra-budgetary support to staff them properly, noting that the then-37 mandate holders did not have even one full time staff person each.

In a December 4, 2002 interview about Iraq, Vieira de Mello indicated his familiarity with at least one special procedure: the Special Rapporteur on Iraq, Andreas Mavrommatis, who had visited Iraq and was "currently discussing with the Iraqi government another possible visit." Vieira de Mello commended the Rapporteur's "very detailed" recommendations.[58]

---

[51] *A Global Agenda: Issues Before the 53rd General Assembly of the United Nations*, eds. John Tessitore & Susan Woolfson (Rowman & Littlefield, 1998) 175.

[52] Ted Piccone, *Catalysts for Change: How the UN's Independent Experts Promote Human Rights* (Washington, DC: Brookings Institution Press, 2012) 21.

[53] *Fact Sheet No. 27: Seventeen frequently asked questions about United Nations Special Rapporteurs*, OHCHR, 2001, http://www.ohchr.org/Documents/Publications/FactSheet27en.pdf.

[54] Paulo Sergio Pinheiro, "Being a Special Rapporteur: a delicate balancing act," *International Journal of Human Rights*, Vol. 15, No. 2, 162–171 (February 2011) 167.

[55] Interview with author, October 2, 2012.

[56] OHCHR, *2002 Annual Report*, 6.

[57] Ibid., 161.

[58] Sergio Vieira de Mello, press conference, December 4, 2002 (reply to question from Lisa Schlein, ABC). See also Gustavo Capdevila, "RIGHTS-IRAQ: UN Preparing to Protect Civilians – High Commissioner," *Inter Press Service*, December 9, 2002.

Some months later, after the US invasion, Kofi Annan sent Vieira de Mello to serve as his Special Representative to Iraq. Although High Commissioner Vieira de Mello closely followed events related to Iraq, he reportedly did "nothing" to get the Special Rapporteur into the country. He did not undercut the Rapporteur, but he "did not go out of his way" to show support for the Rapporteur's views. Mavrommatis did not get into Iraq again nor did OHCHR help continue the mandate after the invasion. "In order to avoid criticism," Mavrommatis reflected, "...most if not all High Commissioners keep their distance" from the special rapporteurs.[59]

Bertrand Ramcharan

Acting High Commissioner Bertrand Ramcharan publicly supported the special procedures, defended them from criticism, and encouraged more attention to their administrative and substantive needs. He saw himself as their partner, facilitator, and protector.

Ramcharan was an architect of the special procedures, dating from his service as Special Assistant to Human Rights Division Director Theo van Boven.[60] An insider with extensive experience in human rights, Acting High Commissioner Ramcharan shaped relationships with the special procedures. Serving 1998–2003 as Deputy to Robinson and then Vieira de Mello, he facilitated many logistical changes to support the special procedures.[61] As Acting High Commissioner, Ramcharan encouraged expanding each special rapporteur's public report from a five-minute summary at the Commission to an interactive dialogue with many states, not only those visited.[62]

At the 2003 special procedures meeting, in Vieira de Mello's absence, Ramcharan raised the growing criticism of rapporteurs by Member States, and encouraged participants to reflect on how to rationalize and enhance the effectiveness of their machinery.[63] There is no evidence that the special rapporteurs engaged with him on this topic. Ramcharan also tried to strengthen a 'quick response' desk, noted that operational standards for

---

59 Author email exchange with A. Mavrommatis, October 2, 2012.

60 Joanna Naples-Mitchell, "Perspectives of UN Special Rapporteurs on their role: inherent tensions and unique contributions to human rights," *International Journal of Human Rights*, Vol. 15, No. 2, February 2011, 232.

61 Ramcharan says he initially pressed to create the Special Procedures Branch in the Secretariat. Bertrand Ramcharan, *A High Commissioner in Defence of Human Rights* (The Hague: Martinus Nijhoff, 2004).

62 *Report of the United Nations High Commissioner for Human Rights,* UN Doc. A/58/36 (2003) para. 64.

63 Ramcharan, *A High Commissioner in Defence of Human Rights*, 176–7.

urgent appeals needed serious attention, and proposed professionalizing the selection process.

Ramcharan claims he was always ready to protect the special procedures under challenge: "I met with them whenever they asked and I sought to come to their support each time they faced attacks by governments."[64] He defended special rapporteurs when denounced publicly by government representatives: the Special Rapporteur on torture, who was criticized by Brazil, the staff of the expert on Cuba, who was excoriated by that government, and the Special Rapporteur on the right to food, who was also challenged publicly. Ramcharan later defended the Special Representative on human rights defenders regarding an interaction in Thailand that he called a personal attack.[65]

At the General Assembly, Ramcharan praised the "crucial role" of special procedures in "early warning and preventive action," noting they are often the first to recognize problems in a country and inform other UN bodies.[66] This idea would stick: both of his successors advert to it in their reports and strategic plans.

Louise Arbour

As High Commissioner during 2004–8, Louise Arbour presided over the UN's reform of its principal intergovernmental human rights body, replacing the Commission with the new Human Rights Council. Secretary-General Annan had criticized the Commission for losing credibility and professionalism, and impugning the legitimacy of the UN itself. Governments, he said, competed for membership to shield themselves from criticism, severely politicizing the body.

Arbour supported universalizing the membership of the Human Rights Council and establishing a peer review mechanism to scrutinize every country. She convinced governments to double funding for UN human rights programs, for use outside Geneva. But Arbour reportedly distanced herself from the contentious political negotiations which aimed to review and reform the special procedures.[67] Participants in the prestigious Wilton

---

64 Ibid., 241.

65 Piccone describes it differently. See Piccone, *Catalysts for Change*, 77.

66 *Report of the United Nations High Commissioner* (2003), para. 64.

67 "[T]he Special Procedures occupied an important but contested place in this process. ...[T]hose states which would have been happy to relegate the Special Procedures to marginality, if not quite oblivion, had to deal with the fact that the Human Rights Council's overall credibility, and thus its capacity to achieve its other objective, depended in the eyes of most observers on its ability to do two things: to respond to crisis situations and grave

Park annual conference on human rights expressed concern that the leadership and visibility of the High Commissioner was missing when it was most needed.[68] The new Council maintained the special procedures, but established term limits and new selection procedures.

Saying little about the special procedures in her annual reports or Plan of Action, Arbour's 2006–07 strategic plan noted their independence and "crucial role" in efforts to protect and empower people "to realize their rights."[69] Arbour supported the review of special procedures by states launched after the Secretary-General raised concerns in 2002. However, Arbour claimed that annual meetings, a coordination committee, manuals, a quick response desk, and other methods already addressed any shortcomings. The key issue now was lack of resources.[70] As she departed, Arbour urged strengthening the "vital functions" of the special procedures.[71]

Although the special procedures mandate holders had, in 2005, created a coordination committee to receive complaints, the same governments that had demanded rationalization, review and reform of the machinery still called for more. They demanded a code of conduct to govern the methodology – and even the public remarks – of every rapporteur. Many saw this as aimed to diminish the independence of these mechanisms.[72] Ultimately, the 2007 code of conduct became part of an overall agreement to extend the special procedures system. It requires mandate holders to cross-check facts, take into account information provided by the state concerned, and evaluate data according to human rights norms applicable to each state. It instructed them to act with impartiality, transparency,

violations, and to undertake routine monitoring which covered all states, rather than just a handful of pariahs." Alston, "Hobbling the Monitors," 587.

68 The participants urged Arbour to become "more visible, consulting regularly, and spending more time among delegations. Some express concern that the High Commissioner appears to be standing back from the Council at a time when her leadership is needed more than ever." Wilton Park Conference WP835, January 19–21, 2007.

69 OHCHR, *High Commissioner's Strategic Management Plan 2006–2007*, 26.

70 Ibid., 10 and 26. Arbour also told the Human Rights Council she appreciated maintenance of the rapporteurs' independence. "High Commissioner addresses the Human Rights Council," OHCHR news release, September 13, 2007.

71 "In final speech to Human Rights Council, Arbour notes 'tangible progress,' but warns against pursuit of narrow political agendas," UN press release, June 2, 2008.

72 Alston, "Hobbling the Monitors" (presents the history of the code of conduct and demands for accountability of special procedures under the Council). For views of the mandate holders, see "A Note by the Special Procedures' Coordination Committee in Response to Discussions on a Code of Conduct and Annex: Possible Elements of a Code of Conduct," April 13, 2007, http://www2.ohchr.org/english/bodies/chr/special/docs/note_code_of_conduct.pdf.

even-handedness, and to engage in constructive dialogue, taking into account the positions of the states. Philip Alston describes the code as a "concerted effort to limit the mandate-holders' scope of action, introduce extensive delays in their work, and put governments firmly in the drivers' seat. ..."[73] Nonetheless, the code's stated purpose is to "enhance the effectiveness" of the special procedures, and it refers to their independence seven times. Surprisingly, the special procedures emerged largely intact from the review by Member States that led to adoption of the code of conduct.

When the code of conduct was invoked publicly during Human Rights Council sessions, it was in an accusatory context.[74] States complained that mandates were exceeded by the Special Rapporteur on arbitrary executions (Kenya), the Special Rapporteur on the right to food (Brazil), the Special Rapporteur on torture (Equatorial Guinea), and the freedom of expression Special Rapporteur (Zambia for the African group). In the end, none of these claims resulted in ouster of a mandate holder. Arbour's views on these controversies were not always public.

Canada and some NGOs asked Arbour to condemn then-Special Rapporteur on the right to food Jean Zeigler, as the Secretary-General had.[75] Zeigler had directly compared Israeli soldiers to Nazi concentration camp guards, and complainants reminded Arbour that the European Union monitoring agency and others defined such comparisons with Nazi symbols as anti-Semitic slurs. In a private letter, Arbour responded, emphasizing the independence of special rapporteurs, insisting they were accountable solely to the Commission on Human Rights, and disassociating herself from Zeigler's "inflammatory" remarks.[76] Her spokesman later explained that it was a matter of policy not to comment publicly on the reports of special rapporteurs.[77]

---

[73] Alston, "Hobbling the Monitors," 595.

[74] Ibid., 591.

[75] There were several complaints. See letter from UN Watch to High Commissioner Louise Arbour, July 7, 2005, http://www.unwatch.org/atf/cf/%7B6DEB65DA-BE5B-4CAE-8056-8BF0BEDF4D17%7D/letter_arbour.pdf.

[76] Letter from Louise Arbour to Ambassador Alfred Moses and Hillel Neuer, July, 19 2005, http://www.unwatch.org/atf/cf/%7B6DEB65DA-BE5B-4CAE-8056-8BF0BEDF4D17%7D/ARBOUR_LETTER190705.PDF. Arbour noted that Zeigler claimed his remarks were in his private capacity.

[77] Spokesman Rupert Colville stated in e-mail to FOXNews.com, "As a matter of practice, we do not offer commentaries on individual special rapporteurs." Joseph Abrams, "Critics Demand Resignation of U.N Official Who Wants Probe of 9/11 'Inside Job' Theories," *FoxNews.com*, July 16, 2008, http://www.foxnews.com/story/0,2933,369122,00.html.

In 2007 Arbour made public remarks to the Human Rights Council that helped protect two Special Rapporteurs facing threats because they were also Pakistani human rights defenders – Asma Jahangir and Hina Jilani.[78] Arbour initially raised concerns also when Sigma Huda, the Special Rapporteur on trafficking, was allegedly harassed. Huda faced criminal charges in 2007 for corruption in Bangladesh and was eventually sentenced to three years in prison. The Secretary-General later stated the incident had nothing to do with Huda's position or functions as a special rapporteur, and urged that in any trial or detention, she should be afforded all her human rights.[79] Arbour stated that she would seek clarification on Huda's conviction and possible appeal, but reiterated the Secretary-General's view.[80]

Navi Pillay

Like her predecessors, Navi Pillay has often complimented the special procedures. In September 2009, she reminded Human Rights Council members that the work of the special procedures is of the "utmost importance" and urged all states to ensure that "their recommendations help shape reform at the national level." She urged better support for their "independence and freedom" as it underpins their "integrity, impartiality, and effectiveness."[81]

At an October 2009 seminar at UN headquarters, Pillay said the contribution of the special procedures "could not be overemphasized" and that they "were in an ideal position to function as early warning mechanisms."[82]

In June 2011, the General Assembly completed its 5-year Review of the Human Rights Council, citing "the integrity and independence of the special procedures mandate holders" and the importance of "ensuring a robust

[78] See Louise Arbour remarks to the Human Rights Council, December 11, 2007.

[79] Secretary-General Ban Ki-moon, "Statement Attributable to the Spokesperson for the Secretary-General on Legal proceedings in Bangladesh against the Special Rapporteur on trafficking in persons, Ms. Sigma Huda," July 17, 2007. The Special Rapporteur on independence of the judiciary earlier raised questions about due process. While UN experts on mission would normally be granted immunity, in this case Ban Ki-moon stated that the allegations against her "appear not to be related to, or otherwise fall within, her functions as special rapporteur." Caitlin Price, "UN legal counsel backs convention on criminal accountability of UN officials," *Jurist*, October 16, 2007.

[80] "Bangladesh: UN seeks confirmation on conviction of human rights expert," *UN News Centre*, August 30, 2007.

[81] "Statement of Ms. Navanethem Pillay United Nations High Commissioner for Human Rights at the 12th session of the Human Rights Council," September 15, 2009.

[82] Office of the High Commissioner for Human Rights, "Human rights experts have a key role in early warning," November 23, 2009.

system of special procedures."[83] The Review encouraged cooperation by countries, urged adequate and equitable funding, including extra-budgetary resources, and rejected intimidation or reprisals against mandate holders.[84]

In March 2012, Pillay called the special procedures "more relevant than ever, including for identifying urgent situations"[85] and in September she stressed their past underutilization.[86] She has paid similar homage to commissions of inquiry (COIs).

In the controversy over so-called 'defamation of religions,' Pillay dispatched the special procedures to participate in regional workshops addressing the various norms at issue. Governments had clashed over the threshold for limiting the rights to freedom of expression and freedom of religion in order to prevent incitement to racial or religious hostility, violence, or discrimination. The relevant Special Rapporteurs – on expression, religious freedom, and racial discrimination – explored this topic at each of the sessions, and their presence reportedly played a key role in clarifying the relevant thresholds.[87]

OHCHR continues to provide services to the special procedures, including staffing, logistical and travel support for country visits, communications, and annual meetings. OHCHR has revised the Manual of the Special Procedures and has also begun "induction sessions" for new mandate holders. These address basic administrative procedures and working relationships, not only with OHCHR staff but with states, media, and sources of information.

Navi Pillay has also faced the issue of defending rapporteurs from criticism. In 2011, referring to Richard Falk, Special Raporteur on the Occupied Palestinian Territories, Secretary-General Ban Ki-moon spoke to the Human Rights Council and stated:

> Recently, a special rapporteur suggested there was an 'apparent cover-up' in the 2001 terrorist attacks on the United States. I want to tell you, clearly and directly. I condemn this sort of inflammatory rhetoric. ... It is the responsibility of the Human Rights Council to uphold, at all times, the highest standards ...[88]

---

83 General Assembly. Resolution 65/281, "Review of the Human Rights Council," UN Doc. A/RES/65/28, July 20, 2011, see Annex, para. 24.

84 Ibid., Annex, paras 31, 33.

85 Navi Pillay, "United Nations High Commissioner for Human Rights / Introduction of her Annual Report 2011 to the Human Rights Council," March 2, 2012.

86 Navi Pillay, "Opening Statement by Ms. Navi Pillay, United Nations High Commissioner for Human Rights," February 27, 2012.

87 See Office of the High Commissioner for Human Rights, "Articles 19–20," http://www.ohchr.org/EN/Issues/FreedomOpinion/Articles19-20/Pages/Index.aspx.

88 Ban Ki-moon, "Secretary-General's Remarks to the Human Rights Council," Geneva, Switzerland, January 25, 2011.

Ban's chief of staff, Vijay Nambiar said this applied to experts "however eminent they may be in their fields...." The Secretary-General later criticized Falk, calling a cartoon posted on Falk's personal website anti-Semitic. Ted Piccone, in his book on the special procedures, has described Falk as "an egregious example of a rapporteur who has lost sight of his mandate."[89]

In July, Pillay also addressed these complaints. She affirmed the independence of the special procedures but, like Arbour, declared that she is not responsible for their statements or actions, as the rapporteurs report to the member states.[90] She disassociated herself from the action that provoked the criticism, declaring "... Mr. Falk is neither a representative nor an employee of my Office. ... I utterly deplore and condemn anti-Semitism, as I do any form of incitement to hatred and racial discrimination."[91]

This statement underscores the limits of the High Commissioner's capacity to sanction other than verbally. Since the creation of the Coordination Committee of Special Procedures and the adoption of the code of conduct, which requires the special procedures to act with integrity and "conduct consistent with their status at all times," there has been much less public criticism of the mandate holders by states. A complaint to the Coordination Committee has been made once by a member state, but the details of this are not yet known, due to confidentiality of the Internal Advisory Procedure. Most complaints take place in bilateral meetings with government officials, where Pillay reportedly reminds them of the independence of the special procedures.

An Ongoing Challenge: Country Visits

Country visits by special procedures have become their most well-known function and, according to Piccone, "yield the most attention and results" and are their "most important tool."[92] Considering the number of country visits that both they and the High Commissioner are undertaking, this tool

89 Piccone, *Catalysts for Change*, 77.

90 Pillay wrote: "As you are aware, special procedures mandate-holders are neither representatives nor employees of the Office of the United Nations High Commissioner for Human Rights. The Member States of the Human Rights Council appoint mandate-holders. ...Mandate holders serve in their independent capacities and report directly to the Member States of the Human Rights Council." Letter from Navi Pillay to Hillel Neuer, July 11, 2001, http://www.unwatch.org/atf/cf/%7B6deb65da-be5b-4cae-8056-8bf0bedf4d17%7D/PILLAY%20ON%20FALK.PDF.

91 Ibid.

92 Piccone, *Catalysts for Change*, 21, 23.

could be put to better use. Mandate holders often complain that the High Commissioners have not consulted them before or after statements made by the High Commissioners about their country visits. The country visits are aimed at investigating human rights conditions at the national level, and consulting directly with alleged victims, human rights defenders and government officials. Navi Pillay reports that in her first 3 years, she visited 39 countries, an average of 13 such visits annually.[93] Special procedures make many more country visits: 67 in 2010, 82 in 2011, and 80 in 2012.[94]

Some OHCHR staff members in Geneva, particularly those assisting country rapporteurs, state that they are consulted regarding the visits and statements of the High Commissioner, but others say the opposite. Expert mandate holders themselves commonly state they are not consulted. One expert reported that it took seven months to schedule a meeting with the High Commissioner, despite his own proximity to Geneva. Others complained at the annual special procedures meeting or in private interviews conducted for this chapter. Perhaps the High Commissioner's aides think they are consulting the specialists by contacting members of the OHCHR staff. However, the mandate holders feel they are neither consulted before nor briefed afterwards. The annual special procedures meetings often feature an hour-long speech and question-and-answer session with the High Commissioner. However, these formal sessions commonly address technical, staffing or logistical issues, not strategic country-specific options.

In 2012, special procedures mandate holders made 334 statements, 16% of which were joint (i.e., by more than one mandate holder). The High Commissioner makes far fewer public statements: between the 12 months between December 2011 and December 2012, the High Commissioner made 72 statements, of which 20 were country-specific and half of these were made during visits to the country concerned; the High Commissioner also issued 40 press releases addressing 38 countries.[95] In total, at least 50–60 of the High Commissioner's statements or press releases annually address country situations.

---

93 Based on the annual reports of OHCHR.

94 OHCHR, "Facts and Figures 2010," "Facts and Figures 2011," and "Facts and Figures 2012," http://www.ohchr.org/EN/HRBodies/SP/Pages/Publications.aspx.

95 The High Commissioner's statements are available at OHCHR, and "Facts and Figures 2012," http://www.ohchr.org/EN/NewsEvents/Pages/NewsSearch.aspx?PTID=HC&NTID=STM, and her press releases are available at http://www.ohchr.org/EN/NewsEvents/Pages/NewsSearch.aspx?PTID=HC&NTID=PRS. The statements by the Deputy High Commissioner are not included. Items appearing on both websites were counted only once as statements.

During the ten country visits in 2012 in which the High Commissioner made detailed public statements at press conferences, specific mention of special procedures was made only three times: Indonesia, Algeria, and Pakistan. In Indonesia, the High Commissioner complimented Indonesia's acceptance of a future visit. In Algeria, she remarked that many special procedures had already visited the country and that the Working Group on Disappearances would shortly accept an invitation. She encouraged the government to invite two additional rapporteurs. In Pakistan, the High Commissioner welcomed the expected visit of the first special procedure in 13 years and the government's invitation to the freedom of expression rapporteur. She also urged the government to invite the Special Rapporteur on summary and arbitrary executions. The High Commissioner's four published press statements on country visits in 2011 (Maldives, Moldova, Russia, and Senegal), show that the High Commissioner mentioned follow-up regarding rapporteurs' concerns about the Transdnestria region, but did not refer to similar matters in the other countries. This is surprising since each of the others had received at least four visits from special rapporteurs in the years before her visit.[96]

These figures do not count whether the High Commissioner may have also reinforced substantive points raised by special procedures. The High Commissioner normally has a broader agenda on her country visits than that of the individual rapporteurs. Still, the comments delivered at the end of a visit are the most closely watched and publicized statements. Whatever the reason for the High Commissioner's reluctance to cite the special procedures directly, there is surely room for more coordination and consultation about follow up to reinforce conclusions from the special procedure visits and communications.

Recommendations for Further Study

Much has changed since José Ayala Lasso declared that he, the first High Commissioner, would facilitate the activity of the special procedures. Now,

[96] OHCHR, "Special Procedures of the Human Rights Council," http://www.ohchr.org/EN/HRBodies/SP/Pages/CountryvisitsF-M.aspx and http://www.ohchr.org/EN/HRBodies/SP/Pages/CountryvisitsN-Z.aspx. Russia has received visits from several special rapporteurs since 2003, including those on internally displaced persons, violence against women, racism, independence of judges and lawyers, and indigenous people. Senegal has received four special procedures (arbitrary detention, sale of children, migrants, and education). The Maldives also received four (religious freedom, independence of judges and lawyers, housing, and freedom of expression).

almost 20 years later, High Commissioner Navi Pillay states that it is the other way around: the special procedures facilitate the work of the High Commissioners as they address human rights crises worldwide. Pillay, Arbour, and Ramcharan have all commended the special procedures as early warning mechanisms that alert the world and press for reforms at the national level. The High Commissioner's briefings at the Security Council are many, and are awaited by the media and diplomats seeking authoritative information on rights violations. More could be done to support the capacity of special procedures to respond effectively to human rights abuses and crises. Similarly, the work and knowledge of special procedures could be more effectively utilized by the High Commissioner.

Intellectual and Policy Leadership

As the overall official in charge of the human rights program, the High Commissioner has a key role in providing leadership – on both intellectual and policy priorities – to the special procedures.

The High Commissioner can strategically shape and utilize the expertise of the special procedures to defend universality of human rights and the application of standards. Challenges about universality have emerged anew, despite the Vienna World Conference's Declaration. A number of states have promoted condemnation of 'defamation of religions' which has tried to establish that religions, rather than individuals, have rights. Several 'incitement' workshops mentioned above show how the High Commissioner can bolster support for the human rights paradigm by engaging special procedures and others. Recently, some states have been pressing to elevate 'traditional values' over universal rights. Still others assert extremist and even discriminatory interpretations of religious freedom. Greater use of strategic partnership and more coordination with special procedures by the High Commissioner can uphold universality of human rights norms, especially when challenged.

The High Commissioner should plan policy-focused consultations and retreats with relevant special rapporteurs on the challenges of 'traditional values' and other items aimed at undermining the scope and content of universal human rights. If the Secretary-General's plan for a new world conference to mark Beijing Plus 20 advances, the High Commissioner will want to ensure it upholds all the human rights of women affirmed in the 1995 Beijing Declaration and Programme of Action and thereafter. Other topics meriting strategic consultations include the 'right to truth' and non-discrimination on grounds of sexual orientation.

Similarly, the High Commissioner should organize meetings and separate discussions with relevant special procedure mandate holders regarding key countries. The situation in Syria and its implications for the region is one obvious example, as are other countries already examined by special procedures or commissions of inquiry. The High Commissioner should be present throughout these consultations.

Better Partnerships

High Commissioners have occasionally endorsed and reiterated the findings and recommendations of the special procedures. Much more can be done so that the High Commissioner consults directly regarding country visits and priority topics, enhancing collaborative partnerships.

The High Commissioner is not and need not be a 'super-rapporteur,' but could certainly do more to utilize the expertise of the human rights mechanisms. The 48 special procedures possess an extraordinary array of sophisticated insight. Yet, on substance, former and current special procedures that I have interviewed claim they have not been consulted when the High Commissioner speaks on an issue squarely within their competence. Inside the Secretariat, special efforts now enable the special procedures to offer joint statements on issues within their competence.

The High Commissioner should plan to meet and consult with relevant mandate holders in connection with each of her country visits and prior to issuing public statements, whenever possible. The High Commissioner should bring one or more special rapporteurs with her to New York headquarters, when appropriate, or on her travels to other venues to demonstrate that they are valued resources of the UN's human rights programs.

Ongoing Protection

High Commissioners have provided protection for the special rapporteurs when the latter were challenged, either individually or jointly by governments. Despite the years that have passed and the growth of the special procedure system, the antipathy of states towards these independent experts has continued, leading to a code of conduct, a coordination committee, and more formalized selection techniques.

The High Commissioners have the responsibility to enhance the trustworthiness of the special procedure system. When confronted with cases that do not meet those standards, they have faced a dilemma: to criticize the rapporteur would call into question the independence of the mandate holder and feed into the political agenda of those seeking to stop country-specific scrutiny of human rights violations. Not to criticize creates doubt regarding the credibility and principles of the High Commissioner, and the integrity of the UN human rights system as a whole.

Though the code of conduct is in place as an accountability mechanism for the special procedures, there is currently no impartial means of enforcing it. Moreover, the special procedures are not accountable to the High Commissioner, who neither creates their mandate nor appoints the mandate holder. The High Commissioner is left in charge but not in charge, and is most effective when speaking out, but unable to speak out strongly in criticism of the system she coordinates. The High Commissioner should find added opportunities to support the independence of the mandates and to enhance their credibility. The High Commissioners should also provide more prominence to the special procedures in their annual reports. Finally, the High Commissioner should explore means of ensuring an effective accountability mechanism, which is impartial and recognized as fair by all parties.

Greater Resources and Logistical Support

The High Commissioners have overall managerial responsibility for the secretariat office that services rapporteurs with staff, research, and logistical and financial support.

The special procedure mandate holders routinely request an enhanced level of logistical and financial support. Indeed, they criticize every High Commissioner and the OHCHR about facilitation issues. The High Commissioners have had neither the time, nor resources, nor inclination, to micro-manage such matters, as they face so many other substantive crises of their own. Coordination takes time and resources, and brings little credit to the High Commissioner engaged in the world of media, governments, and popular demands. Yet resources are key to the effectiveness of the special procedures. The High Commissioner should make extra efforts to facilitate the special procedures' work by prioritizing greater regular budget funding for them, by raising voluntary funds for their work, and by enabling them to continue to raise funds independently. The High Commissioner should ensure adequate secretariat services for each special procedure, as well as improve training, background preparation, and logistics for country visits by the mandate holders. The larger number of country visits by special procedures, and their role in the Universal Periodic Review, makes this particularly urgent.

Enhanced Visibility and Follow Up

The High Commissioners are also engaged in enhancing the visibility of the special procedures, both inside the UN system and to the public. The High Commissioners have affirmed the importance of addressing human rights violations and reporting publicly on them, but do not appear to assign the special procedures a high priority in their own statements. Written and oral statements referencing the special procedures are comparatively few, and, as indicated above, the mandate holders complain of a lack of consultation.

Although she has many other responsibilities and her own separate mandate on preventing violations, the High Commissioner should make every effort to cite recommendations by special procedures in her public remarks on every country visit, particularly when she has consulted with them before the travel commences.

The High Commissioner should make every effort to be present, in person, when the special procedure mandate holders present their reports and conduct interactive dialogues at the Human Rights Council and General Assembly. The High Commissioner should consider asking questions at those sessions, reinforcing the findings of each special procedure, and raising relevant follow up matters.

Finally, the High Commissioner should continue to assign a separate media specialist to the special procedures.

Conclusion: The Need for Strategic Management

One would expect that the High Commissioners, based at the top of the UN human rights hierarchy, and facing criticisms, would be able to comment upon or amplify the voices of the mandate holders, as circumstances require. That has not happened. The relationship of the High Commissioners and the special procedures is still largely arm's-length. In part this is because the special procedures are 'independent.' But it also stems from the overlap of their roles, particularly with regard to country visits and public statements on violations. As a result, the High Commissioners and the special procedures are occasionally rivals. Both focus on violations, with the High Commissioner having the much broader mandate. Country visits involve investigations as well as dialogues with officials. The High Commissioner has a separate mandate to play an active role in preventing violations worldwide, in addition to the mandate to manage and coordinate the human rights machinery, including the special procedures.

The High Commissioner should be more strategic in utilizing the expertise of the special procedures, particularly in finding ways to follow up on their recommendations. The High Commissioner should also consult special procedures about which countries to visit, what to seek, and how to press afterwards to implement their recommendations.

As the special procedures are accountable to the states, not the High Commissioner, they have had little incentive to accept oversight or coordination from the High Commissioner. This relationship merits serious re-examination, as the system of special procedures has grown so large as to be unwieldy, with 48 separate mandates, many of which overlap with one another.

The High Commissioner, as a leader and manager, has a responsibility to ensure the credibility of the human rights program, which is itself affected by the credibility of the world organization as a whole. The reverse is also true. The special procedures have brought expertise, facts, and reality into the work of the UN's human rights program, which has long been consumed by theoretical standards and aspirational goals. Some of the procedures have been challenged by governments for what appear to be political reasons – because their conclusions are unwelcome – or in an effort to weaken or silence them. But some of the rapporteurs have also confronted the world body with credibility problems, either because of bias, lack of judgment, or questionable integrity. Senior UN officials, including the High Commissioners, have been reluctant to criticize the independent special procedure mandate holders, particularly for crossing the line into inappropriate actions.

Faced with such challenges and problems, the High Commissioners have tried to speak positively about the special procedures, to strengthen and protect them, and to move on with their own work. Future leadership by the High Commissioner will require ensuring that the independence of the special procedures is maintained and protected, the eradication of human rights violations remains a pre-eminent goal, and the special procedure mandate holders can be reasonably accountable to their diverse stakeholders, victims as well as governments. By focusing more on strategic coordination and using the levers of leadership – rhetorical, substantive and organizational – the High Commissioner can make strides towards a stronger and more effective special procedure system, and strengthen the post in the process.

PROTECTION THROUGH PRESENCE: THE OFFICE OF THE HIGH COMMISSIONER FOR HUMAN RIGHTS IN THE FIELD

Christen L. Broecker

Introduction

Since the establishment of the post of UN High Commissioner for Human Rights, the individuals who have served in the position have overseen a significant expansion of the UN's human rights activities outside Geneva. The OHCHR field presences created to date have varying mandates; some are complex, with both 'protective' and 'promotional' mandates; some are focused solely on delivering technical assistance; some provide support to the human rights sections of peace operations managed by the Department of Political Affairs (DPA) or the Department of Peacekeeping Operations (DPKO); some advise UN Country Teams (UNCTs); and some are regional or sub-regional presences.[1] All OHCHR field presences are expected to assist in human rights capacity building, coordinate activities related to human rights, advocate for non-governmental organizations (NGOs) vis-à-vis the Government to facilitate the work of NGOs on the ground; serve as a focal point on human rights for all non-governmental institutions; participate in various human rights activities; disseminate human rights materials; and provide information on human rights and relevant international and domestic laws.[2]

This chapter details the efforts of the various High Commissioners to expand OHCHR's presence in the field; describes emblematic examples of such field presences, highlighting both examples of success and of shortcomings encountered; and identifies challenges that the current and future High Commissioners will face in ensuring that the field activities of OHCHR make as significant a contribution to human rights protection as possible in the coming years.

---

1 OHCHR, "Making a Difference Where it Matters Most: OHCHR's Support to Implementation at Country Level," http://www.ohchr.org/EN/Countries/Pages/MapOfficesIndex.aspx.

2 OHCHR, *2011 Annual Report*, 426–437.

Background

Prior to the end of the Cold War, the UN's human rights activities were largely carried out in Geneva, including through the formulation of standards, the carrying out of debates and adoption of resolutions by the Commission on Human Rights, the work of the independent UN treaty bodies; and, beginning in the 1980s, though the establishment of 'special procedures': working groups with a mandate to investigate the commission of certain violations and though brief visits to states by a handful of thematic and country-specific special rapporteurs, who then reported their findings to the Commission on Human Rights. The Centre for Human Rights in Geneva supported the work of the treaty bodies and the special procedures, and also offered a small technical assistance program to governments aimed at training officials abroad or promoting in-country structural changes that would increase human rights protection.[3] The UN's peacekeeping missions did not monitor human rights violations or protect civilians; rather, they were principally devoted to monitoring cease-fires, controlling buffer zones between countries, supervising and observing elections, and training officials.[4]

By 1990, some states that had turned to the UN for assistance in negotiating peace settlements in the aftermath of conflict and political transitions became receptive to the new idea of mandating UN staff abroad not only to monitor cease-fires and elections but also to monitor and promote human rights. Accordingly, human rights components were integrated into four UN field missions over the early 1990s, in El Salvador, Haiti, Colombia, and Guatemala.[5] These human rights missions were directed from New York, rather than from Geneva, and on a somewhat ad-hoc basis. A review of these missions by the Aspen Institute in 1995 concluded that "every human rights mission mounted by the United Nations has been hampered by the need to reinvent the bureaucratic wheel. ... The absence of a permanent professional office within the United Nations to establish and guide these missions has exacerbated problems for field

---

[3] OHCHR, "Advisory Services and Technical Cooperation in the Field of Human Rights," UN Fact Sheet No.3 Rev.1 (1996).

[4] See United Nations, "Honouring 60 Years of United Nations Peacekeeping," http://www.un.org/events/peacekeeping60/1980s.shtml for a chronology of all UN peacekeeping operations with descriptions of their mandates.

[5] Ian Martin, "A New Frontier: The Early Experience and Future of International Human Rights Field Operations," *Netherlands Quarterly of Human Rights*, Vol. 16/2 (1998), 121–139.

staff."[6] The assessment noted that the Geneva-based Centre for Human Rights lacked adequately experienced staff to serve this function and that its relationship with the UN's New York headquarters was far from close.

The creation of the post of High Commissioner presented an unprecedented opportunity for the expansion of the UN's human rights activities, both in Geneva and into the field. While the High Commissioner is given the responsibility in UN General Assembly Resolution 48/141 for promoting universal respect for and observance of human rights, including "providing, through the Centre for Human Rights and other appropriate institutions, advisory services and technical and financial assistance, at the request of the State concerned,"[7] there is no specific requirement to seek the approval of the political organs of the UN in order to establish a human rights field presence abroad. The establishment of the post of UN High Commissioner for Human Rights in 1993 thus presented an opportunity to extend the UN's human rights protection efforts outside Geneva and into the field in a systematic manner. However, it was not without significant challenges: prior to 1993, the UN Secretariat, and particularly the Centre for Human Rights, had little experience in establishing, staffing, coordinating, or running human rights field presences. Developing this capacity would be a major challenge for the High Commissioner, one that remains pressing today.

The Role of the High Commissioners in Building OHCHR's Presence in the Field

The High Commissioners have accomplished the expansion of UN human rights activities outside Geneva as a result of both the merging of the Centre for Human Rights into the Office of the High Commissioner for Human Rights (OHCHR) in 1998 and, more significantly, the establishment of an impressive network of field presences.

José Ayala Lasso

At the time that José Ayala Lasso began his term as High Commissioner for Human Rights in April 1994, the Office of the High Commissioner was formally assigned only three professional staff (the High Commissioner,

[6] The Aspen Institute. *Honoring Human Rights*, ed. Alice H. Henkin (The Hauge: Kluwer Law International, 2000).

[7] UN General Assembly. Resolution 48/141, "High Commissioner for the promotion and protection of all human rights," UN Doc. A/RES/48/141, December 20, 1993.

his assistant, and a representative in New York).[8] The rest of the UN's human rights bureaucracy was designated to remain within the UN Centre for Human Rights, under the direction of a separate official, the Assistant Secretary-General for Human Rights. Around 80 professional staff were responsible for administration, handling communications, supporting the special procedures, supporting the activities of the human rights treaty-monitoring bodies, providing technical advisory services, issuing publications, and managing other priorities of the Centre.[9] After his appointment as the High Commissioner, Ayala Lasso began the difficult work of restructuring the Centre to increase its effectiveness. The relationship between the Office of the High Commissioner and the Centre for Human Rights nevertheless proved contentious.[10] After Ayala Lasso's resignation in February 1997, the Secretary-General placed the Centre under the management of the High Commissioner, within the OHCHR.

Despite the meager size of his office and the unprecedented nature of his office and work, Ayala Lasso expended significant time and energy during his term as High Commissioner in creating a series of nine OHCHR field offices and an additional nine smaller OHCHR presences abroad. In part, this effort was driven by necessity, as Ayala Lasso began his work as High Commissioner the day before the presidents of Rwanda and Burundi were killed in a plane crash on 6 April 1994, an event which sparked the genocide in Rwanda and threatened to do the same in Burundi. Ayala Lasso went on to establish a field office in Rwanda staffed by nearly 150 field officers, as well as an office in Burundi, for which he secured voluntary commitments from donor states to fund a $3.14 million technical assistance program over three years. Ayala Lasso also established a field office in Cambodia in 1993 following the end of the mandate of the UN Transitional Authority there and established a significant human rights field office in Colombia in 1997. He also facilitated the establishment of technical assistance projects in a number of other countries – with over 400 such activities reported to have occurred in 1996 alone.[11] In his farewell address to the Commission on Human Rights, Ayala Lasso explained

---

[8] See Andrew Clapham, "Creating the High Commissioner for Human Rights: The Outside Story," European Journal of International Law, Vol. 5, 556–568 (1994), 565.

[9] Alfred De Zayas, "The United Nations High Commissioner of Human Rights," (Lecture, University of Postdam, Berlin, 1994), http://alfreddezayas.com/Lectures/HIGHcompotsdam_de.shtml.

[10] Academy of European Law, "The Protection of Human Rights in Europe Volume VIII Book 2," (The Hague: Kluwer Law International, 1997), 156.

[11] Report of the Secretary-General, *Technical Cooperation in the Field of Human Rights*, UN Doc. E/CN.4/1997/86, February 25, 1997, para. 16.

that he had sought to expand the human rights technical assistance program "to the maximum degree."[12]

At the time of his resignation in February 1997, Ayala Lasso had come to preside over a vastly increased UN human rights field presence, comprising 289 field workers and consultants, largely concentrated in Rwanda, Cambodia, and Burundi, but also present in Bosnia-Herzegovina, Croatia, the Former Yugoslavia, Mongolia, Zaire, Georgia, Haiti, Latvia, Malawi, Gaza, Papua New Guinea, and Togo.[13]

Mary Robinson

Upon assuming the High Commissioner post in September 2007, Mary Robinson sought to address the lack of resources allocated to it. Here, Robinson benefited from the above-mentioned merger of the Office of the High Commissioner and the Centre for Human Rights in 1998. She also enjoyed significant success in increasing the amount of voluntary contributions received by the Office, launching the first annual funding appeal in 2000 and raising $44 million in the process.[14]

Robinson also continued Ayala Lasso's pattern of engaging both in technical assistance agreements with states and seeking to expand the presence of human rights monitors in the field. For example, she was able to establish a field operation for Kosovo within a week of the beginning of the emergency there in 1999. Robinson expanded the operation of the OHCHR office in Cambodia to a total of 40 staff and also facilitated the expansion of the OHCHR office in Colombia. She also enabled greater participation of OHCHR staff with other parts of the UN system, such as by deploying a member of OHCHR to participate in the Integrated Mission Task Force on Afghanistan. By 2001 OHCHR had field presences in 26 countries and technical cooperation agreements and projects in over 50 countries.[15]

---

[12] Philip Alston, "Neither Fish nor Fowl: The Quest to Define the Role of the UN High Commissioner for Human Rights," European Journal of International Law, Vol. 8.2 (1997), 321–33.

[13] *Report of the United Nations High Commissioner for Human Rights*, UN Doc. A/51/36 (1996).

[14] Andrew Clapham, "UN High Commissioner for Human Rights: Achievements and Frustrations" (paper presented at the Symposium on the United Nations High Commissioner for Human Rights: The First Ten Years of Office and the Next, Columbia Law School, New York, NY February 17–18, 2003), http://www2.law.columbia.edu/hri/symposium/ClaphamPaper.htm.

[15] UN General Assembly, "Report of the United Nations High Commissioner for Human Rights," UN Doc. A/56/36 (2001), 11.

Sergio Vieira de Mello and Bertrand Ramcharan

Shortly after he assumed the post of High Commissioner in 2002, Sergio Vieira de Mello stated that "the principal goal of OHCHR work" was "the creation of strong national protection systems, working with and through UN country teams, and where they exist, UN peace support missions."[16] Vieira de Mello was instrumental in securing a role for OHCHR human rights officers in the humanitarian hubs in Cyprus and Jordan established before and during the US war in Iraq in 2003. Unfortunately, his untimely death prevented him from having as significant of an impact on the management and functioning of the OHCHR and its field presences as observers had hoped. Bertrand Ramcharan would serve as Acting High Commissioner for Human Rights from May 2003 to July 2004, and during this time, he presided over a modest expansion of the Office's presence in the field.

By 2004, the High Commissioner's office managed 33 OHCHR field presences,[17] including six regional/sub-regional offices, as well as a number of technical cooperation missions in countries including Azerbaijan, China, Mongolia, Morocco, Russia, and Sri Lanka, with a total of 350 staff members in those presences. OHCHR maintained several types of field presences: for example, in Africa alone, it had three regional representatives (Eastern, Central, and Southern Africa), two stand-alone offices (Burundi and DRC), technical cooperation projects in cooperation with UN country teams (UNCTs) (Angola, Sudan, and Liberia), and a human rights component of a UN peacekeeping mission (Sierra Leone).

Louise Arbour

Louise Arbour's tenure as High Commissioner was marked by a significant expansion of the Office's field presences, made possible by a significant increase in resources resulting from the 2005 World Summit. That event marked the 60th anniversary of the UN, and the Secretary-General recommended that the Office's funds be doubled. At that point the Office expended $265 million annually, with one-third coming from the regular

---

16 Sergio Vieira de Mello, "Statement" (Heads of Field Presences Meeting, Geneva, Switzerland, November 18, 2002), http://www.unhchr.ch/huricane/huricane.nsf/view01/68103BF81D03FF49C1256C7600353A2B?opendocument.

17 Afghanistan, Angola, Bolivia, Bosnia-Herzegovina, Burundi, Cambodia, CAR, Colombia, Cote D'Ivoire, DRC, Ethiopia/Eritrea, Georgia, Guatemala, Guinea-Bissau, Guyana, Haiti, Liberia, Macedonia, Mexico, Nepal, Sierra Leone, Sri Lanka, Sudan, and Tajikistan; also regional/sub-regional field offices in Cameroon, Ethiopia, South Africa, Lebanon, the Occupied Palestinian Territories, Thailand, Kazakhstan, and Chile.

budget and two-thirds from voluntary contributions. Arbour's Plan of Action for the OHCHR, published the same year, emphasizes that "engagement and dialogue with countries will be the primary means through which OHCHR works to ensure the implementation of human rights," and as its first area of action anticipated "greater country engagement though an expansion of geographic desks [in Geneva], increased deployment of human rights staff to countries and regions, the establishment of standing capacities for rapid deployment, investigations, field support, human rights capacity building, advice and assistance, and work on transitional justice and the rule of law."[18]

During Arbour's tenure, the staff of OHCHR increased to 947 people, and in-country offices grew significantly. She opened offices in Nepal, Guatemala, and Uganda in 2005 and in Togo in November 2006, and signed a host country agreement with Bolivia in February 2007. During her term in office, Angola refused to renew the agreement for the OHCHR office and OHCHR closed its technical cooperation program in Skopje and its country offices in Sarajevo and Belgrade. Arbour opened a regional office for West Africa in Dakar, Senegal, entered into an agreement with Kyrgyzstan for the opening of a Regional Office in Central Asia, and, at the request of the General Assembly, began negotiations with Qatar for the establishment of a regional human rights training and documentation centre for the South-West Asia and the Arab region. At the time of Arbour's departure in July 2008, OHCHR was running and supporting a total of 53 field presences, including nine regional presences, nine country offices, human rights components in 17 UN peace missions, and human rights advisers to 16 UN country teams.[19]

Arbour took another significant step in establishing in 2006[20] a Rapid Response Unit to support the work of OHCHR by swiftly deploying personnel to the field, whether by conducting or supporting fact-finding missions and commissions of inquiry that investigate serious allegations of human rights abuses or providing technical assistance to governments in transition or turmoil, at the request of the Human Rights Council or another political organ of the UN, or at the initiative of the High Commissioner.[21]

---

[18] Louise Arbour, "Plan of action drawn up by the United Nations High Commissioner for Human Rights," in Report of the Secretary-General, *In larger freedom: towards development, security and human rights for all,"* Addendum 3, UN Doc. A/59/2005/Add.3, May 26, 2005.

[19] OHCHR, *2008 Annual Report*, 68. Note that this figure includes OHCHR's Angola office, which closed in mid-2008.

[20] OHCHR, *2006 Annual Report*, 15.

[21] See e.g. OHCHR, *2012 Annual Report*, 320–321.

Navi Pillay

In her four years as High Commissioner, Navi Pillay has presided over a modest expansion of the OHCHR field presences. Pillay entered into agreements for the establishment of OHCHR country offices with Mauritania in September 2009 and Guinea in May 2010 and inaugurated offices in Tunisia in 2011 and Yemen in 2012. Pillay also opened an OHCHR regional office for Europe in October 2009, for South America in September 2009 and for North Africa in 2012; and opened the United Nations Human Rights Training and Documentation Centre for South-West Asia and the Arab Region in Doha, Qatar, in May 2009. At the end of 2012, OHCHR was running or supporting 59 field presences, including 13 country or stand-alone offices[22] 13 regional presences,[23] human rights components in 15 UN peace missions,[24] and human rights advisers to 18 UN Country Teams.[25]

One development over the course of Navi Pillay's tenure as High Commissioner has been the increasing use of OHCHR's rapid-response capacity, on the initiative of the High Commissioner as well as at the instruction of the Human Rights Council. While the rapid-response capacity has been deployed in the context of supporting fact-finding missions and commissions of inquiry created by the Human Rights Council during Pillay's tenure,[26] OHCHR has also fielded rapid response missions on its own initiative. Some examples of the use of this capacity include missions to Honduras following the coup in 2009; to Madagascar to provide

22 Ibid., 181–183. These include country offices in Bolivia, Cambodia, Colombia, Guatemala, Guinea, Mauritania, Mexico, Togo, Tunisia, Uganda, and Yemen and two stand-alone offices in Kosovo and the Occupied Palestinian Territory.

23 Ibid. This includes regional offices in East Africa (Addis Ababa), North Africa (temporarily in Tunisia), Southern Africa (Pretoria), West Africa (Dakar), South-East Asia (Bangkok), the Pacific (Suva), the Middle East (Beirut), Central Asia (Bishkek), Europe (Brussels), Central America (Panama City) and South America (Santiago de Chile); a sub-regional centre for human rights and democracy for Central Africa (Yaoundé); and a Training and Documentation Centre for South-West Asia and the Arab Region (Doha).

24 Ibid, 207. These are in Afghanistan, Burundi, Central African Republic, Côte d'Ivoire, the Democratic Republic of the Congo (DRC), Guinea-Bissau, Haiti, Iraq, Liberia, Libya, Sierra Leone, Somalia, South Sudan, Sudan (Darfur) and Timor-Leste.

25 Ibid. These are in Chad, Ecuador, Honduras, Kenya, Madagascar, Moldova, Niger, Papua New Guinea, Paraguay, Russian Federation, Rwanda, Serbia, Sri Lanka, the Southern Caucasus (based in Tbilisi and covering Armenia, Azerbaijan and Georgia), Tajikistan, the former Yugoslav Republic of Macedonia and Ukraine, and as of year-end 2012, the Office was in the process of recruiting advisers to the UN Country Teams in Timor-Leste, Malawi, and Mali, to be deployed in 2013.

26 See the chapter in this volume by Suzanne Nossel and Christen Broecker for more on cases in which OHCHR's rapid response capacity has been deployed to support commissions of inquiry and OHCHR fact-finding missions.

technical assistance during a political crisis in 2009; to Gabon to monitor human rights during presidential elections in 2009; to Iraq to provide temporary assistance to the UN Assistance Mission; to Haiti in the aftermath of the January 2010 earthquake; to Togo to monitor human rights during elections in 2010; to Guinea to monitor human rights during elections in 2010; to Mali to serve as human rights advisers to the UN Country Team in 2012; and to South Sudan to support the UN peacekeeping mission's human rights investigations in 2012.[27]

OHCHR's Field Presences and Protection – Emblematic Cases and Challenges

The following examples of OHCHR field presences established at various points in time since the creation of the post of High Commissioner illustrate some of the complexities of human rights field officers' work and the challenges they and the High Commissioners for human rights have faced in implementing their mandates. It should be noted that this section, and the recommendations that follow, are particularly focused on challenges facing OHCHR in connection with its 'stand-alone' field presences (country and regional offices) rather than its 'collaborative' presences (advisers to UN Country Teams and components of peacekeeping missions). William G. O'Neill's chapter in this volume specifically addresses the unique set of challenges that arise in the context of 'collaborative' field presences, and particularly human rights components of peacekeeping missions.

Complex 'Protective/Promotional' Missions

Field presences with both a protective and promotional mandate face a number of challenges. These include discerning how best to strike a balance between human rights monitoring activities and the provision of technical assistance, how to ensure that monitoring activities result in effective human rights protection by the host country, and how to ensure that technical cooperation activities have a measurable impact on the ongoing human rights crises necessitating the existence of the monitoring component of the mission. High Commissioners have grappled with these challenges in a variety of contexts.

---

[27] OHCHR, "Office of the High Commissioner for Human Rights in the World: Making Human Rights a Reality on the Ground," http://www.ohchr.org/EN/Countries/Pages/WorkInField.aspx. See also OHCHR Annual Report 2012, 330.

The OHCHR office in Colombia, established by José Ayala Lasso, is one example of a complex field presence. The objectives of the office were "to provide technical assistance, monitor the human rights situation in the country, receive complaints and allegations of human rights violations and other abuses, including breaches of humanitarian norms ... follow up the complaints and allegations received with the national authorities and international human rights bodies, and report periodically to the High Commissioner, who would in turn report to the Commission on Human Rights." The office continues to operate today, and has often been referred to as a very successful effort by the OHCHR. As Mary Robinson detailed in a January 2000 speech,

> Its constant monitoring through regular visits to the field and contacts with the relevant authorities, the different parties to the conflict, the NGO community, the church, the displaced and representatives of civil society allow the Office to have an understanding of the highly complex situation that Colombians face in their day-to-day lives. The Office, through its interventions with the authorities, exercises its preventive function by alerting them to imminent massacres or displacements of people. Efforts are currently being undertaken to set up an alert system that will increase the Colombian authorities' capacity to intervene in time to prevent human rights violations. On several occasions the Office has been invited to present views concerning national legislation. ... [T]he Office has concluded six agreements with key local authorities ... [that] aim at, for example, assisting the government to elaborate a National Plan of Action on Human Rights; improving the system of reception of complaints of the Office of the Ombudsperson; assisting the Office of the Public Prosecutor in improving the system for protection of witnesses and victims of human rights victims...[28]

Additionally, the presence of the OHCHR office in Colombia appeared occasionally to facilitate the work of other UN officials working to negotiate a settlement to the ongoing conflict there. In a 2004 survey of UN personnel on their views on the OHCHR's field work, officials from the Department of Political Affairs (DPA) described the OHCHR office in Colombia as playing a useful role as 'bad cop,' and enabling staff from DPA to take a harder line on significant human rights issues in discussions between the parties to the conflict in the country, and providing information and draft language to the Secretary-General on the situation there in advance of a statement by him on negotiations between the parties.

---

[28] Mary Robinson, "Human Rights Activities in the Field" (Speech, Spanish Diplomatic School, Madrid, January 2000), http://www.unhchr.ch/huricane/huricane.nsf/view01/86B36FD19520CC058025686D0036631B?opendocument. See Victor Rodriguez-Rescia's chapter in this volume for more on the OHCHR office in Colombia.

Another successful example of a 'complex' OHCHR field presence was the OHCHR office in Nepal. An evaluation of the office by a private firm said of the office's performance between 2005 and 2008:

> The office rapidly and quite boldly extended itself in the field, combining advocacy and visible presence towards the objective of direct physical protection against abuses. It established sub-offices throughout the country, assisting human rights defenders facing grave threats, issuing prominent reports calling attention to serious abuses during the conflict, visiting arrested human rights defenders and political party activists in detention and calling attention to the dubious legality of their detention. At key moments of public unrest between 2005 and the April 2008 elections, the office mobilized all its resources to have a prominent preventive presence at demonstrations ... this presence is widely credited with reducing the risk of massive violence.[29]

Both the independent evaluator and NGOs that worked closely with the office stated that the Nepal office's placement of field officers outside the capital city had served as a critical source of information through their monitoring and investigations, and provided political space for the parties to the conflict in Nepal during the course of a multi-year peace process.[30]

However, in 2010 and 2011, the government, in the context of a resurgence of the political influence of the army, began pressing OHCHR for a significant reformulation of the office's mandate. Over time, the government insisted that the office's field posts outside the capital be closed and that the OHCHR cease monitoring human rights cases and transfer this responsibility to the country's National Human Rights Commission (NHRC). NGO observers voiced concern that due to the persistence of a culture of impunity in Nepal, the absence of OHCHR monitors in the field could put local human rights defenders in jeopardy. Advocates also argued that that the NHRC clearly lacked the capacity to handle the caseload previously shouldered by OHCHR, and that some NHRC members had publicly been calling for OHCHR's withdrawal from the country for more than a year.[31] Indeed, an independent evaluation had described the

---

29 Fieldview Solutions, "Evaluation of the work of OHCHR in Nepal," 12 November 2010, http://www.fieldviewsolutions.org/fv-publications/Evaluation_of_the_work_of_OHCHR_in_Nepal.pdf.

30 Ibid.

31 See in Asian Centre for Human Rights, "OHCHR Nepal and the log frame for impunity," June 3, 2011, 9, n. 24, http://www.achrweb.org/countries/nepal/OHCHR-NEPAL2011.pdf (citing Commissioner Dr. K.B. Rokaya as saying that OHCHR "must leave as soon as possible because it has been weakening human rights movement in Nepal...").

relationship between the NHRC and the OHCHR as "poisonous."[32] By January 2011 OHCHR-Nepal's mission had been redefined as supporting the government's three-year National Human Rights Action Plan (NHRAP), despite the fact that the Action Plan did not include plans to pursue accountability for the many human rights violations, including those perpetrated by the army, previously documented by OHCHR-Nepal. Critics of the OHCHR's dramatically altered mandate in Nepal argued:

> ... [E]ngagement is a means to an end, not an end [in itself]. There is value in engagement but not, as is so often the case, when it is mistaken for influence. ... The political risk ... is that the engagement provides *de facto* political support for a continuance of the current direction of policy; a policy that seeks to avoid accountability and in so doing undermines large sections of the peace agreement and the aspirations of the people of Nepal.[33]

Regrettably, the mandate of the Office in Nepal was not renewed by the Government of Nepal at the end of 2011, with the result that the Office ceased all new substantive work in early December 2011 and formally closed on March 31, 2012.[34] Yet the work of the Nepal Office would continue to bear fruit: in October 2012, over the objections of the Nepalese government, OHCHR Geneva published a groundbreaking 233-page report, based in part on information gathered by the Nepal Office, analyzing conflict-related violations of international human rights law and international humanitarian law perpetrated in Nepal between February 1996 and 21 November 2006. OHCHR also made public a Transitional Justice Reference Archive (TRJA) to accompany the report. This database, which OHCHR originally developed to be an offline reference tool for the use of the Nepali transitional justice commissions, was modified[35] and released to the public when these commissions had not been created six years after the conclusion of the conflict. In a foreword to the report, High Commissioner Navi Pillay noted that Nepal had failed to enact the necessary legislation to create transitional justice mechanisms to hold perpetrators of serious violations of international human rights and humanitarian law accountable or for the state to acknowledge the

---

[32] Final evaluation of European Union support to the United Nations Office of the High Commissioner for Human Rights Field Operation Nepal Evaluation undertaken by independent consultants Daniel Alberman and Govinda Bandi in August 2008. Asian Centre for Human Rights, "OHCHR Nepal and the log frame for impunity," June 3, 2011, n. 23.

[33] Ibid.

[34] OHCHR, "Welcome," http://nepal.ohchr.org/en/index.html.

[35] OHCHR, "The Nepal Conflict Report," http://www.ohchr.org/EN/Countries/Asia Region/Pages/NepalConflictReport.aspx.

suffering of victims and their families, and suggested that the Nepal Conflict Report and TJRA would assist the government and people of Nepal in addressing these shortcomings.[36]

Technical Assistance Missions

Field presences with a purely technical assistance mission also face a number of challenges. These include ensuring that the cooperation activities agreed upon between OHCHR and the host country actually give rise to discernible changes in law, policy, or the behavior of the authorities, and that local observers are able to recognize these positive changes when they are achieved.

One example of a technical assistance effort undertaken by OHCHR that enjoyed some success was a project on promotion and protection of human rights in Guatemala from 2002–2003. The project aimed in part to strengthen the Guatemalan government's capacity to undertake verification/monitoring and reporting with regard to its international and national human rights obligations; to provide technical advice on and facilitate coordination and cooperation with international human rights mechanisms; and to provide assistance and advice to the UN system on human rights in Guatemala. A review of the program in late 2003 found that the project had been successful with regard to several of its goals, despite the fact that its total budget was ultimately only fifty percent of that anticipated when it was designed. In particular, the project had successfully supported workshops and seminars for NGOs, raising their awareness regarding international human rights norms; and had also stimulated the interest of NGOs in writing alternative reports to UN treaty bodies on the human rights situation in the country. The project also raised the awareness of government officials regarding human rights norms and treaty reporting obligations, not least through very successfully planning and facilitating the visits of special rapporteurs to Guatemala, whose visits received significant media and government attention and whose reports were seen as very helpful by local human rights activists. In this case, despite the fact that it did not have a protective mandate and was ultimately forced to operate on a much lower budget than originally anticipated, OHCHR could point to clear achievements through its programs in the country.

---

[36] OHCHR, "Nepal Conflict Report 2012,"http://www.ohchr.org/Documents/Countries/NP/OHCHR_Nepal_Conflict_Report2012.pdf.

On the other hand, the effectiveness of some technical assistance missions seems to have been undermined by problems related to the staffing of missions with an adequate number of properly trained personnel, over-ambitious mandates, and questionable lasting impact of the projects carried out. One presence which, despite some successes, exhibited these problems was the OHCHR office in Malawi. OHCHR opened an office in Malawi in late 1994. OHCHR began its technical assistance projects by providing assistance to the government in drafting a National Action Plan for human rights, and thereafter entered into a cooperation agreement with the government that established a range of projects to be undertaken beginning in 1996. These included continuing to support the development and implementation of the national human rights action plan and building the capacity of the Malawi Human Rights Commission.

An assessment of OHCHR-Malawi's performance on these activities from 1996–2002 found that the majority of the programs undertaken by the office had not been as productive as originally hoped. While the Malawi Human Rights Commission was eventually established, as of 2002 the Commission was described as "certainly not fully effective," and it appeared that while OHCHR and other donors hoped that the Commission would dedicate its minimal resources to investigating past human rights abuses, the Commissioners placed a higher priority on carrying out civic education and research on human rights. Regarding the National Human Rights Action Plan, OHCHR first provided support to the drafting process, and following the government's adoption of the plan, the office focused its attention on raising popular awareness about the plan rather than on encouraging the government to implement it. Ultimately, the plan was never put into operation by the government. Nevertheless, the OHCHR office agreed in 2001 to work with the government on drafting another national plan, a decision the evaluators likened to "reinventing the wheel." One justification for the "few" successes of the "over-ambitious and under-funded" office put forward by the evaluators was the "discontinuity of staff" that the office had faced and the failure of a regional office established in Pretoria during that time to ameliorate the problem. Another was the fact that the office had engaged in "no systematic needs assessment, planning, review and impact assessment methodologies" related to its programs.

Enduring Challenges to Effective Protection

With the ability to independently design and deploy field missions came the potential for the High Commissioner to provide protection on the ground and demonstrate to the world the ability of the UN and the international human rights system to make a positive impact on the everyday lives of those imperiled by gross and systematic human rights abuses. However, with the freedom to expand the Office's work and create field offices comes a host of challenges. Many lessons have been learned, while some challenges to effective protection through field presence still remain. Over the course of the past two decades, the High Commissioners have attempted to review and to improve the performance of OHCHR field presences in enhancing human rights protection worldwide. These reviews have revealed a number of enduring challenges to effective field protection, many of which remain relevant today. In particular, the High Commissioners have occasionally come under criticism for insufficient provision of leadership, guidance, and support to OHCHR field operations to ensure they have appropriate mandates, political backing, direction, resources, staff, and training to carry out their work successfully.

The High Commissioners' leadership is critical, in the first instance, in ensuring that all field presences have an appropriate mandate, and one that is structured in such a way as to be achievable and also effective at visibly improving human rights protection on the ground in a reasonable period of time. This has been a challenge for the High Commissioners in part because they are obligated to reach an agreement upon the mandate of every OHCHR field presence with each host government concerned, while simultaneously ensuring that such presences are able adequately to balance monitoring, protection, advocacy, and technical cooperation objectives.

Some observers have noted, for example, that monitoring is a critical function of all human rights field presences, even those that exist solely to provide technical assistance.[37] A key responsibility of the High Commissioner is to ensure that field staff are empowered to conduct research and investigations necessary to reveal what projects and goals should be priorities and whether OHCHR activities in the field are achieving their intended results. High Commissioners should also ensure that reporting undertaken by human rights presences on human rights violations is made available to the public in a timely manner whenever possible, and to refrain from publicizing the findings of human rights monitors on the

[37] Peggy Hicks, "The UN High Commissioner for Human Rights: Conscience for the World," (remarks at conference convened by the Jacob Blaustein Institute for the Advancement of Human Rights, New York, NY, February 7–8, 2012). See also William G. O'Neill's chapter in this volume.

ground for the reason that this could impede efforts at private diplomacy only in truly exceptional cases.[38]

Aside from their role in reaching agreements with host governments on mandates for OHCHR field workers, High Commissioners must also ensure that the mandates agreed upon will be perceived by local human rights defenders and other observers as appropriate and positive in the broader context of the country situation and are achievable and appropriate given the anticipated project budget. High Commissioners should also ensure that the technical cooperation activities to be undertaken by human rights field officers are unique from those undertaken by other donors and that adequate planning procedures are in place.

Another critical role of the High Commissioners has been soliciting funding for the OHCHR to enable it to carry out its human rights objectives in the field. At the time of the establishment of the High Commissioner post, the budgets allocated to the Centre for Human Rights and the OHCHR out of the general UN fund were very small, and even today, OHCHR remains heavily dependent on voluntary contributions. While some of the High Commissioners have been successful in obtaining additional resources, in 2012 OHCHR's total budget still remained a dismal three percent of the entire UN budget.[39] This lack of resources presents a significant obstacle to maintaining effective field presences that future High Commissioners will need to strive to address.

High Commissioners must also ensure that field presences are adequately staffed and that personnel have the training and technical skill to carry out mandated projects. Indeed, critics have noted that high vacancy rates for OHCHR field office positions have had a crippling effect on the work of some presences – as seen in the example of the OHCHR field presence in Malawi, as well as in Nepal, where the leadership position in the OHCHR stand-alone office remained vacant for a significant period of time at a moment in which the host government sought to redefine the office's mandate and limit its activities.[40] On the training front, some have lamented the failure of the High Commissioner and OHCHR staff in Geneva to develop effective guidance and training materials for

38 Ibid.

39 OHCHR, "About OHCHR Funding," http://www.ohchr.org/EN/ABOUTUS/Pages/FundingBudget.aspx.

40 Asian Centre for Human Rights, "OHCHR Nepal and the log frame for impunity," Fieldview Solutions, "Evaluation of the work of OHCHR in Nepal," 12 November 2010, http://www.fieldviewsolutions.org/fv-publications/Evaluation_of_the_work_of_OHCHR_in_Nepal.pdf, 13.

field-based staff. One positive development in this regard, however, has been the High Commissioners' development of an annual 'Meeting of Heads of Field Presences,' at which human rights field officers can exchange information, learn lessons from one another's experiences, and have an opportunity to interact with the High Commissioner in person.

Once field presences have been established, High Commissioners must also show political support for OHCHR personnel and their work so that these are not compromised by the host government or other UN agencies. In the case of stand-alone offices like those in Nepal and Colombia, High Commissioners must work to defend mandates and ensure that personnel in the field receive sufficient administrative support and communication from Geneva. In cases where the OHCHR field presence is integrated into a UN Country Team or peacekeeping force, the High Commissioner should ensure that the work of human rights field offices is sufficiently supported by the resident coordinators and Special Representatives of the Secretary-General leading such efforts. Critics have regretted, for example, the relatively minor role that the High Commissioner and OHCHR seem to play relative to DPKO in guiding the work – both practically and doctrinally – of human rights field staff attached to peacekeeping missions, which represents a particularly significant proportion of the UN's overall field-based human rights activity.

Finally, when High Commissioners visit countries with a human rights field presence, they should ensure that their visits have the effect of mitigating, rather than exacerbating, challenges the field presence may be experiencing. Some have critiqued the High Commissioners for failing to take necessary steps and engage in planning so that visits to countries in which a human rights field presence is operating result in the High Commissioner making public statements and raising popular awareness of her work while achieving tangible gains for the mission and for human rights on the ground. In the absence of such gains, the visits of High Commissioners to such countries may disappoint the raised expectations of the population and damage the credibility of the UN, including the country team.

Conclusion

The High Commissioners' work to expand the activities of the OHCHR on the ground throughout the world over the past decade represents a considerable achievement for the Office and the UN. While some field presences have encountered considerable challenges, others have very clearly demonstrated the unique value and potential of on-the-ground monitoring, protection, training, and capacity-building. The High Commissioners should thus strive to increase the presence of OHCHR in the field in the coming decades. In doing so, however, they must be mindful of the need to increase their leadership, guidance, and support for field staff in the future so that all field presences are able to realize their fullest protective potential.

ENHANCING UN HUMAN RIGHTS WORK ON THE GROUND

William G. O'Neill

Introduction

More than 20 years have passed since the first UN human rights field operation deployed to El Salvador. Over 100 international civilians, with nothing more than an agreement between the two warring parties brokered by negotiators from the UN's Department of Political Affairs (DPA), arrived in a country still at war, with landmines, checkpoints, no-go areas and death squads roaming the landscape.

The United Nations had never mounted such an operation in its then 45-year history. Human rights work largely consisted of the important task of creating treaties and standards, organizing the annual meetings of the Human Rights Commission and its Sub-Commission, and supporting the work of a number of special rapporteurs and working groups. While this standard-setting, annual meetings, and the work of 'special procedures,' in UN parlance, was crucial, it was a radically different challenge to identify, recruit, and deploy civilians to a war zone. These human rights officers would have to monitor, verify, and report on violations of human rights and the laws of war by both parties to the conflict. They would need vehicles, communications equipment, offices, housing, and other logistical support. Moreover, they would need guidance on how to do their work: how to interview victims, witnesses, and government officials. They would need to know how to conduct a proper prison visit, monitor a demonstration, and then write up a report that captured the key details and propose recommendations to address the violations documented.

The human rights officers would not be there for just a week or so, but would stay for months, following up with visits, meetings, and other interventions. They were to enjoy functional diplomatic immunity and their correspondence, offices, living quarters, and vehicles were immune from search. They were to establish offices all over El Salvador and be able to travel freely, enter any place of detention without prior notice, examine case files, observe trials, and talk to anyone without threat of reprisals.

Where would the UN find people with the experience, skills, and language (Spanish in this case) ability to do such stressful, sensitive, and demanding work? Who would train them at the outset, and what would the training include? No one had answers to these questions in 1991 yet time was of the essence. The war had been going on for 20 years, over 70,000 people had been killed, and a chance for peace was there but fleeting.

The Human Rights Centre in Geneva had no role in the conception, organization, or realization of the first UN human rights field operation, ONUSAL, known by its Spanish acronym. UN officials in New York, relying on their own personal network of leading human rights experts at organizations like Amnesty International, the Lawyers Committee for Human Rights, and Human Rights Watch, convened meetings where human rights priorities, reporting, and recruiting personnel were discussed. The Mission soon began work.

Barely two years later, in 1993, Haiti was facing a crisis following a violent military coup in late 1991 that had chased from office the hugely popular and recently elected President, Jean-Bertrand Aristide. Gross human rights violations were rampant, with murder, disappearances, torture, and rape leading the way; the perpetrators were the Haitian army, police, and their paramilitary death squads. Again, due to political negotiations led by UN's DPA, the Haitian military, in an effort to defuse the crippling sanctions imposed by the US and the Organization of American States, agreed to the deployment of human rights officers to monitor and report on violations. This time, working off the El Salvador template, UN officials in New York with the same representatives of major human rights NGOs, hammered out 'terms of reference' for the human rights officers who would be sent to Haiti. Challenges regarding recruitment, deployment, logistics, and securing agreement from the illegitimate de facto military regime to allow the officers to do their work proved daunting.[1] Yet with the experience gained from El Salvador and a growing body of work and experience, the mission was on the ground in Haiti by February 1993.

The tidal wave of human rights field operations picked up speed throughout the 1990s. After El Salvador and Haiti came Guatemala, Bosnia-Herzegovina, Angola, Sierra Leone, Democratic Republic of the Congo, Timor Leste, Kosovo, Liberia, and the Central African Republic. Rwanda in 1994, following the April genocide, marked the first time that the UN Geneva office had responsibility for a human rights field operation,

---

[1] Ian Martin, "Paper versus Steel: The First Phase of the International Civilian Mission in Haiti," in *Honoring Human Rights and Keeping the Peace*, ed. Alice H. Henkin (The Hague: Kluwer Law International, 1995): 73–118.

HRFOR. The position of the High Commissioner for Human Rights had just been created in 1993 as a result of the Vienna Conference. José Ayala Lasso, the first High Commissioner, was literally on the job for one week when the Rwandan genocide began on April 6. The Human Rights Centre in Geneva had never fielded a major human rights office before, its only experience being the establishment of a one-person office in Bosnia in 1993.[2] Deploying over 100 people to post-genocide Rwanda was an entirely different matter.[3]

The drive to put human rights officers on the ground for extended periods of time did not end with the dawn of the new century. Human rights officers deployed to Nepal, Iraq, Afghanistan, Côte d'Ivoire, Burundi, Haiti (again in 2004), Colombia, Darfur, South Sudan and Libya, to name a few.[4] While the Office of the High Commissioner assumed a greater role in establishing and managing these operations over time, the bulk of the officers worked as part of a UN peacekeeping operation, usually in a human rights department. The Department of Peacekeeping Operations in New York (DPKO) had primary responsibility, while OHCHR participated in recruiting and received regular reports from the unit. The real power and authority, however, remained with the Special Representative of the Secretary-General (SRSG), who in turn reported to the Secretary-General and the Security Council in New York.[5]

When Louise Arbour took over as High Commissioner for Human Rights in 2004, she made field presences a high priority.[6] In addition to the human rights components in peace operations, Arbour wanted to

---

[2] For details, see Michael O'Flaherty and George Ulrich, "The Professionalization of Human Rights Field Work," *Journal of Human Rights Practice* 2, no. 1 (2010): 1–27.

[3] Todd Howland, "Mirage Magic, or Mixed Bag?: The United Nations High Commissioner for Human Rights' Field Operation in Rwanda," *Human Rights Quarterly* 21, no. 1 (February 1999): 1–55.

[4] The missions to which they were attached are UNMIN, the United Nations Mission in Nepal (January 2007-January 2011). UNAMI, the United Nations Assistance Mission in Iraq (August 2003-present). UNAMA, the United Nations Assistance Mission in Afghanistan (March 2002-present). UNOCI, the United Nations Operation in Côte d'Ivoire (April 2004-present). ONUB, the United Nations Operation in Burundi (March 2005-January 2007). MINUSTAH, the United Nations Stabilization Mission to Haiti (June 2004-present). UNAMID, the United Nations/African Mission in Darfur (July 2007-present). UNMISS, the United Nations Mission in the Republic of South Sudan, (July 2011).

[5] The Secretary-General's 2000 Note of Guidance affirms the SRSG's role as establishing "the political framework for, and provid[ing] overarching leadership to, the UN team in country." Inter-Agency Standing Committee, "Note of Guidance of the Secretary-General on Relations between Representatives of the Secretary-General, Resident Coordinators and Humanitarian Coordinators," news release, October 1, 2000.

[6] See OHCHR, "The OHCHR Plan of Action: Protection and Empowerment," May 2005, http://www2.ohchr.org/english/planaction.pdf.

establish stand-alone human rights presences and also pushed for UN Country Teams (UNCTs) to include a human rights officer to assist in implementing Secretary-General Kofi Annan's directive to 'mainstream' human rights in all the UN's work. At the end of 2012, there were 18 human rights officers in UNCTs.[7]

The last 20 years have seen an explosion of on-the-ground long-term field presences in various guises working on human rights around the world. This is a tectonic shift from the UN's approach in the first 45 years of its existence. It has brought human rights down from a high conceptual, some would argue abstract, level, to improving people's lives in real, measurable, and concrete ways. As with any venture that is so ambitious and sensitive, remember the UN Charter's proviso about not interfering in the domestic affairs of Member-States, and with on-going resistance from some states to the very notion of human rights (despite Article 1 of the Charter which states one of the purposes of the UN is "promoting and encouraging respect for human rights and for fundamental freedoms..."),[8] there have been setbacks. The efforts continue, however, and the UN has tried to learn from its mistakes.

UN human rights field officers deployed in integrated peacekeeping operations literally face a smoldering, ravaged terrain and a terrified, often largely displaced population. Education and literacy levels among police, corrections, and even judicial officials are often very low. Rape has been used as a weapon of terror or ethnic cleansing, leaving a legacy of horror and trauma across huge swathes of the population. Corruption is often endemic, and the post-conflict governance vacuum has created a culture of criminality, often highly organized, well-funded, and lethal. Finally, the general population may have lost all faith in systems of government and justice, with good reason. The state has rarely respected human rights and the relationship with the population has been one of mutual distrust and fear, often tinged with contempt.

This post-conflict reality requires pragmatism, patience, and a fair dose of humility. Building capacity, giving technical advice, and (re)forming institutions in places like Afghanistan, Sierra Leone, and Burundi are a world apart from tinkering with some shortcomings in the judiciary,

---

[7] At the end of 2011, OHCHR had Human Rights Advisers in Chad, Kenya, Madagascar, Maldives, Niger, Rwanda, Ecuador, Honduras, Paraguay, Papua New Guinea, Sri Lanka, South Caucasus Region, Republic of Moldova, the Russian Federation, Tajikistan, Ukraine, former Yugoslav Republic of Macedonia and Serbia, and the recruitment of three new advisers for Timor-Leste, Malawi, and Mali was underway. OHCHR, *Annual Report 2012*.

[8] Charter of the United Nations (1945), Ch. I, Art. 1(3).

prisons or police in countries like Chile, Mexico, Slovakia, Jordan, Mongolia, or Morocco.

Capacity-Building in UN Peace Operations

UN human rights field officers enjoy several advantages over the 'typical' advisory services or capacity-building initiatives undertaken by OHCHR or other UN agencies in more stable countries. The most important benefit is on-going presence. Human rights officers deploy to the mission country for comparatively long periods, months sometimes years. This contrasts with other capacity-building or technical assistance missions that might last weeks at best and consist of episodic visits. A lengthy presence offers the possibility for the human rights officer to develop an in-depth knowledge of the country, including an understanding of what went wrong and the urgent priorities for fixing the problem. When officers leave for a new assignment, their successors pick up the work.

In most mission countries, human rights officers are present throughout the territory. Even in vast countries like Sudan and DRC, human rights officers can be found in even the most remote provinces.[9] Their presence for sustained periods allows them to create working relationships with local partners, to gain their trust by demonstrating competence and good faith. And the importance of consistent follow-up should never be underestimated. When the prosecutor knows, for example, that the human rights officer will be back next week, and the week after that, to check on the status of cases, the odds of seeing real action and accountability for inaction increase. Officers respond to questions and requests while enlisting support from other UN actors. Forging relationships with civil society, especially local human rights defenders, develops since UN human rights officers live in their town, understand the reality, and will be there for advice, constructive criticism, and support.

Another advantage resides in the existence of the other sections of the UN integrated peace missions. Learning how to leverage the greater numbers and resources of UN military, UN police, and the various humanitarian and development agencies, and tapping into their expertise, is an important skill.

---

[9] In the DRC, for example, outside of its headquarters in Kinshasa, the UN Mission has 15 field offices throughout the country. United Nations Organization Stabilization Mission in the DR Congo, "Office Locations," http://monusco.unmissions.org/Default.aspx?tabid=10686&language=en-US.

Exploding the Myths

Several myths persist about the work of human rights field officers, even after 20 years of experience.

First, 'monitoring is a separate activity from technical assistance or capacity-building.' This myth is widespread and dangerous. Monitoring the human rights situation is a pre-requisite for effective programming to strengthen institutions. Without an understanding of the weaknesses in the judiciary, police, or other state institutions, capacity-building efforts are likely to fail. Monitoring provides the diagnosis of the problem which must then help define the cure. Monitoring also reveals whether the cure is working; without on-going investigations into the situation the human rights officers will not know whether their training programs, logistical support, oversight capacity building, or awareness-raising campaigns are having a positive impact on the ground so that people enjoy greater respect for their human rights.

A related myth is that capacity-building initiatives should come later in a mission cycle and that only monitoring occurs at the start. From the earliest days in a mission, officers should exploit opportunities for capacity-building, often with limited or no resources. Building links and trust with locals via project activities must start immediately.

The second myth is that capacity-building efforts must focus on government entities only. Human rights officers should work with key members of civil society, strengthening their ability to monitor, advocate, and promote human rights. Addressing the 'demand' side, in addition to the 'supply' side is a critical strategy in peace operations. Helping civil society to develop ways to push the authorities to do their jobs (*responsabiliser l'état* in the French formulation) must be part of capacity-building.

Third, many working in peace operations believe they cannot work on economic, social, and cultural rights and emphasize civil and political rights. While these latter rights may be priorities, especially in the early phases of a peace operation, some human rights officers have used creative approaches to engage both state and non-state actors in programs on food, shelter, education, and medical care, enlisting UN agencies and bilateral donors to support projects. Finally, detecting discrimination in the access to education, food, shelter, and medical care is a crucial component of the field officer's work and can help prevent further conflict while assuring equitable enjoyment of these human rights.

Fourth, human rights is often seen as a specialist task, best left to the human rights section, and in particular, lawyers. Human rights officers need to overcome this myth by forging alliances with other sections of the mission and the UNCT. These partnerships can be especially fruitful in the areas of economic, social, and cultural rights. Learning how to leverage the larger resources and greater numbers of people in other parts of the UN mission increases the impact of the human rights section.

Fifth, many in the host society and even in the UN family see human rights as essentially 'confrontational.' For them, human rights means naming, shaming, and public criticism. While these may be important tools, they are not the only ones and it is by designing effective programs to assist government institutions and their civil society counterparts to promote and protect human rights that the field officers can best defuse this myth. "We have to show them that we are here to try to help them and not only to criticize them," says one experienced human rights officer in Haiti. Another noted, "We must convince them that we are not here only to bother them."

Sixth, another myth holds that 'capacity-building' essentially means training local counterparts to do their jobs. While training is necessary, it is not sufficient to insure that both capacity-building and institutional reforms occur. Human rights officers must adopt the approach used by their counterparts in the development world: the Project Cycle of assessment, analysis, design, implementation, monitoring, and evaluation.[10] All are crucial to successful human rights programming. And one should always ask: which capacity are we trying to build and what is our overall strategy? How does what we are doing mesh with efforts by the UNCT, the Mission, bilateral donors, and the international financial institutions (World Bank, regional banks, IMF)?

'Good Practices' in Human Rights Field Operations

Most of the following examples come from my own work and from discussions with colleagues in the field over the years. I have attempted to place the examples in broad themes rather than by country since I think the thematic approach would be more useful.

Use 'Emblematic Cases'

Human rights officers have identified an 'emblematic case,' whether for the courts, police, prison administration, or the military, as a way to

[10] See, for example, the use of the project cycle at the World Bank and the African Development Bank Group. World Bank, "How the Project Cycle Works," http://web.worldbank.org/WBSITE/EXTERNAL/PROJECTS/0,,contentMDK:20120731~menuPK:41390~pagePK:41367~piPK:51533~theSitePK:40941,00.html.

identify institutional weaknesses and strengths; test the state's commitment to reform; judge whether it is 'safe' to perform your job properly; and engage civil society.

This practice addresses four potential gaps identified by OHCHR: knowledge, capacity, commitment, and security.

Human rights officers investigated a case of a young girl who was raped and murdered while in detention at a Nepal Army base. The office provided its findings to the military prosecutor and the courts. It offered to supply evidence and testimony it had gathered and to find additional expertise to help in the prosecution. The office also used the case to advocate for changes in the way the military operated, especially concerning arrest, detention, and conditions of detention. The government and the army for a long time failed to respond to these initiatives, thus showing that the political will for change was not there. This is a crucial factor since why bother with training, providing equipment, or offering study programs abroad if the institution itself is not really interested in reform.

This high visibility case also showed the donors that the army was not interested in protecting rights so their programs needed to reflect this reality. Unless the girl's case was treated seriously, all technical assistance and capacity-building risked being a waste of time and money.

Use Public Opinion Surveys to Identify Priorities and Generate Base-Line Data

Several human rights departments have conducted public opinion surveys to gauge the population's concerns, goals, and perceptions of the state's performance. As with monitoring, these surveys are tools for human rights officers to pinpoint problems or weaknesses in all areas of rights. For example, in Afghanistan, the Human Rights Section and UNHCR, in partnership with local groups, created and distributed a questionnaire for internally displaced persons (IDPs) that generated solid information to base programming on, especially for economic, social, and cultural rights.[11]

The human rights officers in Abkhazia used a questionnaire to get information about the nature and extent of violence against children and then used this information along with UNICEF to design training and

[11] World Bank and UNHCR Afghanistan, "Research Study on IDPs in urban settings – Afghanistan," May, 2011, http://siteresources.worldbank.org/EXTSOCIALDEVELOPMENT/Resources/244362-1265299949041/6766328-1265299960363/WB-UNHCR-IDP_Full-Report.pdf.

education campaigns for officials and NGOs.[12] Without this data and the relationships that developed from the very process of gathering information, the programs and the capacity of local counterparts would have been weaker. This program had the additional positive impact of enhancing the government's capacity to gather, maintain, analyze, and then use data. Without the first survey, there would be no way to measure the impact of the training or other initiatives. This underscores a crucial lesson for capacity building and institutional reform: "you cannot improve what you cannot measure."

Twin Results-Based Monitoring with Results-Based Capacity-Building

Monitoring is a means to an end and not an end in itself. The main purpose of monitoring is to lead to improved protection and promotion of rights. Similarly, capacity-building and institutional reform are more than just a series of training activities or logistical and financial support. The activities must lead to identifiable change in performance. This culture of 'results' has often been lacking in UN human rights field work but there are signs that a new rigor and accountability are emerging. Concrete examples will be cited below, but emphasizing activities that lead to change and knowing how to identify change is an important lesson that needs to be applied in all UN human rights field work.

Provide Program Budgets for Activities

All UN field presences, whether as part of a peace operation, a stand-alone office, or even a solitary human rights officer in a country team, need money for programs and not only for staff salaries. If the human rights presences bring nothing to the table, only monitoring and reporting, they will lose credibility, access, and ability to effect change. UN human rights work must be more than just denouncing violations. "We must be able to say: we are here to help solve these problems and prevent future violations; it's paradoxical that human rights offices don't have program budgets since it must be central to what we are doing," according to a UN humanitarian officer in Burundi who supported human rights and saw its importance to the overall success of the UN in Burundi.

---

12 Margaret A. Lynch, Lia Saralidze, Nina Goguadze, Aadam Zolotor, "National Study on Violence Against Children in Georgia," (Tbilisi: UNICEF Georgia 2008), http://www.unicef.org/georgia/Violence_Study_ENG_final.pdf.

Having something to offer also buys good will from the national authorities and makes it easier to raise the inevitable criticisms and 'negative' news. A UNICEF official in Burundi noted, "There is a lot of human rights talk, but you need money to do this work, human rights do not come cheap, yet the human rights section is always the poor cousin."

Human rights officers with even a minimal budget for programming (Burundi, Haiti, and Nepal) have seen greater impact, results, and thus success. With just $300/month per province in Burundi (about $30,000/year), the section was able to conduct important promotion and protection activities. Financing must be flexible and quickly available. When I was head of the UN field operation in Rwanda in 1997, $10,000/month for programming made a crucial difference to our work and made our criticisms of government performance more palatable for all sides.

OHCHR should be more assertive at the mission planning stage and in staffing and budgetary discussions in the Advisory Committee on Administrative and Budgetary Questions for peace operations and in programming within UNCTs. The need for an assured budget line for human rights programming cannot be overstated.

Consult with your Beneficiaries before Embarking on Assistance Efforts

Sometimes human rights officers, in an excess of enthusiasm, design programs that they think are priorities without first consulting the intended beneficiaries. 'Participation' is too often honored in the breach. Meaningful, early participation with key stakeholders is always a good practice. Human rights officers should take the time to identify who are the most important local counterparts, governmental and civil society actors, and insure that they participate in every stage of the project. This is time-consuming but essential.

In addressing female genital mutilation in Eritrea, the Human Rights Section of UNMEE (Ethiopia/Eritrea) worked closely with the National Union of Eritrean Women who engaged with women's organizations to conduct a needs assessment and gathered reliable data.[13] Along with UNICEF, the section supported meetings with local government and civil society (including religious leaders) to design a campaign to combat female genital mutilation. For HIV/AIDs, local youth groups led

[13] These efforts ultimately contributed to the Eritrean government banning female genital mutilation in 2007. See *Proclamation 158/2007, A Proclamation to Abolish Female Circumcision* [*Eritrea*], No. 158/2007, 20 March 2007, available at: http://www.unhcr.org/refworld/docid/48578c812.html.

awareness-raising campaigns as part of a 'human rights week.' These groups learned how to gather information, analyze it, and hone their advocacy skills. The Human Rights Section found not only that their key local counterparts could run effective promotion activities, but also could collect and analyze masses of information that contributed to the Section's own monitoring and reporting capacity. Everyone emerged a winner.

Identify Allies as Senior as Possible in the Government Hierarchy

This is especially true in organizations like the police, intelligence services, and the military where command structures are paramount. Without their leaders' support for institutional change, it doesn't matter how many human rights workshops, how many people you train, or how many thousands of copies of the Universal Declaration of Human Rights you distribute.

One police reform expert emphasizes the importance of 'integrity management' which requires managers and administrators in a police force to enforce constantly the rules that govern police behavior. It is not enough to have policies in place, written up nicely in terse language and posted in procedural manuals. Unless managers make integrity a top priority and take action when necessary to address corruption or abuse of power, then slowly integrity will erode due to peer pressure and demands from outsiders who offer opportunities for material gain and symbolic rewards. This holds equally true for the judiciary, penal administration, and other state bodies.

"You have to get the senior leaders on board, then they will pass the orders down the hierarchy," says a UN human rights officer in Burundi. Otherwise, "the training will go in one ear and out the other once they are back in their workplace." An officer in the Haitian National Police's Inspector General's office echoed this advice: "You have to have the right person in the Station Command post. He or she sets the tone for everything and is responsible for discipline and good order." Selecting the right people for key posts is crucial (see the section below on 'Registration, Certification, and Vetting').

Work with Parliament and National Legislatures

National parliaments should protect and promote human rights. In addition to helping parliamentarians draft and review laws to insure they are consistent with international human rights standards and the state's treaty obligations, human rights officers should help legislatures meet their responsibilities to oversee behavior by government ministries. Human rights sections in Haiti, Burundi, Timor Leste, Liberia, and Kosovo have worked to enhance the skills of parliamentarians to investigate human rights issues, hold hearings, draft laws, and write reports.

In Sudan, the Human Rights Division of UNMIS has worked with Parliament on analyzing national budgets.[14] The members of parliament (MPs) have learned to assess financial information so that they can question the Executive Branch. This is important for economic, social, and cultural rights. A 'human rights-based approach to budget monitoring' insists on progressive realization of rights and examines whether 'maximum available resources' are being devoted to education, housing, health care, and access to clean water as required by the International Covenant on Economic, Social, and Cultural Rights. Greater public debate on how government funds are spent, priorities identified, and increased transparency and accountability for spending decisions lead to greater knowledge and capacity of MPs. The impact of this capacity-building is better governance as MPs engage in the budget process and probe for information and demand explanations from the ministries.

Use Treaty Bodies and Special Procedures Strategically

Human rights officers should use treaty body conclusions and recommendations, the reporting process, and visits and findings by special rapporteurs and working groups. In the early days of human rights field work there was a divorce between the work on the ground and the whole treaty body and special procedures world. Designing a process to channel treaty body and special procedures' findings into programming should become routine practice for human rights officers. The concluding observations and recommendations provide an entry point for human rights officers to raise delicate issues with the authorities.

The recommendations and conclusions should become the basis for programming to address the deficiencies identified by the experts. In Sudan, the human rights section has used the Convention on the Elimination of All Forms of Discrimination Against Women (CEDAW) reporting process to launch a national discussion on the relationship between Shari'a and women's rights. The Human Rights Section's role has also made it 'safer' to have such discussions on sensitive issues.

---

[14] See for example Estzer Farkas, "Bridging the Gap: Finding alternatives to the oil revenue," *United Nations Mission in Sudan* (June 2011): 6, http://unmis.unmissions.org/Portals/UNMIS/2011Docs/inSUDAN-June-2011-eng-web.pdf.

The Independent Expert's report on Haiti helped establish the human rights section's priorities when MINUSTAH deployed in 2004.[15] Later reports by the expert led to funding from one UN Member State to address priorities identified, such as establishing a legal aid program and intensifying human rights promotion. The Human Rights Section funded a 10-segment radio program produced by a well-known Haitian author and filmmaker on Human Rights and Law Enforcement; the programs used characters based on Haitian reality speaking Créole to convey important lessons about the police, judiciary, and the citizen's role. In recent years, the Independent Expert on Haiti and the human rights team in MINUSTAH exchange information and analysis with the Expert relying on the priorities identified by officers on the ground.[16]

The Special Rapporteurs on torture and internally displaced persons (IDPs) came to Abkhazia and their visits started a dialogue with the authorities that was supported by the human rights team.[17] Both Rapporteurs offered to return to run workshops for the authorities on how to implement their respective recommendations. Also, the other members of the UNCT are now involved in this dialogue so the special procedures have helped integrate further human rights within the UN family.

A good practice developed by the Timor Leste Human Rights Section in their 2008–9 Strategy is to include special procedures-related indicators: number of communications and missions/visits by mandate holders, percentage of government responses to communications from mandate holders, number of invitations by government to special rapporteurs and working groups, percentage of special procedures recommendations implemented by government, NGOs' follow-up on special procedures recommendations, NGOs submitting information to mandate holders, and the level of UN agencies' participation in supporting the work of mandate holders.[18] The Section also had a goal of supporting the submission of at least two 'shadow reports' to treaty bodies.

---

15 UN Commission on Human Rights, *Situation of Human Rights in Haiti / Report prepared by the independent expert, Mr. Louis Joinet*, UN Doc. E/CN.4/2003/116, December 23, 2002.

16 UN Human Rights Council, *Report of the Independent Expert on the situation of human rights in Haiti, Michel Forst*, UN Doc. A/HRC/20/35, April 23, 2012.

17 See UN Commission on Human Rights, *Report of the Special Rapporteur on Torture and other cruel, inhuman or degrading treatment or punishment, Manfred Nowak / Mission to Georgia*, UN Doc. E/CN.4/2006/6/Add.3, September 23, 2005; Human Rights Council, *Report of the Representative of the Secretary-General on the human rights of internally displaced persons, Walter Kälin, Addendum, Mission to Georgia*, UN Doc. A/HRC/10/13/Add.2, February 13, 2009.

18 See Office of the High Commissioner for Human Rights in Timor-Leste, "OHCHR in Timor-Leste (2008–2009), http://www.ohchr.org/EN/Countries/AsiaRegion/Pages/TL

Parliament is often unaware of the treaty body conclusions or recommendations by the special rapporteurs. Human rights officers should provide parliament with relevant recommendations from the treaty bodies and special procedures and advise on implementing relevant findings. The teams in the Sudan and DRC have done this and others should be encouraged to do likewise.

The Universal Periodic Review establishes a new and promising tool for human rights field officers to feed information and analyses while offering to help and monitor implementation of the UPR recommendations.

Strengthen Local Ownership and Management and Leadership Skills

"Stay one step behind the locals, let them take the credit and gain the visibility, even if the UN has done all the work," said one experienced field officer. And the sooner the locals can do the bulk of the work the better. The team in Haiti has adopted this approach, providing all of the documents, materials, and logistical support for Haiti's national human rights institution's events celebrating International Human Rights Day, while staying in the background and allowing the *Office de Protection du Citoyen* (OPC) to get visibility and credit.[19] The team also provides support for OPC investigations (logistics, material, and personnel) with the goal of raising the OPC's stature so that more people will use it, have confidence in it, and funders will see that it is worth supporting.

UNPOL in Haiti has adopted a similar approach that human rights officers could use. UNPOL provides logistical and material support to the Haitian National Police (HNP) to increase their presence: on patrol, directing traffic, visiting schools, and interacting more with the public.[20]

Summary0809.aspx. Office of the High Commissioner for Human Rights and United Nations Integrated Mission in Timor-Leste (UNMIT), *Report on Human Rights Developments in Timor-Leste: 1 July 2008 to 30 June 2009*, http://www.ohchr.org/Documents/Countries/UNMIT01072008_300609.pdf.

19 Office de la Protection du Citoyen & de la Citoyenne, "Commémoration de la Journée Internationale des Droits Humains et Lancement de l'Unité de Protection de l'Enfant [Commemoration of International Human Rights Day and Launch of the Child Protection Unit]," news release, http://www.protectioncitoyenhaiti.org/index.php?option=com_content&view=article&id=109:commemoration-de-la-journee-internationale-des-droits-humains-et-lancement-de-lunite-de-protection-de-lenfant-&catid=41:note-de-presse&Itemid=57.

20 See UN Office of Internal Oversight Services, Internal Audit Division, *The Haitian National Police development programme in MINUSTAH*, internal audit report, Assignment No. AP2011/683/10, May 17, 2012.

The population gained confidence in the HNP while the HNP likewise gained competence and confidence in itself. Some units demanded even more training so they would not be 'left behind' and the UNPOL deputy police commissioner noted a 'cultural change' in the HNP. The incentives have changed and officers see that competence and good behavior are rewarded while incompetence and malfeasance are punished. This builds capacity leading to long-term institutional change and illustrates 'integrity management' as described above.

The UN human rights officers in Abkhazia developed good practices even in that difficult environment before they were expelled in late 2008. All human rights projects were implemented directly by local partners.[21] The UN human rights team provided advice and sometimes support (documents, access to experts, and limited financial help). Training on project management, fund-raising, and reporting to donors and budgeting made these local NGOs more self-sufficient, independent, and effective. They were also well placed to raise certain 'taboo' topics like domestic violence that international observers would have found hard to do. One local NGO established a 'hot-line' and received over 130 calls for domestic violence incidents in the first few weeks. Police later received specialized training on how to handle domestic violence.

In Sierra Leone, the Human Rights Section of UNIOSIL supported the creation of an umbrella organization of human rights NGOs in 14 districts.[22] UNDP's financial support allowed the office to hold workshops on monitoring and reporting, advocacy, and how to intervene with the authorities. The human rights section documented greater activity by these organizations and intensified reporting which led to the removal of several local officials for corruption and abuse of power. Civil society grew more assertive about demanding rights and accountability from the authorities. "We support and they lead," said a UN official in Freetown.

In Burundi, UNIFEM and the Human Rights Section/Office work jointly with the local traditional leaders ("*Bashingantahe*") on sensitive issues like women's rights, inheritance, early marriage, and HIV/AIDS.[23] Without the

---

[21] See UN Security Council, *Report of the Secretary-General on the situation in Abkhazia, Georgia*, UN Doc. S/2008/219 (Apr. 2, 2008).

[22] United Nations Integrated Peacebuilding Office in Sierra Leone, "Second DHRC National Consultative Conference and training takes place in Bo," news release, http://unipsil.unmissions.org/Default.aspx?tabid=9611&ctl=Details&mid=12590&Itemid=10769&language=en-US.

[23] UNIFEM, *Annual Report 2008–2009*, (New York: United Nations Development Fund for Women, 2009): 5, http://www.unifem.org/attachments/products/annual_report_2008_2009_en.pdf.

leadership from these local chiefs, raising awareness and the capacity of local organizations to discuss these issues and seek change would be unthinkable.

Co-Locate and Mentor/Coach

As a follow-up to more formal class room training, placing experts as mentors inside institutions, government and non-state, has produced positive results. The opportunity to observe and react quickly to local counterparts' actions has an immediate and lasting impact on performance.

In Timor Leste, human rights officers worked alongside colleagues in the *Provedoria's* (Ombudsman's) office for several years.[24] Applying the mantra 'reinforce, not replace,' the mentors advise national officers on complaint handling, hearing procedures, report writing, and human rights education. Study after study shows that adults learn best by doing, so what better way to build capacity than to provide advice and constructive criticism while someone is 'on the job'?

Yet Burundi also underscores the importance of building strong leadership, oversight capacity, and putting a premium on integrity. Without these, mere training and mentoring will not be enough. For example, one senior UN official in Burundi summed up the challenge: "How do we insure a transfer of what is learned in the classroom to the work place and the skills and knowledge from the training does not get drowned out in the daily routine?" The police in Burundi continue to commit abuses despite many training sessions and workshops. One officer who had just received his certificate following a UN-sponsored human rights training session beat and nearly tortured a politician to death. When asked how he could do this, he responded, "I went back into the system, and the system was the same."

Efforts at mentoring judges and prosecutors in Cambodia, Haiti, and Kosovo are also worth replicating. Kosovo CIVPOL created a 'Field Officer's Training Manual' which shows the mentor how to advise and assess the local officer's performance and contains checklists for each police function and questions to pose to the officers to insure they understand their tasks.[25]

---

[24] See UN Development Programme Timor-Leste, "Provedoria Project Supported," news release, Dec. 22, 2009, http://www.tl.undp.org/undp/Provedoria%20Project%20Supported.htm.

[25] Colette Rausch, "From Elation to Disappointment: Justice and Security Reform in Kosovo," in *Constructing Justice and Security after War*, ed. Charles T. Call (Washington, D.C.: United States Institute of Peace, 2007): 289–298.

Develop Capacity to Handle Data

As was mentioned, "you can't improve what you can't measure." The capacity to gather, analyze, maintain, retrieve, and use sound data is a fundamental part of all human rights work. An important lesson is that the amount of time and effort spent on helping the state and NGOs to handle all aspects of data is a worthwhile investment.

The human rights teams in Haiti and Timor Leste have helped the national human rights institutions in both countries, the *Provedoria* and the *Office de Protection du Citoyen*, to establish databases and have trained officers on how to use the software and the UN HURIDOCS system.[26] The team in Liberia is helping the Justice Ministry to develop a database on trends, patterns, and concerns within the judiciary on harmful traditional practices that will help define a strategy to address this problem.[27]

Link with UNCTs and "Mainstream" Human Rights

Human rights officers must try to forge closer links with the UNCT. This includes possibilities for increased programming on economic, social, and cultural rights (ESCRs). In Sudan, human rights officers worked with UNCT to promote awareness of ESCRs among the population in the south and the Government of South Sudan. Burundi's human rights officers have trained other UNCT members on the rights-based approach and participated in CCA-UNDAF formulations to ensure human rights content in these core planning documents.[28]

In the DRC, MONUC's human rights officers informed UNCT members of the work of the special procedures and their recommendations and arranged for meetings with UNCT during experts' visits. The officers have also set as a target that at least thirty percent of UN agencies' country programs incorporate a human rights perspective.

"Pick a right – water, food, housing, health, education – then team up with a UN agency, budget programs in your cost plan, and then tackle the ESCR you have targeted" a human rights field officer recommends, offering a sound formula that should be regular good practice in all missions.

---

[26] UN Office on Drugs and Crime, "Law enforcement officers receive computer-based training in Timor-Leste," news release, September 9, 2009.

[27] United Nations Mission in Liberia, "Legal and Judicial Systems Support Division," http://unmil.unmissions.org/Default.aspx?tabid=3958&language=en-US.

[28] UN Development Group, *Action 2 Global Programme: 2008 Final Report for Burundi*, report, October 31, 2008, http://www.undg.org/docs/8676/ACTION2-UNCT-FINAL-EVALUATION-REPORT—Burundi.doc.

Register, Certify, and Vet Judicial and Security Personnel

Many government institutions in post-conflict countries do not even know how many staff they have, where they are deployed, their backgrounds, qualifications, or past performance records. Registration and certification programs can strengthen institutions by identifying all personnel, revealing their qualifications and providing information on gender, ethnic, religious, and racial composition. This capacity to know and manage your staff is crucial, especially for insuring competence, integrity, and diversity.

In Haiti, the Human Rights Section supported a registration and certification program for the police. The head of the Haitian National Police had no idea how many officers he had, where they were stationed, and whether they had been appointed legally. And this was true before the devastating January 2010 earthquake. Many people claimed to be police officers who really were not. A significant number were implicated in serious human rights abuses and criminal activity. So a registration program was crucial for all further reform work. Building a solid database on all personnel was a capacity that the HNP never had before.

Vetting serving officers is a bridge between addressing impunity and reforming institutions. Any government official who by his/her past behavior is unworthy of continuing in office should be removed following a fair and open procedure. The population and the organization itself sees that the old ways will not be accepted and those vetted out pay a price for their crimes by losing a good job.

See the Human Rights Section as a 'Convener'

UN human rights officers can exploit their role as 'outsiders' to bring together institutions that often have not worked together or even communicated much before. This facilitating role can help strengthen the state's ability to identify problems, forge concerted action to respond, and create programs to prevent future violations. The mere fact of getting people in the same room to discuss issues can enhance government performance and reinforce links to civil society, whose representatives should be included whenever possible. One human rights officer noted: "We're a facilitator, we bring people together who should be talking but are not."

The human rights and justice sections in BINUB regularly convened meetings between the Ministry of Justice and the Ministry of Human Rights to discuss problems affecting their work. This had rarely happened before and it quickly yielded results, such as the collaboration between the two in reforming the penal and criminal procedure codes. The Office also held periodic workshops for human rights groups, trade unions, political parties, and the press.[29] Much less expensive and time-consuming than formal training sessions, these workshops nonetheless provided an opportunity to build the knowledge and skills of local counterparts and habituate them to consulting and communicating across sectors. They offered a regular forum to meet and follow up on issues and included more people than a formal training would have allowed. Formulating arguments and learning how to make demands on the government are skills that were honed in these meetings.

Another good practice employed by the OHCHR Office in Burundi was the weekly 'protection meeting' chaired by the Office and attended by senior representatives of the police, army, intelligence service, and security service, the ICRC, and a few international NGOs. These meetings became mini-training sessions in themselves where human rights officers conveyed to their government counterparts certain key principles and garnered their 'buy-in' to prevent violations and punish those responsible for violations. One participant noted that "The weekly protection meetings help build government capacity by pressing the army, police, and intelligence services to do their jobs the right way and to take corrective action when needed. And we are there to remind them each week of their responsibilities."

Include National Human Rights Officers

One of the most effective, efficient, and sustainable ways of building capacity is to include nationals in the UN's human rights mission teams. In some places and times, certain issues cannot be assigned to nationals for reasons of their security or for broader concerns about confidential information. But these are often the exceptional situations. Most times national human rights officers can and should do just about anything that internationals do.

The advantages of national officers are obvious: language ability, knowledge of local history, culture, the patterns and sources of human rights violations, and good contacts with key local players. Most national officers will stay in the country when the mission departs so one of the most important legacies a human rights office can leave is a well-trained corps of national human rights professionals who will take their knowledge,

29 Zenja Bašagic, *UN integration in Burundi in the context of the peacebuilding office BINUB: Taking stock and lessons learned from June 2006 to November 2007*, report (2008): 9.

skills, and work ethic into a variety of jobs, including national human rights institutions, government posts, or with non-governmental organizations. The UN could learn a lot from the OSCE, an organization that has pioneered the use of national human rights officers.[30] The ultimate goal of all UN human rights officers should be to make themselves obsolete, to work themselves out of their jobs, and who better to hand the work over to than national counterparts?

Focus on Youth

The Human Rights Section of UNMIL in Liberia has supported 'Human Rights Clubs' in high schools throughout the country.[31] Using teachers and NGOs, the section has provided guidance, materials, and financial support to these clubs. The goal is to make the clubs completely self-sufficient and self-governing.

In Abkhazia, the human rights officers worked with local NGOs specializing in children's rights.[32] One in Sokhumi had children write and produce a puppet play that conveyed human rights problems and principles using traditional Abkhaz stories and characters. Enormously popular with children and adults, the puppets will be used for future human rights activities.

The team in Timor Leste integrated human rights into the primary school curriculum and trained trainers at the Ministry of Education on human rights issues.[33] The office has joined UNICEF to lead a national campaign for children's rights.

Assess Training's Impact on Performance

Human rights officers must identify ways to evaluate how training achieves the goal of improving capacity, knowledge, and commitment leading to improved performance by those trained. It is not enough to pass around a questionnaire at the end of a workshop asking people what they think of the training.

---

[30] See, for example, Organization for Security and Co-operation in Europe Office of Democratic Institutions and Human Rights, *Annual Report 2011* (Warsaw: OSCE Office for Democratic Institutions and Human Rights (ODIHR), 2011), 38–49.

[31] UNIMIL,"Human Rights Protection," http://unmil.unmissions.org/Default.aspx?tabid=3957&language=en-US. See also United Nations Security Council, *Eighth progress report of the Secretary-General on the United Nations Mission in Liberia*, September 1, 2005, UN Doc. S/2005/650: 11.

[32] OHCHR, *Quarterly Reports of Field Offices: Europe Central Asia, and North America region*, report (June 2005): 26–27.

[33] See UNICEF, *Evaluation of UNICEF's Education Programme in Timor Leste* (New York: United Nations Children's Fund, 2010).

Periodic evaluations to gauge the impact of training are necessary. Effective human rights officers link their overall monitoring to issues covered in various trainings. Their monitoring strategy includes obtaining information showing whether or not training improves the performance of those trained. For example, has a workshop for judges on international human rights law led to an increased use of these laws in the judges' work?

In Sierra Leone, after workshops held for the police on juvenile justice and the Convention on the Rights of the Child, follow-up monitoring by the section has shown that prisons and police lock-up facilities now refuse to admit juveniles and insist that they be taken back to court and assigned to appropriate juvenile facilities or released.

In Burundi, the National Intelligence Service (SNR) was implicated in serious cases of rights violations, including routine beatings of detainees and holding people incommunicado for long periods. SNR leaders attend weekly meetings convened by the UN Human Rights Office in Burundi where serious cases were raised with government officials, including representatives of the army, police, and SNR.[34] The SNR leadership requested training for its agents on the rights of detainees and the proper use of force. Human rights officers helped organize these training sessions based on real cases. Afterwards, human rights officers noted a decrease in cases alleging violations by the SNR. Inspections showed that cells were not overcrowded and detainees were treated humanely. SNR improved its capacity and its will to investigate and bring perpetrators to justice. One officer noted, "I can see the impact, I review the orders given by commanding officers and they have improved and include references to human rights and humanitarian law principles where they never did before."

Another effective tool is to create after each training session a '*Comité de Suivi*' or 'Follow-up Committee,' which should include some participants, the UN human rights officers, and relevant government or NGO officers.

The Guiding Principles for Human Rights Field Officers Working in Conflict and Post-Conflict Environments

Much of the preceding analysis has been distilled into ten Guiding Principles for Human Rights Field Officers Working in Conflict and

[34] Human Rights Watch, *Pursuit of Power: Political Violence and Repression in Burundi* (New York: Human Rights Watch, 2009): 73.

Post-Conflict Environments (the 'GPs').[35] A group of leading experts on human rights field work reviewed and commented on early drafts of the GPs, culminating in a day-long meeting at the Scuola Sant'Anna in Pisa in March 2008. Senior officials from OHCHR participated in every phase of the development of the GPs and they were officially introduced in Geneva in 2009. They "do not purport to be a comprehensive field manual or to exhaustively address every aspect of the issues explored. They are intended to provide a professional framework for the individual human rights field officer – in the main reflecting consensus as to international law and practice, but also pointing critically to how field practice may be enhanced."[36]

Initial reactions from practitioners to the GPs have been positive with most noting the GPs are practical, attuned to field realities, being both accessible and comprehensive. One mystery, however, is OHCHR's ambivalent attitude toward the GPs. Despite significant and sustained participation by OHCHR officials, the Office has not fully embraced the GPs nor, more importantly, used them or made them available to UN human rights field officers. The High Commissioner should formally endorse the GPs and have her Office incorporate them into training, doctrine, and evaluations of field work.

Greater awareness and application of the GPs would help to improve the quality of UN human rights field work while instilling a more coherent, consistent, and effective approach allowing for the variation in context that is the essence of field work. The challenge of doing principled work in diverse environments is precisely what makes human rights field work so difficult and rewarding.

---

[35] Full disclosure, the present author was the principal drafter of the Guiding Principles. William O'Neill, *Guiding Principles for Human Rights Field Officers Working in Conflict and Post-conflict Environments* (Nottingham: Human Rights Law Centre, University of Nottingham 2009).

[36] The GPs are also available online at www.hrfoguidingprinciples.org.

THE HIGH COMMISSIONER AND NATIONAL HUMAN RIGHTS INSTITUTIONS

Tseliso Thipanyane

Introduction

The year 1993 marked a momentous point in the struggle for the promotion and protection of human rights at the international, regional, and national levels. Following a lengthy process that formally began in the 1940s,[1] the UN General Assembly in December 1993 endorsed the Principles Relating to the Status and Functioning of National Institutions of Human Rights (Paris Principles).[2] These principles provide for the competence, responsibilities, composition, guarantees of independence, and methods of operation of national human rights institutions (NHRIs) and are used as a minimum standard to assess and accredit them by the International Coordinating Committee of National Institutions for the Promotion and Protection of Human Rights (ICC).[3]

During the same period, the General Assembly also adopted a resolution establishing the post of the UN High Commissioner for Human Rights – the principal UN official for human rights.[4] Support for the establishment and strengthening of NHRIs became one of the main responsibilities of the UN High Commissioner for Human Rights.[5]

---

[1] UN Centre For Human Rights, *National Human Rights Institutions: A Handbook on the Establishment and Strengthening of National Institutions for the Promotion and Protection of Human Rights: Professional Training Series No. 4* (Geneva: UN, 1995), 4.

[2] UN General Assembly. Resolution 48/154, "National Institutions for the Promotion and Protection of Human Rights," annex, UN GAOR A/RES/48/134, December 20, 1993.

[3] The ICC "is the international association of national human rights institutions (NHRIs) from all parts of the globe" established in 1993 by NHRIs. Its main objective is to support the establishment and strengthening of national human rights institutions in accordance with the Paris Principles. See "A Brief History of the ICC," International Coordinating Committee for National Human Rights Institutions, http://nhri.ohchr.org/EN/AboutUs/Pages/History.aspx.

[4] UN General Assembly, Resolution 48/141, "High Commissioner for the Promotion and Protection of All Human Rights," UN Doc. A/RES/48/141, December 20, 1993.

[5] This is through the provision of 'advisory services and technical and financial services' to states by the UN Centre for Human Rights and other relevant institutions for 'actions and programmes in the field of human rights,' see ibid, para. 4(d). See also, UN Centre for Human Rights, "Fact Sheet No 19, National Institutions for the Promotion and

The support for the establishment and strengthening of NHRIs provided by successive UN High Commissioners over the years has led to an impressive growth in the number of these institutions and to their significant and increasing impact on the advancement of human rights and involvement with the UN human rights system. There were, for example, about 15 NHRIs that were regarded to be compliant with the Paris Principles in 1994 when the first UN High Commissioner took office. This number increased to 31 in 2001, to 45 and 50 in 2003 and 2004 respectively, and stood at 69 in 2012.[6] Today these institutions make statements in intergovernmental bodies, submit information to both the treaty-monitoring bodies and the Human Rights Council, contribute to the development of international human rights norms and standards, and are increasingly gaining recognition in importance in the advancement of human rights. Ban Ki-moon in acknowledging the role and importance of these institutions observed:

> National human rights institutions compliant with the Paris Principles are key elements of a strong and effective national human rights protection system. They can help to ensure the compliance of national laws and practices with international human rights norms; support governments to ensure their implementation; monitor and address at the national level core human rights concerns such as torture, arbitrary detention, human trafficking and human rights of migrants; support the work of human rights defenders; and contribute to eradicate all forms of discrimination.[7]

Despite the proliferation of NHRIs and their increasing role in the advancement of human rights,[8] there are concerns about the compliance of many of these institutions with the Paris Principles and the effectiveness of

---

Protection of Human Rights," April 1993, http://www.ohchr.org/Documents/Publications/FactSheet19en.pdf.

6 See UN Commission on Human Rights, *National institutions for the promotion and protection of human rights / Report of the Secretary-General*, UN Doc. E/CN.4/2005/106, January 7, 2005, para. 12; "Chart of the Status of National Institutions (Accreditation Status as of May 2012)," International Coordinating Committee of National Institutions for the Promotion and Protection of Human Rights, http://nhri.ohchr.org/EN/Documents/Chart%20of%20the%20Status%20of%20NIs%20%2830%20May%202012%29.pdf.

7 See OHCHR, *Annual Report 2011*; UN Human Rights Council, *National Institutions for the Promotion and Protection of Human Rights / Report of the Secretary-General*, UN Doc. A/HRC/13/44, January 15, 2010, para. 108.

8 See C. Raj Kumar, "National Human Rights Institutions (NHRIs) and Economic, Social and Cultural Rights: Toward the Institutionalization and Developmentalization of Human Rights," *Human Rights Quarterly* 28, no. 3 (2006): 755–779; Linda C. Reif, "Building Democratic Institutions: The Role of National Human Rights Institutions in Good Governance and Human Rights Protection," *Harvard Human Rights Journal* 13, no. 1 (2000): 2.

many of those regarded to be in compliance with these principles.[9] These concerns also bring into question the effectiveness of the support these institutions receive from the UN and respective High Commissioners.

A review of the support successive High Commissioners have given to NHRIs is both opportune and important. It would benefit the current High Commissioner and future High Commissioners in their role and responsibility towards the establishment and effectiveness of these institutions. As a contribution to such a review, this chapter provides a critical assessment of the support national human rights institutions have received from respective High Commissioners and the achievements and weaknesses/challenges pertaining to such support.

Part I analyzes the main achievements of the support successive High Commissioners have provided for the establishment, strengthening, and integration of NHRIs in the UN human rights system. Part II deals with weaknesses and challenges of this support while Part III addresses several measures the current High Commissioner and future High Commissioners could consider in providing better support to these institutions.

Support for National Institutions

José Ayala Lasso: 1994–1997

José Ayala Lasso, the first UN High Commissioner for Human Rights,[10] provided important support to NHRIs that successive High Commissioners built upon and helped to develop a framework for ongoing assistance for these institutions. At the second session of the ICC held in Geneva in 1995, the High Commissioner indicated that one of his priorities would be the establishment and strengthening of NHRIs[11] and announced that the Centre for Human Rights, in consultation with the ICC,[12] was formulating

---

9 See Human Rights Watch, *Protectors or Pretenders? Government Human Rights Commissions in Africa* (New York: Human Rights Watch, 2001), http://www.hrw.org/reports/2001/africa. C. Raj Kumar sees some of these institutions as 'institutions that legitimize the functions of the state and do not intervene even when blatant violations of civil, political, economic, social, and cultural rights occur.' He refers to them as 'another arm of the state apparatus, producing less accessible bureaucratic styles of responding to human rights violations.' Kumar, "National Human Rights Institutions," 758–760.

10 See OHCHR, "José Ayala-Lasso," http://www.ohchr.org/EN/AboutUs/Pages/Ayala.aspx.

11 See UN General Assembly, *National institutions for the promotion and protection of human rights / Report of the Secretary-General*, UN GAOR A/50/452, September 20, 1995, para. 12.

12 See, e.g., Commission on Human Rights, *Report on the Fifty-Third Session (10 March-18 April 1997)*, UN Doc. E/CN.4/1997/150, (1997) 136, para. 12.

a policy that would guide and inform his support of NHRIs. The emergence of independent and effective national institutions that comply with the Paris Principles; the promotion of cooperation among national institutions at regional and sub-regional levels; and support for NHRIs in developing countries were the main thrusts of this policy.[13]

Ayala Lasso also initiated a process to restructure the organizational and operational structure of the UN Centre for Human Rights,[14] which, after his departure, led to the consolidation of the Centre for Human Rights with the Office of the High Commissioner for Human Rights (OHCHR) in September 1997.[15] The appointment of Brian Burdekin – the former Australian Human Rights Commissioner – as special adviser on national human rights institutions in July 1995 made a significant contribution to the support given to national human rights institutions by the High Commissioner.[16]

Establishment and Strengthening of National Human Rights Institutions

The establishment and strengthening of NHRIs was a central theme of many of José Ayala-Lasso's country visits. His visits included countries that were in transition to democracy, such as Malawi, Rwanda, Burundi, Lithuania, and Nepal.[17] During his October 1994 visit to Lithuania, for example, he met with the country's president to discuss the establishment of a national human rights commission in the country.[18] The opening of offices of the High Commissioner for Human Rights in Burundi (October 1994) and Malawi (January 1995) and the eventual establishment of NHRIs in these countries were a result of these visits.

The High Commissioner also received requests from several countries such as Nigeria, Indonesia, Panama, Kuwait, Pakistan, Slovenia, and Sri Lanka for assistance in the establishment of NHRIs.[19] Assistance was

---

13 *National Institutions*, A/50/452, paras. 21–22.

14 See UN General Assembly, *Report of the Secretary-General on the Work of the Organization*, UN GAOR A/51/1, August 20, 1996, para. 624.

15 UN General Assembly, *Report of the United Nations High Commissioner for Human Rights*, UN GAOR A/52/36, October 29, 1997, para 8.

16 See Chris Sidoti, "National Human Rights Institutions and the International Human Rights System," in *Human Rights, State Compliance, and Social Change: Assessing National Human Rights Institutions*, eds. Ryan Goodman and Thomas Pegram (New York: Cambridge University Press, 2012), 94; Peter Rosenblum, "Tainted Origins and Uncertain Outcomes: Evaluating NHRIs," in Goodman and Pegram, *Human Rights*, 302–303.

17 See UN General Assembly, *Report of the United Nations High Commissioner for Human Rights to the General Assembly*, UN GAOR A/49/36, January 1995.

18 Ibid., para. 42.

19 *National Institutions*, A/50/452, para. 33.

provided to several countries such as Latvia, Moldova, and other countries and entailed expert advice on enabling legislation for the establishment of NHRIs in Sri Lanka, Thailand, Georgia, and Nepal amongst other countries.[20]

Human rights training, the development and provision of training materials, expert advice, and capacity needs assessments for national institutions in countries like Papua New Guinea and Latvia were some of the measures provided and supported by the High Commissioner towards the strengthening of these institutions.[21] The publication of a handbook on NHRIs by the UN Centre for Human Rights in 1995 provided useful information on their establishment and strengthening.[22]

Significant support was also provided to the International Coordinating Committee of National Institutions for the Promotion and Protection of Human Rights (ICC) for its activities and meetings pertaining to the establishment and strengthening of national institutions and for the promotion of cooperation amongst them. In this regard, the High Commissioner convened and participated in the second session of the ICC held in Geneva in February 1995[23] and set a trend for future High Commissioners.

The High Commissioner also supported the establishment of regional networks of national institutions and their activities and meetings. The National Commission of Human Rights and Freedoms of Cameroon received financial and technical assistance from the Office of the High Commissioner to organize the first regional conference of African NHRIs. It was during this conference held in Yaoundé, Cameroon, from February 5 to 7 1996 that representatives of 12 African national institutions decided to establish the Coordinating Committee of African National Institutions[24] – later renamed the Network of African National Human

---

[20] UN General Assembly, *Report of the UN High Commissioner for Human Rights*," UN GAOR A/51/36, September 18, 1996, para. 27. See also, UN Commission on Human Rights, *Technical cooperation in the field of human rights / Report of the Secretary-General*, UN Doc. E/CN.4/1997/86, February 25, 1997, for detailed information on support provided by OHCHR to national human rights institutions.

[21] *National Institutions*, A/50/452, para. 32. See also, Anna-Elina Pohjolainen, *The Evolution of National Human Rights Institutions: The Role of the United Nations* (Copenhagen: Danish Institution for Human Rights, 2006), 66.

[22] See UN Centre for Human Rights, Training Series No. 4: National Human Rights Institutions: A Handbook for the Establishment and Strengthening of National Institutions for the Promotion and Protection of Human Rights (Geneva: United Nations, 1995).

[23] See Report of the Secretary-General, 'National institutions for the promotion and protection of human rights,' A/50/452 of 20 September 1995, para. 12.

[24] Report of the UN High Commissioner for Human Rights, A/51/36/ of September 18, 1996, para. 27.

Rights Institutions (NANHRI). Similar support was given for a July 1996 meeting of NHRIs in the Asia Pacific region held in Darwin, Australia that led to the formation of the Asia Pacific Forum of National Human Rights Institutions (APF).[25]

Integration of National Human Rights Institutions in the UN Human Rights System

Following the adoption of the Paris Principles, NHRIs were allowed to participate in meetings of the intergovernmental UN Commission on Human Rights, though in a limited capacity and as part of the official delegation of their respective governments. However, through the support of the High Commissioner and his staff, these institutions, beginning in 1996, were allowed to participate in meetings of the Commission on Human Rights in their own right, though they were only allowed to speak on the agenda item pertaining to their activities.[26] This support, nevertheless, contributed to a process that would eventually lead to greater integration of NHRIs in the UN human rights system.

Mary Robinson: 1997–2002

Mary Robinson[27] continued and consolidated the work started by her predecessor. More NHRIs were established during her term of office than under her predecessor.[28] As illustrated in her 2001 address to the International Coordinating Committee of NHRIs, she was particularly concerned about the effectiveness and independence of these institutions:[29]

> [T]he support of my Office is contingent on a demonstrated willingness to meet internationally accepted standards and a genuine commitment to produce results. In the case of institutions which are subservient to

[25] See Catherine Renshaw and Kieren Fitzpatrick, "National Human Rights Institutions in the Asia Pacific Region: Change Agents Under Conditions of Uncertainty," in Goodman and Pegram, *Human Rights*, 150–151.

[26] See UN Commission on Human Rights, *National Institutions for the Promotion and Protection of Human Rights / Report of the Secretary-General*, UN Doc. E/CN.4/1998/47, December 30, 1997, paras. 6, 15.

[27] UN General Assembly, *Report of the High Commissioner for Human Rights* (1997) para. 2. See also, Office of the High Commissioner for Human Rights, "Mary Robinson," http://www.ohchr.org/EN/AboutUs/Pages/Robinson.aspx.

[28] See Report of the Secretary-General on national human rights institutions, E/CN.4/2005/106 of 7 January 2005, para. 12.

[29] "Address by Mary Robinson, United Nations High Commissioner for Human Rights to the International Co-Coordinating Committee of National Institutions for the Promotion and Protection of Human Rights," April 18, 2001.

Governments that violate their international human rights obligations, support has not been forthcoming – nor will it be.

More significant progress in the integration of these institutions in the UN human rights system was made during her term of office. She also played an important role in forging greater cooperation among UN bodies for the support of these institutions.[30]

Establishment and Strengthening of National Human Rights Institutions

In order to enhance the support given to NHRIs, the High Commissioner had an evaluation of her Office conducted in 1998. The evaluation highlighted the need to increase the capacity of OHCHR in supporting these institutions in response to increasing demands for such assistance.[31]

Efforts by the High Commissioner to promote greater cooperation between OHCHR and other UN bodies for the support of national institutions led to a memorandum of understanding between OHCHR and UNDP signed on March 4, 1998.[32] This resulted in several joint projects between the two bodies pertaining to the establishment and strengthening of NHRI in several countries including Albania, Bangladesh, Latvia, Uganda, and the Republic of Moldova,[33] and the development and implementation of national plans of action for human rights in countries such as Australia, Bolivia, Brazil, Ecuador, Indonesia, Latvia, Malawi, Mexico, the Philippines, South Africa, and Venezuela.[34]

Support by the High Commissioner for the development and adoption of the ICC's rules of procedure on April 6, 1998, helped to improve the

---

30 Her efforts and the high priority her Office gave to the support of national institutions was acknowledged by the Commission on Human Rights. See UN Commission on Human Rights. Resolution 1998/55, "National Institutions for the Promotion and Protection of Human Rights," UN Doc. E/CN.4/1998/55, April 17, 1998, paras. 5–6.

31 UN General Assembly, *Report of the United Nations High Commissioner for Human Rights*, A/54/36 UN GAOR A/54/36 (New York: United Nations, September 1999), para.50.

32 Ibid., paras. 41and 61.

33 See Commission on Human Rights, *Report of the Secretary-General submitted in accordance with Commission on Human Rights resolution 1998/55*, UN Doc. E/CN.4/1999/95, February 3, 1999, para. 11.

34 UN General Assembly, *Report of the High Commissioner*, A/54/36, para. 46. By 2001, OHCHR was responding to requests from 60 states for assistance in the establishment and strengthening of national human rights institutions. See UN General Assembly, *Report of the Secretary-General on the Work of the Organization*, UN GAOR A/56/1 (September 2001), para. 201. OHCHR also published a handbook to assist national institutions in the development and implementation of national human rights action plans. See OHCHR, *Professional Training Series No. 10, Handbook on National Human Rights Plans of Action* (New York and Geneva: UN, 2002).

accreditation system and ensure greater compliance with the Paris Principles by NHRIs. Compliance with the Paris Principles became a prerequisite for full membership and participation in the ICC and its activities for NHRIs thereafter. OHCHR provided secretarial support to the ICC for assessing the requisite compliance.[35] The development of a website for NHRIs in 2002 in collaboration with the Danish Centre for Human Rights promoted greater cooperation amongst these institutions.[36]

Regional networks of NHRIs and their activities also continued to be supported by OHCHR. The High Commissioner in this regard gave a keynote address at the second conference of African national institutions held in Durban, South Africa, from June 30 to July 3, 1998. Support was also provided for the establishment of the network of NHRIs of the Americas in 2000.[37]

Integration of National Human Rights Institutions in the UN Human Rights System

Further integration of NHRIs in the UN human rights system was supported by the High Commissioner. In 1998, the Commission on Human Rights allowed NHRIs to have their own seats separate from those of government delegations.[38] This positive development was a further recognition of the role these institutions could play in the UN human rights system.[39]

The High Commissioner, mainly through the National Institutions Team, also promoted greater interaction between NHRIs and the UN treaty bodies. Treaty bodies were advised of the role national institutions could play in the application and monitoring of the implementation of international human rights standards at national levels by OHCHR.[40] The adoption of General Comment No. 10 on the role of NHRIs in the protection of economic, social, and cultural rights by the Committee on Economic, Social and Cultural Rights in 1998[41] and General Comment

---

35 *Report of the Secretary-General*, E/CN.4/1999/95, paras. 47, 51.

36 UN Commission on Human Rights, *National institutions for the promotion and protection of human rights / Report of the Secretary-General*, UN Doc. E/CN.4/2003/110, December 31, 2002, para. 12.

37 Ibid., paras. 12, 14.

38 *Report of the Secretary-General*, E/CN.4/1999/95, para. 58.

39 See UN Commission on Human Rights, Resolution 1998/55; UN Commission on Human Rights, Resolution 1997/40, "National Institutions for the Promotion and Protection of Human Rights, UN Doc. E/CN.4/1997/40, April 11, 1997.

40 *National institutions*, E/CN.4/2003/110, para. 41.

41 *Report of the Secretary-General*, E/CN.4/1999/95, para. 4.

No. 2 (2002) on the role of NHRIs in the promotion and protection of child rights by the Committee on the Rights of the Child[42] was an acknowledgement of this role.

Through the support of the High Commissioner,[43] national institutions participated in the World Conference against Racism, Racial Discrimination, Xenophobia and Related Intolerance, held in Durban, South Africa, from August 31 to September 7, 2001.[44] This was the first time national institutions participated in a UN conference independently.[45]

Sergio Vieira de Mello: 2002–2003 and Bertrand Ramcharan (Acting High Commissioner): 2003–2004

Despite the short period Sergio Vieira de Mello served as High Commissioner, he continued the work of his predecessors and also contributed to the increasing role and recognition of NHRIs in the international human rights system. His view was that the establishment of effective and Paris Principles compliant NHRIs was crucial for sustainable human rights protection worldwide, and he identified the support of these institutions as a priority of his office.[46]

Establishment and Strengthening of National Human Rights Institutions

Several initiatives to promote and coordinate support for NHRIs by UN bodies were taken by OHCHR. As an example, a UN interagency workshop on national human rights institutions was organized by OHCHR in May 2003. This was followed by the request of the UN Secretary-General for OHCHR to prepare a plan of action to strengthen the UN's work on human rights including support for the establishment and development of national human rights promotion and protection systems.[47] Consultations also

---

42 *National institutions*, E/CN.4/2003/110, para. 51.

43 UN Commission on Human Rights, Resolution 2000/76, "National Institutions for the Promotion and Protection of Human Rights, Un Doc. E/CN.4/RES/2000/76, April 26, 2000, para. 8. This resolution encouraged the participation of national institutions in preparations for the World Conference.

44 See UN Commission on Human Rights, *National institutions for the promotion and protection of human rights / Report of the Secretary-General submitted in accordance with resolution 2000/76,* UN Doc. E/CN.4/2001/99, December 26, 2000, para. 9.

45 See World Conference against Racism, Racial Discrimination, Xenophobia and Related Intolerance, "Durban Declaration," UN Doc. A/CONF.189/12, September 8, 2001.

46 Sergio Vieira de Mello, address at the Annual Meeting of the ICC in Geneva, Switzerland, April 15, 2003.

47 UN General Assembly, *Report of the Secretary-General on the Work of the Organization*, UN GAOR A/58/1, August 2003, para.172.

took place between OHCHR, UNDP, and the United Nations Educational, Scientific and Cultural Organization (UNESCO) on how these organizations could best support national human rights institutions.[48]

Over 70 national human rights institutions received support during the Vieira de Mello and Ramcharan terms of office. This entailed support for international and regional workshops to promote the establishment of NHRIs and to enhance the capacity of existing institutions. One example of this was the workshop for Portuguese speaking African countries that OHCHR helped to organize in Maputo, Mozambique from January 27 to 29, 2003, under the theme 'National human rights institutions, their role, the Paris Principles and guidelines for their establishment and functioning.' The workshop led to the establishment of a national human rights institution in Mozambique a few years later. OHCHR also supported an international workshop on the effectiveness of national institutions organized by the British Council in Belfast in October 2003.[49]

The publication of a handbook on economic, social, and cultural rights for national institutions by OHCHR was intended to enhance the effectiveness of NHRIs in dealing with economic and social rights issues and challenges. OHCHR also continued to support the website for NHRIs.[50]

Integration of National Human Rights Institutions in the UN Human Rights System

The decision of the Sub-Commission for the Promotion and Protection of Human Rights, a subsidiary body of the UN Commission on Human Rights, in its fifty-fifth session to allow accredited NHRIs to speak on *any* substantive agenda item in their own right was another significant development attributed to the support of OHCHR to some extent. Another important development was the participation of NHRIs in the Working Group of the Ad Hoc Committee on a Comprehensive and Integral Convention on Protection and Promotion of the Rights and Dignity of Persons with Disabilities, which Sergio Vieira de Mello supported.[51] This was the first time national institutions took part in the drafting of a UN human rights

48 UN Commission on Human Rights, *National institutions for the promotion and protection of human rights / Report of the Secretary-General*, UN Doc. E/CN.4/2004/101, January 28, 2004, para. 28.

49 Ibid, paras. 4, 17, 24.

50 Ibid., paras. 7, 32.

51 Ibid., paras. 9, 33.

treaty as distinct actors and reflected an increasing integration of these institutions in the UN human rights system.

OHCHR also continued to organize and support conferences and workshops for national institutions in order to promote their integration in the UN human rights system. A training workshop on how NHRIs could engage treaty bodies was convened and included representatives of national institutions from Colombia, Guatemala, Latvia, the Russian Federation, and Sri Lanka.[52]

Louise Arbour: 2004–2008

Like other High Commissioners, Louise Arbour also focused on ensuring effective support for NHRIs. As she explained in November 2004, "the UN can do little to ensure respect for human rights without the support of national actors" and the "need for strong national human rights institutions...is greater than ever." Her activities in support of NHRIs were based on a three-prong approach: strengthening of the capacity of national institutions, enhancing international support for them, and working with them as a partner.[53]

The High Commissioner released a report on May 20, 2005, detailing her vision for the future direction of OHCHR. The strengthening of national systems of human rights protection was one of the main features of her vision and entailed amongst other things, support for the development of national human rights action plans, human rights education, and strengthening of NHRIs in terms of monitoring and investigative techniques.[54] This was followed by the release of the High Commissioner's first biennial strategic plan on key focus areas for her Office.[55]

Establishment and Strengthening of National Human Rights Institutions

In addition to measures focused on establishing and strengthening NHRIs and support for the ICC and its activities, the High Commissioner collaborated with the International Council on Human Rights Policy to review

---

52 Ibid., para. 25.

53 Louise Arbour, address of the High Commissioner at the 7th International Conference of National Institutions, Seoul, Republic of Korea, September 14, 2004.

54 UN General Assembly, *Report of the Secretary-General on the Work of the Organization*, A/60/1, August 2005, paras. 182, 192. See also *OHCHR Plan of Action: Protection and Empowerment*, May 2005, paras. 45–50 and 63–66.

55 UN General Assembly, *Report of the Secretary-General on the Work of the Organization*, A/61/1, August 2006, para. 117.

the effectiveness of NHRIs. The study proposed appropriate recommendations to enhance the effectiveness of NHRIs and their compliance with the Paris Principles.[56] OHCHR also partnered with the International Service for Human Rights, a leading human rights organization, to determine effective cooperation between NHRIs and non-governmental organizations.[57]

Integration of National Human Rights Institutions in the UN Human Rights System

The 2005 resolution of the UN Commission on Human Rights allowing NHRIs compliant with the Paris Principles to speak on all agenda items of the Commission was a major development in the integration of these institutions in the UN human rights system. This was a culmination of efforts of OHCHR amongst other actors and was, according to the UN Secretary-General, a "significant development that would enhance the status of national institutions within the international human rights system."[58]

OHCHR also assisted over 36 national institutions to participate in the sixtieth session of the Commission on Human Rights. National institutions were also accorded their own document series – E/CN.4/2004/NI/ – which allowed them to submit written documents to the Commission.[59]

OHCHR also continued to support and encourage the participation of NHRIs in the work of UN treaty bodies. The adoption and entering into force of the Convention on the Rights of Persons with Disabilities in May 2008 was another important development in the integration of NHRIs in the UN human rights system. The Convention contains specific provisions regarding the monitoring, reporting and complaints handling roles of NHRIs.[60]

---

[56] International Council on Human Rights Policy and the Office of the High Commissioner for Human Rights, *Assessing the Effectiveness of National Human Rights Institutions* (Geneva: International Council on Human Rights Policy, 2005).

[57] UN Commission on Human Rights, *National institutions for the promotion and protection of human rights / Report of the Secretary-General.* UN Doc. E/CN.4/2005/106, January 7, 2005, para. 10.

[58] *Report of the Secretary-General*, A/60/1, para. 184.

[59] *National Institutions*, E/CN.4/2005/106, para. 117.

[60] UN General Assembly, *Report of the Secretary-General on the Work of the Organization*, A/63/1, August 2008, para. 70.

Navi Pillay: 2008–2014

Under Navi Pillay, whose term as High Commissioner will end in July 2014,[61] national institutions compliant with the Paris Principles have continued to increase in number, impact, and recognition in the UN human rights system. OHCHR under her leadership has continued to work closely with the ICC in the establishment and strengthening of NHRIs.[62]

Establishment and Strengthening of National Human Rights Institutions

Over 40 national institutions were supported during the High Commissioner's first year in office and this number continues to increase. The support provided by OHCHR to these institutions includes assistance in the selection of commissioners and their training and assistance in the accreditation process of these institutions by the ICC. OHCHR also collaborates with UNDP, other UN bodies, and various NHRIs in this regard.[63]

A survey of national institutions was conducted by OHCHR in order to identify priority areas for the support of NHRIs by the UN.[64] A fellowship program introduced by OHCHR in 2008 allows staff members of national institutions that comply with the Paris Principles to spend time in Geneva gaining experience in the UN human rights system.[65] A new website for national institutions supported by OHCHR began operating in 2011.[66]

OHCHR and UNDP developed a toolkit to help UN country teams provide more effective assistance to national institutions[67] and also agreed

61 See UN Department of Public Information, "United Nations High Commissioner for Human Rights, Navi Pillay, to Serve Two More Years, By Geneva Assembly Decision," UN press release GA/11244, May 24, 2012.

62 Navi Pillay, "Statement by the UN High Commissioner for Human Rights at the 10th International Conference of NHRIs: Human Rights and Business: The Role of NHRIs, Edinburgh, Scotland, UK, October 8–10, 2010."

63 UN General Assembly, *Report of the UN High Commissioner for Human Rights*, UN GAOR A/64/36, August 2009, para. 40.

64 Ibid., para. 42.

65 See OHCHR, "Fellowship Programme," http://www.ohchr.org/EN/AboutUs/Pages/FellowshipNHRIStaff.aspx.

66 See International Coordinating Committee of National Institutions for the Promotion and Protection of Human Rights, "UN Human Rights Committee Outlines Relationship with NHRIs," January 7, 2013 http://nhri.ohchr.org/EN/News/Lists/News/DispForm.aspx?ID=90.

67 UN General Assembly, *Report of the United Nations High Commissioner for Human Rights*, UN Doc. A/65/36, August 11, 2010, para. 38.

on a joint global strategy in 2011 to ensure greater support for NHRIs.[68] The development of a manual for the assessment of national institutions that is increasingly being used to determine the needs of many national institutions is a result of this strategy.[69]

Integration of National Human Rights Institutions in the UN Human Rights System

OHCHR facilitated the participation of national institutions in the 2009 Durban Review Conference, held in Geneva. The attendance and participation of NHRIs in the conference, including the reading of their joint statement, was confirmation of their increasing integration in the UN human rights system.[70]

The involvement of NHRIs in the Universal Periodic Review (UPR) process of the UN Human Rights Council is the latest and by far the most significant example of the integration of NHRIs in the UN human rights system. This process allows NHRIs to make their own submissions on human rights developments in their respective countries, advise and engage their governments on the process, and cooperate with other national institutions in the sharing of experiences. OHCHR assisted many NHRIs to engage with the UPR process by providing training and facilitating information exchanges among NHRIs on the process, and it continues to do so. It also facilitated the interaction between national institutions, UN country teams, and civil society organizations on the process.[71]

Efforts of the High Commissioner in assisting the integration of NHRIs in the UN human rights system, particularly the Human Rights Council and its UPR process and the UN treaty bodies, were commended by the General Assembly in resolution 64/161 of December 18, 2009.[72] Resolution 16/21 of March 25, 2011 of the Human Rights Council provides a greater role for NHRIs in the UPR process and allows NHRIs to nominate special procedures mandate holders, highlighting another acknowledgement of

---

[68] UN General Assembly, *National Institutions for the Promotion and Protection of Human Rights, Report by the Secretary-General*, UN Doc. A/66/274, August 8, 2011, para. 19.

[69] See Asia Pacific Forum of National Human Rights Institutions (APF), UNDP, and OHCHR, *Capacity Assessment Manual for National Human Rights Institutions* (Bangkok: UNDP, 2011).

[70] "Statement to the Durban Review Conference by National Human Rights Institutions, Geneva, April 24, 2008," http://www.un.org/durbanreview2009/pdf/closing_stm_draft2.ENG.final.pdf. The author read the statement on behalf of the chairperson of the ICC.

[71] *Report of the United Nations High Commissioner*, UN Doc. A/65/36, para. 18.

[72] Ibid., para. 37.

the increasing role and impact of these institutions.[73] This was followed by resolution 20/14 of the Human Rights Council supporting the participation of Paris Principles-compliant NHRIs in all relevant UN human rights mechanisms, including the General Assembly.

Overall Support

Successive High Commissioners have strived to enhance the independence of NHRIs, the effectiveness of these institutions in promoting and monitoring human rights at the national level, and their participation in the international human rights system. The main vehicle in this regard has been a unit maintained within OHCHR that pays attention to the interests of NHRIs, trains and assists these institutions to function better, promotes regional and international co-operation amongst them, and supports their participation in appropriate international human rights activities and forums.

Much of the funding provided to OHCHR for the support of NHRIs is used to maintain the international network and support meetings of the NHRIs and the ICC. OHCHR serves as the ICC's secretariat and, in this capacity, organizes meetings of the ICC in Geneva and the two annual sessions of the ICC's Sub-Committee on Accreditation (SCA). The interpretation and translation services costs for activities of the ICC are also covered by OHCHR. The ICC's biennial international conferences are also funded by OHCHR. In some cases, travel of NHRIs from the least developed countries to attend the annual or biennial meetings are funded by the OHCHR too. OHCHR also regularly provides a grant to the NHRI assuming the chairpersonship of the ICC and also provides grants to regional networks of NHRIs.[74]

OHCHR also pays for consultants to work directly with relevant NHRIs to enhance the capacity and effectiveness of these institutions. Substantive support, such as legal advice on draft laws for the establishment of many NHRIs; workshops, seminars, and training sessions for newly appointed Commissioners and/or staff; and other field-based activities for establishing and strengthening these institutions is also provided by OHCHR.[75] This support has been increasing over time as more NHRIs are established and more deeply integrated in the UN human rights system.

---

[73] *National Institutions*, UN Doc. A/66/274, para. 70.

[74] Private communication, September 9, 2012, and prior knowledge and experience of the author.

[75] Ibid.

Challenges and Weaknesses in the Support of National Human Rights Institutions

Overview

Establishment and Strengthening of National Human Rights Institutions

While there has been a substantial growth in the number of NHRIs that comply with the Paris Principles, a significant number of NHRIs are not compliant with these principles due to weaknesses in their founding laws or instruments, their composition, and powers that negate their independence and denude their effectiveness. A significant number of states are yet to establish these institutions.

Many NHRIs that are deemed to be in compliance with the Paris Principles are not very effective due to factors such as lack of adequate resources, poor or weak leadership, and inadequate cooperation and support from their governments. Inadequate resources render many of these institutions inaccessible to many victims of human rights violations.[76] Limited knowledge of human rights within the leadership of many of these institutions, power struggles related to poor governance systems, and weak leadership that is subservient to governments also undermine the effectiveness and credibility of many NHRIs.

The survey on NHRIs conducted by the UN Office of the High Commissioner for Human Rights in 2009 also points out many challenges faced by national institutions in relation to their work and impact. The failure of many national institutions to follow up on their own recommendations in relation to human rights issues and their inadequate interaction with civil society organizations are some of the concerns highlighted by the survey.[77]

---

[76] In its report on the re-accreditation of the Bolivian national human rights institutions, Defensoria del Pueblo, the Sub-Committee on Accreditation Committee of the ICC whilst recommending an "A" status re-accreditation for the institution expressed a concern that more than 50 percent of its budget including staff salaries was from external sources. See International Coordinating Committee of National Institutions for the Promotion and Protection of Human Rights, *Report and Recommendations of the Sessions of the Sub-Committee on Accreditation* (*SCA*), March 2012, p 17. http://nhri.ohchr.org/EN/AboutUs/ICCAccreditation/Documents/SCA%20MARCH%202012%20FINAL%20REPORT%20ENG%20WITH%20ANNEXURES.pdf.

[77] OHCHR, *Survey on National Human Rights Institutions: Report on the Findings and Recommendations of a Questionnaire* (Geneva: OHCHR, 2009), pp 33- 34, 57.

Integration in the UN Human Rights System

Notwithstanding developments and institutional arrangements to promote the integration of NHRIs in the UN human rights system, many NHRIs that comply with Paris Principles have not adequately and effectively engaged the UN human rights system and its mechanisms. According to the OHCHR survey on NHRIs, only about 50 percent of NHRIs engaged adequately and meaningfully with the UN human rights system. More NHRIs participated in the UPR process, whilst the treaty bodies had the lowest level of such participation according to the survey.[78] Financial and capacity constraints and lack of adequate knowledge and expertise in the international human rights system for many NHRIs contributed to this situation.[79]

Support provided by the High Commissioners and OHCHR

The above-mentioned challenges of national institutions are indicative, to some extent, of limitations and weaknesses in the support provided by OHCHR to these institutions. These challenges can be attributed to the following four factors affecting the supportive role of OHCHR: funding and capacity, coordination of UN bodies, accreditation system for national institutions, and lobbying of governments.

Funding and Capacity

The biggest challenge that has faced OHCHR and that continues to do so is the lack of adequate resources and capacity. This affects the requisite support needed for NHRIs and also undermines the ability of OHCHR to monitor and follow-up on the impact and effectiveness of the support provided to NHRIs.

Inadequate resources and expertise on NHRIs were blamed for the limited support the Centre for Human Rights was able to avail to these institutions in the early stages of the term of the first High Commissioner.[80] In her 1998 report, Mary Robinson expressed a concern about inadequate resources availed to her Office and the impact of this on the support her Office provided to national human rights institutions. She also indicated that there had been no significant improvements in the budget allocation

---

78 Ibid., pp 42–43.

79 See Sidoti, note 16 above, p. 103.

80 See Pohjolainen, note 21 above, p. 66.

to OHCHR from 1995 to 1998 and that her Office also experienced a loss of staff posts between 1996–1997 and 1998–1999.[81]

While financial support to OHCHR from the regular UN budget and voluntary contributions of Member States for the assistance of NHRIs has been increased over the years, this is still not adequate to meet increasing demands for support of NHRIs. In 2002, for example, OHCHR received $1.2 million for a two-year period for the support of NHRIs and expended $866,948 in 2002 on activities related to its national institutions unit.[82] In 2010, OHCHR received $1.3 million for the support of NHRIs and this increased to $1.8 million in 2011 while it expended about $1.6 million for each of the years.[83]

This financial situation has negatively affected the extent and quality of support the OHCHR provides for the engagement of national institutions with UN treaty bodies, the UPR process, the accreditation process of the ICC, and interaction between NHRIs and civil society organizations. The inadequacy of funds also affects the monitoring by OHCHR of the impact of support provided to NHRIs.[84] The survey conducted by the Office of the High Commissioner on national institutions highlights this challenge very well.[85]

Coordination of UN Bodies

Poor and inadequate coordination by OHCHR – a key responsibility of the High Commissioner – of the support various UN entities such as UNDP and UNICEF should and can provide for the support of NHRIs exacerbates the financial and capacity challenges of OHCHR. While the memorandum of agreement between UNDP and OHCHR has promoted better cooperation between these two entities, the absence of such an agreement between OHCHR and other UN bodies such as UNICEF which also work with NHRIs does not augur well for the desired support for NHRIs.

---

[81] UN General Assembly, *Report of the United Nations High Commissioner for Human Rights,* UN GAOR A/53/36, October 1998, para. 62.

[82] See OHCHR, *Annual Report 2002,* paras. 108–109.

[83] See OHCHR, *Annual Report 2011,* para. 140. OHCHR's 2011 Report shows an increase from US$1,600,800 in 2010 to US$1,673,400 in 2011 in terms of what OHCHR has expended on national institutions.

[84] As an example, OHCHR provided technical assistance for the drafting and adoption of the South African National Action Plan for the Protection and Promotion of Human Rights in 1998 but did not have the means to monitor the implementation of this plan. The plan was never fully implemented and was not revised after its three-year lifespan. Based on the author's knowledge and involvement with the process.

[85] OHCHR, *Annual Report 2002.*

Accreditation Process

Resource challenges have also affected the accreditation process of the ICC supported by OHCHR. Due to lack of adequate resources, the ICC's accreditation process has not been very effective – it lacks rigor and does not have frequent reviews of NHRIs. This resulted in several NHRIs with questionable compliance with the Paris Principles being accredited or remaining accredited while in flagrant violation of these principles.[86] This situation has cast doubt on the effectiveness and credibility of the accreditation process and is compounded by the fact that the ICC's accreditation system has for a long time largely focused on formal compliance with the Paris Principles by NHRIs with limited focus on the actual effectiveness of the institutions.[87] Some scholars like Peter Rosenblum have ascribed many of these challenges to the initial failure of OHCHR to have NHRIs evaluated in the context of "their actual contribution to human rights" and the "notoriously difficult bureaucratic environment" in OHCHR, which makes meaningful and necessary changes difficult to effect.[88]

While the new measures taken by the ICC to improve the accreditation system in order to make it more 'rigorous and transparent' are acknowledged,[89] it is not clear whether these measures will succeed in enhancing the effectiveness of NHRIs and be effectively implemented in view of the resource and capacity constraints of OHCHR.

Lobbying of Governments

While there are on-going interactions between OHCHR and governments in relation to the establishment and strengthening of NHRIs, the challenges experienced by many NHRIs in terms of their funding, effectiveness, and support and cooperation from their governments highlight

[86] It took more than a year (October 2007) for the National Human Rights Commission of Nigeria to lose its "A" status with the ICC following the removal of the Commission's executive secretary, Mr. Bello in June 2006 by the Nigerian government in violation of the Commission's independence. See International Coordinating Committee, *Report and Recommendations of the Sub-Committee on Accreditation* (*SCA*), (Geneva: ICC, October 2007), p. 10.

[87] See International Council on Human Rights Policy and OHCHR, *Assessing the Effectiveness of National Human Rights Institutions,* note 56 above.

[88] See Rosenblum, note 16 above, pp. 302–303.

[89] The accreditation process now considers the 'effectiveness of NHRIs and their engagement with the international human rights system. Non-Governmental organizations can also make inputs in the assessment of relevant national institutions. See International Coordinating Committee, *Report and Recommendations of the Sub-Committee on Accreditation* (*SCA*), May 2011.

weaknesses in these dialogues.[90] This is despite the many resolutions of the UN General Assembly and the UN Human Rights Council urging for such support from states and UN bodies.[91]

Recommendations: Towards Better Support of National Institutions

Funding and Capacity

The increase in the capacity of OHCHR to effectively support national human rights institutions is a crucial matter that needs to be attended to by the current High Commissioner and future High Commissioners. This would require extensive lobbying of the UN and Member States to provide more funds to OHCHR for its support of NHRIs.

Coordination of UN Bodies

The current High Commissioner and future High Commissioners need to ensure that there is better coordination within the UN human rights system for more effective support of NHRIs. This would require greater attention to management and process issues and the improvement of working relations between relevant UN bodies, particularly UNICEF and UNDP. Greater coordination of UN entities for the support of NHRIs can minimize the resource and capacity constraints of OHCHR.

Accreditation Process

More material support by OHCHR would enhance the requisite rigor and frequency of the ICC's accreditation process, which in turn would improve the effectiveness of NHRIs and help these institutions to exert their independence and demand better support from governments.

Lobbying Governments

The establishment of independent and effective national institutions would make the work of OHCHR easier and more effective. Well-functioning national human rights institutions are crucial for the success

90 Annual reports of the Sub-Committee on Accreditation of the ICC highlight many of these challenges.

91 See UN Human Rights Council. Resolution 20/14, "National institutions for the promotion and protection of human rights," UN Doc. A/HRC/RES/20/14, July 16, 2012.

of OHCHR and for the advancement human rights worldwide. The current High Commissioner and OHCHR should make more effort to tap and maximize this potential. In engagements and interactions with respective governments and political leaders, the High Commissioner should make a stronger case for NHRIs.

Conclusion

While the support for the establishment and strengthening of national human rights institutions by OHCHR has certainly contributed to the large increase in the number of these institutions and their impact in the promotion and protection of human rights, much more should be done by OHCHR to support these institutions. Much of this support should entail lobbying respective governments to establish effective and well-resourced institutions as required by the Paris Principles and numerous resolutions of the UN General Assembly and the Human Rights Council. This will require bold and courageous leadership in the Office of the High Commissioner that is appreciative of the role and future of these institutions in the promotion and protection of human rights.

PART FOUR

INFLUENCING OTHER BODIES TO ACT

THE HIGH COMMISSIONER FOR HUMAN RIGHTS AND THE UN HUMAN RIGHTS COUNCIL

Suzanne Nossel and Christen L. Broecker

Introduction

Beginning in the fall of 2009, the UN High Commissioner for Human Rights and her Office (the Office of the High Commissioner for Human Rights, or OHCHR) experienced a significant increase in engagement with the UN Human Rights Council, the political body with primary responsibility for human rights issues within the UN system. At that time, the Council became more active in addressing serious human rights crises worldwide than at any point since its creation in 2006. In part, the Council's increased activity came in reaction to the emergence of significant political unrest in the Middle East and North Africa that commenced in late 2010. It also resulted from concerted efforts by a number of Council Member States to improve the body's responsiveness in the face of abuses, and particularly the United States, which first joined the Council in 2009.

During this time period, the Council demonstrated a newfound willingness to create new mandates to address human rights issues worldwide, including thematic and country-specific special rapporteurs, fact-finding missions, and international commissions of inquiry. While the Council's blessing was a necessary prerequisite for the creation of these mechanisms, the responsibility to provide the administrative and staff support necessary for them to succeed fell squarely on the High Commissioner and OHCHR. Thus, the Council's increased activity provided the High Commissioner with important opportunities to make an impact on the world's response to human rights crises, but also with significant new and unanticipated responsibilities.

High Commissioner Navi Pillay made clear that she welcomed the opportunities presented by the newly energized Council. During this period she took advantage of 'special sessions' of the Human Rights Council, at which she was invited to present key facts, highlight patterns of abuse, and draw global media attention to crises. Pillay framed the narrative surrounding these crises, identified the controlling human rights standards, and offered suggestions for how the Council should react. The High

Commissioner was also responsive to the Council's operational demands, mounting the monitoring and investigative mechanisms it created to address situations of concern.

In the future, however, the present and future High Commissioners could do even more to engage and support the work of the Human Rights Council. Following the reelection of the United States to a second term on the Council, which will extend its presence there to 2015, the High Commissioner can expect that its increased activity and responsiveness will be sustained. She should take advantage of this opportunity by engaging diplomatically with Member States on key issues; undertaking independent investigation and reporting activities to a greater extent in order to provoke the Council to act; and providing additional support to independent force-multipliers such as the Council's special procedures. The High Commissioner must also urgently undertake institutional reforms within OHCHR to enable it to adequately conduct sustained human rights fact-finding and monitoring as needed on a global scale.

The observations on the work of the High Commissioner for Human Rights and her Office during this time period detailed in this chapter are derived from first-hand experience. Suzanne Nossel served as US deputy assistant secretary of state for international organizations from August 2009 through October 2011 and had significant responsibility for US engagement at the UN Human Rights Council. The reflections in this paper are thus confined to that catalytic, though limited, period of time.

Background

In its first years of operation, the Human Rights Council did not live up to the hopes that it would improve upon the shortcomings that plagued its predecessor institution, the UN Commission on Human Rights. A majority of the states comprising the initial membership of the Council rejected the practice of 'naming and shaming' human rights violators.[1] These states were often reluctant to support efforts to investigate and promote

[1] The Council's initial Member States were: Algeria, Argentina, Azerbaijan, Bahrain, Bangladesh, Brazil, Cameroon, Canada, China, Cuba, Czech Republic, Djibouti, Ecuador, Finland, France, Gabon, Germany, Ghana, Guatemala, India, Indonesia, Japan, Jordan, Malaysia, Mali, Mauritius, Mexico, Morocco, Netherlands, Nigeria, Pakistan, Peru, Philippines, Poland, Republic of Korea, Romania, Russian Federation, Saudi Arabia, Senegal, South Africa, Sri Lanka, Switzerland, Tunisia, Ukraine, United Kingdom, Uruguay and Zambia.

accountability for human rights abuse (an exception was made for abuses perpetrated by Israel, which were the subject of frequent Council deliberations). Indeed, during the period between 2006 and fall 2009, despite the emergence of new human rights crises in many places worldwide, the Council did not establish a single new country-specific special procedure. It terminated existing mandates on Belarus and Cuba and came within one vote of ending the mandate of the independent expert on human rights in Sudan, despite the persistently deplorable human rights situations in those countries.

The Council's record with regard to convening 'special sessions' to consider human rights crises was also quite poor in its first years of operation. Four of its first six special sessions focused on Israel. In May 2009, the Council convened its eleventh special session on the human rights crisis in Sri Lanka, but rather than condemning the government for indiscriminately killing tens of thousands of civilians in its attempt to defeat an armed insurgency, it instead congratulated the government on its successful counter-terrorism campaign.[2]

The focus and tempo of the Council began to change in fall 2009. In the two years that followed, the Council would take action in the face of serious human rights abuses in Côte d'Ivoire (convening a special session and creating a commission of inquiry),[3] Libya (convening a special session and creating a commission of inquiry),[4] Syria (holding four special sessions, deploying an OHCHR fact-finding mission, and establishing a commission of inquiry),[5] Iran (establishing a country-specific special rapporteur),[6] and

---

2 UN Human Rights Council. Resolution S-11, "Assistance to Sri Lanka in the promotion and protection of human rights," UN Doc. A/HRC/S-11/2, June 2, 2009, 3.

3 UN Human Rights Council. Resolution S-14, "Situation of human rights in Côte d'Ivoire in relation to the conclusion of the 2010 presidential election," UN Doc. A/HRC/RES/S-14/1, April 1, 2011.

4 UN Human Rights Council. Resolution S-15, "Situation of human rights in the Libyan Arab Jamahiriya," UN Doc. A/HRC/RES/S-15/1, February 25, 2011.

5 UN Human Rights Council. Resolution S-16/1, "The current human rights situation in the Syrian Arab Republic in the context of recent events," UN Doc. A/HRC/RES/S-16-1, May 4, 2011; UN Human Rights Council. Resolution S-17, "Grave Human Rights Violations in the Syrian Arab Republic," UN Doc. A/HRC/ S-17/1, August 18, 2011; UN Human Rights Council. Resolution S-18, "The human rights situation in the Syrian Arab Republic," UN Doc. A/ HRC/RES/S-18/1, December 5, 2011; UN Human Rights Council. Resolution S-19, "The deteriorating situation of human rights in the Syrian Arab Republic, and the recent killings in El-Houleh," UN Doc. A/HRC/RES/S-19/1, June 4, 2012.

6 UN Human Rights Council. Resolution 19/12, "Situation of human rights in the Islamic Republic of Iran," UN Doc. A/HRC/RES/19/12, April 3, 2012.

Belarus (establishing a country-specific special rapporteur).[7] Moreover, the Council called on OHCHR to provide technical assistance on human rights protection to Kyrgyzstan, Guinea, Côte d'Ivoire, Tunisia, South Sudan, and Libya.[8] The Council also addressed thematic human rights challenges, including abuses against lesbian, gay, bisexual, and transgender (LGBT) persons (commissioning a UN report),[9] the rights to freedom of assembly and association (creating a new special rapporteur to monitor abuses)[10] and discrimination against women (creating an independent working group).[11]

Indeed, while the revitalized Council's performance from 2009 to 2011 still left much to be desired, its willingness to address human rights conditions in countries other than Israel improved significantly during this time. Whereas during its first two years of operation, from 2006 to the end of 2008, about 52 percent of its country-specific resolutions targeted Israel, from 2009 to 2011, about 34 percent did so. This pattern continued in 2012, in which about 17 percent of its resolutions targeted Israel. It should be noted that not all of these country-specific resolutions actually criticize a government for committing human rights abuses, let alone with the vigor reserved for resolutions on Israel; some merely call for the provision of 'technical assistance' to the country in question, highlighting challenges but also noting efforts already taken to address abuses. However, even these resolutions improved upon the Council's past silence in the face of the vast majority of situations of serious human rights abuse.

---

[7] UN Human Rights Council. Resolution 20/19, "Technical assistance to Côte d'Ivoire in the field of human rights," UN Doc. A/HRC/RES/20/19," July 17, 2012.

[8] UN Human Rights Council. Resolution 14/14, "Technical assistance and cooperation on human rights for Kyrgyzstan," UN Doc. A/HRC/14/14, June 23, 2010; UN Human Rights Council. Resolution 16.36, "Strengthening of technical cooperation and consultative services in Guinea," UN Doc. A/HRC/RES/16/36, April 13, 2011; UN Human Rights Council. Resolution 16/25, "Situation of human rights in Côte d'Ivoire," UN Doc. A/HRC/RES/16/25, April 13, 2011; UN Human Rights Council. Resolution 16/19, "Cooperation between Tunisia and the Office of the High Commissioner for Human Rights," UN Doc. A/HRC/RES/16/19, April 13, 2011; UN Human Rights Council. Resolution 18/17,"Technical assistance and capacity-building for South Sudan in the field of human rights," UN Doc. A/HRC/RES/18/17, October 17, 2011; UN Human Rights Council. Resolution 17/17, "Situation of human rights in the Libyan Arab Jamahiriya," UN Doc. A/HRC/RES/17/17, July 14, 201.

[9] UN Human Rights Council. Resolution 17/19, "Human rights, sexual orientation and gender identity," UN Doc. A/HRC/RES/17/19, July 14, 2011.

[10] UN Human Rights Council. Resolution 15/21, "The rights to freedom of peaceful assembly and of association," UN Doc. A/HRC/RES/15/21, October 6, 2010.

[11] UN Human Rights Council. Resolution 15/23, "Elimination of discrimination against women," UN Doc. A/HRC/RES/15/23, October 8, 2010.

Country-specific resolutions adopted by the UN Human Rights Council, 2006–2012[12]

Year	Country-specific resolutions	# on Israel
2006	7	7
2007	11	4
2008	15	6
2009	17	7
2010	18	8
2011	29	7
2012	30	5
TOTAL	127	44

The Council's practice with regard to convening special sessions to address human rights emergencies (which requires the consent of one-third of Council members) also improved from 2009 to 2011. From 2006 to 2008, the Council convened seven country-specific special sessions, four of which (or 57 percent) were on Israel. From 2009 to 2011, the Council convened eight country-specific special sessions, two of which (or 25 percent) were on Israel.

Special Sessions Convened by the Human Rights Council on the Situation of Human Rights in Specific Countries, 2006–2012[13]

Year	Country-Specific Special Sessions	# on Israel
2006	4	3
2007	1	0
2008	2	1

(Continued)

[12] See Jacob Blaustein Institute for the Advancement of Human Rights, "Country-specific scrutiny by the UN Human Rights Council: Changes documented since US membership began," March 1, 2013, http://www.jbi-humanrights.org/jacob-blaustein-institute/2013/03/country-specific-scrutiny-by-the-un-human-rights-council-changes-documented-since-us-membership-bega.html. Some commentators have employed a different methodology for calculating country-specific resolutions adopted by the Council. For example, some do not count resolutions that discuss the human rights situation in a country, but without condemnatory language. See, e.g., UN Watch, "Anti-Israel Resolutions at the HRC," http://www.unwatch.org/site/c.bdKKISNqEmG/b.3820041/#1st (reporting that the Council criticized only one country (Burma) other than Israel in 2007, ignoring a resolution on Sudan that extended the mandate of the special rapporteur on that country, Resolution 6/34, "Mandate of the Special Rapporteur on the situation of human rights in the Sudan" (14 December 2007)). This author is of the opinion that all resolutions in which the Human Rights Council addresses the human rights situation in a particular country should be included.

[13] Ibid.

Year	Country-Specific Special Sessions	# on Israel
2009	3*	2
2010	1	0
2011	4	0
2012	1	0
TOTAL	16	6

* Includes the May 2009 special session on Sri Lanka in which the Council failed to condemn the government for its indiscriminate use of force in its conflict against the LTTE. Does not include the May 2008 special session on "the negative impact of the worsening of the world food crisis," the February 2009 special session on "the impact of the global economic and financial crises on the universal realization and effective enjoyment of human rights," or the January 2010 special session on "the support of the HRC to the recovery process in Haiti after the earthquake of January 12, 2010: a human rights approach."

Similarly, the total number of special procedures mandated by the Council rose from a low point of 38 in 2008 to 47 in 2011, reflecting increases in the number of both country-specific and thematic mandate holders.

Special Procedures Mandated by the Human Rights Council, 2006–2012[14]

Year	Country-Specific Mandates	Thematic Mandates	Total
2006	13	28	41
2007	12	28	40
2008	8	30	38
2009	8	31	39
2010	8[15]	31	39
2011	11*	35	47*
2012	12*	36	48*

^ All were established by the Commission on Human Rights and automatically transferred to the Council.
* Includes the Special Rapporteur on Syria, a mandate which was created in 2011 but was to remain inactive until the expiration of the mandate of the COI on Syria.

As Suzanne Nossel has described in detail elsewhere,[16] this increase in Council activity was driven in significant part by the efforts of the

14 Ibid.

15 Same as 2009.

16 Suzanne Nossel, "Advancing Human Rights in the UN System," Council on Foreign Relations International Institutions and Global Governance Program Working Paper, May 2012.

US government, which upon joining the Council sought to demonstrate that greater engagement could increase the body's responsiveness to human rights abuses occurring worldwide and its ability to serve as an important driver of human rights protection. By engaging intensively with other components of the US government and civil society, determining main priorities and strategies in advance, and developing deep, long-term relationships with other Council members, the US team was able to successfully secure the required votes for passage of initiatives it supported, and which responded to some of the most urgent human rights situations of the moment.[17]

Yet no amount of effort on the part of the United States would have been independently sufficient to translate increased attention by the Human Rights Council into more effective human rights protection on the ground. Rather, it would fall to the High Commissioner and OHCHR to capitalize upon the opportunities for action created by a more responsive Council.

The High Commissioner's Response to Crises: Côte d'Ivoire, Libya, and Syria

From 2009 to 2011, High Commissioner Pillay responded to emerging human rights crises that had come to the attention of the Human Rights Council with a two-pronged approach. First, the High Commissioner seized upon the opportunity to 'use the bully pulpit' to present the facts of the crises within a human rights framework, to forthrightly condemn abuses, and to propose future action for the Council to take in response, in doing so gaining the attention of the media and the world and placing pressure on states and other UN entities to take protective action. Second, the High Commissioner ensured that investigative mechanisms created by the Council in response to the crisis received competent staff support from OHCHR and undertook credible, objective fact-finding, so that when their reports were published, they were well-received and again focused the attention of the international community on the human rights violations at the heart of the crisis at hand. The publication of these reports provided the High Commissioner with further opportunities to address the Council, capture the attention of the media and the world, and keep the crises under review at the forefront of the minds of Member States. The High Commissioner's increased engagement with the Council,

[17] Ibid.

in turn, raised her profile with other UN entities, most notably the Security Council, which began inviting Pillay to brief it on emerging crises far more frequently than any of her predecessors.

This strategy proved particularly successful in the cases of the human rights crises in Côte d'Ivoire, Libya, and Syria.

Côte d'Ivoire

Following a highly contested presidential election in Côte d'Ivoire in late November 2010, the incumbent, President Laurent Gbagbo, refused to accept results indicating his defeat by challenger Alassane Ouattara, and the candidates' supporters reacted violently. High Commissioner Pillay issued two press releases, the first anticipating the potential for conflict and the second warning the candidates that they would be held accountable for their supporters' acts of violence.[18] On December 21, the US and Nigeria, acting on behalf of the African Group, formally requested a special session of the Council on the situation in Côte d'Ivoire.[19]

At the special session, held the following day, Deputy High Commissioner for Human Rights Kyung-wha Kang delivered a statement the High Commissioner's behalf, presenting data gathered by OHCHR's field presence in the country, consisting of human rights officers attached to the UN Operation in Côte d'Ivoire (UNOCI), and called on the country's leadership to ensure that abuses were stopped and those responsible for violations held to account.[20] In response, the Human Rights Council unanimously adopted a resolution requesting the High Commissioner to report to it on the situation in the future.[21]

Over the following weeks, the High Commissioner publicized additional UNOCI data on human rights violations in Côte d'Ivoire.[22] The report she had been mandated to prepare recommended that the international community establish an international commission of inquiry and

---

[18] "UN human rights chief urges Cote d'Ivoire presidential candidates and supporters to clearly renounce violence," OHCHR news release, November 26, 2010.

[19] Note Verbale from the Secretariat of the Human Rights Council to all UN Member States of December 21, 2010, http://www2.ohchr.org/english/bodies/hrcouncil/docs/14specialsession/NVbyhteSecretariat.pdf.

[20] Kyung-wha Kang, Deputy High Commissioner for Human Rights, "The situation of human rights in Cote D'Ivoire since the elections on 28 November 2010," (Statement to the Human Rights Council's 14th Special Session, December 23, 2010).

[21] UN Human Rights Council, "Situation of human rights in Cote D'Ivoire in relation to the conclusion of the 2010 presidential election," UN Doc. A/HRC/RES/S-14/1 (4 January 2011).

[22] "Human rights situation in Côte d'Ivoire "deteriorating alarmingly" – Pillay," OHCHR news release, March 10, 2011.

provide UNOCI with the capacity to protect civilians under imminent threat of danger.[23]

On March 25, the Human Rights Council approved a resolution creating the International Commission of Inquiry (CoI) on Côte d'Ivoire recommended by the High Commissioner and tasking OHCHR with providing the administrative, technical, and logistical support necessary for the CoI to carry out its mandate.[24] On March 30, the Security Council unanimously passed a resolution[25] recognizing Ouattara as president and authorizing UNOCI to "use all necessary means" to protect civilians. Thereafter, Assistant Secretary-General for Human Rights Ivan Šimonović led an OHCHR mission to Côte d'Ivoire and met with Ouattara, who pledged to establish a truth and reconciliation commission and to punish those who committed crimes. On April 13, High Commissioner Pillay was invited to brief the Security Council on the situation in Côte d'Ivoire, where she presented new data gathered by UNOCI and stressed the urgent need for a transitional justice process leading to meaningful accountability for perpetrators, regardless of affiliation.[26]

The three-member CoI on Côte d'Ivoire[27] traveled to the country from May 4–28, 2011. Assisted by a team of OHCHR investigators and a medical examiner, the CoI met with hundreds of victims and witnesses, the authorities, and civil society. In its final report, the CoI documented potential war crimes and crimes against humanity, and in a confidential annex, it identified the individuals most responsible for those crimes. It recommended that the Ivorian government investigate and prosecute perpetrators and that OHCHR provide technical assistance to aid the authorities in establishing a "dialogue, truth and reconciliation commission."[28] The Council reacted to the CoI's report by establishing a new mandate of 'independent expert on the situation of human rights in Côte d'Ivoire,' responsible for

---

23 UN Human Rights Council, *Report of the United Nations High Commissioner for Human Rights on the situation of human rights in Côte d'Ivoire*, UN Doc. A/HRC/16/79, February 25, 2011.

24 UN Human Rights Council. Resolution 16/25.

25 UN Security Council. Resolution 1975, "Côte d'Ivoire," UN Doc. S/RES/1975, March 30, 2011.

26 UN Department of Public Information, "Top UN Official Tells Security Council Post-Electoral Crisis in Cote d'Ivoire ended," press release SC/10223, April 13, 2011.

27 Vitit Muntarbhorn (Thailand) (Chair), Suliman Baldo (Sudan), and Reine Alapini Gansou (Benin).

28 UN Human Rights Council, *Report of the international commission of inquiry to investigate the facts and circumstances surrounding the allegations of serious abuses and violations of human rights committed in Cote d'Ivoire following the presidential election of 28 November 2010*, UN Doc. A/HRC/17/48, July 1, 2011.

following up on the implementation of the CoI's recommendations, to be supported in its work by OHCHR, and endorsing its call for OHCHR to provide the government with technical assistance.[29]

Since the summer of 2011, the Ivorian government's efforts to establish accountability, particularly for pro-Ouattara forces implicated in crimes, have been far from satisfactory, and the Truth, Reconciliation and Dialogue Commission has experienced serious operational problems. However, there have been significant steps toward ensuring accountability for those implicated in the post-election violence: former President Gbagbo has been transferred to the ICC, where he is facing charges of crimes against humanity, and scores of Gbagbo supporters have been charged with post-election crimes.[30] Moreover, the CoI's findings have provided the High Commissioner and the Independent Expert on Côte d'Ivoire with a basis from which to critique the Ouattara government's tepid efforts so far to put the necessary transitional justice and accountability initiatives in place.

Libya

In February 2011, Libyan leader Muammar Qaddafi began a violent crackdown against demonstrators rallying against his repressive regime. On February 22, High Commissioner Pillay issued a statement condemning the reported indiscriminate killing of civilians by government forces, noting that they could rise to the level of crimes against humanity, and calling for an international investigation of the abuses.[31] That same day, Hungary requested a special session of the Council on the situation, on behalf of Member States and observers including the United States.[32]

At the special session, convened on February 25, Pillay described allegations of serious human rights abuse in Libya received by OHCHR from human rights groups on the ground. She called again for the establishment of an independent international commission of inquiry and for the Council to "use all means available to compel the Libyan Government to

[29] UN Human Rights Council. Resolution 20/19.

[30] Coalition for the International Criminal Court, "Cases & Situations: Cote d'Ivoire," http://www.coalitionfortheicc.org/?mod=ivorycoast.

[31] "Pillay calls for international inquiry into Libyan violence and justice for victims," OHCHR news release, February 22, 2011.

[32] UN Human Rights Council. "Letter dated 22 February 2011 from the Permanent Representative of the Republic of Hungary to the United Nations Office and other international organizations in Geneva addressed to the President of the Human Rights Council," UN Doc. A/HRC/S-15/1, February 24, 2011.

respect the human rights and heed the will of its people."[33] The Council adopted by consensus a resolution authorizing the creation of an independent international commission of inquiry (CoI) and giving the High Commissioner a mandate to update the Council and to convene an interactive dialogue on Libya in the future.[34] The Council also urged the General Assembly to suspend Libya's Human Rights Council membership, a recommendation that the GA endorsed the following week in the first ever-suspension of a Council member.[35] The day after the special session, the UN Security Council adopted resolution 1970, which referred the situation in Libya to the ICC, among other measures.[36] On March 17, citing concerns that crimes against humanity may have been committed in Libya, the Security Council authorized the use of "all necessary measures... to protect civilians and civilian populations under threat of attack," and established a no-fly zone.[37]

Comprised of Chairperson M. Cherif Bassiouni, Asma Khader, and Philippe Kirsch, and supported by a team of OHCHR human rights officers, the Human Rights Council's CoI made a first trip to Libya in May, during which time it interviewed more than 350 people.[38] The CoI's initial report found that government forces had committed crimes against humanity and war crimes at the behest of Qaddafi and members of his inner circle.[39] In a June 2011 resolution, the Council approved the CoI's request for a mandate extension, providing it with a much-needed opportunity to immediately continue its investigation. It thus came as a major disappointment when the CoI was forced to postpone a planned return visit to Libya in August 2011 because the temporary 90-day contracts for its

---

33 Navi Pillay, "Situation of Human Rights in the Libyan Arab Jamahiriya: Statement by Navi Pillay, UN High Commissioner for Human Rights," (Human Rights Council 15th Special Session, Geneva, February 25, 2011).

34 UN Human Rights Council. Resolution S-15.

35 "General Assembly Suspends Libya from Human Rights Council," UN press release GA/11050, March 1, 2011.

36 UN Security Council. Resolution 1970, "Peace and Security in Africa," UN Doc. S/Res/1970, February 26, 2011.

37 UN Security Council. Resolution 1973, "Libya," UN Doc. S/Res/1973, March 17, 2011. Two days later, French forces began a military operation to defend the population of Benghazi from an attack by Libyan forces; at the end of March NATO assumed control over military operations to protect civilians.

38 UN Human Rights Council, *Report of the International Commission of Inquiry to investigate all alleged violations of international human rights law in the Libyan Arab Jamahiriya*, UN Doc. A/HRC/17/44, June 1, 2011.

39 The CoI also noted that it had received some evidence suggesting commission of international crimes by forces connected with the opposition. Ibid., 7.

OHCHR support staff had expired.[40] OHCHR's failure to put in place a contingency plan to allow the CoI to continue functioning when it received its requested extension meant that rather than returning to the field, it was forced to recruit entirely new staff before it could undertake its second mission. During that recruitment process, which endured until mid-November 2011, conditions on the ground in Libya deteriorated as the conflict escalated, culminating with the capture and killing of President Qaddafi by rebel forces in late October 2011.

Despite the CoI's staffing troubles, in September, the Security Council authorized the establishment of the United Nations Support Mission in Libya (UNSMIL), which included a human rights section headed by a representative of the High Commissioner. OHCHR staff members were temporarily deployed to Libya in connection with the setting up of the section, first to carry out a needs assessment and later to bolster the section's capacity.[41] In January 2012, Pillay was asked to brief the Security Council on human rights developments in Libya, where she stressed the need to end ongoing abuses and establish transitional justice mechanisms.[42]

After Suzanne Nossel's departure from the US government, in early March 2012, the CoI came before the Human Rights Council to present its final report. It had eventually overcome the obstacles resulting from the OHCHR staffing interruption and renewed its investigation on the ground in Libya in December 2011. Its report confirmed that both the Libyan military and opposition forces had committed international crimes. The CoI also compiled a non-public list of 80 individuals responsible for the violations it identified, which it provided to High Commissioner Pillay.[43] The methodology it applied, the extent of its investigation, and its analysis were praised by legal experts.[44] While it remains to be seen whether the High Commissioner's calls for post-conflict accountability in Libya will be

---

40 See UN Human Rights Council, *Report of the International Commission of Inquiry on Libya*, A/HRC/19/68, March 8, 2012, para. 9(a).

41 Navi Pillay, "Statement to the Security Council by Navi Pillay, High Commissioner for Human Rights [Libya] 25 January 2012, New York."

42 Ibid.

43 UN Human Rights Council, *Report of the International Commission of Inquiry on Libya*, para. 14.

44 Kevin Jon Heller, "The International Commission of Inquiry on Libya: A Critical Analysis," Jens Meierhenrich (ed.), *International Commissions: The Role of Commissions of Inquiry in the Investigation of International Crimes*, 2013 Forthcoming, http://papers.ssrn.com/sol3/papers.cfm?abstract_id=2123782 ("It followed the best practices of human-rights fact finding, explaining the law, privileging direct evidence, conducting hundreds of interviews with victims and witnesses, scrupulously corroborating testimony with physical evidence, and conservatively applying its chosen standard of proof.").

heeded, the data delivered to her by the CoI on individual culpability provides her with a basis for encouraging, supplementing, and critiquing the efforts of both the ICC and the Libyan authorities.[45]

Syria

High Commissioner Pillay raised the alarm about the Syrian government's crackdown against peaceful protesters in late March 2011.[46] On April 27, the US, acting on behalf of 16 Member States, requested a special session of the Human Rights Council to discuss the situation. At the special session, Deputy High Commissioner Kyung-wha Kang described "widespread, persistent and gross disregard for basic human rights" by Syrian forces, citing information from Syrian and international human rights organizations indicating that more than 450 people had been killed, and called for an investigation.[47] The Council reacted by requesting OHCHR to urgently dispatch one.[48]

OHCHR quickly established a fact-finding mission, comprised of the Deputy High Commissioner and 13 staff members. While it was unable to travel to Syria, lacking the government's consent to do so, it nevertheless conducted three field investigations to the region. The High Commissioner presented the mission's preliminary findings to the Human Rights Council in June, noting that more than 1,100 people were believed to have been killed in the protests.[49]

In its official report, released on August 18, the fact-finding mission noted that it had learned from local coordinating committees inside Syria of 1,900 civilians killed since March 2011.[50] It concluded that the Syrian

---

[45] As of year-end 2012, the Libyan authorities had challenged the admissibility of the ICC's case against Saif Al-Islam Qaddafi, son of Muammar Qaddafi, and the ICC had demanded that Libya submit evidence that would demonstrate to it that investigations and preparations for a trial were in fact ongoing. See "International Criminal Court prosecutor calls on Libyan authorities to ensure no impunity," UN News Centre, November 7, 2012, and "ICC Says Libya Must Prove It Is Investigating Seif Al-Islam's Case," The Tripoli Post, December 12, 2012.

[46] "Continued killings of protestors risks sending Syria into downward spiral – Pillay," OHCHR news release, March 26, 2011.

[47] "Pillay denounces escalation of Government crackdown in Syria, calls for immediate end to killings," OHCHR news release, April 25, 2011.

[48] UN Human Rights Council. Resolution 16-1.

[49] Navi Pillay, "Statement of Ms. Navi Pillay, United Nations High Commissioner for Human Rights to the Introduction of preliminary report on the situation of human rights in the Syrian Arab Republic," June 15, 2011.

[50] UN Human Rights Council, *Report of the United Nations High Commissioner for Human Rights on the situation of human rights in the Syrian Arab Republic*, UN Doc. A/HRC/18/53, 10, September 15, 2011.

government had committed attacks that could amount to crimes against humanity, compiled a confidential list of 50 alleged perpetrators to aid future investigations, and recommended that the Human Rights Council urge the Security Council to consider referring the situation in Syria to the ICC. The day the report was released, High Commissioner Pillay presented updated data that 2,200 people had been killed and endorsed the mission's recommendation that the Council refer the situation in Syria to the ICC.[51]

Even prior to the report's release, the Human Rights Council prepared to respond to its recommendations by convening another special session on Syria. The session, held on August 22, provided the High Commissioner with yet another opportunity to directly refute the government's version of events and to stress the importance of holding perpetrators accountable.[52] In response, the Council passed a resolution urgently dispatching an Independent International Commission of Inquiry on Syria (CoI).[53] The CoI would be up and running by the end of September, comprised of commissioners Paulo Pinheiro (Chairperson), Yakin Ertürk and Karen Koning AbuZayd, and supported by OHCHR staff.[54]

Just after Nossel's departure from the US government, in late November, the CoI published its first report to the Human Rights Council, based on investigations from September to November 2011.[55] The CoI's report documented widespread, systematic, and gross violations of human rights by Syrian authorities, committed pursuant to state policy and rising to the level of crimes against humanity.[56] The report's publication was followed by a third Council special session on Syria, at which time the High Commissioner revealed that the death toll had risen to more than 4,000. The High Commissioner warned bluntly of the risk of civil war and repeated once again her call for the Security Council to refer Syria to the ICC.[57] The Council passed another resolution recommending that the

---

51 Ibid. The UN published an advance version on August 18.

52 Navi Pillay, statement to the Human Rights Council 17th Special Session on "Situation of human rights in the Syrian Arab Republic," Geneva, 22 August 2011.

53 UN Human Rights Council. Resolution S-17.

54 Later, Yakin Erturk resigned and Ms. Carla del Ponte and Mr. Vitit Muntarbhorn were appointed as Commissioners.

55 UN Human Rights Council, *Report of the independent international commission of inquiry on the Syrian Arab Republic*, UN Doc. A/HRC/S-17/2/Add.1, November 23, 2011.

56 Ibid.

57 Navi Pillay, "Statement by UN High Commissioner for Human Rights Navi Pillay at the Human Rights Council 18th Special Session to examine the situation of human rights in the Syrian Arab Republic," December 2, 2011.

UN's main bodies urgently consider the CoI's report and take appropriate action. It also established a Special Rapporteur on Syria, to become active following the end of the CoI's mandate.[58]

The situation in the country only worsened during the following year. The High Commissioner has continued to press the international community,[59] deploring the failure of the Security Council to take action to resolve the crisis and repeating her call for Syria to be referred to the ICC.[60] The CoI on Syria operated throughout 2012, publishing a second report in February, updates in April, May, and June, a third report in August, and another update in December.[61] Both the second and third reports indicated that the CoI had compiled confidential lists of names of individuals believed to bear responsibility for the abuses it investigated and given them to the High Commissioner.

Throughout 2012, as a result of the escalation of the conflict, OHCHR could not speculate on the death toll in Syria.[62] This changed on January 3, 2013, when the High Commissioner recaptured international headlines with an announcement that OHCHR had commissioned a study by a nonprofit company that had tallied nearly 60,000 conflict-related deaths in Syria by late 2012.[63] In a statement accompanying the release of the study, Pillay rebuked governments for their inaction in the face of the conflict, urged them to use the study as a basis for future investigations, and called on them to begin planning a "massive stabilization effort" for Syria in the post-conflict period.[64]

---

58 UN Human Rights Council. Resolution S-18.

59 "UN human rights chief urges action to halt escalating violence in Syria," OHCHR news release, February 8, 2012.

60 Navi Pillay, "Statement by UN High Commissioner for Human Rights Navi Pillay at The Urgent Debate on the Human Rights and Humanitarian Situation in the Syrian Arab Republic at the Human Rights Council 19th Session," February 28, 2012.

61 All reports of the CoI can be found at UN Office of the UN High Commissioner for Human Rights, "Syrian Arab Republic Homepage," http://www.ohchr.org/EN/Countries/MENARegion/Pages/SYIndex.aspx.

62 The CoI was similarly unable to gather such data, as the government continued to refuse to grant it access to Syrian territory.

63 Megan Price, Jeff Klingner, and Patrick Ball, "Preliminary Statistical Analysis of Documentation of Killings in the Syrian Arab Republic," The Benetech Human Rights Program, January 2, 2013, https://www.benetech.org/download/Benetech-final-SY-report.pdf. The study confirmed 59,648 deaths between March 2011 and November 2012, and as the conflict continued thereafter, the High Commissioner concluded that the 60,000 threshold was crossed by year-end 2012.

64 "Data analysis suggests over 60,000 people killed in Syria conflict: Pillay," OHCHR news release, January 2, 2013.

The High Commissioner's Performance: Evaluation and Recommendations for the Future

Reacting to Opportunities to Speak Out Presented by the Council

On the whole, the High Commissioner successfully reacted to the efforts of certain Member States on the Human Rights Council to bring human rights crises to the international community's attention. Once the political support to convene special sessions of the Council had been mustered, the High Commissioner consistently capitalized on the opportunity to share striking facts about the human rights violations being committed – such as estimated death tolls and records of instances of abuse – with Member States and, even more importantly, the media, which used the authoritative data to anchor coverage. Over time, the High Commissioner's presentation of facts and recommendations became increasingly focused and effective. This presentation of data and the resulting media attention assisted supportive states in gathering the necessary votes to pass resolutions creating mechanisms that required the High Commissioner, OHCHR, or an independent entity supported by OHCHR to report to the Council again in the future.

This strategy resulted in an internationally-mandated cycle of human rights monitoring and reporting by the High Commissioner that helped bolster media coverage of the crises. It also significantly raised the public profile of the High Commissioner and ensured that she had the data and information to enable her to serve as a more authoritative voice within the UN system more broadly – as seen by the increase in requests from the Security Council for her to brief its members.[65] The High Commissioner has been able to directly advise not only the Member States of the Human Rights Council, but also the Security Council and the General Assembly, on the steps needed to address emergent human rights crises.

While this cooperative approach between the High Commissioner and the Human Rights Council did not necessarily lead to the realization of the High Commissioner's goals – the vast majority of perpetrators of gross human rights abuses in Côte d'Ivoire, Libya, and Syria had not been brought to justice at the time of writing – it did succeed in placing

[65] As of February 2011, the time of the conference convened by the Jacob Blaustein Institute for the Advancement of Human Rights on the subject of the High Commissioner for Human Rights, Pillay had been invited to address the Security Council 11 times since her 2008 appointment, whereas all her predecessors combined had been invited to address the Council 8 times.

sustained pressure on the international community and Security Council to act. Human rights crises that occurred during this period that were not made the subject of a special session by the Council received much less scrutiny.[66] In this way, the High Commissioner played a catalytic role in advancing international awareness of human rights crises and efforts at promoting accountability for the most egregious abuses, and was a critical aspect of the US effort to achieve greater impact through the Council.

Undertaking More Active Diplomacy

From 2009–2011, the High Commissioner's role in the Human Rights Council's response to crises was largely reactive. The High Commissioner occasionally tested the waters of a more active approach, for example by raising the alarm about impending crises and seeking to gain the media's attention. However, the High Commissioner and OHCHR did not engage directly with Member States of the Council on crises; for example, by approaching states with information about emerging crises gathered by their personnel in the field or from human rights defenders to persuade them to raise the situation at the Council or by coming to states with recommendations on the operative texts that should appear in Council resolutions on crises. The result is that states were left to rely on their own delegations, which often lacked deep knowledge of the situations, to determine what crises to call to be taken up and draft the text of the resulting Council resolutions.

The US experience with the High Commissioner is illustrative in this regard. Despite the fact that the US had publicly announced its intention to engage with and increase the activity and responsiveness of the Council, and even after the US followed through on these aspirations in the cases of Côte d'Ivoire, Libya, Syria, and others, the High Commissioner and OHCHR did not approach the US delegation or others as potential partners in addressing these or other human rights crises abroad. While the US would on occasion seek out OHCHR's input when it was crafting the text of a resolution that would require it to have an active role, OHCHR did not proactively seek to recommend the form or nature of Council action.

The High Commissioner may have adopted this practice in order to avoid being seen to be working with one or more Member States in an

66 One example is the 2011 crackdown by China against Tibetan protesters, which provoked a joint statement by several Special Procedures in November and a press release by the High Commissioner in 2012, but which had not been addressed by the Council as of January 2013.

effort to bring attention to another state's misconduct. Yet while it is essential for OHCHR to maintain its objectivity with respect to all states and their conduct, this should not stand in the way of cooperation in handling crises of the sort in which many other UN agencies engage. The High Commissioner's arms-length approach has the practical effect of preventing her from assisting to make the Council a more effective and objective body, which affects both the Council's credibility and her own.

In the future, the High Commissioner should consider seeking to play a greater role in shaping the international diplomatic will to address human rights crises and other serious situations, through diplomatic means as well as public appeals, in Geneva as well as in New York. The High Commissioner should engage in more active diplomacy vis-à-vis Member States of the Council, pressing for the most significant and egregious human rights violations to be on the Council's agenda and seeking to bring information about unfolding crises from human rights organizations and defenders to the table. In cases where the Council seems poised to take action on a human rights crisis that will hurt the Council's credibility, as in the case of the special session on Sri Lanka, the High Commissioner should play an active part in seeking to uphold the Council's and UN System's credibility by pressing for adherence to legitimate human rights principles.

Exercising Independent Initiative

During the period from 2009–2011, the High Commissioner demonstrated increasing willingness to take independent action without waiting for a mandate from the Council to do so. One primary example is Pillay's outspokenness in defending of the rights of lesbian, gay, bisexual, and transgender (LGBT) individuals and condemning discrimination and violence on the basis of sexual orientation and gender identity (SOGI). Despite its controversial nature, Pillay took the initiative of appointing an expert to advise her and OHCHR on how to advance the issue within the UN in 2010.[67] She also supported efforts by the US and other delegations to advance the issue, for example by delivering a strong statement at a September 2010 'side event' at the Council hosted by the US government on ending violence and criminal sanctions based on SOGI.[68] The High Commissioner's support helped build momentum in favor of action by

[67] Statement by Ms. Navi Pillay, Side Event on ending violence and criminal sanctions based on sexual orientation and gender identity, Geneva, September 17, 2010, http://geneva.usmission.gov/wp-content/uploads/2010/09/Pillay.pdf.

[68] Ibid.

the Council, and in June 2011, the Council passed its first-ever resolution affirming LGBT rights as human rights and requested OHCHR to produce a report on discriminatory laws and practices and acts of violence against individuals based on SOGI. The High Commissioner personally presented the report to the Council in March 2012.[69]

In another example, in October 2010, the High Commissioner published an OHCHR report that mapped over 600 of the most serious human rights and humanitarian law violations committed in the Democratic Republic of the Congo between March 1993 and June 2003 and offered recommendations for ensuring accountability. Overcoming pressure from the government of Rwanda, identified in the report as responsible for many serious crimes in the country, and the reported misgivings of Secretary-General Ban Ki-moon,[70] Pillay published the groundbreaking report two months after it was leaked to the press in August 2010.

More recently, the High Commissioner seems to have become increasingly willing to take action. In 2012, the High Commissioner published a groundbreaking OHCHR report mapping violations of human rights and humanitarian law committed in Nepal between 1996 and 2006.[71] In early January 2013, the High Commissioner published her independently-commissioned outside study on the casualties resulting from the conflict in Syria, placing her, as well as her call for accountability for perpetrators of abuses, back in the headlines of the global news media.[72] Only a few weeks later, the High Commissioner called for the creation of a Commission of Inquiry into human rights abuses in the Democratic Republic of North Korea, another welcome sign of affirmative initiative that helpfully influenced the debate among states.[73]

In the future, the High Commissioner should exercise her independent authority to investigate and report on human rights abuses even more assertively, undertaking initiatives on her own accord to provoke Member States into action on serious crises.

---

[69] "Pillay presents groundbreaking UN study on violence, discrimination against people because of their sexual orientation," OHCHR news release, March 7, 2012.

[70] Colum Lynch, "Did Ban Ki Moon's Advisors try to Spare Rwanda from Genocide Charge?" Turtlebay.ForeignPolicy.com, September 3, 2010.

[71] OHCHR, "Nepal Conflict Report," http://www.ohchr.org/EN/Countries/AsiaRegion/Pages/NepalConflictReport.aspx.

[72] See e.g. Nick Cumming-Bruce, "More Than 60,000 Have Died in Syrian Conflict, U.N. Says," *The New York Times*, January 2, 2013.

[73] "Pillay urges more attention to human rights abuses in North Korea, calls for international inquiry," OHCHR news release, January 14, 2013. Following Pillay's call, the Human Rights Council created the Commission of Inquiry on the Democratic People's Republic of Korea on March 21, 2013.

Supporting and Leveraging the Work of the Special Procedures

While the High Commissioner supported and embraced the work of the commissions of inquiry created by the Human Rights Council, she was noticeably less inclined to highlight the findings of its special procedures, particularly for the purpose of encouraging the Council to act.[74] More broadly, the High Commissioner did not appear to provide the special procedures mandate holders – who are independent but supported in their operation by OHCHR – with the assistance and visibility that could have amplified their work and heightened their impact.

The special procedures are universally under-resourced, in part a casualty of OHCHR's own chronic struggle to obtain adequate funding for its activities. Special procedures do not work full time, as they receive no salary from the UN and generally need to be employed elsewhere.[75] Moreover, they generally have only a single staff member from OHCHR supporting their work, unless they are able to, through their own initiative, obtain pro-bono assistance. Neither collectively nor individually are they staffed to engage in advocacy with governments on behalf of their recommendations; to utilize the media to publicize their reports, findings, and proposals; to investigate appeals sent to them by persons reporting instances of human rights abuse; or to liaise with NGOs. The thin infrastructure supporting the special procedures limits their visibility and impact.

In her chapter in this volume, Felice Gaer explores this shortcoming extensively, recommending that the High Commissioner devote more attention to strategic coordination of the special procedures in the future. We strongly agree with her conclusions. Indeed, it is all the more important that OHCHR identify ways to provide adequate support to the special procedures at a time in which the performance of the Human Rights Council – which is responsible for their selection – has significantly improved.

In the future, the High Commissioner should seek to endow the special procedures so that they can more fully realize their potential as force-multipliers for the UN human rights system. Without a concerted effort to raise the funds to underwrite the work of the special procedures, it will be increasingly difficult to persuade Member States that such mandates are worth the investment of political energy required to create and periodically re-authorize them. While the High Commissioner may not consider

---

74 However, the President of the Human Rights Council invited the special procedures to submit joint statements to the Council's special sessions on Libya and Syria.

75 See OHCHR, "United Nations Special Procedures, Facts and Figures 2011," May 2012, http://www.ohchr.org/Documents/HRBodies/SP/Facts_Figures2011.pdf.

this to be her responsibility, the mandate-holders lack the time and staff to pursue stable funding. If the High Commissioner does not address this chronic weakness in the system, no one will.

Managing OHCHR

For the most part, OHCHR's performance in response to the crises in Côte d'Ivoire, Libya, and Syria was excellent, particularly considering its limited resources. Indeed, OHCHR ably supported all three CoIs, carried out the fact-finding mission on Syria that preceded the creation of the CoI, and transmitted information from human rights monitors attached to the UN's peace missions in Côte d'Ivoire and Libya from the ground back to headquarters. OHCHR's performance on these crises bolstered the High Commissioner's reputation as a manager with the ability to ensure effective, competent, and prompt support for mechanisms created by the Council.

Yet there have been very significant exceptions to OHCHR's otherwise positive record, first among them its failure to ensure continuity of staffing for the CoI on Libya at a critical point, with the result that the mandated international investigators were down for the count just when the crisis reached its height. This glaring failure highlights an important shortcoming that the High Commissioner should urgently address. A senior OHCHR staff member once described expecting OHCHR to respond ably in crisis situations as akin to expecting someone to drive the Indy 500 in a 1950s car. The institution lacks the operational capacity at present to perform the functions that an improved Human Rights Council – and the world – expect of it.

In this context, the High Commissioner must see herself as an institution builder, nurturing and building up OHCHR's capacity, and not simply a manager perpetually operating in triage mode. One aspect of this institution-building must involve reorienting OHCHR's operations to reflect its identity as an agency with a significant 'expeditionary' role in addition to its research and support functions. OHCHR's development of a rapid response capacity represents such an evolution in thinking, and it has proved successful in improving OHCHR's ability to deploy staff into the field quickly. Over time, though, OHCHR will need to lessen its reliance on redeploying existing staff with jobs to do in order to cover emergencies and new Council mandates. This approach is stop-gap in nature, and creates disruptions both in missions and in the offices from which staff have been redeployed. There is some indication that OHCHR has recently taken steps to address this issue to prevent it from affecting the work of the CoI for Syria. However, the underlying bureaucratic challenges at issue have not yet been fully resolved. OHCHR is not presently managed in a way that anticipates that it will engage in sustained monitoring and reporting on crisis situations; rather, the focus is on completing the discrete mandated tasks assigned to it by the Council and doing nothing further. OHCHR staff supporting fact-finding missions and COIs reported that once they had finalized the reports they were required to complete, even in situations where their Council mandates had not yet expired, they would cease collecting and responding to information on ongoing abuses. In the future, the High Commissioner should strategically aim to make the most of monitoring mandates given to OHCHR by the Council to the maximum degree possible, as these will always be hard to obtain.

Another component of the High Commissioner's managerial role, extensively addressed by other authors in this volume, is her responsibility for establishing OHCHR field presences abroad. As the examples of Libya and Côte d'Ivoire show, such field presences were a vital source of 'early warning' information that the High Commissioner shared with the Council in the earliest days of the crises. Her access to such information helped her gain the attention of Member States and the media and added legitimacy to her recommendations for future action. While OHCHR already has a relatively extensive field presence worldwide, the High Commissioner should aim to establish an OHCHR presence – with a mandate to monitor human rights conditions – in every state where it is feasible to do so, so that in the future, its reach, and by extension that of the High Commissioner, is truly global. The High Commissioner can mitigate costs by placing human rights officers within UN country teams and attaching human rights monitors to peacekeeping operations, rather than attempting to set up stand-alone offices in every situation. This is a strategy that the High Commissioners have increasingly pursued in recent years, and they should continue it in the future.

Finally, the High Commissioner must continue and increase efforts to address the funding challenges that have plagued OHCHR since its inception. In part, this could be ameliorated through changing its approach to funding operations in the field. At present, OHCHR is reluctant to accept voluntary funding from states and private entities for activities mandated by the Council, for fear that such funding could be perceived to detract from the objectivity and credibility of its work. Other entities that rely heavily on private funding, the United Nations Children's Fund (UNICEF) and the United Nations High Commissioner for Refugees (UNHCR) among them, have created private funding divisions that have enabled them to solicit significant additional resources without compromising their independence.[76] The High Commissioner should study the examples set by these institutions to determine if they might be appropriate for OHCHR. She should also develop strategies for building a culture of voluntary funding outside the West, where this is less common, as Valerie Amos has done as the Under-Secretary-General for the UN's Office for the Coordination of Humanitarian Affairs (OCHA).[77]

Additionally, at present, OHCHR does not have an assessment system akin to that developed by the Department of Peacekeeping Operations (DPKO) in which it estimates the size and budget of a field deployment in advance and then raises the resources to fund it.[78] OHCHR should explore the feasibility of such an assessment system; if it did so, and also reconsidered its restrictions on acceptance of voluntary funding for such activities, it could estimate the amount of funding needed for a mission in advance and then approach interested states, seeking their support for the activity.

While these operational and bureaucratic issues may seem somewhat mundane, they have an immense impact on the High Commissioner's ability to take advantage of opportunities created by the Human Rights Council to affect the international community's response to human rights crises as they unfold. Member States must be given an incentive to launch the intense political mobilization efforts required to create commissions of inquiry, fact-finding missions, and special procedures mandates. A first step for the High Commissioner should be to prioritize her institution-building role and to correct the operational shortcomings that presently jeopardize OHCHR's ability to make the most of these opportunities.

Conclusion

From 2009–2011, as the Human Rights Council increasingly embraced its responsibility for responding to the most serious human rights crises

[76] UNICEF, "UNICEF High-Level Structure," http://www.unicef.org/about/structure/files/UNICEF_high-level_structure_2010.pdf; "UNHCR Organizational Structure," June 30, 2011, http://www.unhcr.org/4bffd0dc9.html.

[77] OCHA, "How OCHA is funded," http://www.unocha.org/about-us/ocha-funded. In 2011, donors increased their funding to OCHA by $26.6 million to $213.3 million. OCHA, "Funding and Financial Analysis," *OCHA Annual Report 2011*, http://unocha.org/annualreport/2011/financial-plan.

[78] As early as possible the Department Peacekeeping Operations (DPKO) and Department of Field Service (DFS) send a Technical Assessment Mission (TAM) to the field to determine "mission factors" such as equipment and troop needs/costs. See UN Department of Peacekeeping Operations, *Planning Toolkit*, "http://www.un.org/en/peacekeeping/publications/Planning%20Toolkit_Web%20Version.pdf.

facing the world, the High Commissioner for Human Rights played a catalytic role in supporting and encouraging its work. Her efforts to draw global attention to the need to halt abuses and promote accountability, both by personally speaking out and by ensuring that OHCHR provided competent support to the independent mechanisms the Council created to conduct investigations, were absolutely critical to the US effort to reinvigorate the Council and improve the UN's credibility on human rights. Yet the High Commissioner must do more in the future to capitalize on and encourage this trend. This includes engaging in greater diplomacy directly with Member States, undertaking independent investigations when necessary to provoke international action, empowering the special procedures to aid her in engaging the Council, and building the institution of OHCHR to ensure that it is capable of fulfilling the tasks entrusted to it by the Council.

HUMAN RIGHTS PROSECUTORS? THE HIGH COMMISSIONER FOR HUMAN RIGHTS, INTERNATIONAL JUSTICE, AND THE EXAMPLE OF SYRIA

David Kaye

A few years ago, a long-time international prosecutor – a man who has dedicated his life's work to bringing to justice individuals accused of mass atrocity – spoke to a class of law students. With great detail and honesty, within the bounds of confidentiality requirements, he spelled out for students the complexities of international criminal law, including the difficulties of collecting evidence and gaining the cooperation of governments in hostile environments; the criteria by which alleged perpetrators may be selected for investigation and prosecution; the ways in which prosecutors develop arguments in an area of law with relatively little precedent; and the challenges of communicating with victims and witnesses who live thousands of miles from the tribunal's headquarters. The students were enthralled: here was a prosecutor, in effect a leading descendant of Justice Robert Jackson's prosecutorial team at Nuremberg, a mission-oriented lawyer at the top of the field, the tip of the spear in the effort to hold to account those responsible for the worst crimes under international law.[1]

A student intervened. What, she asked, is your relationship to human rights and human rights law? Do you see yourself as part of the international human rights movement? The prosecutor gave a look as if he had just eaten a bitter lemon and responded, perhaps with a spot of sarcasm, "We don't do human rights." International prosecutors, he averred, are in the business of criminal accountability, punishment, possibly deterrence – in the prosecutor's view, a kind of hard law against the soft law of human rights. Human rights lawyers, he suggested, have different objectives: creating public awareness of human rights abuse, focusing on state and non-state entities rather than individuals, generating political responses to abusive behavior, examining a broader range of legal norms than those found in international criminal law.

[1] The essential account of the inside work at Nuremberg, Telford Taylor's *The Anatomy of the Nuremberg Trial* (New York: Little Brown & Co, 1992), provides a comprehensive assessment of the relationship between prosecuting specific cases and the broader policy aims of holding individuals to account for atrocities.

The prosecutor was right: international criminal law and human rights law operate on different planes, with different objectives, institutions, jurisdictions, mandates, and competencies. Increasingly, however, the boundaries between the central international institutions of individual accountability (The Hague) and human rights (Geneva) are becoming porous. Personnel and leadership move from The Hague to Geneva and back. Such personnel moves happen at the working level, when staffers from the Office of the Prosecutor at the International Criminal Court or the United Nations ad hoc tribunals for the former Yugoslavia (ICTY) and Rwanda (ICTR) transfer to work within the Office of the High Commissioner for Human Rights (OHCHR). Sometimes the moves work in reverse. The sharing of personnel may be most striking at the senior levels of leadership; the last two High Commissioners served first in the institutions of accountability: Louise Arbour as chief prosecutor at the ICTY and ICTR; and since 2008, Navi Pillay, former judge and president of the ICTR and judge at the International Criminal Court (ICC).

The personnel moves themselves – the 'inside baseball' of the international civil service – are less important than what they represent: the merging of the movements of international criminal justice and international human rights, long in the making, and the high profile of accountability for mass atrocity among human rights professionals and the international community more generally. Indeed, the institutional porousness tracks the legal, normative, and jurisprudential links – and controversies – governing the relationship between human rights and international humanitarian law.[2]

To return to our prosecutor: When pressed, prosecutors will recognize the contributions that human rights organizations, including OHCHR, make to international criminal justice. Some may even acknowledge that they don't know what human rights officers do. But in the separation between the two fields, the distinction between human rights and international justice, one detects an undercurrent of superiority felt by one's practitioners over the other's, reflected not only in the private statements of prosecutors but also the discourse of progress inherent in international justice, the press attention to arrests and convictions, and much else.

---

[2] Rene Provost, *International Human Rights and Humanitarian Law* (Cambridge: Cambridge University Press, 2002). See also Alexandra Huneeus, "International Criminal Law by Other Means: The Quasi-criminal Jurisdiction of the Human Rights Courts," 107 American Journal of International Law 1 (2013).

At the same time, human rights and humanitarian assistance professionals also see risks that international justice may impose on their work. Many privately express misgivings about an approach that privileges criminal accountability at an international level over other forms of transitional justice, whether at the international or national level. Many observe institutions, especially the ICC, for which comparatively significant resources are devoted to a process that takes place far from the victim communities – far in distance, in experience, in culture, in other ways as well.[3] They perceive generalists trampling through places that require specialist knowledge. Some worry that international justice can serve to undermine humanitarian efforts, arguments made explicitly in the context of the ICC's investigation of Sudanese leaders over alleged crimes in Darfur.[4]

I am overdrawing the divide here, but I do this to emphasize that the international justice and human rights communities – at the institutional level – do not necessarily perceive one another as natural allies. And yet they are, and they should see each other that way.[5]

I want to explore this relationship between the High Commissioner and international justice and ask what this portends for the future of OHCHR. What are the origins of this relationship and how are these different actors meant to interact? How should OHCHR, and the High Commissioner in particular, engage with international justice? What opportunities exist for the High Commissioner to advance the goals of international justice? What might the framework of a High Commissioner-International Justice relationship look like? Are there any risks involved in the increasing association of OHCHR with international justice? If so, are those acceptable risks? How may those risks be managed?

---

[3] See David A. Kaye, Justice Beyond The Hague: Supporting the Prosecution of International Crimes in National Courts (Council on Foreign Relations 2011).

[4] Julie Flint, "Sudan: Justice And Hunger," *African Arguments* (blog), March 6, 2009, http://africanarguments.org/2009/03/06/justice-and-hunger/.

[5] OHCHR engages in international justice in ways that go beyond the Syria case, whether for the specific purposes of the High Commissioner's mandate reporting and analyzing and recommending, or as a supportive agency for The Hague-based courts. Moreover, the High Commissioner does not enjoy an exclusive role. Other human rights actors – whether under the treaty bodies, UN special procedures, non-governmental organizations, or other variants of the human rights monitor – also play important roles. In a sense, the High Commissioner plays the highest profile role in the field, but she must work to coordinate these other actors as well to ensure the greatest impact in her mandated areas. We may think of the High Commissioner in the specific sense of the person holding the post and also as the coordinator of the broader human rights work happening internationally. See, e.g., OHCHR, *Annual Report 2011*, 13.

Finally, I conclude with some thoughts about key priorities over the coming years.

The Origins

The stories of the creations of both the OHCHR and the international criminal tribunals are well known, but it bears noting that contemporary human rights and humanitarian law both arose, intertwined, from the ashes of World War II and the Holocaust. The first legal responses following the war were landmarks in the development of contemporary international law: first, in June of 1945, the conclusion at San Francisco of the Charter of the United Nations, with Article 1 highlighting not only the priority placed for human rights but also the essential collective security role of the Security Council; and second, two months later, the adoption of the Charter of the International Military Tribunal to be held at Nuremberg. In both legal and institutional senses, the international community determined priorities early on: the maintenance of international peace and security, the promotion of human rights, accountability for massive violations of international law.

The momentum of the post-war years reached its zenith in 1948 and 1949. In December of 1948, the United Nations adopted not only the Universal Declaration of Human Rights but also the Convention on the Prevention of Genocide. Within the year, governments adopted the four Geneva Conventions, the fundamental texts of modern international humanitarian law. Thus, before the terrible decade of the 1940s was finished, the basic outlines of human rights and humanitarian law would be written, often by the same people, with the governments involved in one movement also involved in the other. They were creating distinct bodies of international law, but they were also borrowing themes, principles, and ideas from one another.[6] To be sure, they differ in critical respects, particularly as one dealt with the obligations of belligerents in times of armed conflict while the other dealt with the obligations of governments whether

[6] One may find the sharing of principles, for instance, in the provisions related to fair trials, a fundamental principle of the Universal Declaration that carried over into the Geneva Conventions. Compare, for instance, Articles 10 and 11 of the Universal Declaration with Articles 71 to 73 of the Fourth Geneva Convention. UN General Assembly. Resolution 217A (III), "Universal Declaration of Human Rights," UN Doc. A/810, 71, 1948; International Committee of the Red Cross, Geneva Convention Relative to the Protection of Civilian Persons in Time of War (Fourth Geneva Convention), August 12, 1949.

in peacetime or war. Moreover, while human rights law at the international level imagined enforcement principally in the realm of politics – devising state-governed monitoring mechanisms for each of the treaties adopted – humanitarian law envisioned criminal enforcement through such means as the 'prosecute or extradite' provisions of the Geneva and Genocide Conventions.[7] Still, international justice and international human rights share enough of each other's origins and principles that it should be seen as natural for their principal institutions to cooperate today.

Law and policy in both fields developed extensively over the course of the ensuing forty years. Human rights norms expanded with the International Covenants and an extensive array of specific treaties in such areas as racial discrimination, women's rights, children's rights, and torture. Humanitarian law norms developed as well, especially in the case of the Additional Protocols to the Geneva Conventions in 1977 and the Convention on Conventional Weapons in 1980. Enforcement provisions failed to keep up. The international community failed to provide a permanent and universal successor institution for the international tribunals at Nuremberg and Tokyo, and the deep politicization of the United Nations during the Cold War prevented it from serving as a vigorous champion for human rights.

The end of the Cold War provided a moment of East-West, North-South and government-civil society cooperation that directly contributed to the development of innovative tools of enforcement. First among those institutions were the UN's ad hoc tribunals, the ICTY and ICTR, and OHCHR. Both the ICTY and OHCHR were born in 1993, in the same optimistic, opportunistic moments following the end of the Cold War. The ICTY, established by the Security Council in the spring of that year, emerged in the face of the siege of Sarajevo and the widespread and systematic abuses across Bosnia. The following year saw the genocide in Rwanda and the creation of the ICTY's sibling institution, the ICTR. Though movement toward an international criminal court had already been underway at that time, the ad hoc tribunals gave impetus and optimism to the negotiations that led to the Rome Statute and the ICC in 1998, and beyond that to hybrid courts in Cambodia and Sierra Leone, among other places.

---

[7] Fourth Geneva Convention; UN General Assembly, Resolution 260 (III) A, "Convention on the Prevention and Punishment of the Crime of Genocide," U.N.T.S. No. 1021, vol. 78 (1951), 277, December 9, 1948.

After Nuremberg, the ICTY, ICTR and ICC are often seen as the first steps in the progressive historical process of building accountability for the worst abuses of human rights. As Louise Arbour put it upon her departure from the High Commissioner post,

> It's a small miracle to see how far we have come since the 50 years of silence after Nuremberg … All things considered, in human rights law we have achieved more in the past 15 years than in the previous 50 in taking personal criminal accountability to where it is now.[8]

The tribunals may be seen as an extension not only of Nuremberg but also of the increased attention paid to enforcement of human rights norms, a part of the same spirit that has seen the development of treaty bodies and the European, Inter-American and African human rights systems. Antonio Cassese, as the first president of the ICTY and caught up in the spirit of the moment, characterized the Tribunal in broad terms, arguing that "[t]he role of the Tribunal cannot be overemphasized. Far from being a vehicle for revenge, it is a tool for promoting reconciliation and restoring true peace."[9] The Security Council had a less idealistic view of its innovation: In adopting the ICTY Statute, it decided "to establish an international tribunal *for the sole purpose* of prosecuting persons responsible for serious violations of international humanitarian law …"[10] Gabrielle Kirk McDonald, the second president of the ICTY, emphasized this point succinctly at the opening of the Tadic trial in 1996, noting her goal of "ensuring that this first trial will be conducted as fairly and as expeditiously as possible with justice being both done and being seen to be done. Regardless of all of the apparent trappings of today, that is our sole *raison d'etre*."[11] Fair trials, doing justice, meeting the mandate set out by the Security Council: these were the objectives of international criminal justice.

The goal of prosecution, of course, leaves out quite a bit, and this is where the High Commissioner should be stepping in, as OHCHR has a set of responsibilities both broader and more malleable than the ad hoc

---

[8] Marlise Simons, "Departing Rights Official Raised Volume on Issues," *The New York Times*, July 6, 2008.

[9] UN General Assembly and UN Security Council, *Report of the International Tribunal for the Prosecution of Persons Responsible for Serious Violations of International Humanitarian Law Committed in the Territory of Former Yugoslavia Since 1991*, UN Docs A/49/342 and S/1994/1007, August 29, 1994.

[10] UN Security Council. Resolution 827, "Tribunal (Former Yugoslavia)," May 25, 1993 (emphasis added).

[11] The International Criminal Tribunal for the Former Yugoslavia, "The Prosecutor v. Dusko Tadić," Case IT-94-1-T, trial transcript of May 7, 1996, http://www.icty.org/x/cases/tadic/trans/en/960507IT.htm.

tribunals and the ICC. The High Commissioner's fundamental responsibility is to "promote and protect the effective enjoyment by all of all civil, cultural, economic, political and social rights."[12] Yet over time, the High Commissioner's role has expanded well beyond the idea of being merely "the United Nations official with principal responsibility for United Nations human rights activities."[13] The UN General Assembly resolution creating the post provides that the High Commissioner shall "carry out the tasks assigned to him/her by the competent bodies of the United Nations system in the field of human rights and to make recommendations to them with a view to improving the promotion and protection of all human rights."[14] Relying on this provision, the Security Council and the General Assembly have established a critical role for the High Commissioner as a key, if not lead, investigator for human rights violations worldwide, particularly in conflict situations. It is largely under this rubric – the High Commissioner as investigator in conflict situations – that the role has become so essential in the field of international justice.

A Case Study: Syria

The situation in Syria since the middle of March 2011 has tested the role of OHCHR and the High Commissioner herself. She consistently called for international responses to the severe violations she and commissions she supports identified in extensive reporting. The West has imposed sanctions on Syria, but Russia and China have resisted coercive measures, with Moscow supporting the government. As a result, the ability of the High Commissioner to shape the situation on the ground has been limited. In the absence of international criminal investigation and prosecution, the lack of enforcement tools of the High Commissioner seems stark. In this environment, even if the conflict remains ongoing at the time of publication of this volume, it is possible to make some observations about the key trends in the High Commissioner's work and draw a few conclusions about them.

Background

When the uprisings of the so-called Arab Spring spread across the Middle East and North Africa, the regime of Bashar al-Assad "was not alone in

[12] UN General Assembly. Resolution 48/141, "High Commissioner for the promotion and protection of all human rights," UN Doc. A/RES/48/141, December 23, 1993, paragraph 4(a).
[13] Ibid., paragraph 4.
[14] Ibid., paragraph 4(b).

believing in a form of Syrian exceptionalism that would shield it from serious popular unrest."[15] The international community only slowly responded to the violence that began in the middle of March 2011, when the regime responded with a mixture of superficial engagement with protester demands and violent repression of political gatherings around the country. Even so, the High Commissioner was among the first voices to be heard, and she subsequently played an important external role in the tragic drama of Syria in 2011 and 2012. The response of the High Commissioner, in particular her engagement with the language and processes of international justice, deserves reflection as a marker of the change in the relationship between OHCHR and the principles, if not the institutions, of international justice.

The High Commissioner's engagement in Syria began soon after the government began using violent measures to put down protests. As early as March 24, 2011, High Commissioner Pillay warned the Syrian government that responding with violence "risks creating a downward spiral of anger, violence, killing and chaos."[16] She was among the earliest international officials to call for an investigation into the killings.[17] Her words were prescient: The regime's violent response, rather than pushing protesters back into their homes, triggered further protest nationwide, followed in turn by renewed violence, a cycle that continued through 2011 and 2012. At the same time, the regime cut citizen access to domestic and international communication, creating an atomized environment in which Local Coordinating Committees worked town-by-town, often without connections to others inside the country.[18] The Free Syrian Army developed in similar ways. Ultimately, the regime's violence was met with resistance that itself became violent, to the point that the unrest could be characterized as a civil war.[19]

As the violence in Syria worsened, the High Commissioner's role deepened in ways that emphasized the role her Office might play with respect to international justice. Less than two months into the conflict, the Human Rights Council asked OHCHR "to dispatch urgently a mission to the Syrian

---

[15] International Crisis Group, *Popular Protest in North Africa and the Middle East (VI): The Syrian People's Slow-Motion Revolution,* July 6, 2011.

[16] "Syria's violent repression of protests risks fuelling further anger – UN official," *UN News Centre*, March 26, 2011.

[17] Ibid.

[18] See Carnegie Middle East Center, Local Coordinating Committees of Syria, December 20, 2012, available at http://carnegie-mec.org/publications/?fa=50426.

[19] See, e.g., "Syria: ICRC and Syrian Arab Red Crescent maintain aid effort amid increased fighting," International Committee of the Red Cross news release, July 17, 2012 (ICRC characterizing the violence as a non-international armed conflict).

Arab Republic to investigate all alleged violations of international human rights law *and to establish the facts and circumstances of such violations and of the crimes perpetrated, with a view to avoiding impunity and ensuring full accountability*."[20] The High Commissioner responded with an oral report in June of that year, in the course of which she "remind[ed] the Syrian authorities that violations of international law are serious crimes for which perpetrators can be held accountable."[21] She followed up with a written report in September 2011 that reviewed the range of alleged crimes committed by the government.[22]

OHCHR's mission became regularized with the establishment of the Independent International Commission of Inquiry on the Syrian Arab Republic by the Human Rights Council, supported by the High Commissioner and her staff.[23] The Independent Commission has reported several times, beginning in the fall of 2011, and the High Commissioner has presented those reports and called for international action before the UN Security Council and the General Assembly.[24] Her views received considerable attention from a media that, because of Syrian governmental restrictions, had substantial difficulty reporting from Syria itself, at least through 2012.[25]

Key Themes and Objectives

Throughout the High Commissioner's engagement in the Syria crisis, observers, led by Ms. Pillay, called for the Security Council to refer the Syria situation to the ICC for investigation and possible prosecution.

---

20 UN Human Rights Council. Resolution S-16/1, "The Current Human Rights Situation in the Syrian Arab Republic in the Context of Recent Events," UN Doc. A/HRC/RES/S-16/1, April 29, 2011 (emphasis added).

21 "Statement of Ms. Navi Pillay, United Nations High Commissioner for Human Rights to the Introduction of Preliminary Report on the Situation of Human Rights in the Syrian Arab Republic," OHCHR news release, June 15, 2011. News media around the world reported Ms. Pillay's statement. See, e.g., "Syria crisis: UN report condemns crackdown on protests," *BBC News*, June 15, 2001.

22 UN Human Rights Council. *Report of the United Nations High Commissioner for Human Rights on the Situation of Human Rights in the Syrian Arab Republic*, UN Doc. A/HRC/18/53, September 15, 2011 (hereinafter OHCHR Report of September 15, 2011).

23 UN Human Rights Council. Resolution S-17/1, "Grave Human Rights Violations in the Syrian Arab Republic," UN Doc. A/HRC/ S-17/1, August 18, 2011.

24 See, e.g., "Statement by UN High Commissioner for Human Rights Navi Pillay at the Human Rights Council 18th Special Session to examine the situation of human rights in the Syrian Arab Republic," OHCHR news release, December 2, 2011. "Statement by Navi Pillay, High Commissioner for Human Rights to the Human Rights Council 19th Special Session on "The deteriorating human rights situation in the Syrian Arab Republic and the killings in El-Houleh,," OHCHR news release, June 1, 2012.

25 Reporters without Borders, "Syria," last accessed February 10, 2012, http://en.rsf.org/report-syrie,163.html. See the chapter in this volume by Suzanne Nossel and Christen

However, no such steps were taken, with action in the Council on Syria generally blocked. As a result, OHCHR became the principal international body focused on accountability for alleged violations in Syria. The High Commissioner has taken on that role and, in the process, served a number of key functions connected to international justice. A review of the High Commissioner's actions indicates the following types of roles:

Framing and Defining

Early in the conflict, the High Commissioner framed it in the traditional human rights terms of an abusive government repressing a peaceful population. She also went further, characterizing the aims of the protests themselves. In her June 15, 2011 oral report, she said,

> [T]he people of Syria are eager to attain dignity, equity, and justice for all in their country. They are calling for change and seek a democratic system of government that respects their human rights and fundamental freedoms. The Government has responded with excessive violence against unarmed protestors. I am gravely concerned about the human rights and humanitarian crises that the country is facing.[26]

This kind of framing suggests a role beyond what might be appropriate for an international criminal tribunal. The High Commissioner, for one thing, characterized the broad pattern of the conflict rather than specific individual culpability. In doing so, she presented an early version of the conflict that aimed to be authoritative, even while noting the mission's inability to enter Syria itself. The first report annexed a chronology of the conflict up to that point in order to underline the patterns the report itself described. Moreover, she sought to establish that the conflict implicates Syria's "obligations under international human rights law."[27] She claimed a role for human rights law and institutions early on, even as the conflict was moving onto the stage of global politics centered around the Security Council.

As the conflict worsened, the reporting took on a broader sweep, not only urging the Government to cease violations. The Independent Commission's report of August 16, 2012, for instance, also found "reasonable grounds to believe that anti-Government armed groups committed war crimes and abuses of international human rights law and

---

Broecker on the High Commissioner and the UN Human Rights Council for additional analysis of the High Commissioner's response to the crisis in Syria.

26 "Statement of Ms. Navi Pillay, United Nations High Commissioner for Human Rights to the Introduction of Preliminary Report on the Situation of Human Rights in the Syrian Arab Republic," OHCHR news release, June 15, 2011.

27 Ibid.

international humanitarian law."[28] This kind of framing puts the High Commissioner squarely into the realm of international justice, where the governing legal frameworks – whether crimes against humanity or the *jus in bello* – impose obligations on state and non-state actors.[29]

Beyond framing the conflict itself, the High Commissioner sought to place the Syrian situation in the broader context of the Responsibility to Protect (R2P). She urged Syria to recall this responsibility, as "agreed at the 2005 Summit," and clarified that the doctrine "entails the prevention of such crimes, including their incitement."[30] Claiming a role for R2P showed a High Commissioner who was thinking not only of the current conflict and accountability but of the broader regime of atrocity prevention as it applies globally.

Identification of the Legal Framework

While claiming a governing role for human rights, the High Commissioner asserted that three bodies of law governed in Syria: international human rights law, by virtue of Syria's ratification of treaties such as the International Covenant on Civil and Political Rights and the Convention against Torture; international criminal law, in particular the Rome Statute of the ICC, even though Syria had merely signed but not ratified the Statute; and domestic law. Yet with respect to the third, the High Commissioner noted that "Syrian domestic law cannot be adequately relied on because it violates constitutional guarantees and encourages impunity."[31]

Identification of Potential Crimes and Perpetrators

In OHCHR's first written report, the High Commissioner went beyond legal frameworks and identified a pattern of violations committed by the government "that constitutes widespread or systematic attacks against the civilian population, which may amount to crimes against humanity" under the Rome Statute of the ICC.[32] She expressed concern with

---

28 Human Rights Council. *Report of the Independent International Commission of Inquiry on the Syrian Arab Republic*, UN Doc. A/HRC/21/50, August 16, 2012 (hereinafter Syria CoI report of August 16, 2012).

29 Compare, for example, with the language of The Rome Statute of the International Criminal Court, U.N. Doc. 2187, 2187 U.N.T.S., entered into force July 1, 2002, at 3.

30 OHCHR Report of September 15, 2011, note 22 above.

31 Ibid., 3–4.

32 Ibid., 13.

respect to murder and disappearances, torture, deprivation of liberty, and persecution. Strikingly, the first report notes that OHCHR's fact-finding mission "compiled a list of 50 alleged perpetrators at various levels of government and its agencies in connection with incidents documented in this report."[33] Though the information with respect to individual perpetrators was held in confidence and not made public, OHCHR appeared to be laying the groundwork for specific efforts at holding those individuals accountable. At the same time, the language directed to the government and its military and security forces – particularly where focused on the accountability for violations – appeared aimed to deter future violations, putting potential perpetrators on notice.

Providing Overarching Context in History, Law, and Politics

The High Commissioner, as well as the Independent Commission that followed, attempted to place the conflict, even as it was evolving, into historical and political context. Thus, in the first written report, the High Commissioner presented a picture of Syria "characterized by gross human rights violations under the cloak of emergency legislation in force since 1963."[34] Subsequent reports aim to do the same thing, if in brief, describing the legal, security, military, and political situations in the country. Unlike fuller historical treatments found in past human rights inquiries, such as the Commission of Inquiry on Darfur and the Goldstone Commission established in the wake of the 2008–2009 war in Gaza, the Syria material is concrete and succinct, without wading into controversial historical issues.[35]

Accusing and Engaging the Government

OHCHR aims to some level of transparency in order to demonstrate its efforts to engage the government. The annexes in the reports are valuable

---

[33] Ibid., 2. Subsequent reports also indicate that OHCHR is compiling lists of potential perpetrators. *See, e.g.*, Syria CoI report of August 16, 2012, note 28 above.

[34] Syria CoI report of August 16, 2012, note 28 above.

[35] International Commission of Inquiry on Darfur, *Report to the Secretary-General*, September 18, 2004, http://www.un.org/news/dh/sudan/com_inq_darfur.pdf. UN Human Rights Council, *Report of the United Nations Fact-Finding Mission on the Gaza Conflict*, UN Doc. A/HRC/12/48, September 29, 2009. See also David Kaye, "The Goldstone Report," *ASIL Insights (blog), the American Society of International Law*, October 1, 2009, http://www.asil.org/insights091001.cfm.

documentation of the diplomacy of the High Commissioner. OHCHR sought but was refused entry into Syria and thus relied on interviews with witnesses and refugees along with other sources. The High Commissioner noted to Syrian authorities that her team's work underscored not merely a "dire human rights situation … a matter of the gravest concern[,]" but also "egregious violations" of human rights law.[36] The High Commissioner's role here is not as a prosecutor but as an investigator, aiming to learn the full scope of violations occurring in the country, but at the same time, she directly warns the government of its accountability and the possibility of criminal enforcement.

Generating Recommendations to Key Actors

Whereas the international tribunals aim to protect their independence from political actors, OHCHR operates expressly as an organ of the United Nations. While it maintains the independence required of all UN bodies, it nonetheless has political functions: carrying out tasks assigned by the Human Rights Council, Security Council, and General Assembly; reporting to the political bodies; and advising the political bodies and governmental actors of particular steps that they ought to adopt. The recommendatory function of OHCHR comes through clearly in the Syria reporting, with the High Commissioner making recommendations to the Syrian government to cease its human rights violations and hold perpetrators accountable, including through legal reform, and to armed groups to "adopt, publicly announce and abide by rules of conduct that are in line with international human rights law and international humanitarian law standards, and hold perpetrators of abuses to account."[37] OHCHR also urges the Security Council, through the Human Rights Council, "to consider referring the situation" to the ICC.[38] As the conflict extended in time, the reporting also took into account the broader political situation, urging international actors "to put pressure on the parties to end the violence and to initiate all-inclusive negotiations for a sustainable political transition process in the country."[39] Thus, while OHCHR sees its role as consistent with and supportive of the aims of international justice, it also

36 OHCHR Report of September 15, 2011, note 22 above, 27–28.
37 Syria CoI report of August 16, 2012, note 28 above.
38 OHCHR Report of September 15, 2011, note 22 above, 24–25.
39 Syria CoI report of August 16, 2012, note 28 above.

sees a political mandate that would be inappropriate for an international prosecutor.

Media and Public Impact

The High Commissioner's statements and reporting received substantial media attention over the course of the conflict's first eighteen months. In part, the media lacked sources for consistent on-the-ground reporting; OHCHR provided analysis, based on its own investigations, that was more difficult to find than in other conflicts. The High Commissioner, however, did more than mere reporting of facts. The framing, the legal assessment, the recommendations, the overarching context: all of these elements gave the High Commissioner a message. Rather than report that message merely in the bureaucratic, methodological style characteristic of most UN human rights reporting, she spoke to the media and sought to provide a voice for outrage.

Consider, for instance, Ms. Pillay's briefing to the UN General Assembly on February 13, 2012. While she specified Syrian governmental behavior with facts and figures – thousands killed by security forces, tens of thousands arrested, many more thousands internally displaced – she also deploys first-person, emotive, consonant language apparently designed to trigger political response. "I am particularly appalled by the ongoing onslaught on Homs," she said, where "[t]he humanitarian situation ... is simply deplorable." "I am outraged by these serious violations. I am very distressed that the continued ruthless repression and deliberate stirring of sectarian tensions might soon plunge Syria into civil war," she adds. And she concludes, "The longer the international community fails to take action, the more the civilian population will suffer from countless atrocities committed against them."[40]

International Justice and Syria

Throughout the extensive reporting of OHCHR and its independent missions, the High Commissioner highlighted and prioritized international justice as the conflict in Syria spread and deepened. The work was critical to the international community's understanding of the conflict and the

---

[40] "Briefing to the General Assembly by Navi Pillay [Syria], High Commissioner for Human Rights," OHCHR news release, February 13, 2012.

nature of the Syrian government's attacks on civilians and civilian populations. It was also sensitive to the risks, some of which came to fruition, that armed groups would themselves commit violations, shedding light on a conflict that became more complicated over time.[41] There was some risk that, as the continual calls for justice and political settlement were met with inaction by a stalemated Security Council, the High Commissioner might develop an image as an ineffectual actor, unable to generate political response that would lead to accountability. During the course of the conflict, however, it is more likely than not that the High Commissioner enhanced OHCHR's role in the investigation, analysis, coordination, and publication related to massive human rights abuses in an ongoing conflict.

As important as the High Commissioner's public role in Syria has been, one theme received comparatively less, if any, attention from OHCHR. While some of its work may be quietly confidential, out of public reporting, OHCHR seems to have left out Syrian civil society. Civil society, or civilians more generally, are depicted as victims mainly, though the evolution of the conflict has required OHCHR to report more fully on civil society's move toward self-protection in a civil war scenario. Yet the constituent elements of civil society – the individuals and organizations that make up Syria's non-governmental environment – are active actors in Syria, and they have played a significant role in organizing the resistance to Ba'ath regime repression since long before March 2011.[42] The High Commissioner should have highlighted the role of civil society not only for contextual accuracy but also to prioritize the role of independent organizations as Syria moves, one hopes inevitably, from civil war to transitional governance, rule of law building, and transitional justice. OHCHR's technical expertise should have been deployed beyond the reporting of the various fact-finding missions and commissions, so that actors who are likely to make up the future of Syria's leadership – whether governmental or not – have the tools early on not only to press for transitional justice but to lay the groundwork for society-wide support for and understanding of accountability. In the future, reporting should be deployed not only for the traditional 'naming and shaming' goals of human rights work but also to build domestic constituencies for accountability.

---

41 See International Crisis Group, "Syria's Mutating Conflict," *Middle East Report* no. 128, August 1, 2012.

42 Ignacio Alvarez-Ossorio, "The Syrian Uprising: Syria's Struggling Civil Society," *Middle East Quarterly* 19, no. 2 (Spring 2012): 23–32.

Risk Management

As noted above, the current and immediate past High Commissioners were former leaders within the international criminal tribunals. Of all the High Commissioners, only one – Sergio Vieira de Mello – did not have a degree in law. With these kinds of backgrounds, one might expect strong support. The risk, however, might be a conflation of roles, so that a High Commissioner sees herself or himself in the role of prosecutor or lawyer, adopting legalistic approaches when strong moral ones might be called for. Vieira de Mello was alive to this potential problem.[43] Subsequent High Commissioners also seem to understand that they have roles that go beyond prosecutor; certainly High Commissioner Pillay, who brought the sense of personal commitment to the case of Syria, has gone beyond lawyerly approaches to her role. The High Commissioner serves very different functions from lawyer or prosecutor, operates according to different standards of proof, and aims not to move judges but to influence action by states and other organizations inside and outside the UN system. The High Commissioner should not be constrained by prosecutorial norms.

Still, when the post of High Commissioner was created, there was already an ICTY, but no prosecutor. The High Commissioner could be the 'conscience for the world' without any other individual below the rank of Secretary-General really claiming that mantle. The Rome Statute changed that. The days of one 'conscience for the world' came to an end when the ICC had a prosecutor who saw for himself quite a similar role. Harold Koh once said that "the world needs a human face for human rights."[44] Over the past several years we have found that we have two faces for human rights. We need to think through the implications, most importantly how these two high profile posts may be coordinated in ways that protect the independence of each and yet enable them to get their respective messages out to a wide audience.

In addition, any High Commissioner should take care to manage two particular risks:

First, the High Commissioner has a mandate that is much broader than that of the prosecutors of the ICC or ad hoc tribunals. Her mandate requires her "to promote and protect the effective enjoyment by all of all

---

43 Samantha Power quoted Sergio Vieira de Mello as telling close associates, "this place is just infested with [expletive] lawyers." Samantha Power, *Chasing the Flame: Sergio Vieira de Mello and the Fight to Save the World* (New York, the Penguin Press 2008): 356.

44 Harold Hongju Koh, "A Job Description for the U.N. High Commissioner for Human Rights," *Columbia Human Rights Law Review* 35 (Summer 2004): 495. See also Koh's chapter in this volume.

civil, cultural, economic, political, and social rights," including the right to development. It is true, again as Harold Koh put it, that the High Commissioner can be a kind of first-responder in human rights crises.[45] While attention has been driven by Syria since 2011, the High Commissioner operates not only in crises, but must work to press human rights concerns in all sorts of environments. There is a risk that crisis – in particular the kinds of crises that consume an ICC focused on ongoing conflict – will inexorably pull the High Commissioner away from her core mandate of universal promotion and protection. This is not to suggest that the High Commissioner cannot choose her battles. But the role was devised for purposes broader than international justice.

Second, to the extent the High Commissioner engages with institutions of international justice, she may be tied increasingly to notions of individual accountability instead of broader principles of transitional justice. The present High Commissioner uniquely brings to the position experience not only in international criminal justice but also truth and reconciliation, based on her time as a senior jurist in South Africa. The risk in Syria, as in other conflict situations, is that she may be seen to prioritize international criminal accountability – with its focus on the most senior levels of state and non-state actors – over other mechanisms, such as community reconciliation, domestic trials and inquiries, institutional change, rule of law development, and other issues essential to long-term observance of human rights norms.

Evaluating the High Commissioner's Role in International Justice

The Syria example provides just one of many potential cases which demonstrate the High Commissioner's role in international justice. Yet a review of the global range of human rights work surely goes beyond the scope of this essay. Here I want to recommend ways to conceive of the High Commissioner's work in international justice, drawing only superficially and briefly on other examples of OHCHR work beyond Syria.

First, borrowing from Harold Koh's notion of a first-responder, the High Commissioner may be seen as running an *early warning* system. OHCHR's field presence, though modest itself, extends well beyond the jurisdiction of the ad hoc tribunals and the ICC, which enjoy a field presence only in

45 Ibid., 494.

those places where the Office of the Prosecutor may be pursuing investigations or prosecutions. As such, the High Commissioner's statements and reports should be followed closely by those in The Hague, readying them for the possibility of referral or the necessity of *proprio motu* action by the prosecutor. Even beyond Syria, numerous examples of potential early warning may be found in OHCHR's presence in the Middle East, which by the end of 2012 included field officers in the Palestinian territories, Mauritania, Tunisia, Lebanon, Iraq, and Libya.[46] The functions in these six field presences include technical assistance to governments and NGOs, but they also serve to highlight critical problems that may be on the horizon.

A second way of thinking of the High Commissioner's role is, to borrow a military term, as a *force multiplier*. Recall that the ICC's staff is quite small, and though that is also true of OHCHR, its missions often gain access to conflict zones and translate that access into important and highly detailed reports on human rights abuses. Its reports, or the commissions of inquiry it staffs, may help the ICC Prosecutor direct her investigations.

Apart from the detailed Syria reporting, a strong example of force multiplication is the Commission of Inquiry on Darfur.[47] OHCHR staffed the Commission, led by the late Antonio Cassese, whose report is in many respects a model of careful human rights reporting. The Commission laid out the legal framework by which the Security Council should assess the conflict in Darfur, focusing on both human rights and international humanitarian law. It then evaluated specifically the question whether Sudan "pursued a policy of genocide."[48] It created a file of potential perpetrators that it urged be passed to the prosecutor of the ICC, while also recommending that the Security Council refer the situation in Darfur to the Court for investigation and prosecution.[49] The Commission, through

---

46 OHCHR, *Annual Report 2012*, 181–183. The Beirut office serves as a regional headquarters for OHCHR.

47 International Commission of Inquiry on Darfur, *Report*, note 25 above.

48 The Commission concluded that Sudan had not pursued such a policy. Ibid. By contrast, the prosecutor of the ICC concluded that President Omar al-Bashir had pursued genocide as a policy, generating considerable controversy. International Criminal Court, "Warrant of Arrest for Omar Hassavn Ahmad Al Bashir," March 4, 2009. Andrew Cayley, "The Prosecutor's Strategy in Seeking the Arrest of Sudanese President Al Bashir on Charges of Genocide," *Journal of International Criminal Justice* 6, no. 5 (2008): 829–840.

49 Under Article 12 of the Rome Statute, the Security Council may refer situations to the ICC for prosecution, even if – or rather, especially if – the situation is occurring in the territory of a non-state party. The Rome Statute of the International Criminal Court, art 3.

the High Commissioner, passed to the Court the files that served as the basis for the Commission report, providing investigators a valuable head start at the time the Security Council actually referred the situation to the ICC.[50]

Related to force multiplication, the High Commissioner may also share information she and her staff collect through a regular process of cooperation with the ICC Prosecutor. At a very basic level, the High Commissioner and OTP should engage in regular consultations to ensure that each know what the other is doing in areas of overlap. Such consultation can be done without intruding on either's independence or mandate, and it need not involve sharing of information related to investigations and prosecutions. Given the Court's limited presence in conflict situations, it benefits from the expertise and experience of OHCHR field missions. To be sure, cooperation must be managed carefully so as not to put at risk either's independent role in particular countries. Indeed, the experience in the Lubanga case – in which UN information from the DRC shared with the ICC became the subject of intense litigation and the near collapse of the case – provides a cautionary tale for both institutions.[51] Nonetheless, a mechanism for information-sharing of one kind or another should be in place, if one is not already, to satisfy, among other equities, the High Commissioner's need for confidentiality and the ICC's need for disclosure of evidence material to the defense.

Third, OHCHR can serve as *advisor* to the Court, beyond the Office of the Prosecutor. In the Sudan case, for instance, the Court adopted amicus procedures in which friends of the court provided guidance or information based on experience. The chambers in the Darfur case sought the advice of OHCHR in the context of witness protection, though the judges seemed to be doing this in part as a rebuke to what they perceived to be the prosecutor's inability to pursue the referred situation. So this is a controversial instance of the advisory function. Nonetheless, the High Commissioner at the time, Louise Arbour, filed an extensive amicus with

---

50 "After the Security Council's referral to the ICC, the High Commissioner handed over to the ICC Prosecutor 9 boxes of evidentiary material gathered by the Commission. International Criminal Court, "Situation in Darfur: Observations of the United Nations High Commissioner for Human Rights invited in Application of Rule 103 of the Rules of Procedure and Evidence" October 10, 2006, paragraph 56. See also UN Security Council. Resolution 1593, "Violations of International Humanitarian Law and Human Rights Law in Darfur, Sudan," UN Doc. S/RES/1593, March 31, 2005.

51 ICC documents detailing the stay of the proceedings in the Lubanga case can be found at Coalition for the International Criminal Court, "Lubanga Case," http://www.iccnow.org/?mod=drctimelinelubanga.

the Court in which she reviewed the procedures OHCHR followed to try to protect witnesses who provided assistance to missions. While she reflected an understanding, based on experience, of the risks to witnesses, she also expressed delicately the view that the ICC should take those risks. As she put it:

> In the particular case of the ICC investigation in Darfur, this balancing [of factors concerning protection and the goals of the referral] may require amongst other things a determination of whether the possible risks created by victims' contact with ICC investigators are greater than the danger they face daily by the continuation or escalation of the conflict and commission of related crimes. The determination in turn must take into account the potential deterrent effect of ICC investigations on the perpetrators of the very crimes that put the civilian population at risk and thus of its impact on the general reduction of violence.[52]

According to sources in the Court, this was taken by the Prosecutor at the time as a rebuke of his position that he could not put his investigators at risk in Darfur.[53] Regardless, the kind of extensive advisory function illustrated by the High Commissioner's submission to the Court should be seen as a model for future cooperation.

Fourth, the High Commissioner addresses issues *beyond the scope of the ICC's jurisdiction,* triggering or supporting national or international mechanisms of accountability. Perhaps the best example of this is OHCHR's production of the Mapping Report for the DRC, covering 1993–2003. The Mapping Report did not result – not yet, at least – in an accountability process for the DRC, but it does provide the model for this kind of engagement.

Fifth, the High Commissioner, in her 2010 Annual Report, privileged *"impunity and the rule of law"* as a key subject matter for her Office. This is right, for as the report says, "OHCHR engages in dialogue with states on the best ways to achieve legal protection of human rights and accountability for violations." The High Commissioner may take on an ever important role of promoting justice at the national levels, not only in ICC states but elsewhere. This would dovetail the logic of complementarity under the Rome Statute and could support the notion of positive

52 "Situation in Darfur: Observations of the United Nations High Commissioner for Human Rights invited in Application of Rule 103 of the Rules of Procedure and Evidence" October 10, 2006, paragraph 68.

53 International Criminal Court, "Statement of the Prosecutor of the International Criminal Court, Mr. Luis Moreno-Ocampo, to the UN Security Council Pursuant to UNSCR 1593 (2005)," December 14, 2006.

complementarity promoted widely but not really pressed with funding or long-term and sustainable programming. OHCHR should consider taking an even fuller role in the area of domestic accountability, perhaps as coordinator of the overlapping, duplicative work done by dozens of actors in the field.[54]

Conclusion

I will close here simply by noting that the High Commissioner has an important role to play in the institutions of accountability at the national and international levels, and in encouraging states and others to act in the face of atrocity. Yet the relationship may go both ways. In this essay I have treated the 'relationship' as a one-way ratchet: the High Commissioner has a role to play in international justice, but what of the role for the institutions of international justice, especially the ICC, in human rights? It is less clear that the relationship can work in both directions, given the limited mandate of the ICC. Nonetheless, the ICC has the responsibility to undertake its mandate in ways that are sensitive to basic rule of law principles, whether in terms of investigations and the rights of those not charged with crimes or prosecutions and the right of defendants to fair and public trials. In this sense, the relationship is two ways, as the ICC can support broader efforts – if even only by example – to spread the basic human rights principles that are at the heart of the High Commissioner's mandate. Part of that relationship requires that both parties, ICC and OHCHR, be open to the ideas of the other, sensitive to each other's mandates, and respectful of the different competencies and equities each brings to the table.

[54] David Kaye, "Justice Beyond The Hague: Supporting the Prosecution of International Crimes in Domestic Courts," *Council on Foreign Relations Special Report* No. 61 (June 2011).

PART FIVE

HARD CASES: CAN THE HIGH COMMISSIONER MAKE A DIFFERENCE?

THE HIGH COMMISSIONER, OHCHR, AND CHINA 1998–2005: CHALLENGES AND ACHIEVEMENTS

Stephanie T. Kleine-Ahlbrandt

Introduction

The UN, and especially the High Commissioner for Human Rights, faces a dilemma in its need to hold governments accountable for performance on human rights issues while maintaining good relations to keep channels open for diplomacy and influence. The High Commissioner is mandated to be both the voice for victims of human rights violations around the world, and to also engage in dialogue with governments.[1] On both of these counts, the People's Republic of China (hereafter, China) represents a particularly daunting challenge.

A permanent member of the Security Council with burgeoning economic and political clout, China welcomed certain parts of the UN and vigorously opposed others. China ratified six of the nine core international human rights treaties and invited in special rapporteurs and working groups for fact-finding visits. It held activities in support of regional frameworks and world conferences on human rights. In 2004, China revised its constitution to include a reference to human rights.

At the same time, not only was China's own record – particularly on civil and political rights implementation – problematic, but it also firmly rejected any public criticism of its domestic policies. Notwithstanding some progress on economic and social rights,[2] human rights violations committed by China have consistently been brought to the attention of the UN's monitoring mechanisms – mostly in the areas of freedom of expression, religion and assembly, due process rights, and participation rights.[3] But the Commission on Human Rights was always heavily divided

---

1 UN General Assembly, Resolution 48/141, "High Commissioner for the Promotion and Protection of All Human Rights," UN Doc. A/RES/48/141, December 20, 1993.

2 China reduced the incidence of poverty (using the World Bank's $1 a day definition) from 49% in 1990 to 6.9% in 2002, but it faced major challenges in realizing all economic, cultural, and social rights. While it ratified the ICESCR, it filed a reservation against Article 8 on freedom of association.

3 See UN Commission on Human Rights, *Report of the Special Rapporteur on torture and other cruel, inhuman or degrading treatment or punishment, Manfred Nowak / Mission to*

in response to efforts to condemn China.[4] Partly this was due to the robust diplomacy China carried out to re-orient the Commission away from its 'adversarial' concern with violations in specific states towards one emphasizing dialogue and cooperation.[5]

The High Commissioner could not ignore China; nor engage on China's terms. Mary Robinson's approach as High Commissioner (1997–2002) was to initiate a two-pronged strategy of systematically raising human rights problems with the government, while at the same time engaging in a technical cooperation program to help improve the human rights situation.[6] By the time Robinson's five-year term ended in 2002, she had visited China seven times, each time combining both public and private criticism of the authorities with engagement with them on issues of concern. In itself this was no small achievement, given the reluctance of the Chinese government to issue invitations to human rights officials to visit the country, let alone carry out workshops on the issue of human rights.

During this time, the Office of the High Commissioner for Human Rights (OHCHR) established the first UN-led dialogue and technical cooperation program on human rights with the Chinese government.

China, UN Doc. E/CN.4/2006/6/Add.6, March 10, 2006; UN Committee on the Rights of the Child, "Concluding Observations: China," UN Doc. CRC/C/CHN/CO/2, November 24, 2005; UN Committee Against Torture, *Report of the Committee Against Torture*, A/55/44, 2000; UN Human Rights Council, *Report of the Special Rapporteur on Torture and Other Cruel, Inhuman or Degrading Treatment of Punishment, Manfred Nowak / Follow-up to the recommendations made by the special rapporteur / visits to China, Georgia, Jordan, Nepal, Nigeria, and Togo*, UN Doc. A/HRC/10/44/Add.5, February 17, 2009; UN Commission on Human Rights, *Report of the Working Group on Arbitrary Detention / Mission to China*, UN Doc. E/CN.4/2005/6/Add.4, December 29, 2004; Commission on Human Rights, *Report submitted by Mr. Abdelfattah Amor, Special Rapporteur, in accordance with Commission on Human Rights resolution 1994/18*, UN Doc. E/CN.4/1995/91, December 22,1994; UN Committee on the Elimination of Racial Discrimination, *Report of the Committee on the Elimination of Racial Discrimination*, UN Doc. A/56/18 (SUPP), October 30, 2001.

[4] See Sonya Sceats and Shaun Breslin, *China and the International Human Rights System*, (London, UK: Chatham House, October 2012).

[5] As part of the Asian Group's emphasis on 'constructive' approaches, it pressed the Commission to undertake an overall review of the special procedures in 1998. Philip Alston, "Hobbling the Monitors: Should UN Human Rights Monitors be Accountable," *Harvard International Law Journal* 52, no. 2 (Summer 2011): 584.

[6] "My approach is two-fold – that I'm working very closely and deepening the working relationship through our memorandum of understanding with the Chinese authorities. .... But I must, and do, retain a critical voice. I have to speak out. I spoke yesterday evening about the issue of torture. ... I'm pressing for a visit by the special rapporteur on torture, Nigel Rodley, and it's very important that the Chinese have accepted that I operate very firmly in raising human rights issues as well as discussing how we can move forward constructively." See "Q&A: Mary Robinson on China's Human Rights Record," *CNN.com*, February 26, 2001.

The program was designed to capitalize on OHCHR's expertise in helping to prepare governments to ratify and implement the two main international human rights covenants. Indeed, during the initial years of the program, China signed and ratified the International Covenant on Economic Social and Cultural Rights (ICESCR) and signed the International Covenant on Civil and Political Rights (ICCPR). This gave rise to a certain momentum and belief that OHCHR could play a role in seeing through China's ratification of the ICCPR while supporting the changes needed for implementation of both covenants. Technical cooperation was also designed to support reform-minded individuals and institutions to tackle some of the country's most pressing human rights issues.

The High Commissioner was able to help keep certain issues on the agenda in China through regular and high profile visits and both public and private outreach. But the balance between engagement and criticism with China was so delicate as to prove impossible to sustain. While Mary Robinson's successor, Louise Arbour, was able to continue to both criticize and engage China, the technical cooperation program essentially came to an end by 2007. The program faced numerous practical challenges, alongside the larger political impediments of an increasingly restrictive environment and the government's growing defensiveness on human rights.

This chapter first describes a selection of the activities implemented by OHCHR in the course of its technical cooperation program with China, to familiarize readers with the objectives and its impact. It then identifies challenges faced both by the High Commissioner and OHCHR in carrying out the program and discusses how these were tackled. It concludes with an analysis of the High Commissioner's performance in balancing the responsibility to both engage with and criticize the Chinese government.

Background

In early 1998, Mary Robinson held a series of meetings with the Chinese Ambassador to the UN in Geneva, Wu Jianmin, which led to the signing of a Memorandum of Intent (MOI) to pursue a program of technical cooperation in late 1998.[7] The MOI was followed by a two-week OHCHR

[7] In those days, the Ministry of Foreign Affairs (MFA) had more influence within the Chinese bureaucracy than is the case at present. See International Crisis Group, *Stirring up the South China Sea (I)* (Brussels, Belgium: International Crisis Group, 2012), 14–16.

Needs Assessment Mission (NAM) to China in March 1999 to identify cooperation projects. The NAM recommended that OHCHR focus on the administration of justice, human rights education, and legislative reform; identified short, medium, and long-term objectives; and recommended activities with the ministries of justice, public security, and education, the Supreme People's Procuratorate (SPP), the Supreme People's Court (SPC), and various academic institutions which met a "minimum threshold" for meaningful cooperation (i.e. would justify OHCHR's involvement in China). The program envisaged working with these institutions in reviewing Chinese training practices and incorporating additional content based on international standards and UN materials.

In September 2000, following consultations with Chinese ministries regarding proposed project activities, OHCHR undertook another mission to China to negotiate the text of a Memorandum of Understanding (MOU) with the MFA. Mary Robinson signed the MOU, which provided for a two-year cooperation program, during her second visit to China in November 2000. The various references in the MOU to international human rights treaties and to China's international obligations under them reflect the outcome of difficult negotiations between OHCHR and the MFA. While OHCHR pursued discussions with the MFA to establish an OHCHR project officer in Beijing, these were fraught and ultimately unsuccessful.

Selected Activities Implemented under the Technical Cooperation Program

Re-Education through Labor

One of the areas targeted under the program was reform and abolition of Re-Education Through Labor (RETL). A widely discredited system, RETL is a measure administered by the police which can entail imprisonment for up to four years for those accused of minor offences that do not fall under Chinese criminal law.[8] The UN Working Group on Arbitrary Detention

[8] Those subject to RETL had no access to a lawyer, no opportunity to defend themselves in an independent hearing, and no right of appeal. RETL could be applied to a range of vaguely defined offences ranging from low value theft to drug addiction, prostitution, and membership of Falun Gong. Although the measure was targeted at minor crimes, many of those sentenced received harsher punishments than those found guilty of criminal offences. For the police, RETL had become an important mechanism of crime control largely outside any external regulation.

found that RETL led to violations of Article 9 of the ICCPR in its 1997 report and follow-up report of 2005.[9] Reform of RETL was on the legislative plan of the National People's Congress (NPC) in 1999, and OHCHR's approach was therefore to complement and strengthen research underway in China on alternative ways of punishing minor crimes in order to contribute to the debate and possible legislation on reform.

The first activity, a workshop in Beijing in February 2001, attracted significant international and domestic attention as the first workshop to be held in China on this relatively sensitive issue with UN participation. It focused on the requirements of international human rights law, particularly the guarantees regarding detention and a fair trial provided by Articles 9 and 14 of the ICCPR, and drew on the conclusions of the Working Group on Arbitrary Detention. Participants considered comparative experiences of punishment of minor crimes in conformity with international law in other countries and their relevance to China. Working groups identified a number of issues for further study, including research on the implications of international law for Chinese penal policy and comparative treatment of minor offenders. The conference report concluded that OHCHR should follow up by publishing the workshop proceedings online, holding an expert meeting in Geneva, and forming an informal consultative group to produce recommendations for revising Chinese law.

The second activity was a round-table meeting in September 2001 in Geneva. While a necessary next step, it did not meaningfully take forward the debate on RETL reform. By then, reform of RETL had hit a roadblock in China – the legislative reform process in the NPC had been suspended – and this was immediately evident in the more difficult implementation of technical cooperation activities.

In the end, and after two changes of date, a one-day workshop on Alternatives to Incarceration in the Punishment of Minor Crimes took place in Beijing in March 2003, attended by two international experts, three UN professionals, six Chinese experts and two representatives from the MFA. Although debate at the workshop was open and many of the national participants voiced criticisms of the RETL system, there was almost no discussion of the more substantial reform challenges. While Chinese participants provided information on the ways in which RETL sentences were being carried out, the discussion would have benefited

---

[9] *Report of the Working Group on Arbitrary Detention / Mission to China*, UN Doc. E/CN.4/2005/6/Add., para 74.

from visits by participants to pilot projects, as had been requested by the UN.

The various workshops demonstrated Chinese academic and official interest in both international law and the practical implications of reform to RETL, but the suspended government commitment to reform the system inevitably affected the project. It became clear that without high-level political commitment, further activities in this area were not worthwhile. It was also clear that discussions regarding potential collaboration should be held with the Ministry of Public Security (MPS), the agency with most responsibility in this area.

Police Training

Police training was another key area of activity under the MOU. The NAM had highlighted that many human rights-related problems linked to the administration of justice fell within the purview of the MPS, in particular torture, unlawful and prolonged detention, and substantial, largely unregulated police powers regarding administrative penalties. OHCHR sought to develop a human rights training program for basic level police, outlining a step-by-step approach, from translating UN materials into Chinese for workshops to the setting up of pilot training courses in several locations and using them to train trainers.

A workshop on Human Rights and the Police in July 2001 brought together international experts with representatives of the MPS and recommended designing a work plan to incorporate human rights into existing Chinese police training. A meeting following up on this recommendation took place in January 2002 in Geneva.

In cooperation with the MFA and MPS, OHCHR then organized a scoping mission to China on 8–16 March 2003 to determine the training materials being used by police training academies in China; to understand the methodology of police training in China and how best to develop and deliver additional training; and to agree with the MPS on co-designing and delivering a course and materials on human rights. The OHCHR delegation visited Zhengzhou People's Police Training School in Henan Province and was provided with police training materials for analysis against international standards.[10] The school also indicated that it would welcome the opportunity to host an OHCHR-sponsored pilot training scheme on

[10] "Training Materials for Investigative Police, Zhengzhou Peoples' Police Training School, December 30, 2002."

human rights, but it was clear that the MPS had little interest in a program outside of Beijing that it could not directly control, so OHCHR was never able to follow-up on this possibility.

A course to train 12 Chinese police trainers from around the country was held at the UK Police Staff College in Bramshill from 20 November to 12 December 2003. The aim of the course was to jointly develop a training module and training materials on the prevention of abuse of power in arrest, detention, and custody reflecting international standards. It was expected that international experts would be invited back to China to launch the pilot training scheme at a Chinese police-training academy.

Prior to the course, participants visited key organizations in the English criminal justice system, observing first-hand how international human rights standards had been incorporated into operational policing and the administration of justice. Participants then engaged in a combination of practical exercises involving human rights issues and training methodology, and information and discussion on human rights standards in relation to Chinese laws.

The course provided participants with information on international standards relating to law enforcement and made clear the value of training for all levels of police officers and leadership in setting standards of behaviour and conduct. It also emphasized the importance of understanding where domestic law fell short of human rights standards. Participants discussed problems encountered on the ground, including the lack of detailed guidance on police action in China and the difficulty of halting the process of detention and arrest of a suspect once the police and prosecution machinery engaged.

The training program greatly benefited from having been organized directly with the MPS. This was the first time that OHCHR had been able to work directly with a line ministry without involving the MFA as a conduit for communications. The MPS later confirmed that the study visit and training course had been useful in clarifying police powers in relation to arrest and detention through detailed implementing regulations. The visit also provided simple, practical examples of how detainees could be informed of their rights, such as though the use of posters, which were then introduced in police stations in China. The project also laid the foundation for a working relationship between OHCHR and the MPS, a ministry central to improving human rights protection and one with which foreign organizations had almost no history of engagement on the issue of human rights.

Yet the challenges inherent in strengthening the human rights component in Chinese police training were substantial. It was unrealistic to expect participants in a two-week overseas course to achieve not only a sufficient understanding of international standards and their implications for police training, but also to thrive with training methodologies with which they were unfamiliar and sceptical. Indeed, the flexible, participatory, self-critical training approach employed in the course significantly differed from Chinese training methods, which rely on large group lectures. The methodology was challenging for some trainees. There was also sensitivity over whether China's record was being attacked during some of the sessions. The successful transfer of a more participatory training model to the Chinese context would have required significant investment in training trainers and in developing appropriate teaching materials, as well as a commitment from the MPS to ensure that funds would be available for smaller training groups. In the short term, resource constraints – human and financial – made this very challenging to achieve. However, it was thought that the small group of very active participants could be potential project champions in a position to advocate for a stronger human rights component in police training within the MPS – for example, one of the most enthusiastic participants was a high-ranking MPS officer in Beijing.

While the police had a stated commitment to improving human rights protection and awareness, conflicting incentive structures meant that putting human rights into practice was very difficult for a local police officer under pressure to break cases. Further revision of the law, independent monitoring, credible reporting, and reparation mechanisms would also be necessary. Furthermore, any successful work in this area would need to be based on an understanding that international standards should be translated not only into national laws, but also into codes of conduct that would ensure implementation in practice. In meetings with the MPS it seemed that future collaboration along these lines was possible.

Prison Administration

In early discussions with OHCHR, the Ministry of Justice acknowledged the need to improve the protection of prisoners' rights. UN human rights mechanisms consistently expressed concern regarding harsh treatment of prisoners including torture, the denial of medical care, and the use of forced labor.[11] OHCHR recommended working with the Ministry to

[11] See, e.g., *Report of the Committee Against Torture*, UN Doc. A/55/44, paras. 106–145.

incorporate international standards into the training of prison officials and to examine the relevance of such standards for legislative and institutional reform.

The first activity was a two-day workshop in Beijing in June 2002. Workshop participants acknowledged the need for prison reform and proposed follow-up activities such as further workshops on inspection and monitoring; study visits to countries offering examples of good practice; the establishment of a committee of experts comprising international and Chinese resource persons; the training of trainers; and the distribution in China of a Chinese version of OHCHR Professional Training Series No. 9 *Human Rights and Prisons* and *Pocket Guide* (a translated version was made available to all participants).

A follow-up to the workshop took place in Switzerland from 29 September to 2 October 2003, comprised of a round-table and a program of visits to the Swiss prison system for a delegation of 15 senior Chinese prison administrators, trainers, legislators, and MFA officials. International experts from New Zealand, Switzerland, and the U.S. attended both the Beijing workshop and the Geneva round-table, providing continuity. Discussions involved the treatment of prisoners and the recruitment, training, and responsibilities of prison officers.

An independent evaluation found that participants were satisfied with the activities, with the main regret being insufficient time for discussions. While specific recommendations for prison reform had not been clarified, Chinese participants were interested in continuing cooperation.

Given capacity issues at OHCHR and the strong role of Switzerland in these activities, it was agreed that the Swiss government would undertake further activities with the Chinese in this area. As the MOU had expired, this was a practical response to ensure that potentially valuable cooperation continued. While useful in the circumstances, when initiatives are handed over for funding and implementation to other governments or agencies, the instigating agency naturally loses the ability to have any real influence over future outcomes.

Judges and Lawyers

The Needs Assessment Mission had identified the need to promote examination of international human rights standards for the administration of justice and highlighted concerns within China regarding corruption and other interference with law enforcement. While the mission also rightly recognized that fundamental reform would require difficult political decisions, it determined that technical cooperation activities could encourage greater understanding of and attention to the relevance of these decisions to China's international obligations.

In August 2002, High Commissioner Mary Robinson and China's Vice Foreign Minister Wang Guangya opened a high level workshop on judges and lawyers, with a focus on the independence of the judiciary and comparative training approaches. The two-day workshop, held in Beijing, brought together Chinese senior officials and practitioners with international experts. As a high level activity, it drew significant attention to the issue in China and was widely covered in the press. But there was not a clear follow-up agenda.

This is another area where successful technical cooperation depended on political decisions. The underlying problems were already well understood by Chinese scholars and reform-minded officials, and proposals by Chinese scholars for substantial legal revisions that would have increased judicial independence reportedly had been shelved. It was decided that there was little necessity for further technical assistance in the absence of a political breakthrough and a request from the Supreme People's Court for assistance with the reform process.

Human Rights Education

In meetings between OHCHR and the Ministry of Education, discussions took place regarding the training of primary, secondary, and university-level teachers on human rights. OHCHR believed there was a joint commitment to train teachers on human rights education as had been reflected in the MOU. It developed an incremental approach, envisaging an initial workshop to introduce UN materials (the UN publication *The ABCs of Human Rights* and a Resource Kit of UN human rights education material for schools, which was translated into Chinese), followed by activities to integrate international material with existing Chinese materials to strengthen teacher training in human rights education.

Vice Premier Qian Qichen and High Commissioner Mary Robinson opened a national workshop on human rights education in primary and secondary schools in Beijing in November 2001. The workshop sought to develop a common understanding of human rights education in schools, as defined in human rights instruments; to identify key components for the effective incorporation of human rights education in the Chinese school system; to present relevant experiences from other countries, particularly in Asia; and to develop a strategy for strengthening such teaching in China. A study visit to the Philippines then took place in September

2002 to introduce Philippine practice in incorporating human rights in primary and secondary school curricula, but it was not able to elicit common ground or a strategy for continued cooperation.

Overall, these activities were not successful in taking forward the stated aim of jointly developing teacher-training materials for human rights education. This was in large part because of a key difference in how the two sides defined human rights education. In meetings with the Ministry of Education, officials were keen to present China's experience in teaching legal education, but appeared to have little interest in joint collaboration on teacher training. China was clearly proud of its own efforts in this area and provided copies of primary and middle school legal education textbooks to OHCHR which showed material with reference to specific rights protected by Chinese law. But not all the rights discussed were human rights and the emphasis was more on encouraging respect for national law rather than international human rights law. OHCHR made clear to the Chinese side that while legal education activities may provide a good foundation for human rights education, the two were not the same. OHCHR decided that there was little scope for further collaboration with China on this issue without a clearer political commitment from the government.

Human Rights Support to Academic Institutions

OHCHR assisted in the publication of a *Chinese Yearbook on Human Rights* with the Chinese Academy of Social Sciences (CASS) Institute of Law.[12] CASS is an influential government-affiliated research institution with high standing in China's academic community and is also home to one of the first human rights centers in China. Given that the publication was dually edited by OHCHR and CASS and published by Brill, content selection and quality control was rigorous. The bilingual publication included both Chinese and international authors' articles on key human rights issues of relevance to China.

Human Rights Fellowships and Study Tours

Human rights fellowships for government officials and academics relevant to the technical cooperation program were listed as an agreed activity

---

[12] Sun Shiyan and Stephanie Kleine-Ahlbrandt, eds., *Chinese Yearbook of Human Rights*, Vol. 4 (Leiden, Netherlands: Brill, 2006), http://www.brill.com/chinese-yearbook-human-rights-volume-4-2006.

in the MOU. Several were provided in 2002 at the International Institute of Human Rights in Strasbourg and in 2004 at the Åbo Academi Institute for Human Rights in Finland. These courses were highly appreciated by the MFA officials who attended. On completion of the course, participants were required by the MFA to write a report, which, according to one participant, was later published in the Ministry's internal publication.

Despite expressed Chinese interest in continued workshops and study tours, it was decided that general human rights training for MFA officials was not the best use of available funding. OHCHR decided not to provide future fellowships unless recipients could contribute new insights and understanding to the implementation of the program, since the OHCHR mandate was to encourage structural change in Chinese law, policy, or practice.

Disability Rights

OHCHR cooperated with UNDP in a Project on Disability Rights, in which OHCHR provided expertise.[13] OHCHR also participated in the development of a handbook on best practice, *Protecting the Rights of Persons with Disabilities: International and Comparative Law and Practice*, the first publication of its kind in Chinese, which was launched in Beijing on the International Day of Disabled Persons 2003. The China Disabled Persons Federation (CDPF) distributed the publication to its offices at the provincial, city, and county level and carried out local trainings of trainers utilizing the publication and the OHCHR-UNDP disability rights training methodology.[14]

Challenges to the Program

Commitment of the High Commissioner and the Chinese Leadership

The success of technical cooperation depends on political will to use project outcomes. In a field as sensitive as human rights, it was difficult to

[13] For example, OHCHR provided expert trainers for workshops on disability rights held in Chengdu (2002) and Xi'an (2003).

[14] The China Disabled Persons Federation (http://www.cdpf.org.cn/english/) is one of the key Government-supported non-governmental organizations in China. Deng Pufang, President of the CDPF (himself a victim of the Cultural Revolution, when he became paralyzed from the waist down), the elder son of Deng Xiopang, was a recipient of the 2004 UN Human Rights Prize.

keep government partners active in implementing activities at the working level unless they knew that they were obliged by a high-level agreement. The personal commitment of both High Commissioners and the Chinese leadership was essential. As long as the High Commissioner was travelling regularly to China and meeting with high level officials, momentum was created at the working level to ensure project implementation. When High Commissioners subsequent to Mary Robinson inevitably travelled less to China, it was not surprising that technical cooperation also encountered difficulties. But in the end, nothing could make up for a lack of political will from the Chinese side to implement and follow-through on projects, which became clearer as time went on.

Lack of an OHCHR Presence in China

The lack of a field presence in China was another significant challenge to the effective implementation of the technical cooperation program. While the MFA could understand the technical reasons for OHCHR's request to place a staff member in Beijing, it had strong reservations about the proposal, arguing that the 'public perception' of an OHCHR presence would confuse technical cooperation with monitoring. The Ministry also pointed out that OHCHR did not provide human rights technical assistance to any Western country nor to many other countries in the Asia-Pacific region.

As a second-best option, OHCHR tried to secure the appointment of a human rights advisor to work within the UN country team. The advisor's responsibilities would have included advising the country team on integrating human rights throughout all UN programming, a stated goal of the UN. But the government never agreed to such a presence, mostly out of fear that it would facilitate monitoring and reporting on human rights. Unfortunately, there was also resistance to the idea from certain members of the UN country team on the ground, who made their views known to the government.[15]

With a program so large and complex, establishing strong and sustained contacts with Chinese partners in the interest of more effective project management was not a task that could be undertaken successfully

[15] Several UN agencies on the ground were highly supportive of OHCHR's activities and wanted access in-country to a human rights expert. However, the UN Resident Coordinator at the time refused to support the establishment of an OHCHR presence. But this was hardly a consistent UNRC approach; his predecessor had been very supportive of OHCHR's work in China.

from Geneva. A focused program of activities with clear and shared objectives unquestionably required a project office in China. Yet even though the NAM identified failing to achieve a presence in China as a risk, the program's goals were never reassessed in light of the fact that a field office was impossible to establish.

MFA "Gate Keeper" Resulted in Limited Access to Line Ministries

One of the factors responsible for delays in the implementation of activities was the MFA's role as the main implementation partner and coordinator of the program. There were constant shortages of available project staff given other priorities in the MFA, and it would have been inappropriate for OHCHR to subsidize staff positions within a Chinese ministry. In order to minimize the administrative burden, OHCHR recommended signing an overall framework agreement with the MFA but working more closely with the other relevant line ministries for day-to-day project implementation. The MFA never agreed to this arrangement, even though in some cases, direct relationships with line ministries were established anyway.[16] The insistence for the MFA to be a 'gatekeeper' seemed to be an attempt to control access to the program and attempt to maintain its own position vis-à-vis other ministries. On several occasions, the MFA went too far, trying unsuccessfully to assert influence over OHCHR's choice of international staff in Geneva to manage the program.[17]

Bureaucracy

While having to work through an understaffed Chinese MFA slowed implementation considerably, things were almost as slow on the UN side, due to bureaucratic constraints in the organization's headquarters in Geneva. OHCHR, which is administratively part of the UN Secretariat, does not have the ability to administer its own programs, and instead

---

[16] This was the case with the Ministry of Public Security, in part because it far outranked the foreign ministry.

[17] The MFA pressured OHCHR to hire a "Chinese candidate" for the program management team in Geneva, and then provided the office with a list. Of course this meant a candidate selected by the Chinese Government, as there were several Chinese nationals already working in OHCHR, whom they did not want to take the position. This was part of a larger effort by China to get more of its candidates into the UN system. They would often say to OHCHR that it "had too few Chinese." OHCHR repeatedly explained to the MFA that there were established recruitment procedures and that any interested candidates should apply through them.

depends on the UN's Geneva Office to do so. Every single action – for example a consultant's contract – had to go through lengthy processes in two separate UN bureaucracies, neither of which showed much flexibility. For example, it was necessary to get pre-approval of all expenses weeks in advance of all travel and activities, with no expense facility outside the multiple step authorization process in Geneva. Trying to implement technical cooperation between OHCHR and the Chinese MFA was therefore like being stuck between two dinosaurs. Whenever it was possible to get one to move, the other held things up. On several occasions, opportunities that presented themselves on the Chinese side were impossible for OHCHR to grasp because the bureaucracy moved so slowly.

Similarly, OHCHR's ambition with its program with China was far greater than the resources devoted to it. The original vision for technical cooperation with China was to engage in meaningful cooperation on the key human rights challenges facing the country. As such, assigning only one staff member to be responsible for the program was a mismatch – particularly when that person was simultaneously given numerous other responsibilities both in China and in the Asia-Pacific region.[18] Although China did not want an OHCHR staff member permanently based in Beijing, it facilitated the program officer spending significant periods of time working from Beijing without any problems. But it soon realised that OHCHR did not intend to devote significant resources to the project – in contrast with other organizations looking to cooperate with the MFA. This led to its decision to give the OHCHR program less importance.

A related issue was the lack of a Chinese language website to bring together all existing UN human rights standards, reports, treaty body documentation, and training materials. Given the keen demand in China for more easily accessible UN documents concerning China, this was an obvious project. But in the absence of an in-house capacity to develop this, the China program officer had to personally manage such translation and dissemination of relevant reports and training materials.

Clash in Methodologies

Beijing made clear early on its principles of cooperation: mutual trust, mutual benefit, equality, and a step-by-step 'building blocks' approach.

[18] The China program manager also served as China Desk Officer, which meant that she supported the monitoring and reporting work of the treaty body and special procedure systems as it related to China, including by accompanying the visit to China in November-December 2005 of the Special Rapporteur on torture, Manfred Nowak, and

This incremental approach was supposed to allow for the development of productive working relationships, mutual learning, and adaptability to changing circumstances. On the one hand, this approach was understandable as both sides did need to build trust, especially since this was the first experience of a UN agency undertaking a project with the MFA on human rights.

But on the other hand, the need to go slowly made it difficult for OHCHR to advance quickly to more meaningful activities. For example, China insisted on agreeing to a 'Memorandum of Intent' before proceeding to a 'Memorandum of Understanding.' Then, as soon as an MOU expired, either a new MOU or an Agreed Note was always necessary, which took weeks and sometimes months to negotiate. According to OHCHR project methodology, MOU and MOI agreements are not necessary for technical cooperation activities and can risk over-politicizing them. On the other hand, the utility of such a document in the Chinese context lay in its ability to provide high-level cover to partners working with OHCHR on sensitive topics. It also helped to lock in Chinese partners; they felt the pressure of needing to implement MOU activities or face criticism. But the difficulty of negotiating these documents slowed down implementation of program activities.

Another example of the different approaches preferred by each side was the organization of workshops. These were designed as initial activities in each area, in order to foster discussion on subsequent project activities – since it was difficult to get detail for projects from OHCHR visits to Beijing alone. But particularly in the very beginning, the workshops served as platforms for each side to reiterate their views without enough time allotted for meaningful discussion of the issues. OHCHR was able to negotiate a methodology for workshops that moved quickly past the plenary stage into smaller working groups with time to discuss specific issues and work on recommendations. This allowed for some very lively and frank discussion on current problems and next steps for cooperation. Meanwhile, OHCHR strived to ensure continuity with international experts and pushed the Chinese side to do the same.

It was also challenging to try to ensure that workshops and trainings were not standalone activities, but integrated into a more focused approach with agreed outcomes to improve, via pilot projects, specific areas of criminal justice practice. In the Chinese context, there was

---

assisting in the drafting of his reports to the Commission on Human Rights and the General Assembly.

reluctance to agree to a long list of outcomes as opposed to initial, exploratory activities.

Another difference in approach was that of emphasis on the different types of human rights. The MFA periodically raised concerns that far fewer events took place in the domain of economic, social, and cultural rights when compared with civil and political rights. However, OHCHR believed that technical cooperation should draw on its comparative advantages and focused its efforts to make the most effective use of its limited resources in a large country. OHCHR felt that economic, social, and cultural rights could best be promoted by supporting and drawing on the resources in the wider UN system (UNDP, ILO, UNICEF, etc.). Yet these agencies did not always use the normative or rights-based approach in their work.[19]

China's Growing International Clout

At the beginning of cooperation in the early 2000s, China saw OHCHR as a relatively neutral and effective way to get the expertise that it wanted, in contrast with working directly with Western governments or organizations. When engagement started, Chinese institutions were working on several potentially significant legal reforms. In contrast to Western government partners, which generally pushed their own legal systems, OHCHR could bring points of view from experts from various countries who would focus on best practice in different countries in trying to meet the requirements of international law. It also helped that there was a strong body of material from treaty bodies and special procedures that could be used in designing technical cooperation.

Another reason China engaged in technical cooperation with OHCHR was for the image value it provided. When China commenced technical cooperation with OHCHR, there was still a credible effort in the then-Human Rights Commission to adopt a country resolution against China.

As the years went on, however, concerns about its international reputation became less important for Beijing. Chinese diplomats knew that China was widely perceived as a serious human rights abuser and a

---

19 An OHCHR-supported "Human Rights Strengthening" Mission visited China from August 9–20, 2004 to begin a dialogue with UNDP China about applying a human rights-based approach to its development programs. While UNDP had policy on human rights (Integrating Human Rights with Sustainable Human Development), getting the organization to apply the human rights based approach on the ground was a continual challenge, especially in China.

protector on the international stage of other human rights abusing states. While they were uncomfortable with this image, they were increasingly far less comfortable with being seen domestically as caving in to international pressure.[20]

As China started to gain more international clout, it also started to take a less cooperative attitude towards the international community on human rights. Even during its early days of technical cooperation, OHCHR was often reminded that it did not have technical cooperation in other P5 or Western countries. As China's economic clout rose, Western countries became even less supportive of giving attention to human rights in China. The progressive weakening of the bilateral human rights dialogues of Western countries was a demonstration of this fact.[21] In one example, China applied pressure to bring to an end the so-called 'Berne process' of dialogue between Western countries maintaining bilateral human rights dialogues with China.[22] China completely halted technical cooperation with OHCHR in 2007.

The High Commissioner's Conflicting Roles: Engaging and Criticizing Governments

The High Commissioner needs to fulfil the obligations of a UN official accountable to Member States, while also being the chief global

[20] In recent years, the MFA has been increasingly criticized by nationalist elements from the Chinese public and harder-line agencies, which accuse it of selling out China's interests. Members of the public have reportedly long sent calcium pills to the ministry in allusion to a weak spine, with others calling it the 'ministry of traitors' (外交部 to 卖国部). See International Crisis Group, *Stirring Up*, 16. See also Susan Shirk, *China: Fragile Superpower* (Oxford, UK: Oxford University Press, 2007), 101.

[21] See Campbell Clark, "China Turns Chilly on Human Rights Dialogue," *The Globe and Mail*, August 22, 2012.

[22] Starting in 2001, the Swiss Government led a series of informal consultations of representatives of governments which participated in bilateral dialogues with China on human rights issues, referred to as the 'Berne Process.' The meetings often involved around 25 participants from 10 Western countries as well as the EU Commission and EU Council Secretariat. Consultations were held in April 2001 (Berne), March 2002 and March 2003 (Geneva, Palais Wilson) (addressed by then-High Commissioners Mary Robinson and Sergio Vieira de Mello), February 2004 (Berne), January 2005 (London), December 2005 (Brussels) and June 2006 (Berne). Participants discussed how to render more effective their bilateral dialogues with China and shared information on technical cooperation projects in the interest of better coordination and avoiding overlap. In later years, the meetings focused on developing benchmarks to evaluate the progress of the human rights dialogues, as well as sharing information on effectively raising individual cases and key thematic issues with Chinese authorities. Starting in 2006, the Chinese Government expressed

spokesperson for human rights.[23] Particularly in the Chinese context, the personal style of the High Commissioners became important in their approach and how the Chinese reacted to them and to OHCHR.

Crucial to the establishment of OHCHR technical cooperation with China was the level and terms of engagement set by Mary Robinson. During her seven visits between 1997 and 2002, she engaged in a 'two-pronged' strategy of continually raising human rights problems with the authorities while at the same time engaging in technical cooperation to help improve the human rights situation. This was not an easy balance to strike, not least because China's practice was to hold out dialogue and engagement as a reward only for countries that refrained from criticizing its human rights record. Robinson enjoyed the political clout that came from being a former head of state – which helped her secure meetings with China's top leadership – and she leveraged this to the maximum into a true exchange with China's leaders.[24] In doing so, she parted ways with the previous High Commissioner, José Ayala Lasso, who favoured quiet diplomacy.[25]

By being a credible and consistent voice for human rights victims, High Commissioners arguably create more power for themselves to go up

---

displeasure with the group and its meetings. One participating government was told that China would suspend indefinitely their bilateral rule of law programs in China if the process were not abandoned. The 'Berne process' name as such was discarded but participants affirmed that they had the right to hold any discussions they chose amongst themselves as a part of normal international diplomacy.

23 In doing so, that individual needs to punch above his or her weight, as OHCHR has never received more than three per cent of the total UN budget. International Service for Human Rights, "High Commissioner Calls 3% UN Budget for Human Rights 'Scandalous', in Third Committee Dialogue," October 19, 2011.

24 Mary Robinson met with the following high-level officials, among others: 1st visit (6–15 Sept.1998) President Jiang Zemin, Vice Premier Qian Qichen, Governor of the Tibetan Autonomous Region Mr. Lek Chok, and Vice Mayor of Shanghai Mr. Zhou Muyao; 2nd visit (19–21 Dec.1999) President Jiang Zemin and the Foreign Minister; 3rd visit (29 Feb.–2 Mar. 2000) Chief Executive of the Hong Kong Special Administrative Region, Mr. Tung Chee-hwa, Vice Premier Qian Qichen, and Vice Foreign Minister Wang Guangya; 4th visit (20–21 Nov. 2000) President Jiang Zemin, Vice Premier Qian Qichen; 5th visit (25–27 Feb.2001), Mr. Li Tieying, member of Politburo, State Counsellor, Foreign Minister Tang Jiaxuan, Minister of Justice Mr. Zhang Fu-Sen, and Mr. Deng Pufang; 6th visit (8–10 November 2001), Vice Foreign Minister, President Jiang Zemin; 7th visit (18–20 August 2002), Vice Foreign Minister, Minister of Justice and Vice Premier.

25 Robinson's predecessor, José Ayala Lasso, said that the proof of success of his low-key approach to China was that he received an invitation to visit. He also stated, "I'm not convinced that simply speaking out is the best way of obtaining results. We have a history of countries speaking out, U.N. institutions speaking out. I'm asking if the results obtained have been enough." Elif Kaban, "UN Rights Chief for Quiet Diplomacy in China, Cuba," *Reuters*, March 5, 1997.

against problem governments and certain corners of the UN that are not always human-rights friendly. High Commissioners are bolstered significantly by the existing treaty body and special procedures systems serviced by OHCHR which engage in reporting and monitoring. High Commissioners have consistently drawn on this body of work when engaging the Chinese authorities on human rights. Mary Robinson started the practice of presenting the Chinese authorities with an Aide-Memoire summarizing the conclusions, observations and recommendations of the treaty bodies and special rapporteurs, to serve as background to discussions during her visits.

At the end of every visit, she gave press conferences and spoke openly about several of the human rights issues she raised in private meetings, something that the government disliked but tolerated.[26] These press conferences ended up being significant events with a massive presence of both Chinese and foreign journalists, none of whom were accustomed to hearing a UN official publicly criticize China – let alone from within a UN building in Beijing. It was uncomfortable and unprecedented for most UN officials based inside the country, some of whom tried to distance themselves from her positions in meetings with Chinese officials.

Chinese officials certainly did not like Robinson's criticism – especially her practice of bringing long lists of individual cases and both privately and publicly raising them – but they came to respect her for it. On her last visit to China, the authorities tried to give her less time during her highest-level meetings in an effort to prevent her from raising as many individual cases, but she just read her list twice as fast.[27] They also strongly criticized her meeting with the Dalai Lama in August 1999 and during her subsequent visit lectured her on the differences of being a president and a UN official. In addition to mainland China, Robinson also focused attention on the situation in Hong Kong, travelling there during the height of tensions over the highly controversial Right of Abode case and met top officials including the Chief Executive to discuss a number of issues of concern to the Human Rights Committee in its review of Hong Kong's periodic report four months earlier.

Robinson also used her clout to hold conferences in China on sensitive issues that otherwise would not have been addressed – and certainly not

---

26 In her memoirs, Robinson describes how she strived for balance in those press conferences between recognising progress made and criticizing on-going violations of human rights. Mary Robinson, *Everybody Matters* (London, UK: Hodder & Stoughton, 2012), 226.

27 Afterwards, MFA officials commented that they didn't like it, but "we are used to her ways by now."

at such high levels in the Chinese bureaucracy. The conferences that her office organized were never attended by less than the Vice Minister level, and she also managed to get Politbureau member Qian Qichen to open a conference with her on the highly sensitive issue of Re-Education Through Labor.

Sergio Vieira de Mello continued in this vein. Early in his tenure he established good relations with the Chinese MFA, yet also sent personal letters on various cases of alleged human rights violations. Once, just after signing such a letter, Sergio wondered out loud: "we'll see if they still want me to visit now."[28] Vieira de Mello had a long history of cooperation with the Chinese, including when China sent peacekeepers to East Timor while he was the head of that operation, and he intended to carry on both engaging and criticizing China.

When Louise Arbour took over, she continued to engage without shying away from criticizing China, though understandably with a different personal approach. Unlike Mary Robinson, she did not meet the Dalai Lama and saved some of her harshest criticism for her private meetings with government officials, but she never shied from the protection aspect of her mandate.[29] The rank-conscious Chinese had to adjust to a High Commissioner who they considered lower in political seniority in comparison with Robinson. But Louise Arbour was taken very seriously by the Chinese, as a formidable and trustworthy interlocutor who was absolutely solid on the issues. She quickly gained the respect of the MFA with her commitment to engaging with them while also being quite tough on several human rights issues. For example, she regularly raised with the authorities issues such as the need for judicial review of all decisions regarding deprivation of liberty and the extensive use of the death

[28] Vieira de Mello sent a personal letter on behalf of Tenzin Deleg Rinpoche to Ambassador Sha Zukang dated 13 December 2002 in which he expressed concern at "reports that the trial of Tenzin Deleg Rinpoche and Lobsang Dhondup had been unfair, that the two men did not have access to a lawyer, and that the evidence linking them to the crimes they allegedly stand accused of was vague and unsubstantiated." The late High Commissioner sent a strongly worded follow-up letter dated 23 January 2003 following Lobsang Dhondup's execution.

[29] In an interview, Arbour acknowledged that she had taken a more diplomatic approach to promoting human rights in places such as China and Russia than elsewhere, saying she had chosen a strategy of private engagement "that is likely to yield some positive results" over one that "would make me and a lot of others feel good." She said that as a UN official she was constrained by the reality of the organization's power centers, including China, Russia and the Group of 77, a bloc of more than 130 developing countries. In that context, she said, "naming and shaming is a loser's game." Colum Lynch, "U.N. Human Rights Chief to Leave Post," *Washington Post*, March 3, 2008.

penalty, including for offences that do not meet the international standard of the most serious crimes. She also raised a number of individual cases illustrative of the changes that needed to be made as China prepared to ratify the ICCPR.

During her visit to China in 2005, Louise Arbour was successful in securing meetings with some genuinely independent NGOs, in addition to the usual government-sponsored NGOs that Beijing insisted high-level officials must meet. This was the first time that a High Commissioner was able to meet with genuine civil society organizations, and it was the result of significant negotiation between the two sides. Arbour also met with academics playing a role in advancing human rights in the country through pilot projects (for example, providing lawyers and videotaping police interrogations) and public interest law cases.

Arbour placed a lot of emphasis on ICCPR ratification, which she consistently raised with the authorities. For example, in a meeting with one high-ranking official during her 2005 visit, she said that a target date of the 2008 Beijing Olympics would provide the opportunity to showcase China and leave a unique and positive legacy. In response, this official suggested that rather than linking ICCPR ratification to a specific sporting event, the focus should instead be to bring China's law and practice up to standards to the maximum extent possible before ratification in order to minimize reservations. Arbour then urged the authorities to take concrete, tangible steps that would indicate their seriousness in preparing for ratification, and said that OHCHR would offer support and expertise in this regard. Eight years later, China still has not ratified the ICCPR.

Louise Arbour also asked – for her second visit – to visit Tibet.[30] While the Chinese responded that the "timing was not convenient," her request provided a future High Commissioner with the possibility to follow-up by repeating the request for a visit.[31]

Conclusion

In the end, the demise of OHCHR's program in China was the result of combined factors. But a key, overriding reason was the increasingly

---

[30] Stephanie Nebehay, "Tibet: China Blocks 'Inconvenient' Visit," *The Guardian*, April 11, 2008.

[31] Unfortunately, High Commissioner Navi Pillay had not visited China by mid-2013, despite having visited nearly 40 countries in the first three years of her mandate. China was the first country to request that she visit.

restrictive atmosphere in which OHCHR struggled, no matter the level of administrative support or personal clout of the High Commissioner. The golden years of technical cooperation were from the mid-1990s to early-to-mid-2000s, before the Chinese government began to focus in 2005–2006 on ensuring a successful 2008 Olympics. Then the environment became much more restrictive, with a more sophisticated level of human rights abuse and control and a more defensive and hubristic attitude towards the international community, alongside a number of concrete setbacks which included the removal of the head of the Supreme People's Court.

It is impossible to know now whether an appropriate level of administrative, financial, or political support would have enabled the OHCHR program to continue or whether Beijing would have curtailed it anyway. It is likely that with a more supportive arrangement, OHCHR might have been able to accomplish a more meaningful program that might have lasted a few more years. But the differing priorities, goals, and methodologies of each side meant that the program was unlikely to operate successfully over a significant period of time.

THE HIGH COMMISSIONER FOR HUMAN RIGHTS AND NORTH KOREA

Roberta Cohen[1]

The Democratic People's Republic of Korea (DPRK or North Korea) is best known internationally for its development of nuclear weapons and for the chronic hunger and malnutrition endured by much of its population. Less publicized have been its widespread and grave human rights violations, which North Korea has taken great pains to conceal. The country is by far the world's most inaccessible and 'most secretive,' with its population often described as 'the hidden people.'[2] Since 1948, the Kim dynasty has ruled North Korea with an ideology of nationalistic self-reliance (*juche*) effectively minimizing ties with much of the rest of the world. While there have been recent inroads into this closed society, North Koreans cannot exit their country freely, are not allowed to telephone outside the country or listen to radio broadcasts from abroad, and only a small number are allowed access to the internet.[3] Between North and South Korea today, "there is no telephone service…no postal service, no email."[4] Foreigners allowed entry are limited in their ability to communicate with North Koreans. Even during the great famine of the mid 1990s when North Korea invited in international food agencies to counter starvation (at least one million reportedly died), it restricted the access and involvement of aid workers with the North Korean people.[5] Kim Jong-il, who in 1994 inherited the leadership of North Korea from his father Kim Il-sung, is

[1] The author wishes to thank JBI Associate Director Christen Broecker for her valuable research assistance and editorial suggestions.

[2] See Ralph Hassig and Kongdan Oh, *The Hidden People of North Korea: Everyday Life in the Hermit Kingdom* (Lanham, MD: Rowman & Littlefield, 2009), 3–5.

[3] See UN General Assembly, *Report of the UN Secretary-General, Situation of human rights in the DPRK*, UN Doc. A/65/391, September 24, 2010, para.19; Hassig & Oh, *The Hidden People*; and Melanie Kirkpatrick, *Escape from North Korea: The Untold Story of Asia's Underground Railroad* (New York: Encounter Books, 2012), 275–279.

[4] Barbara Demick, *Nothing to Envy: Ordinary Lives in North Korea* (New York: Spiegel & Grau, 2010), 10.

[5] See Andrew S. Natsios, *The Great North Korean Famine* (Washington, DC: US Institute of Peace Press, 2001), 5, 48–9, 140, 174–5, 215, 224.

quoted as saying, "We must envelop our environment in a dense fog to prevent our enemies from learning anything about us."[6]

Origin of Concern about Human Rights in North Korea

Largely because of the restrictions, inaccessibility, and resulting lack of hard information, the first in-depth human rights report about North Korea was not published until 1988, 40 years after Kim Il-sung first assumed power. Two non-governmental organizations (NGOs) in the United States – the Minnesota Lawyers International Human Rights Committee and Asia Watch decided to bring to light whatever information they could find even though they could not visit and had to rely on unverified interviews and second hand reports. Their findings described draconian controls imposed on the population reinforced by regularized torture and summary executions.[7] Earlier, in 1979, Amnesty International published the accounts of a Venezuelan and Frenchman detained in the North on political grounds from 1967 to 1974 and introduced North Korea's political prison camp system to an international audience.[8] By 1991, Amnesty reported that, "Tens of thousands of people, including prisoners of conscience, appear to have been detained since the 1960s under various forms of arbitrary detention.... Thousands more appear to have been victims of 'disappearances,' torture or summary execution."[9]

Neither the United Nations Division of Human Rights nor the UN Centre for Human Rights – the predecessors to the Office of the High Commissioner for Human Rights (OHCHR) – played a significant role in bringing to light the situation in the DPRK. To be sure, an expert body of the Commission – the Sub-Commission on Prevention of Discrimination and Protection of Minorities – adopted a resolution on human rights in North Korea in 1997,[10] and the following year called on the Commission to

---

6 Demick, *Nothing to Envy*, opening page.

7 Minnesota Lawyers International Human Rights Committee and Asia Watch, *Human Rights in the Democratic People's Republic of Korea*, 1988.

8 David Hawk, *The Hidden Gulag: The Lives and Voices of "Those Who are Sent to the Mountains,"* 2nd ed. (Washington, DC: Committee for Human Rights in North Korea, 2012), 42–3.

9 Amnesty International, "North Korea: Summary of Amnesty International's concerns," October 13, 1993. Amnesty International was allowed to pay restricted visits in 1991 and 1995, the only times an international human rights NGO was allowed entry to North Korea.

10 UN Sub-Commission on Prevention of Discrimination and Protection of Minorities, Resolution 1997/3, "Situation of human rights in the Democratic People's Republic of Korea," UN Doc. E/CN.4/1998/2, August 21, 1997, 18.

take up the situation.[11] But it was not the High Commissioner or her staff that flagged the situation even though that Office took initiatives on other countries.[12] Rather, the Sub-Commission's resolutions originated with the author of the 1988 Minnesota Lawyers Committee report, David Weissbrodt, who became an expert member of the Sub-Commission from 1996 to 2003.

In 2003, the Commission on Human Rights for the first time adopted a resolution on North Korea and in 2004 appointed a Special Rapporteur to investigate and report on the human rights situation.[13] The 2003 resolution was the result of the efforts of NGOs and Western states, especially France, which was influenced by the publication in French in 2000 of a first-hand account by a North Korean survivor of a prison labor camp.[14] The resolution in 2004 appointing a Special Rapporteur was in part the initiative of the United States and its head of delegation Richard Williamson[15] as well as of the EU. Reinforcing the effort was a report submitted to the Commission by the OHCHR Secretariat summarizing UN activities on human rights in North Korea.[16] But the overall effort came from the outside, and even then these Commission resolutions were adopted more than 50 years after the Kim dynasty assumed power and 15 years after the first NGO report on the human rights situation.

---

[11] UN Sub-Commission on Prevention of Discrimination and Protection of Minorities, Resolution 1998/2, August 19, 1998. The 1997 and 1998 resolutions cited reports of "mass internments" in detention centers, the deaths of "many" political prisoners, "frequent reports of extrajudicial execution and disappearances," and "serious restrictions" on free movement. They expressed concern about the "virtual impossibility of obtaining information or visiting that country" and urged greater international attention to the problem so as to help North Korea's population emerge "from the isolation in which it is maintained."

[12] See Bertrand Ramcharan, *A UN High Commissioner in Defense of Human Rights* (Leiden: Brill, 2004), 12. The author reports initiatives that he undertook as Acting High Commissioner (August 2003-July 2004) on countries such as Liberia, Sudan (Darfur), Iraq, and Ivory Coast.

[13] See UN Commission on Human Rights, Resolution 2003/10, "Situation of human rights in the Democratic People's Republic of Korea," UN Doc. E/CN.4/RES/2003/10, April 16, 2003; and UN Commission on Human Rights, Resolution 2004/13, "Situation of human rights in the Democratic People's Republic of Korea," E/CN.4/RES/2004/13, April 15, 2004.

[14] See Kang Chol-hwan and Pierre Rigoulot, *The Aquariums of Pyongyang: Ten Years in the North Korean Gulag* (Paris: Editions Robert Laffont, 2000) [in French], English trans. Yair Reiner (New York: Basic Books, 2001).

[15] Conversation of February 8, 2012 with Ambassador Richard Williamson, head of the US Delegation to the Commission on Human Rights in 2004. He pointed out that President George W. Bush read *The Aquariums of Pyongyang*, met with former North Korean prisoner Kang Chol-hwan, and supported strong UN action on human rights in North Korea.

[16] See UN Commission on Human Rights, "Situation of human rights in the Democratic People's Republic of Korea," Note by the Secretariat, UN Doc. E/CN.4/2004/31, February 17, 2004; and Ramcharan, *A UN High Commissioner*, 100–101.

UN treaty bodies, composed of independent experts and serviced by the Office of the High Commissioner, provided some help. As a result of its accession to four international human rights treaties,[17] the DPRK was obliged to submit reports every few years on its compliance to the expert bodies set up to monitor their implementation. Its reports, however, were mostly sparse and sometimes not forthcoming at all.[18] In fact, the Human Rights Committee observed in 2001 that 17 years had lapsed since the last dialogue with the DPRK and that the lack of information provided by North Korea made it difficult to address effectively "credible and substantiated allegations" brought to its attention by other sources.[19] The Committee nonetheless made extensive recommendations as did other treaty bodies and provided an information base that helped states draft the Sub-Commission and Commission resolutions.[20]

Notwithstanding this supporting role, the impetus for unearthing and publishing information about the human rights situation in North Korea and pressing states to take action came from non-governmental organizations, not the United Nations.

Role of the High Commissioner

In looking at the role played by the High Commissioner prior to the adoption of the 2003 resolution, two questions arise. When grave human rights violations are *suspected* in a country and verifiable information is difficult to come by, what role should the High Commissioner or her Office play in unearthing that information and trying to publicize it? And second, what role should the High Commissioner or her Office be expected to play in a situation where no official intergovernmental UN body (i.e. a body of states as opposed to independent experts) calls for an investigation of the human rights situation?

[17] North Korea is a party to the International Covenant on Civil and Political Rights, the International Covenant on Economic, Social and Cultural Rights, the Convention on the Rights of the Child and the Convention on the Elimination of All Forms of Discrimination against Women. See UN Treaties Collection, http://treaties.un.org/Pages/Treaties.aspx?id=4&subid=A&lang=en.

[18] See UN Commission on Human Rights, "Situation of human rights in the Democratic People's Republic of Korea," para.11.

[19] UN Human Rights Committee, "Concluding Observations of the Human Rights Committee: Democratic People's Republic of Korea," UN Doc. CCPR/CO/72/PRK, August 27, 2001, para.2.

[20] See UN Commission on Human Rights, "Situation of human rights in the Democratic People's Republic of Korea," para.11.

Appointed in 1994, the High Commissioner for Human Rights is intended to be 'the conscience for the world' and the UN authority expected to play an active role in responding to and preventing the continuation of human rights violations internationally. According to the resolution creating this post, the High Commissioner's mandate is to "promote and protect the effective enjoyment *by all* of all civil, cultural, economic, political and social rights" [emphasis added].[21] The High Commissioner therefore has a scope of action far wider than countries on which UN human rights bodies take action. Despite many political and resource constraints, the Office can and does take initiatives.[22] Yet in the case of North Korea, the High Commissioner's Office did not begin to act on human rights in North Korea until nine years after the creation of the position; and even then it acted only because the 2003 resolution of the Commission on Human Rights directly requested the High Commissioner to engage in "a comprehensive dialogue" with North Korea with a view to establishing "technical cooperation programs in the field of human rights."[23]

Establishing Dialogue and Technical Cooperation with North Korea

It was Acting High Commissioner Bertrand Ramcharan who carried out the Commission's request for a dialogue with North Korea in 2003. At the time, the High Commissioner's Office already had technical cooperation agreements with more than 50 countries,[24] but unlike most other countries, the DPRK refused "to identify potential areas of cooperation."[25] It charged that the 2003 resolution was "adopted under pressure by the EU" and was "the product of political collusion with the anti-DPRK policy of the United States."[26] Subsequent High Commissioners were similarly unsuccessful in establishing a dialogue. In 2006, Louise Arbour reported to the Human Rights Council (which replaced the Commission on Human Rights) that although her Office had been "actively trying to encourage the

21 UN General Assembly, Resolution 48/141, "High Commissioner for the promotion and protection of all human rights," UN Doc. A/RES/48/141, December 20, 1993.

22 See Ramcharan, *A UN High Commissioner*, 12.

23 UN Commission on Human Rights, Resolution 2003/10.

24 UN Commission on Human Rights, "Situation of human rights in the Democratic People's Republic of Korea," para.3.

25 Ibid. 2–3.

26 Note Verbale dated 4 February 2004 from the Permanent Representative of the Democratic People's Republic of Korea addressed to the Office of the United Nations High Commissioner for Human Rights, contained in Commission on Human Rights, Note by the Secretariat, 9–10.

Government to avail itself of our [technical] assistance," to date "our efforts have yielded no result." "I have been unsuccessful," she told the Council, "in engaging in dialogue with the Government."[27] Navi Pillay also made no progress in her efforts from 2008 to 2012.[28]

The UN Secretary-General backed the dialogue and urged North Korea to allow entry to the High Commissioner.[29] When Ban Ki-moon dispatched a Special Envoy to Pyongyang in 2010, one of the items on that envoy's agenda was to press the government to cooperate with OHCHR and set up a technical assistance program.[30] Many governments also called upon North Korea to establish a dialogue with the High Commissioner and cooperate on technical assistance programs, whether in the Universal Periodic Review[31] or the General Assembly.[32]

North Korea, in recent years, hinted at a *quid pro quo*: an end to UN resolutions and mandates criticizing North Korea's human rights record in exchange for a visit by the High Commissioner and technical assistance programs.[33] In early 2012, High Commissioner Pillay privately raised the possibility of setting aside country specific mandates and resolutions in order to gain access to North Korea.[34] But the resolutions in the General Assembly and Human Rights Council were the work of UN Member States, not the High Commissioner, and it was unlikely these states would forego

---

[27] Louise Arbour, "Statement of Ms. Louise Arbour, United Nations High Commissioner for Human Rights, to the Human Rights Council," (UN Human Rights Council, Geneva, June 23, 2006).

[28] See UN General Assembly, *Report of the UN Secretary-General / Situation of human rights in the DPRK*, UN Doc. A/64/319, August 24, 2009, paras. 24–27.

[29] Ibid. para.58(a).

[30] UN General Assembly, *Report of the UN Secretary-General / Situation of human rights in the DPRK*, UN Doc. A/65/391, September 24, 2010, paras. 2–5, 86.

[31] See Human Rights Council, *Draft Report of the Working Group on the Universal Periodic Review: DPRK*, UN Doc. A/HRC/WG.6/6/L.12, December 9, 2009, paras.25, 42, 51, 53, 55, 110 and 111.

[32] UN General Assembly, Resolution 66/174, "Situation of human rights in the Democratic People's Republic of Korea," UN Doc. A/RES/66/174, December 19, 2011, para. 5(e).

[33] *Report of the UN Secretary-General, Situation of human rights in the Democratic People's Republic of Korea*, UN Doc. A/64/319, para.26. See also UN Human Rights Council, "Note Verbale dated 1 February 2012 from the Permanent Mission of the Democratic People's Republic of Korea to the United Nations Office at Geneva addressed to the President of the Human Rights Council," UN Doc. A/HRC/19/G/1, February 14, 2012. According to the Note, "The position on country-specific mandates will therefore remain a criterion for determining whether or not one aspires to genuine dialogue and cooperation."

[34] Discussions at the Conference on the United Nations High Commissioner for Human Rights: Conscience for the World, The Jacob Blaustein Institute for the Advancement of Human Rights, February 7–8, 2012.

their detailed resolutions on North Korea in exchange for a dialogue that could yield few results. NGOs objected to such an arrangement, pointing out it would *reward* North Korea for a dialogue, making it an exception among governments that agreed to hold dialogues.[35] Later that year, Pillay moved away from this approach, especially as it became clear that North Korea's new leader Kim Jong-un, who in 2012 took over from his father, intended to continue the same policies of non-cooperation with the UN.[36]

Issuance of Public Statements

From 1994–2012, no High Commissioner issued a public statement devoted entirely to North Korea. High Commissioner Mary Robinson in 1999 expressed concern at a press conference in Seoul that North Koreans fleeing to China for food were being "forced to return" and faced "extremely serious" consequences in North Korea, but it was not a formal statement about North Korea.[37] High Commissioner Arbour, when reporting her lack of success in establishing a dialogue in 2006, mentioned "reports" from North Korean refugees describing "dire conditions in labour camps, grave food shortages and a lack of the most basic freedoms, such as freedom of expression, religion and assembly,"[38] but it was in the course of a much longer statement on human rights conditions in many countries. Pillay for nearly four years adopted the same strategy, saying very little publicly about North Korea's human rights situation.[39] But by mid-2012, she directly expressed "serious concern" about its "political prison camps," and "public executions" without linking these concerns to the reports received from refugees.[40] Further, she called on the North Korean authorities "to allow access to independent experts and organizations," and urged China, albeit indirectly ("neighboring countries"), not to forcibly return North Koreans seeking international protection abroad. At the same time, Pillay's 2012 statement, like Arbour's before her, was but a small paragraph in a much longer statement encompassing sixteen countries.

---

[35] Ibid.

[36] "Pillay urges more attention to human rights abuses in North Korea, calls for international inquiry," OHCHR news release, January 14, 2013 [henceforth Pillay Statement 2013].

[37] See Jacob Adelman, "Top U.N. Official Says N.K. Refugees Situation Serious," *The Korea Herald*, October 14, 1999.

[38] Louise Arbour, June 23, 2006.

[39] See "Study: UN rights chief Navi Pillay turned blind eye to world's worst abusers," UN Watch, June 7, 2011.

[40] Navi Pillay, "Opening Statement by Navi Pillay, High Commissioner for Human Rights," (UN Human Rights Council, Geneva, June 18, 2012).

This caution, even neglect, in large measure emanated from the assumption that the quest for a dialogue with North Korea (from 2003 to 2013) had to rule out strong public pronouncements about the country. Pillay and other High Commissioners for years had given weight to the fact that when the European Union introduced a public resolution at the UN critical of North Korea, the DPRK ended its human rights dialogue with the EU.[41] So for ten years, most public pronouncements were off-limits.

A second impediment to speaking out was the belief that it was necessary to assess the situation directly first. For years, successive High Commissioners held the view that an on-site visit was essential to verify the reports of serious crimes coming out of the country. Pyongyang's "closed door" policy, Arbour explained, "barred" the UN "from forming its own, independent diagnosis of the human rights situation."[42] Pillay likewise in 2011 pointed to the "very little information" available from North Korea "due to the absence of independent media and suppression of the freedom of expression."[43]

This changed dramatically on January 14, 2013 when Pillay issued a sweeping separate statement on the human rights situation in the country, describing it as having "no parallel anywhere else in the world."[44] She recounted the details of "harrowing" testimony from two survivors of the prison camp system with whom she met in December 2012, and concluded that the "rampant" violations being perpetrated within the camps "may amount to crimes against humanity." Expressing alarm that the international community had allowed its concern over North Korea's nuclear program to overshadow its record of abuse, Pillay roundly condemned the Kim Jong-un regime for failing to improve the human rights situation in the country during its first year in power. Noting the persistent refusal of the North Korean government to cooperate with successive Special Rapporteurs on the country and with her Office, Pillay called on the international community to authorize an independent international inquiry into the human rights situation in North Korea, a step she said was "long overdue."

Meetings with camp survivors helped shift Pillay's position. She became the first High Commissioner to directly meet with survivors and was

41 Note Verbale 2004, 9–10.

42 Louise Arbour, June 23, 2006.

43 Navi Pillay, "Statement of Navi Pillay, United Nations High Commissioner for Human Rights" (UN Human Rights Council, Geneva, May 30, 2011).

44 Pillay Statement 2013.

reportedly deeply "moved" by the experience.[45] In her January 2013 statement, she gave credence to their testimony, saying that "what we do know should compel the international community to action."[46] The mistreatment of North Korea's citizens, she underscored, was "to a degree that should be unthinkable in the 21st century." She apparently also realized that her Office's constant calling of attention to the lack of verifiable information on North Korea could have had the unintended effect of lending support to Pyongyang's claims that reports of human rights abuses were based on "unfounded information" propagated by those who had betrayed their country.[47]

Another major factor in Pillay's decision to break with previous practice was the failure of North Korea's new leader Kim Jong-un to bring any "positive change to his country." Although there were "initial hopes" internationally when he first took over from his father,[48] she saw that the DPRK's persistent refusal to meet with her Office was not about to change and that "a much firmer step" was required.[49] She also saw that the Council could act more forcefully in 2013 because China, Russia, and Cuba would not be members.[50]

Growing international publicity in 2012 mustered by NGOs and former prisoners about "crimes against humanity" in the country also influenced Pillay. The new book *Escape from Camp 14*, David Hawk's updated *Hidden Gulag* and a well-attended conference organized in Washington, DC on the North Korea gulag brought worldwide attention to the crimes in the camps.[51] Additionally, a coalition of 40 leading NGOs launched a

---

45 Interviews with human rights advocates knowledgeable about the meeting, January 19, 2013.

46 Pillay Statement 2013.

47 "Human Rights Council adopts outcomes of Universal Periodic Review on Bhutan, Dominica and Democratic People's Republic of Korea," OHCHR news release, March 18, 2010.

48 Pillay Statement 2013.

49 Ibid; see also Roberta Cohen, "Human Rights Progress In North Korea; Is It Possible?" *38 North*, March 20, 2012.

50 These three states had to go off the Council for a year because they had already served two terms.

51 See Blaine Harden, *Escape from Camp 14*, (New York: Viking, 2012); Hawk, *The Hidden Gulag*. Hawk's report, 7–24, also lists the many Seoul-based organizations collecting information, for example the Korea Institute for National Unification (KINU), the Citizen's Alliance for North Korean Human Rights, the Network for North Korean Democracy and Human Rights, the Database Center for North Korean Human Rights and the South Korean Commission on Human Rights. The Committee for Human Rights in North Korea and the Jacob Blaustein Institute for the Advancement of Human Rights held a widely attended

campaign to set up an international inquiry.[52] And experts and NGOs directly began to call on Pillay to speak out.[53] The forced repatriation of North Koreans from China also made headlines in 2012 when South Korean parliamentarians and NGOs undertook demonstrations and hunger strikes in Seoul.[54] Even UN Secretary-General Ban Ki-moon made a public statement on the forced repatriations, as did US Secretary of State Hillary Clinton,[55] and US Congressional hearings were held.[56]

Of course, the reports of the UN Special Rapporteur appointed in 2004 to investigate and report on the human rights situation in North Korea[57] also contributed immensely to raising the profile of the human rights situation at the UN and internationally. Thai lawyer Vitit Muntarbhorn crafted his reports so well that they were regularly cited worldwide. In fact, the words "harrowing and horrific" will always be linked to the human rights situation in North Korea because of Muntarbhorn.[58] On the basis of his findings, the resolutions of the General Assembly became filled with strong and detailed language about the "systematic, widespread and grave violations" in North Korea.[59] By 2011, a total of 123 states in the General Assembly were voting in favor of such resolutions (with 16 opposed and

---

and publicized conference in Washington DC on April 12, see "North Korea's 'hidden gulag,'" Editorial, *Washington Post*, April 13, 2012.

52 See The International Coalition to Stop Crimes Against Humanity in North Korea, http://www.stopnkcrimes.org/about_01.php.

53 See for example Statement of Roberta Cohen at the Conference on the United Nations High Commissioner for Human Rights, February 8, 2012, which called on the High Commissioner to make a stand alone statement on North Korea and meet with survivors of the camps; Jared Genser and the International Coalition urged Pillay to endorse a commission of inquiry in meetings in Geneva in 2012.

54 "Seoul, Parliament urges China to stop the forced repatriation of North Koreans," *AsiaNews.it*, February 28, 2012.

55 "UN chief voices concern over North Korean defectors in China," *Yonhap News*, March 9, 2012; see also "Ban Ki-moon wants to visit N. Korea," *Chosun Ilbo*, October 30, 2012; and "Clinton urges China to stop repatriation of N.Korean defectors," *Korea Herald*, March 10, 2012.

56 See *China's Repatriation of North Korean Refugees*, Hearing before the Congressional-Executive Commission on China, March 5, 2012, Washington, D.C.

57 UN Commission on Human Rights. Resolution 2004/13, "Situation of human rights in Democratic People's Republic of Korea," UN Doc. E/CN.4/RES/2004/13, April 15, 2004 (requesting the appointment of a Special Rapporteur).

58 See UN Human Rights Council, *Report of the Special Rapporteur on Situation of human rights in the Democratic People's Republic of Korea, Vitit Muntarbhorn*, UN Doc. A/HRC/13/47, February 17, 2010, summary and para. 86.

59 See for example, UN General Assembly, Resolutions on "Situation of human rights in the Democratic People's Republic of Korea," UN Doc. A/RES/63/190, December 18, 2008; UN Doc. A/RES/65/225, December 21, 2010; and UN Doc. A/RES/66/174, December 19, 2011.

51 abstentions).[60] In 2012, the 193-member Assembly adopted its resolution on North Korea *by consensus* without the need to bring it to a vote.[61] That same year, Muntarbhorn's successor Marzuki Darusman called on states to consider setting up "a more detailed mechanism of inquiry" because of North Korea's "egregious human rights abuses."[62] This paved the way for Pillay's 2013 call for an international inquiry.[63] Darusman then skillfully collected the information that would form the basis for a determination of crimes against humanity.[64]

The Role of Other Human Rights Mechanisms in Addressing Human Rights in North Korea

In addition to the role of the Special Rapporteur, other independent experts associated with the High Commissioner's Office have called on North Korea to provide information, in particular on individual cases. These include the Special Rapporteur on Torture; the Special Rapporteur on Extrajudicial, Summary, or Arbitrary Executions; the Working Group on Arbitrary Detention; and the Working Group on Enforced or Involuntary Disappearances.[65] While in most instances, the DPRK has failed to provide the information requested, it did do so in 2012 to the Working Group on Arbitrary Detention about the imprisoned family of Oh Kil-nam,[66] which marked a breakthrough in the case.[67]

---

60 See "General Assembly Adopts More Than 60 Resolutions Recommended by Third Committee, Including Text Condemning Grave, Systematic Human Rights Violations in Syria, Also Adopts New Protocol to Child Rights Convention; Wide Range of Resolutions On Social, Humanitarian Issues; Texts on Iran, Democratic People's Republic of Korea," UN news release GA/11198, December 19, 2011.

61 UN General Assembly, *Report of the Special Rapporteur on the situation of human rights in the Democratic People's Republic of Korea*, UN Doc. A/67/370, September 13, 2012, para.13 (transmitting report of Marzuki Darusman). Earlier in the year, the Human Rights Council composed of 47 states also adopted its annual resolution on human rights in North Korea by consensus.

62 Ibid., para.13.

63 Pillay Statement 2013.

64 See UN Human Rights Council, *Report of the Special Rapporteur on the situation of human rights in the DPRK*, UN Doc. A/HRC/22/57, February 1, 2013.

65 See UN General Assembly, *Situation of human rights in the Democratic People's Republic of Korea / Report of the Secretary-General*, UN Doc. A/66/343, September 7, 2011, paras.33–35.

66 North Korea reported that Oh Kil-nam's two daughters who had been imprisoned with their mother when he defected in 1986 are still alive, see "N.Korea Must Prove Its Claims About S.Korean's Death," *Chosun Ilbo*, May 9, 2012.

67 As a result, UN Secretary-General Ban Ki-moon pledged to "keep pushing" for a reunion of the family, see "U.N. chief vows to seek release of 'abducted' S. Korean family in N. Korea," *Yonhap News Agency*, August 14, 2012.

Rapporteurs who have requested entry to discuss human rights in North Korea have not been allowed in.[68] Only in one case was an independent expert from OHCHR's special procedures invited to visit North Korea – the Special Rapporteur on Violence against Women, Radhika Coomeraswamy. But the subject of the meeting was *not* human rights in North Korea but 'military sexual slavery' perpetrated by Japan during World War II against Asian women, and because her plane to the North was delayed Coomeraswamy actually did not reach Pyongyang. However, her staff held meetings with North Korean officials, academics, and former 'comfort women' in 1995, and these enabled DPRK officials to become familiar with how the UN conducts human rights missions.[69]

Still another part of the UN human rights system that has been involved with North Korea is the treaty bodies. As of this writing, North Korea is notably delinquent in its reporting. It has owed a report to the Human Rights Committee since 2004, to the Committee on the Elimination of All Forms of Discrimination against Women since 2006, and to the Committee on Economic, Social, and Cultural Rights since 2008.[70] It also tried to withdraw from its obligations under the International Covenant on Civil and Political Rights,[71] but the UN declared that international law did not permit it to do so.[72] At the same time, North Korea has cooperated to a limited extent with the Committee on the Rights of the Child, although the Committee has reported that its recommendations "have been insufficiently or only partly addressed."[73]

---

68 In addition to the Rapporteur on the situation of human rights in the DPRK, the Rapporteur on the right to food, the Rapporteur on religious freedom and the Rapporteur on freedom of opinion and expression have been denied entry. See UN General Assembly, *Situation of human rights in the Democratic People's Republic of Korea / Report of the UN Secretary-General*, UN Doc. A/63/332, August 26, 2008, para. 11.

69 UN Commission on Human Rights, *Report of the Special Rapporteur on violence against women, its causes and consequences, Ms. Radhika Coomeraswamy, in accordance with Commission on Human Rights resolution 1994/45 / Report on the mission to the Democratic People's Republic of Korea, the Republic of Korea and Japan on the issue of military sexual slavery in wartime*, UN Doc. E/CN.4/1996/53/Add. 1, January 4, 1996.

70 See *Situation of human rights in the Democratic People's Republic of Korea / Report of the Secretary-General*, UN Doc. A/66/343, paras.37–8.

71 See UN Sub-Commission on Prevention of Discrimination and Protection of Minorities, Resolution 1999/5, August 25, 1999, preambular para.11 and operative para.4.

72 Ibid., preambular para.7.

73 North Korea invited the Chair and one member of the Committee to visit in 2004, and has reported on changes it has made in its laws on families and disabilities. See UN Committee on the Rights of the Child, "Concluding Observations: Democratic People's Republic of Korea," UN Doc. CRC/C/PRK/CO/4, March 27, 2009, para. 3; and *Situation of human rights in the Democratic People's Republic of Korea / Report of the Secretary-General*, UN Doc. A/66/343, paras. 42–3.

Conclusions and the Way Forward

North Korea is one of the most difficult countries confronting the High Commissioner. Its government has energetically kept itself and its country at a distance from her and from the special rapporteurs and treaty bodies associated with her Office. It has failed to invite the High Commissioner for a visit despite the many entreaties of governments and the Secretary-General. It is the only country where the Special Rapporteur for that country has never been allowed to visit or even have a dialogue about human rights with DPRK representatives at the UN. Nor has it allowed other rapporteurs to visit or made an effort to implement the recommendations contained in UN resolutions and reports.[74] At the same time, it has felt the need to add the words "respect for human rights" to its Constitution, make some cosmetic changes to its laws,[75] and on one or two occasions, provide information about individual prisoners to UN human rights bodies.[76] But this information has been sparse, and on some occasions misleading.[77]

The paucity of information provided has been intended to obscure violations and prevent UN human rights bodies from addressing them. In fact, North Korea has predicated its willingness to cooperate with the UN on the discontinuation of critical resolutions and an end to the mandate of the Special Rapporteur, whom it depicts as "a marionette running here

[74] Of the 167 recommendations made to North Korea in the Universal Periodic Review in 2009, it has not implemented a single one. See Office of the High Commissioner for Human Rights, "Human Rights Council adopts outcomes of Universal Periodic Review on Bhutan, Dominica and DPRK," March 18, 2010; and UN Human Rights Council, *Draft Report of the Working Group on the Universal Periodic Review: Democratic People's Republic of Korea*, UN Doc. A/HRC/WG.6/6/L.12, December 9, 2009, paras. 90–92.

[75] It reformed its Criminal Procedure Code and reported that it shortened pre-trial detention, restricted nighttime interrogations, and made reforms in laws on children, family law, and disabilities. See Kim Yong Hun, "North Passes Showpiece HR Laws," *Daily NK*, June 14, 2011; UN Human Rights Council, *Report of the Special Rapporteur on the Situation of human rights in the Democratic People's Republic of Korea, Vitit Muntarbhorn*, UN Doc. A/HRC/10/18, February 24, 2009, para.3; and Choe Sang-Hun, "New Constitution Reinforces Kim Jong-il's Hold on Power," *New York Times*, September 29, 2009. See also UN Human Rights Council, *Report of the Special Rapporteur on the Situation of human rights in the Democratic People's Republic of Korea, Marzuki Darusman*, UN Doc. A/HRC/19/65, February 13, 2012, paras. 36–37.

[76] See, for example, "Arbitrary detention," *Korea Herald* editorial, *Asia News Network*, June 1, 2012.

[77] For example, it reported that only six offenses carry the death penalty, whereas the Special Rapporteur unearthed an addendum to the Criminal Code that brings the number to 22. See *Report of the Special Rapporteur on the Situation of human rights in the Democratic People's Republic of Korea, Marzuki Darusman*, UN Doc. A/HRC/19/65, paras.36–37.

and there, representing the ill-minded purposes of string-pullers such as the United States, Japan and the States Members of the European Union."[78]

Although High Commissioner Pillay at one time flirted with the idea of making a deal with North Korea, her January 2013 statement charted a new course. It condemned human rights violations in the country on the basis of testimony from survivors of the prison camps and families of abducted foreigners,[79] characterized the abuses perpetrated as possible crimes against humanity, and called for an international inquiry.

What is not yet clear at this writing is whether this statement is part of a new and broader strategy. If so, then several features need to be added.

First, a new approach for treating information coming from those who have escaped North Korea must be developed. As late as 2011, OHCHR's Deputy High Commissioner was publicly lamenting in Seoul that the UN "cannot access information" directly about North Korea.[80] And Pillay in her 2013 statement even repeated: "We know *so little* about these camps and what we do know comes largely from the *relatively few refugees* who have managed to escape from the country" [emphasis added].[81]

But refugees providing information are not at all few in number. Hundreds of former prisoners and prison guards have fled to South Korea over the past decade and have been providing first-hand information about their experiences. Because their testimony often corroborates the testimony of other prisoners,[82] it is time such information was treated as factual by OHCHR. Moreover, satellite photographs of the camps have become much clearer and more detailed and have been verified by former prisoners and guards. It is estimated that some 150,000 to 200,000 political prisoners are incarcerated in the camps. The locking away of entire families and the high death rates because of forced labor, torture, and starvation must be carefully looked at as part of a strategy for dismantling the camps.

Since the testimony of Shin Dong Hyuk and Kim Hye Sook clearly affected Pillay, it is important that she meet with more camp survivors and issue regular statements about the carefully hidden crimes perpetrated

---

78 See "Note Verbale dated 1 February 2012 from the Permanent Mission of the Democratic People's Republic of Korea."

79 For those abducted, see Committee for Human Rights in North Korea, *Taken: North Korea's Criminal Abduction of Citizens of Other Countries*, 2011.

80 See Kwon Eun Kyoung, "North Korea Must Cooperate with UN on Human Rights," *Daily NK*, July 15, 2011.

81 Pillay Statement 2013.

82 See Hawk, *The Hidden Gulag*.

against North Koreans. Her Office should also provide greater staff support and resources to Special Rapporteur Darusman so that he can glean increased information from survivors and include the findings in his reports.[83]

OHCHR also should provide full backup for the work and recommendations of the 'commission of inquiry' established by the Human Rights Council on March 21, 2013. It is composed of three experts, including Darusman, who will look into North Korea's "systematic, widespread and grave violations of human rights," and the extent to which these violations constitute crimes against humanity.[84] A significant amount of its work will have to be based on the testimony of survivors.

Second, now that the High Commissioner has chosen a more public course of action, she should consider whether the situation in North Korea might merit a special session of the Human Rights Council. And she should explore whether former prisoners can be invited to provide testimony at such a session.[85] Even at a regular session, the High Commissioner could encourage states to introduce an 'interactive dialogue' with the representative of North Korea.[86]

Third, should North Korea respond to increased pressure by offering to engage in a dialogue, the High Commissioner should identify what her Office's priorities would be: access for independent human rights experts in camps and other facilities, legal reform, progress on human rights cases, the setting up of a national human rights commission, or ratification of more human rights treaties? She also will have to decide how to reward progress without undermining international responses to ongoing abuses.

Fourth and most importantly, the High Commissioner should enlist the support of other parts of the UN so that the totality of the system is behind the human rights effort. Within OHCHR, other human rights mechanisms

---

83 For the different kinds of support the High Commissioner can give special rapporteurs, see Felice Gaer, "The High Commissioner and Special Rapporteurs: Colleagues and Competitors," in this volume.

84 UN Human Rights Council, Resolution, "Situation of human rights in Democratic People's Republic of Korea," UN Doc. A/HRC/22/L.19, adopted March 21, 2013. See also Roberta Cohen, "North Korea Faces Heightened Human Rights Scrutiny," *38 North*, March 21, 2013.

85 For a summary of Council special sessions, see International Service for Human Rights, "Special Sessions," http://www.ishr.ch/sessions/special-sessions.

86 For an example of such a dialogue, see International Service for Human Rights, "Belarus criticises politicisation of the Council during interactive dialogue on the country," September 27, 2011, http://www.ishr.ch/council/376-council/1150-belarus-criticises-politicisation-of-the-council-during-interactive-dialogue-on-the-country.

should be encouraged to lend support to the North Korea Special Rapporteur. In 2012, a group of special rapporteurs jointly sent a letter to the DPRK about the labor camps.[87] At the Human Rights Council in 2013 the group issued a joint press release in support of creating an international commission of inquiry.[88] These and other rapporteurs should be encouraged to continue to act jointly so as to strengthen the Special Rapporteur's and the commission's hand. The treaty bodies also could do more. When North Korea fails to send in information, these bodies should not move on to the next country but review the DPRK's compliance in light of *other* available information and propose a dialogue with its representatives on the basis of that information. The High Commissioner should also propose stronger ways to deal with delinquent countries.

The Secretary-General, who reports each year to the General Assembly on the human rights situation in North Korea, should be encouraged on a regular basis to make private intercessions, issue public statements, and take other initiatives. Engaging the Security Council should also be explored. In his last report to the Human Rights Council in 2010, Muntarbhorn suggested the possible involvement of the Security Council and the International Criminal Court in taking up North Korea's systemic human rights violations.[89] Now that a commission of inquiry has been established, both bodies may become involved if crimes against humanity are determined.

A system wide strategy should further explore closer cooperation with humanitarian agencies like the World Food Program. Not only should greater access and enhanced monitoring of food distribution be promoted but an effort made to identify how the UN might provide food to the prisoners in labor camps who are deliberately kept on starvation rations. Humanitarian organizations, after all, are supposed to reach 'the most vulnerable,' and in North Korea, these should include political prisoners. Not to speak of incarcerated children, whom UNICEF should be expected to try to reach. Promoting the engagement of the International Labor Organization with North Korea must also be examined, given the DPRK's reported practice of forced labor and other serious violations of workers' rights.

---

[87] UN Human Rights Council, *Report of the Special Rapporteur on the situation of human rights in the DPRK, Marzuki Darusman*, UN Doc. A/HRC/22/57, February 1, 2013, para. 28.

[88] "UN experts call for an international inquiry into North Korea human rights abuses," OHCHR news release, February 27, 2013.

[89] *Report of the Special Rapporteur on Situation of human rights in the Democratic People's Republic of Korea, Vitit Muntarbhorn*, UN Doc. A/HRC/13/47, para.58.

Fifth, the High Commissioner's Office should be more proactive about North Koreans' learning their rights set forth in agreements their government has endorsed. The UN Department of Public Information and UNESCO should be called in to find ways to promote the dissemination to schools, government offices, and institutions in North Korea of a Korean translation of the Universal Declaration of Human Rights and human rights instruments to which North Korea has acceded. In North Korea today, there are a million cell phones (although North Koreans cannot call outside the country) and DVDs and CDs are making their way inside. Using new technology and social media to send in UN human rights standards and instruments should be explored by OHCHR.

Sixth, a strategy should be devised for dealing with China, from which most if not all North Korean asylum seekers are forcibly turned back and then subject to arrest, beatings, torture, forced abortions, and even execution. UN reports and resolutions on North Korea, as well as public statements, have assiduously avoided mentioning China by name although some do now call on "neighboring countries" to respect the principle of *non-refoulement* and not forcibly repatriate North Koreans.[90] A dialogue is needed with China and also with UNHCR to bring this issue to the fore and to press for adherence to international refugee and human rights standards to protect North Koreans from being forcibly returned to conditions of danger.

In sum, a comprehensive strategy needs to be developed that brings in the entirety of the UN system, and what better Office than the High Commissioner's to coordinate this strategy in the human rights arena? In 1997, an American historian warned that "if and when the regime falls, we will probably learn of larger numbers [of people held in camps] and various unimaginable atrocities..."[91] When change does take place, the High Commissioner should not be among those who wonders why her Office didn't do more.

[90] See for example *Situation of human rights in the Democratic People's Republic of Korea / Report of the Secretary-General*, UN Doc. A/66/343, para. 79. By contrast, UN treaty bodies, which monitor states' compliance with their obligations under international human rights treaties, do call on China by name to cease forcible repatriations of North Koreans, see Roberta Cohen, "Legal Grounds for Protection of North Korean Refugees," *Life & Human Rights in North Korea* 57 (Fall 2010), 12–14.

[91] Bruce Cumings, *Korea's Place in the Sun* (New York: Norton, 1997), 398, as cited in Hawk, *The Hidden Gulag*, 41.

THE ROLE OF THE HIGH COMMISSIONER IN PROTECTING AND PROMOTING HUMAN RIGHTS IN AFGHANISTAN AND SUDAN

Sima Samar

Introduction

Since the establishment of the post of UN High Commissioner for Human Rights by the UN General Assembly in 1993, advocates have sought to encourage those holding the post to increase the UN's effectiveness in combatting human rights violations and preventing the commission of violations in the future, and to symbolize the commitment of the UN to the goal of human rights protection.

The people who have served as High Commissioner over the course of the past 20 years have pursued different approaches to human rights protection and the promotion of the universality of human rights in a global context. My experiences have led me to believe that while the High Commissioners have not developed entirely consistent strategies for ensuring the protection and promotion of human rights; importantly, they have constantly emphasized principles such as the universality of rights and have rejected calls from some to compromise these principles for the sake of realizing short-term political gains in various parts of the world.

This commitment to principle is particularly important for individuals holding the post of High Commissioner, as their role is to seek to promote and protect universal human rights worldwide despite the many differences between countries.[1] While human rights challenges in countries such as Afghanistan and Sudan might be different from one other, the people of both counties deserve to live with full rights and dignity, and it is important that the High Commissioners not be misled by those who seek to use calls for respect for culture and religion as an excuse to deny the universality of human rights. That being said, it is also important for High Commissioners to find useful and practical approaches for the promotion and protection of human rights in very different contexts. In some cases, diplomacy might be most appropriate; in other cases,

[1] UN General Assembly. Resolution 48/141, "High Commissioner for the Promotion and Protection of All Human Rights," UN Doc. A/RES/48/141, December 20, 1993.

outspokenness might be needed. Again, the focus of the High Commissioner should be on ensuring impact on the human rights situation on the ground.

The following article explores how the High Commissioners for Human Rights have addressed these challenges with regard to the particular cases of Afghanistan and Sudan, and are based on my personal experience with the work of the High Commissioners and the Office of the High Commissioner for Human Rights (OHCHR) in those countries.

Afghanistan

Background

Afghanistan has been at war since 1978, the climax of the Cold War. Since that time, several different regimes have come to power in Afghanistan. While many of these regimes had extremely poor human rights records, the Taliban regime nevertheless stood out as a result of its commission of gross violations of human rights, and particularly of women's rights. It is not an exaggeration to say that during the period of Taliban rule, from 1994 to 2001, all of Afghanistan was rendered a prison for Afghan women, who were deprived of basic human rights such as access to education, health, and the ability to work outside of the home.[2] Afghan men were also subjected to a restrictive code of conduct. Indeed, life in Afghanistan during that period was popularly coined 'a peaceful graveyard.'

During this period, the United Nations was not unaware of human rights violations being perpetrated in the country. The Commission on Human Rights created a mandate for a Special Rapporteur on Afghanistan tasked with reporting on the situation there from 1984 to 2003.[3] Unfortunately, the effectiveness of the special rapporteurs was

---

[2] See, e.g., Human Rights Watch, *Humanity Denied: Systematic Violations of Women's Rights in Afghanistan*, accessed December 17, 2012.

[3] The post of Special Rapporteur was held by Mr. Felix Ermacora of Austria from 1984–1995, by Mr. Choong-Hyun Paik of the Republic of Korea from 1995–1998, and by Mr. Kamal Hossain, a lawyer and former minister of the government of Bangladesh, from 1998–2003. OHCHR, "Special Rapporteur/Independent Expert on the situation of human rights in Afghanistan," http://www2.ohchr.org/english/countries/af/mandate/index.htm. In 2004, the Commission on Human Rights did not renew the mandate of the Special Rapporteur, but created a new mandate: the Independent Expert on human rights in Afghanistan. The expert was tasked with developing, together with Afghan government bodies and the OHCHR and UNAMA, "a program of advisory services and to seek and receive information about and report on the human rights situation in Afghanistan in an effort to prevent human rights violations." Egyptian professor M. Cherif Bassiouni held this post from

impeded by the fact that they were denied access to certain areas of the country by the regimes controlling Afghanistan.[4]

The High Commissioners for Human Rights and Afghanistan

Following the September 11, 2001 attacks on New York and Washington by al-Qaeda, and the subsequent military intervention of Afghanistan by the US and allied forces, the Taliban were forced from power. After the fall of the Taliban regime, the Bonn Agreement,[5] signed on December 5, 2001 and endorsed by the Security Council, resulted in the creation of a new government in Afghanistan. It also created a framework for OHCHR to work towards establishing human rights activities in Afghanistan and called for the establishment of an Independent Human Rights Commission.

Mary Robinson, the second High Commissioner for Human Rights, was very active in supporting the establishment of the Afghanistan Independent Human Rights Commission (AIHRC) in 2002.[6] Robinson also visited Afghanistan in 2002 and her meeting with President Hamid Karzai provided strong political support for the establishment of the AIHRC.[7] Robinson also strove to increase OHCHR's capacity to support human rights projects in Afghanistan.[8] At the beginning of 2002, OHCHR lacked even a full-time desk officer on Afghanistan in Geneva. From 2002–2003, however, OHCHR would substantially increase its capacity, appointing a full-time desk officer in Geneva and sending consultants and experts on field missions to Afghanistan to plan and implement a joint project with the UN Assistance Mission in Afghanistan (UNAMA) and the UN Development Programme (UNDP) to support the work of the AIHRC.[9]

2004–2006. See UN Commission on Human Rights. Resolution 2003/77, "Situation of Human Rights in Afghanistan," UN Doc. E/CN.4/RES/2003/77, April 25, 2003.

4 See e.g., UN Commission on Human Rights, *Report on the situation of human rights in Afghanistan / prepared by the Special Rapporteur, Felix Ermacora, in accordance with Commission on Human Rights resolution 1985/38*, UN Doc. E/CN.4/1986/24, February 17, 1986, paras. 5–10.

5 *Agreement on Provisional Arrangements in Afghanistan Pending the Re-Establishment of Permanent Government Institutions ("Bonn Agreement")*, December 5, 2001.

6 See, e.g., "Robinson Welcomes Establishment of Human Rights Commission in Afghanistan," *UN News Centre*, June 6, 2002.

7 See Patricia Gossman, "Afghanistan: Bring Warlords to Justice," *New York Times*, March 9, 2002; "High Commissioner for Human Rights, in Kabul, Calls for Solidarity with Afghan Women in Working for Equality Everywhere," UN press release, March 8, 2002.

8 Mary Robinson, "In Solidarity with the Afghan people: Towards Implementation of the Human Rights Provisions of the Bonn Agreement," statement delivered at the Afghan National Workshop on Human Rights, Kabul, March 9, 2002.

9 See OHCHR, *Annual Report 2002*; OHCHR, *Annual Report 2003*.

Despite its limited capacity, OHCHR provided substantial support to the AIHRC from the beginning of its existence, including by providing various capacity building projects and seeking to mainstream human rights into Afghanistan's strategic plans, laws, and policies.[10]

During her term as High Commissioner for Human Rights, Louise Arbour visited Afghanistan twice. During her first visit, in 2005, Arbour met with President Karzai and expressed her strong support for an exceptional report on transitional justice that had recently been produced by the AIHRC.[11] This report, entitled "A Call for Justice,"[12] had been prepared based on a national survey on transitional justice in which more than 7,000 people participated. President Karzai eventually accepted the report, and the government consequently adopted a three-year Action Plan on Peace, Justice, and Reconciliation.[13] While this was a positive development, the Afghan government was subsequently unwilling to implement all of the components of the Action Plan.[14]

Louise Arbour, like other High Commissioners for Human Rights, employed a dual approach when speaking out against human rights abuses in Afghanistan, always expressing support for achievements by the government on human rights issues but at the same time pushing the government to expend more attention and effort on key areas of concern, such as access to justice, and particularly women's access to justice, discrimination against women, combatting torture, and protection of civilians in armed conflict.[15] The High Commissioner also criticized the ongoing lack of security in Afghanistan, which made the AIHRC unable to monitor human rights in certain areas of the country.[16]

The current High Commissioner, Navi Pillay, has not visited Afghanistan since she assumed the post of High Commissioner in 2009. However, whenever we at the AIHRC have asked her Office to release a statement or

---

10 See, e.g., OHCHR, *Annual Report 2002*, 86–87.

11 See, e.g., International Center for Transitional Justice, *Afghanistan: Addressing the Past*, briefing note, January 1, 2005, 4.

12 Afghanistan Independent Human Rights Commission, *A Call for Justice*, January 25, 2005 http://www.aihrc.org.af/en/research-reports/752/a-call-for-justice.html.

13 "Action Plan on Peace, Justice and Reconciliation," Harvard Kennedy School: Carr Center for Human Rights Policy – Afghanistan & Pakistan State-Building Policy Documents, June 2005, https://sites.google.com/site/afghanpolicysite/Home/action-plan-on-peace-justice-and-reconcilliation.

14 International Center for Transitional Justice, *Afghanistan: Addressing the Past*, 5.

15 See "High Commissioner for Human Rights Urges Support for Afghans to Deal with Impunity," OHCHR news release, January 29, 2004.

16 See "High Commissioner for Human Rights Concludes Visit to Afghanistan," OHCHR news release, November 20, 2007.

send a letter to the government of Afghanistan, raising concern on serious issues of human rights, she has done so, and we are very appreciative of this.[17] Human rights defenders and activists in Afghanistan hope to receive stronger support from the High Commissioner, and particularly a visit, before her mandate expires in 2014. Past experience shows that the visits of the High Commissioners to the country have been effective tools to pressure governments, including the government of Afghanistan, to do more to support human rights. In-country visits also demonstrate that the High Commissioner has a particular interest in seeing an improvement in the human rights situation in the country, and to a greater degree than press releases and letters to the government from her or her Office.

The OHCHR Field Presence in Afghanistan

The OHCHR Representative Office in Kabul was established in 2002, during Mary Robinson's tenure as High Commissioner for Human Rights. To this day, the Office operates under the umbrella of the United Nations Assistance Mission for Afghanistan (UNAMA). OHCHR's field presence consists of human rights officers attached to UNAMA, and at the end of 2012, had 66 staff.[18] The OHCHR field presence in Afghanistan has significantly enhanced the High Commissioners' efforts to promote and protect human rights in Afghanistan. However, the effectiveness of the field presence has also depended in large part on the personalities of its staff, as well as those of the staff of other UN components. It has been key for international staff to demonstrate commitment, an understanding of the political context in the country, and a willingness to coordinate, rather than compete, with other actors.

Support for the AIHRC

For the most part, OHCHR staff have worked very closely with the AIHRC and cooperated with its members in their work. For example, OHCHR,

---

17 See, e.g., Navi Pillay, "Human Rights and the London Conference on Afghanistan," *The Daily Star* (Lebanon), opinion piece, January 28, 2010, http://www.dailystar.com.lb/News/Middle-East/Jan/28/Human-rights-and-the-London-conference-on-Afghanistan.ashx#axzz2RtWrei4C.

18 As of December 2012, UNAMA Human Rights had 66 human rights staff (28 international human rights officers, 13 national human rights officers, and 25 national human rights assistants) deployed throughout the country at the regional and provincial level. Twenty officers worked in the Human Rights Support Office (head office in Kabul) and 46 were deployed in eight regional and six provincial offices. See, "Human Rights," United Nations Assistance Mission in Afghanistan, accessed December 29, 2012, http://unama.unmissions.org/Default.aspx?tabid=12285&language=en-US.

through UNAMA, and AIHRC produced joint reports on the elections of 2004, 2005, and 2009.[19] These reports provided significant support for the democratization process in Afghanistan. Unfortunately, OHCHR's effectiveness has at times been compromised by the failure of other UN personnel to fully cooperate and coordinate with the OHCHR field representative. Indeed, since 2002, UNAMA human rights officers' activities were occasionally curtailed out of concern that they could jeopardize the mission's work to promote national stability.[20] This lack of coordination and cooperation, which may in part be a result of the UN's institutional structure, has at times affected OHCHR's ability to support the AIHRC and to insist that the government of Afghanistan promote and protect human rights.

Publication of Annual Reports on Human Rights in Afghanistan

As noted above, from 1984–2006, special procedures of the UN Commission on Human Rights were tasked with monitoring and reporting on the human rights situation in Afghanistan. In 2006, the Commission did not renew the mandate of the Independent Expert on human rights in Afghanistan, and instead requested that the High Commissioner monitor and report to the Commission and the UN General Assembly on an annual basis on the human rights situation in Afghanistan and on progress made through technical assistance projects, particularly in the area of capacity-building.[21]

The reports of the High Commissioner on human rights in Afghanistan since 2006,[22] which contain human rights analysis provided by the OHCHR field staff in Afghanistan, have been useful in bringing additional

[19] See, e.g., AIHRC and UNAMA, *AIHRC-UNAMA Joint Monitoring of Political Rights Presidential and Provincial Council Elections: Third Report, 1 August – 21 October 2009*, October 30, 2009.

[20] See, e.g., Una Moore, "The Perils of Mapping Afghanistan's Conflict," *UN Dispatch*, October 19, 2010. See also The Henry Dunant Centre for Humanitarian Dialogue, *Politics and Humanitarianism, Coherence in Crisis?* February 2003, 17, noting that within UNAMA "Strategic imperatives related to peacebuilding…led to the tenuous consensus not to speak out on human rights issues if that was felt to cause problems for the political process, and led to the subordination of accountability for human rights abuses, the majority of which were caused, according to most human rights organisations, by the continuing struggle for power among Afghan leaders."

[21] UN Commission on Human Rights, Resolution 2/113, "Cooperation with the Office of the United Nations High Commissioner for Human Rights: Afghanistan," November 27, 2006.

[22] See, e.g., UN Human Rights Council, *Report of the United Nations High Commissioner for Human Rights on the Human Rights Situation in Afghanistan and Technical Assistance Achievements in the Field of Human Rights*, UN Doc. A/HRC/19/47, January 18, 2012.

international attention to human rights abuses in Afghanistan. These reports have also expressed strong support for the reports of the AIHRC.[23] Although the High Commissioner's reporting mandate came at the expense of a UN mandate for a Special Rapporteur or Independent Expert on Afghanistan, it has nevertheless been used by the High Commissioners successfully to raise awareness of the actual situation on the ground.

Interaction with Civil Society

The OHCHR field staff in Afghanistan have also built important relationships with civil society organizations and local human rights activists. High Commissioners have consistently ensured that civil society and non-governmental organizations are invited to participate in workshops convened by OHCHR at the regional level on promotion and protection of human rights. OHCHR has also actively worked to provide civil society and non-governmental organizations with an opportunity to engage in dialogue with government officials and representatives of national human rights institutions on best practices in involving CSOs and NGOs in the process of monitoring human rights and promoting human rights.[24] OHCHR has also encouraged businesses operating in Afghanistan to join the Secretary-General's Global Compact, in which participants pledge to uphold human rights, labor, and environmental standards.

Sudan

I had the privilege to serve as UN Special Rapporteur on the human rights situation in the Sudan from September 2005 until July 2009. My comments here are limited to the extent of my engagement with Sudan in that context.

Background

Sudan is one of the largest countries in Africa and is home to many different ethnic and tribal groups. The population of the northern part of the

[23] See, e.g., UN Human Rights Council, *Report of the United Nations High Commissioner for Human Rights on the Situation of Human Rights in Afghanistan and on the Achievements of Technical Assistance in the Field of Human Rights*, January 19, 2011, 14.

[24] See, e.g., UN Human Rights Council, *Report of the High Commissioner for Human Rights on the Situation of Human Rights in Afghanistan and on the Achievements of Technical Assistance in the Field of Human Rights*, UN Doc. A/HRC/10/23, January 16, 2009, 5.

country is primarily Arabic in ethnicity and the majority of the people practice Islam as their religion. The southern part of the country – which gained its independence in 2011 and is now the Republic of South Sudan – has a population primarily consisting of African tribes, and the majority of people practice Christianity. In the western part of the country, the majority of the people are of African descent and practice Islam.

Sudan has experienced internal war for nearly three decades. In January 2005, the warring factions from the North and South of the country, which had been at war for 21 years, signed the "Comprehensive Peace Agreement."[25] Separately, parties from the North and West of Sudan engaged in a separate internal conflict in the Darfur region, a conflict which peaked in 2003. Both conflicts featured the commission of gross violations of human rights, but in Darfur these were particularly severe and rose to the level of war crimes and crimes against humanity.[26]

The High Commissioners for Human Rights and Sudan

In 2003, as the conflict in Darfur reached its peak, the then-Acting High Commissioner for Human Rights, Bertrand Ramcharan, issued a statement expressing deep concern over the deteriorating human rights and humanitarian situation in Darfur.[27] He affirmed that systematic human rights abuses were being perpetrated against unarmed civilians and villages were being looted, causing massive displacement and an outflow of refugees. He called on the government of Sudan to respond by investigating these atrocities and taking immediate measures to stop the violation of human rights and to punish those responsible, and he called on all parties to work for peace. The Acting High Commissioner called upon the government of Sudan to extend an open invitation to investigative and fact-finding bodies of the Commission on Human Rights to visit Sudan. Significantly, Ramcharan also proposed that all parties agree on the establishment of an independent international commission of inquiry to assess the humanitarian and human rights situation in Darfur.

Later, acting on his own initiative, Ramcharan sent an OHCHR fact-finding team to Eastern Chad to interview 10,000 refugees from the

25 United Nations Mission in Sudan, "The background to Sudan's Comprehensive Peace Agreement," http://unmis.unmissions.org/Default.aspx?tabid=515.

26 See e.g., "Sudan: Violations in Darfur may constitute war crimes, crimes against humanity, says UN rights office report," OHCHR news release, May 7, 2004.

27 "Acting Rights Chief Concerned Over Deteriorating Situation in Darfur Region of Sudan," OHCHR news release, January 29, 2004.

conflict in Darfur.[28] Ramcharan was invited to brief the Security Council on May 7, 2004, behind closed doors, on the report that resulted from the team's work. He did so, and as a result, he was able to draw even more attention to the findings of the report, which established that massive violations of human rights had been perpetrated by Janjaweed militia whose members had been recruited and armed by the Sudanese government.[29] The report called for the deployment of human rights monitors on the ground in Sudan, among other measures.[30]

Louise Arbour

The next High Commissioner, Louise Arbour, visited Sudan within only a few months of her July 1, 2004 appointment to the post. In September 2004, Arbour, together with the Secretary-General's Special Adviser on the Prevention of Genocide, Juan Mendez, visited Sudan, including the Darfur region.[31] According to Arbour, the Secretary-General had specifically requested that she undertake the visit and focus on atrocity prevention.[32]

On September 18, 2004, the day of Arbour's arrival in Sudan, the UN Security Council enacted resolution 1564, and invoking its authority under Chapter VII of the UN Charter, it asked the Secretary-General to "rapidly establish an international commission of inquiry in order immediately to investigate reports of violations of international humanitarian law and human rights law in Darfur by all parties, to determine also whether or not acts of genocide have occurred, and to identify the perpetrators of such violations with a view to ensuring that those responsible are held accountable."[33] The Commission was supported in its work by a Secretariat – consisting of an executive director, a legal research team, and an investigative team composed of investigators, forensic experts, military analysts, and

---

28 "UN Human Rights Fact-Finding Mission Arrives in Sudan," *UN News Centre*, April 22, 2004.

29 "Violations in Darfur May Constitute War Crimes, Crimes Against Humanity, Says UN Rights Office Report," UN press release, May 7, 2004.

30 Ibid. See also International Commission of Inquiry on Darfur, *Report to the Secretary-General*, January 25, 2005, www2.ohchr.org/english/docs/darfurreport.doc.

31 "High Commissioner for Human Rights to Visit Darfur, Sudan: Louise Arbour to Be Accompanied By Secretary-General's Special Adviser on Prevention of Genocide," UN press release HR/4793, September 17, 2004.

32 Ibid.

33 UN Security Council. Resolution 1564, "Darfur, Sudan," UN Doc. S/RES/1564, September 18, 2004.

gender violence specialists, all appointed by OHCHR – and was led by three international experts appointed by the Secretary-General in October 2004.[34]

The International Commission of Inquiry on the conflict in Darfur submitted a full report on its findings to the Secretary-General on January 25, 2005. It concluded, based on evidence it collected, that a number of individual members of the government of Sudan and Janjaweed militias were responsible for the commission of violations of international human rights law and international humanitarian law in Darfur, including war crimes and, very likely, crimes against humanity.[35] The Commission also found credible evidence that rebel forces were responsible for serious violations, which may amount to war crimes. The Commission strongly recommended that the Security Council immediately refer the situation in Darfur to the International Criminal Court (ICC), to ensure that those responsible for these heinous crimes would be held to account and not permitted to enjoy impunity.

In the weeks following the publication of the Commission of Inquiry's report, the UN Security Council requested a briefing from Arbour on its findings. The High Commissioner took this opportunity to press the Council to act on the Commission's recommendation to refer the case of Darfur to the ICC.[36] She noted that the government of Sudan's purported efforts to deal with the crimes perpetrated in Sudan to date had been "grossly inadequate and ineffective" and frankly expressed the view that the Council should dismiss a new initiative proposed by the government given the extent of official involvement in the crimes perpetrated in Darfur to date. Arbour suggested that referring the situation in Darfur would be less expensive and time-consuming than creation of an ad-hoc or international tribunal. She also emphasized that the victims of the atrocities had little faith in the capacity of the Sudanese justice system to be impartial and fair. Arbour argued, "In my view, the Commission eloquently and powerfully argues that referral to the ICC is the best means by which to halt ongoing violations and to prevent future ones."[37]

---

[34] International Commission of Inquiry on Darfur, *Report*. The international experts appointed to lead the panel were Antonio Cassese (Chairperson), Mohamed Fayek, Hina Jilani, Dumisa Ntsebeza and Therese Striggner-Scott.

[35] Ibid.

[36] "Sudan Cannot be Trusted to Tackle Darfur War Crimes, UN Human Rights Chief Tells Security Council," UN News Centre, February 16, 2005.

[37] "SUDAN: Refer Darfur violations to the ICC, senior UN official urges," *IRIN*, February 17, 2005.

She concluded her briefing with a powerful argument for accountability, saying,

> The pursuit of justice is often said to clash with the pursuit of peace. Whatever the theoretical merit of that proposition, the findings of this Commission of Inquiry irrefutably demonstrate that there is no hope for sustainable peace in Darfur without immediate access to justice.[38]

Weeks later, on March 31, the UN Security Council took the unprecedented step of referring the situation in Darfur since July 1, 2002 to the ICC.[39] In June 2005, the Prosecutor of the ICC, Mr. Luis Moreno-Ocampo, officially opened an investigation into crimes committed in Darfur, and ICC staff began extensive additional investigations.[40]

While the ICC's investigations were ongoing, in May 2006, Arbour again visited Sudan. During the visit, she traveled to Khartoum, Darfur and camps for internally displaced persons (IDPs) from South and West Darfur, and to South Sudan. Arbour stressed the responsibility of the Sudanese government for ensuring protection of human rights in Sudan, including Darfur, and called for significant institutional reform and accountability for officials implicated in human rights violations.[41] She criticized the government for failing to allow her to enter the national security detention center in Khartoum. Arbour also emphasized that the human rights situation in Darfur region had only deteriorated since her 2004 visit. Arbour particularly stressed that the incidence of sexual violence against women was occurring at virtually the same rate. Arbour's visit was instrumental in drawing more attention to sexual violence against women in Darfur, which resulted in an increase of human rights monitors in the field.

In December 2006, following a special session on Darfur, the Human Rights Council dispatched a High-Level Mission (HLM) with the mandate

---

38 Louise Arbour, "Statement by Ms. Louise Arbour High Commissioner for Human Rights to the Security Council on the International Commission of Inquiry on Darfur," February 16, 2005.

39 "Security Council Refers Situation in Darfur, Sudan, to Prosecutor of International Criminal Court: Resolution 1593 (2005) Adopted by Vote of 11 in Favour To None Against, with 4 Abstentions (Algeria, Brazil, China, United States)," UN Press Release SC/8351, March 31, 2005.

40 See Joanne Mariner, "Bringing Justice to Darfur," *CNN Justice*, June 24, 2005; "International Criminal Court Prosecutor Tells Security Council Investigation into Darfur Crimes Initiated June 1," UN Security Council Press Release SC/8429, June 29, 2005.

41 "Statement by UN High Commissioner for Human Rights Louise Arbour Following Her Visit to Sudan from 30 April to 5 May 2006," UN Press Release, May 5, 2006, http://www.unhchr.ch/huricane/huricane.nsf/0/038D5CA37BBF3D4EC12571650053F59E?opendocument.

"to assess the human rights situation in Darfur and the needs of the Sudan in this regard."[42] The mission's participants consisted of Professor and Nobel Peace Prize Laureate Jody Williams (Head of Mission), Professor Bertrand Ramcharan, the Honorable Mart Nutt, H.E. Ambassador Patrice Tonda, and myself.[43] The HLM was supported and accompanied by a team of staff appointed by the High Commissioner for Human Rights. The HLM, which carried out its work from 5 February to 5 March 2007 in Geneva, Addis Ababa, N'Djamena, Abeche, and the refugee camps of Eastern Chad, concluded that critical needs to address the human rights situation in Darfur included (1) enhanced protection, (2) renewed progress toward peace, (3) expanded humanitarian space, (4) increased accountability for perpetrators, (5) programs to address root causes, (6) efforts to ensure the implementation of existing recommendations from authoritative human rights bodies, and (7) compensation for the victims of violations of human rights.[44]

In May 2007, nearly two years after the Security Council first referred the situation in Darfur to the ICC, the ICC issued arrest warrants for Humanitarian Affairs Minister Ahmed Haroun, who held the post of Deputy Minister of Interior and responsibility for the Darfur conflict from 2003–2004, and Janjaweed leader Ali Muhammad Ali Abd al-Rahman, also called Ali Kushayb.[45] Both were accused of commission of war crimes and crimes against humanity including the murder, rape, torture, and persecution of civilians in Darfur. Unfortunately the government of Sudan refused to act on the warrants and has not surrendered either man to the custody of the ICC. Later, in March 2009, the ICC would issue an arrest warrant for Sudanese President Omar al-Bashir for war crimes and crimes against humanity, in the first instance in which the Court issued a warrant for a head of state.[46]

Navi Pillay

The next High Commissioner, Navi Pillay, who took office in September 2008, was also very supportive of my work as Special Rapporteur on Sudan. Regrettably, she did not travel to Sudan prior to the expiration of my

---

42 UN Human Rights Council, *Report of the High-Level Mission on the Situation of Human Rights in Darfur Pursuant to Human Rights Council Decision S-4/101*, UN Doc. A/HRC/4/80, March 9, 2007.

43 Ibid., 6. H.E. Ambassador Makarim Wibisono was also appointed to the HLM but discontinued his participation and did not take part in the drafting of the report.

44 Ibid., 25.

45 "ICC Issues Darfur Arrest Warrants," *BBC News*, May 2, 2007.

46 The ICC would issue a second arrest warrant for al-Bashir, this time for genocide, in June 2010. "ICC Issues Arrest Warrant for Genocide Against Bashir," *Reuters*, July 12, 2010.

mandate in July 2009, so I was not able to observe the effects of her presence on the human rights situation there. However, Pillay did raise human rights violations with Sudanese government officials, and she was very supportive of the mandate of Special Rapporteur.

The OHCHR Field Presence in Sudan

The Office of the High Commissioner for Human Rights had a varied level of field presence in Sudan during the time in which I worked as Special Rapporteur. As previously mentioned, in April-May 2004, OHCHR sent fact-finding missions to Chad and Darfur. In August 2004, OHCHR deployed a team of human rights monitors to Khartoum and Darfur to support protection efforts in Darfur and to monitor, report, and follow up on individual cases.[47] Following the creation of the United Nations Mission in the Sudan (UNMIS), OHCHR's activities were integrated into the human rights component of UNMIS in June 2005.[48] Later, following the creation of the peacekeeping operation UNAMID in 2007, OHCHR worked in Darfur through the Human Rights Section (HRS) of that operation.[49]

In 2005, when I began my term as Special Rapporteur, there were 57 international and 15 national staff deployed as human rights officers and monitors to UNMIS, the majority of whom were located in the three Darfur field offices. By 2009, the end of my time as Special Rapporteur, OHCHR's field presence in Sudan comprised 62 staff deployed in the Human Rights section of UNMIS and 85 staff deployed in the human rights component of UNAMID.[50]

OHCHR's field presence performed a few functions in Sudan that were particularly helpful from my perspective: monitoring and reporting on human rights violations in Sudan and supporting my work as Special Rapporteur.

Monitoring and Reporting

In Sudan, and particularly in Darfur, the presence of OHCHR human rights monitors contributed significantly to the promotion and protection of

---

[47] *Report of the High-Level Mission on the Situation of Human Rights in Darfur*, 20.

[48] The mandate of UNMIS, which covered northern and southern Sudan, expired in July 2011. Since the expiration of the mandate, OHCHR does not have a presence in the Sudan beyond Darfur.

[49] UN Office of Internal Oversight Services, *Audit of Human Rights Programme in UNAMID*, July 25, 2012, 1, http://usun.state.gov/documents/organization/199249.pdf

[50] OHCHR, *2009 Annual Report*, 100–101.

human rights. Although the monitors' movements were frequently restricted due to the security situation, they were able to support local human rights defenders, to speak with the victims of abuse, and to report on their findings to Geneva.[51]

The reports of OHCHR on the situation of human rights in Sudan were helpful and the government of Sudan did take the issues raised in those reports into consideration. Generally speaking, the reports had the effect of placing pressure on the government that led to increased access for the field monitors to detention centers and prisons in Sudan. However, in other cases, OHCHR's human rights reports resulted in the authorities increasing restrictions on the field monitors' access. Often, the effect of a human rights report would depend in part on the personalities of the governors or officials in charge of the different regions discussed in the reports.

Another significant impact of the reports of the OHCHR field monitors was to raise international awareness of the human rights situation in the ground in Sudan.

One aspect of the OHCHR field presence that at times compromised its effectiveness was the fact that it operated from within UNMIS, which was a peacekeeping mission with political objectives other than human rights protection and accountability.[52] The OHCHR human rights officers required the support of the Special Representative of the Secretary-General (SRSG) who headed UNMIS, and could not function and report entirely independently. Indeed, the human rights reports compiled by the field monitors could not be published without the approval of the SRSG. Frequently, SRSGs had different views than the OHCHR staff on the best strategy for dealing with the Sudanese authorities, including in cases of violations of human rights. In my view, this arrangement placed political restrictions on the staff of OHCHR.

Additionally, in the future, OHCHR should make an even greater effort to consult with people on the ground in Sudan. Increased interaction between the field presence and the population could increase its effectiveness in promoting and protecting human rights. This is particularly

---

[51] See, e.g., OHCHR, *Eleventh periodic report of the United Nations High Commissioner for Human Rights on the situation of human rights in the Sudan: Killing and injuring of civilians on 25 August 2008 by government security forces: Kalma IDP camp, South Darfur, Sudan*, January 23, 2009, http://www.ohchr.org/EN/Countries/AfricaRegion/Pages/SDPeriodicReports.aspx.

[52] See, e.g., UN Mission in Sudan & Human Rights Section, *UNMIS Report on the Human Rights Situation During the Violence in Southern Kordofan Sudan*, June 2011, 17.

important since the OHCHR staff members in Sudan come from many different countries with diverse understandings of human rights issues. Greater interaction with the people on the ground would help ensure that their personalities, attitude, and behavior increase, rather than decrease, the effectiveness of their work.

Supporting the Special Rapporteur

While the post of Special Rapporteur on Sudan was created by the political bodies of the UN – first by the Commission on Human Rights and later by its successor, the Human Rights Council – OHCHR was responsible for providing logistical assistance to support its work.

During my time as Special Rapporteur, between 2005 and 2009, the work of OHCHR's human rights monitors in Sudan served as the main source of information available to me. OHCHR staff had contact with the local and international human rights defenders, civil society and NGOs. OHCHR's monitors assisted in facilitating my visits to the country, arranging for and scheduling meetings for me with victims of abuse, local human rights defenders, and government officials. OHCHR staff in Geneva assisted me in preparing my reports as well.

Additionally, the reports of the High Commissioner for Human Rights that discussed Sudan, which were prepared with the assistance of the OHCHR staff, referenced and supported my reports on Sudan as Special Rapporteur.[53]

While OHCHR support was incredibly valuable in my work, even more support would have been helpful. For example, due to shortage of staff at the Sudan desk at OHCHR in Geneva, I occasionally experienced difficulties submitting reports on time. This being said, the support of OHCHR was really vital to my work.

Supporting National Human Rights Institutions

One area of work that will be even more important for OHCHR in Sudan in the future will be support for national human rights institutions (NHRIs) in both Sudan and South Sudan. The CPA calls for Sudan to establish a National Human Rights Institution, but during my time working on the country, the government of Sudan showed no interest in establishing such

---

53 See, e.g., OHCHR, *Tenth periodic report of the United Nations High Commissioner for Human Rights on the situation of human rights in the Sudan / Arbitrary arrest and detention committed by national security, military and police*, November 28, 2008, 40.

an institution.[54] Recently, it has taken steps to create such a commission and to appoint its commissioners, but its accomplishments to date are limited.[55] Conversely, the government of South Sudan moved rather quickly even before gaining independence to establish a human rights commission and enact implementing legislation.[56] It will be vital for OHCHR to support both these NHRIs, as their work will be vital for the promotion and protection of human rights in the ground.

Challenges

One common challenge that all High Commissioners have faced, and which has affected their work on Afghanistan and Sudan as well as elsewhere, is the Office's meager budget. Mary Robinson voiced serious concerns over the OHCHR's low budget, stating that the situation would lead her to reject a second term as High Commissioner.[57] The biennial budget allocation to OHCHR by the UN General Assembly has been inadequate to address all the recent developments in the areas of human rights and the increasing human rights issues that OHCHR has been assigned by the Human Rights Council to address. To illustrate the problem, the biennial budget allocated by UN to OHCHR for 2002–2003 was $50.4 million, which was 1.8 percent of the $2.6 billion total biennial budget of the UN.[58] Indeed, the OHCHR's regular annual budget covers less than 50 percent of its expenditures, while the deficit has been made up through voluntary contributions by states and foundations.[59]

The High Commissioners in both Afghanistan and Sudan have also struggled with OHCHR's lack of independence in its field work, owing to

54 "Human Rights Council holds interactive dialogue with Special Rapporteur on situation of human rights in Sudan," OHCHR news release, June 16, 2009.

55 Human Rights Watch, "UN Human Rights Council: Addressing Deteriorating Rights Situation in Sudan," September 17, 2012, http://www.hrw.org/news/2012/09/17/un-human-rights-council-addressing-deteriorating-rights-situation-sudan.

56 See, e.g., Government of South Sudan, "South Sudan Human Rights Commission," http://www.goss-online.org/magnoliaPublic/en/Independant-Commissions-and-Chambers/Human-Rights-Commisions.html.

57 Mary Robinson, "Are Human Rights Taking Root Around The World?," address at World Affairs Councils of America Conference on "Reconnecting America and the United Nations," January 11, 2001, http://www.unhchr.ch/huricane/huricane.nsf/view01/86D1D7902882BF1FC12569D2004953C7.

58 OHCHR, *Annual Report 2003*, 9.

59 OHCHR, "About OHCHR Funding," http://www.ohchr.org/EN/ABOUTUS/Pages/FundingBudget.aspx.

its integration within larger peacekeeping and support operations. OHCHR has also struggled with a lack of coordination and cooperation with other UN bodies, which has occasionally led to duplication of activities. In my view, all UN bodies should have a human rights-based approach in their projects and activities. Closer and stronger cooperation and coordination among the UN agencies would enable them to be more effective in promoting human rights in the field, and if different UN bodies were to consistently offer strong support to the work of the OHCHR, this would further demonstrate the UN's commitment to the universality of human rights.

Another challenge the High Commissioners have faced in Afghanistan and Sudan has been the occasional tendency of OHCHR staff, whether in headquarters or in the field, to perceive local NHRIs, NGOs, and human rights defenders as competitors rather than partners. Rather, OHCHR should be supportive of local institutions and local human rights defenders, particularly because OHCHR field staff will only be working on those countries for a limited period of time; thus, it should be a priority of OHCHR to build the capacity of local actors, which will always be present in the country.

Recommendations

National Human Rights Institutions

States should be pressured to use the findings and recommendations of NHRIs on human rights issues as a tool to improve their policies and to inform their plans to improve human rights protection in the future. This, in turn, will help to secure peace and stability. In this respect, High Commissioners should maintain and increase their support to national human rights institutions, enabling them to fulfill their mandate to protect and promote human rights. High Commissioners should consider raising the findings of NHRIs in their reports at the international level and urging relevant states, UN offices, and other international actors to consider them.

High Commissioners should also support the establishment of more NHRIs in different countries. The High Commissioners through various mechanisms should put further pressure on states to support the creation of respected national human rights institutions in their countries, and to enable them to fulfill their duties and responsibilities according to the Paris Principles.

OHCHR staff in field offices and Geneva should not see NHRIs as competitors; rather, they should support and build the national capacity of human rights defenders to enable them to hold their respective governments accountable for the promotion and protection of human rights.[60]

Implementation of International Human Rights Standards at the Local Level

High Commissioners should encourage states to ensure that their legislation, policies, institutions, and judiciaries are in compliance with international human rights treaties and standards, and that these effectively protect human rights in their territories. High Commissioners should seek to convince states that good governance and development will not take place unless they improve the administration of justice and take other measures to protect and promote human rights in order to secure people's trust in their governments. High Commissioners can play an effective role by pressuring governments in this respect through advocacy and lobbying.

Supporting Civil Society

Civil society organizations (CSOs) and NGOs play vital roles in the promotion and protection of human rights at the national and global levels, and cooperation between CSOs and NGOs and national human rights institutions further strengthens their effectiveness. High Commissioners should value this cooperation and instruct OHCHR to facilitate it in various contexts.

Improving the Effectiveness of OHCHR Field Presences

The High Commissioners should further strengthen the OHCHR regional offices to operate independently from other UN agencies and to consistently speak out when human rights violations occur.

Visiting Countries with Serious Human Rights Problems

Visits by the High Commissioner to Afghanistan and Sudan have been very effective in demonstrating the commitment of the UN and the international

---

60 For more on the High Commissioners' support for national human rights institutions, see Tseliso Thipanyane's chapter in this volume.

community to human rights principles and values. The High Commissioner should make regular or annual visits to these countries, using their visits as an opportunity to engage in high-level advocacy and to pressure the respective governments on key human rights issues.

Conclusion

A diverse set of conflicts and serious human rights violations have occurred around the world since the establishment of the post of UN High Commissioner for Human Rights, including in Afghanistan and Sudan. It has been up to the individual High Commissioners, based on their abilities and personalities, to choose the most effective policies to advance the promotion and protection of the human rights of victims in both countries. To date, the High Commissioners and OHCHR have made a significant difference in raising awareness of human rights violations in these countries, condemning abuses and calling for accountability, and supporting the creation and strengthening of local mechanisms to enhance human rights protection on the ground. In the future, it will be increasingly important for individuals holding the post of High Commissioner to bring innovative and contextualized approaches to addressing human rights issues in these and other countries, as there is no one single approach best suited to all parts of the world.

THE HIGH COMMISSIONER IN THE RUSSIAN FEDERATION

Karinna Moskalenko, Maria Goldman, and
Catherine A. Fitzpatrick

Introduction

While much positive work has been done in the area of human rights in the past 20 years, much work still remains to be done. This essay focuses on proposals to help ameliorate the human rights situation in the Russian Federation and advance human rights worldwide. First, we will provide a general perspective of the relationship of the Russian Federation and the United Nations as well as a brief overview of some of the visits by High Commissioners to the Russian Federation. Second, we will assess the role of the Office of the High Commissioner in Moscow and make suggestions for improvement of its work. Third, we will address the process of submission of individual cases to the Office of the High Commissioner in Geneva and the need for more transparency and feedback. Finally, we will address the implementation of recommendations of the High Commissioner and propose potential solutions to enhance compliance.

Background – Russia and the United Nations

Russia is one of the founding members of the UN. Even after the collapse of the Soviet Union, it is still a large and influential state which provides the UN with significant financial resources.[1] Russia is a key member of the UN as a permanent member of the Security Council with the right to veto resolutions. These circumstances influence and often define the way in which the Russian government is treated by the UN, and in this context, the extensive use of quiet diplomacy by UN officials seeking to confront human rights abuses in Russia is understandable. Yet at the same time, the UN is a highly-respected entity within the Russian Federation, both as an organization and for the values it promotes. Given the degree to which Russia has a stake in the UN, UN bodies could use their leverage with

[1] See OHCHR, *Annual Report 2011*.

Russia to critique human rights abuses to a greater extent than they do at present.

The Personal Role of the High Commissioner for Human Rights

The post of High Commissioner for Human Rights was established at a critical time in Russia's history. During the early 1990s, the period of active democratic restructuring (*perestroika*) had begun, and citizens had suddenly become aware of the universality of human rights and their 'supra-national' character. Citizens eagerly began to communicate their complaints and letters of concern to the UN's human rights treaty bodies and to the special procedures, the independent human rights mechanisms which received secretariat support from the Centre for Human Rights, an entity that would later be subsumed into the Office of the High Commissioner. During this time, the Russian government invited several of the thematic special procedures to visit Russia.

Russia extended one of the most important of these invitations to Professor Nigel Rodley, the Special Rapporteur on Torture. Rodley visited Russia in July 1994. His visit and subsequent report were widely publicized in the media and were important not only for senior officials in the Russian government but also for the staff of the penitentiary system, who took careful notice of the Special Rapporteur's findings.[2] Although he made frank remarks about the horrific violations of human rights in the prisons, Rodley maintained a balanced attitude and provided constructive suggestions and recommendations.[3] Following his visit, the Russian government began to develop humanitarian principles for the penitentiary system and to adopt the UN's minimum standards for the treatment of prisoners. This positive example demonstrates that impact is a function of reciprocity:

---

[2] Claire Nullis, "Detention Conditions Akin to Torture, Worse than Labor Camps," *Associated Press News Archive*, December 1, 1994.

[3] The Special Rapporteur was particularly critical of conditions in pretrial detention centers (SIZOs), writing: "The Special Rapporteur would need the poetic skills of a Dante or the artistic skills of a Bosch adequately to describe the infernal conditions he found in these cells. The senses of smell, touch, taste and sight are repulsively assailed. The conditions are cruel, inhuman and degrading; they are torturous. To the extent that suspects are confined there to facilitate the investigation by breaking their wills with a view to eliciting confessions and information, they can properly be described as being subjected to torture." UN Commission on Human Rights, *Report by the Special Rapporteur on Torture, Sir Nigel Rodley*, UN Doc. E/CN.4/1995/34/Add.1, November 16, 1994.

when a UN official understands the range of problems, and the government has the will to change the system's flaws, impact is possible.

Despite the strength of Nigel Rodley's report, High Commissioner José Ayala Lasso, whose term began three months earlier, in April 1994, did not comment publicly on the mission or its findings. Subsequently, he designated a member of the UN Human Rights Committee, Fausto Pocar, to serve as his envoy to Chechnya. Unfortunately, Ayala Lasso never made public the report on Pocar's 1995 visit, and issued only a cursory account of the report from Pocar's second visit in 1996. While Ayala Lasso made occasional statements to the press on Chechnya, they were very mild.[4] Ayala Lasso was criticized for taking too soft an approach to Russia and other great powers.[5]

A more positive example of the role in Russia played by the High Commissioner for Human Rights was Mary Robinson's April 2000 visit to the country. In her recently-published memoirs, Robinson recounted that the "prevailing view in Geneva was that no High Commissioner could get away with taking on Russia."[6] When she came into office, however, Robinson and the former Irish ambassador to Moscow, Ronan Murphy, made a concerted effort to gain access to Chechnya and Chechen internally-displaced persons in Ingushetia, and to ensure that the visit was covered by the press. The Russians were reluctant, but finally invited her, although with a requirement that in addition to traveling to Chechnya and Ingushetia, the High Commissioner would also travel to Dagestan to see the impact of Chechen rebel incursions there. Although international human rights groups warned the High Commissioner that such a choreographed trip to Dagestan could be a detour from the most serious atrocities in the war, she accepted Moscow's condition in order to gain access.

At Robinson's insistence, in Ingushetia, she was able to meet with victims of abuses perpetrated by the Russian military and heard appalling accounts of their atrocities, as well as reproach of the Chechen rebels for

---

4 Ayala Lasso was quoted as saying only that "there are violations of human rights in Chechnya." "Russians pound strategic village in Chechnya," *Associated Press*, March 15, 1996.

5 In a paper analyzing the Office of the High Commissioner for a symposium at Columbia, Andrew Clapham wrote, "We have to conclude that the first High Commissioner's strategy with regard to Chechnya proved to have little or no impact." Andrew Clapham, "The UN High Commissioner for Human Rights: Achievements and Frustrations," (Columbia University, 2003). Following Pocar's first visit in 1995, a subsequent visit in 1996 produced a rather cursory report: UN Commission on Human Rights, *Report of the Secretary-General on the situation of human rights in the Republic of Chechnya of the Russian Federation*, UN Doc. E/CN.4/1996/13/Add.1, April 22, 1996.

6 Mary Robinson, *Everybody Matters: A Memoir* (London: Hodder & Stoughton, 2012).

escalating the war.[7] Robinson also met with human rights organizations, including those working in Chechnya, and encouraged them to continue their work. Then the High Commissioner was able to make the trip to Grozny, the capital of Chechnya, and to hear victims' pleas, albeit in the company of a Russian general who yelled at survivors in the bombed-out city that they should stop complaining in her presence. On the way to Dagestan, she was kept circling in the air for hours by local authorities and later reproached by an official who accused her of taking the side of Chechen insurgents. Robinson then returned to Moscow for a tense meeting with the Russian Foreign Minister[8] in which she raised human rights issues including the violations in Chechnya.

Ultimately, Robinson and her colleagues were able to return to Geneva and report to the UN Commission on Human Rights which was in session at the time. For the first time in its history, on the basis of Robinson's report, the Commission passed a resolution[9] condemning atrocities committed by a permanent member of the Security Council.[10] Moreover, unlike Ayala Lasso, who had either declined to publish reports on Russia produced by his Office or ensured that those published were brief, Robinson released a more substantive account of her visit and critique of Russia's conduct in her annual report for 2000.[11] Unfortunately, Robinson's focus on Chechnya gave the Russian government an opportunity to criticize her for lack of attention towards other issues in the Russian Federation.[12] Henceforth, the Russian government began to speak about the purported lack of objectivity of the High Commissioner's Office with regard to Russia, and its alleged political one-sidedness.

After 2000, when the process of reform in the Russian Federation began to disintegrate, human rights institutions including the UN High

---

[7] Ibid.

[8] Note that Mary Robinson met with the Russian Foreign Minister, but not with President Putin. Robinson, *Everybody Matters*, 240.

[9] However, the Commission approved by consensus Chairman's statements in 1992 on the Soviet Union (regarding killings in Lithuania and Latvia) and in 1995 and 1996 on Russia (regarding the war in Chechnya). See *A Global Agenda: Issues Before the 46th General Assembly of the United Nations*, eds. John Tessitore and Susan Woolfson (Maryland, USA: Rowman & Littlefield, 1991), 190–191; *A Global Agenda: Issues Before the 50th General Assembly of the United Nations*, eds. John Tessitore and Susan Woolfson (Maryland, USA: Rowman & Littlefield, 1995), 176–203.

[10] UN Commission on Human Rights. Resolution 2000/58, "Situation in the Republic of Chechnya of the Russian Federation," UN Doc. E/CN.4/RES/2000/58, April 25, 2000.

[11] Mary Robinson, "Statement by Mary Robinson, High Commissioner for Human Rights on the Situation of Human Rights in Chechnya in the Russian Federation," April 5, 2000.

[12] See, for example, Government of the Russian Federation, "The Minister of Foreign Affairs of the Russian Federation received the UN High Commissioner for Human Rights Mary Robinson," news release, April 4, 2000.

Commissioner and the values these institutions promoted lost importance for the Russian government. While the new government tried to keep the established diplomatic status quo, it was more a function of inertia than a genuine appreciation and respect for the UN's human rights work. Therefore, subsequent visits of the High Commissioner, such as the visits of Louise Arbour in 2005 and 2006 and Navi Pillay in 2011, were conducted in a rather low-key manner.[13] Regrettably, none of these visits received significant publicity in the Russian media, so the average Russian citizen would probably not have been aware of the important visits taking place. On the other hand, the visits focused on a much broader range of issues, such as torture, detention, and the penitentiary system as well as judiciary reform. Another positive feature of the low-key approach was that the visits were less confrontational and tended not to provoke outright aggressive disagreement from the Russian government.[14] In Louise Arbour's case, this approach seemed to increase the effectiveness of her visits, because the Russian government was more receptive to the High Commissioner's criticism on less politically sensitive issues.[15]

These examples demonstrate that the High Commissioner should understand the importance of keeping some balance between criticizing governments for human rights abuse and acknowledging areas of progress. Consequently, future visits of the High Commissioner to Russia should place minimal emphasis on broad political topics, but adopt an honest and demanding attitude towards communicating awareness of specific human rights violations to the Russian government. Another suggestion is to ensure that the High Commissioner negotiates the trip and meets with the prime minister and other top officials of the Russian government.

---

[13] "High Commissioner for Human Rights ends visit to Russian Federation," OHCHR news release, February 14, 2005. Michael Mainville, "U.N. envoy checks on Russia's troubled land / Human rights chief slams 'desecration' of Beslan school," *San Francisco Chronicle* (San Francisco, CA), February 23, 2006. Lada Korotun, "UN High Commissioner for Human Rights pays visit to Moscow," *The Voice of Russia* (Moscow), February 18, 2011.

[14] Navi Pillay, "Opening remarks by UN High Commissioner for Human Rights Navi Pillay at a press conference during her mission to the Russian Federation," (press conference, Moscow, February 17, 2011).

[15] However, there is some indication that even the low-key approach is no longer guaranteed to prevent the Russian government's wrath. In July 2012, Navi Pillay expressed concern about "a worrying shift in the legislative environment governing the enjoyment of the freedoms of assembly, association, speech and information in the Russian Federation," following her February 2011 trip to Russia. Office of the High Commissioner for Human Rights, "Russia's new laws could have serious negative impacts on human rights," news release, July 18, 2012. Pillay also protested Russia's continued arming of the murderous Syrian regime. The Russian Foreign Ministry then blasted Pillay in a statement later in July. "Pillay's statements on Russia do not fit her status – ministry (Part 2)," *Interfax*, July 18, 2012.

The Work of the Office of the High Commissioner for Human Rights in the Russian Federation

In order to assess the High Commissioner's influence on Russia beyond trips to the country, one must consider the role of the High Commissioner's Office (OHCHR) in the Russian Federation. Regrettably, the work of this body remains nearly invisible in Russia.

In the 1990s, as his special envoy traveled to Chechnya, Ayala Lasso discussed with Russian officials the possibility of opening a permanent OHCHR office in Moscow the staff of which would undertake regular visits to Chechnya and provide assistance to Russia in meeting its human rights treaty obligations.[16] But these efforts came to naught, possibly because they were not sufficiently forcefully promoted.

By 2000, when Mary Robinson picked up the file on establishing the High Commissioner's office in Moscow, Russian officials were no longer pretending to cooperate on Chechnya or other serious human rights reforms, and worked to ensure that any such 'office' would have as restrictive a mandate as possible. During Robinson's tenure, OHCHR carried out technical assistance projects in Russia, but only on benign subjects such as human rights education.[17]

In February 2005, following a visit by High Commissioner for Human Rights Louise Arbour to Moscow, OHCHR reached a preliminary agreement with the Russian government and the UN Resident Coordinator in

---

[16] "They [Russian officials] welcomed in principle the proposal for the establishment in Moscow of more systematic contacts with the Office of the High Commissioner, either by the formal establishment of an office in Moscow, possibly located within the existing United Nations Office, or through a regular program of visits by the Envoy of the High Commissioner. The Russian authorities also declared their willingness to facilitate regular visits by the High Commissioner's Envoy to the Chechen Republic. Russian officials also proposed that one objective of an enhanced presence of the High Commissioner's Office in the Russian Federation should be the provision of advisory services on the international obligations of the Russian Federation in the field of human rights. The Russian authorities expressed their wish to coordinate with the High Commissioner their own efforts to restore respect for the human rights and freedoms of those affected by the conflict in Chechnya." UN Commission on Human Rights, *The situation of human rights in the Republic of Chechnya of the Russian Federation Report of the Secretary-General: Addendum*, UN Doc. E/CN.4/1996/13/Add.1, April 22, 1996.

[17] "The main objective of the project in Russia is to support human rights educators in developing training materials and increasing the number of qualified human rights teachers and professors. Teaching materials for educators are to be published and nationwide poster competition for school children held in cooperation with other UN partners as well as Russian newspapers." OHCHR, "Human rights in action," February, 2003, http://www2.ohchr.org/english/countries/field/docs/fiche.pdf.

Russia to enlarge OHCHR's technical cooperation program in the country. Negotiations between OHCHR and the Russian government would continue for three more years, with a 'preparatory presence' of national staff established in 2006 and a Framework for Cooperation finalized with the Foreign Ministry in August 2007.[18] Finally, in March 2008 OHCHR established a permanent field presence in Russia, in the form of the deployment of a single human rights adviser to the UN Country Team for Russia.[19]

Today, the OHCHR field presence in Russia consists of a senior human rights adviser to the UN country team and five additional staff members.[20] While the OHCHR 'office' is involved in important activities, such as various educational and awareness-raising lectures, workshops, and conferences, the topics are all completely neutral and non-provocative and only address issues on which Russia already has approved state programs, such as promoting tolerance and combating racism and training judges and lawyers, or which were already permitted to be covered by international development agencies, such as domestic violence and the human rights of HIV/AIDS patients.[21] In keeping with OHCHR's mild interpretation of its mandate, the themes chosen for recent events have been about the environment, public health, employment, culture, persons with disabilities, and refugees. Although the Framework Agreement with Russia does include work on the difficult topics of violence against women, protection of minorities, and juvenile justice, they are tucked under the topic 'rule of law' and are not mentioned explicitly in the description of OHCHR's mandate on the UN team in Russia's website. OHCHR does not undertake any

---

18 OHCHR, "Framework for Cooperation with the Russian Federation for 2007 and beyond," http://www.ohchr.org/EN/Countries/ENACARegion/Pages/RUFramework.aspx.

19 See OHCHR, *Annual Report 2006*. Human rights advisers have a dual reporting line to the High Commissioner and the UN Resident Coordinator and perform the following functions: Advise the Resident Coordinator and the UN Country Team on strategies to build and strengthen national human rights capacities; Advise and provide training to independent national human rights institutions; Advise duty-bearers on how best to promote UN normative values; Liaise with, and provide moral and practical support to, civil society at large; Follow and analyze the human rights situation and provide issue-based or thematic assessments to OHCHR and the Resident Coordinator; and provide operational support to human rights training and/or national capacity-building activities. Between February 2005 and 2008, when the human rights adviser for Russia was actually deployed, OHCHR carried out its technical assistance activities in Russia through the OHCHR desk in Geneva, supported by a consultant and a locally-based national human rights officer. See OHCHR, *2007 Annual Report*, 106.

20 OHCHR, *2012 Annual Report*, p. 259 (noting that the OHCHR field presence in Russia had six staff members as of December 31, 2011).

21 See United Nations in the Russian Federation, "Events," http://www.unrussia.ru/en/un-in-russia/events.

kind of monitoring, advocacy, or support for local litigators working on these issues, even though they might lead to more practical results.[22]

This approach thus ignores the harder subjects of torture in prisons and the armed forces, disappearances and massacres in the North Caucasus, and freedom of the media and assembly. Those living and working in Russia cannot ignore that people are being tortured and even killed in prison and arrested for expressing their opinions. However, judging from the Russian-language and English-language OHCHR pages on the website of the UN team in Russia,[23] none of these issues seem to be on its agenda. Additionally, as a result of its mandate constraints, OHCHR does not act as a representative on high-impact individual cases nor does it assume any monitoring role for the top human rights cases at the national level. For example, when people are arrested *en masse* at demonstrations for peacefully expressing their views, OHCHR's field presence in Russia does not take steps to protest the violation of human rights. It also does not raise high-profile cases that are hotly debated in the media and civil society and on which the involvement of an international body could truly make a difference.

These tough issues are ignored because they do not fit into OHCHR's carefully-constructed and calibrated mandate of human rights education and other less controversial matters. Yet although the mandate does confine the possibilities for UN officials in this regard, there is a sense that they do not use it creatively. For example, OHCHR could hold a public seminar on the new resolution by the UN Human Rights Council affirming the right to freedom of association and invite the special rapporteur on this theme to give a talk, or invite members of the UN treaty bodies that have considered Russia in recent years to discuss their findings, and characterize this as an educational enterprise. Indeed, although OHCHR's Framework Agreement with Russia gives it a broad mandate to disseminate "knowledge of international mechanisms and procedures" and "other relevant UN information," the conclusions of the UN treaty bodies or other procedures that have reviewed Russia's compliance with its human rights obligations are not even published on either the English-language or Russian-language versions of the website of the UN team in Russia. While OHCHR held a roundtable in July 2010 involving both the Russian

---

22 See United Nations in the Russian Federation, "Office of the United Nations High Commissioner for Human Rights (OHCHR)," http://www.unrussia.ru/en/agencies/office-united-nations-high-commissioner-human-rights-ohchr.

23 Ibid.

International Law Association and the Russian Federation Chamber of Accounts on the Universal Periodic Review (UPR) process and its recommendations to the Russian Federation, the official United Nations documents from the UPR session on Russia were not published on the UN Team's website.[24] Instead, only materials on more anodyne topics such as the Millennium Development Goals are published there.

Or to take another example, recently, a comprehensive research work titled *An International Tribunal for Chechnya* was compiled and published by the Nizhniy Novgorod Society for Russian-Chechen Friendship.[25] The authors worked on their research for the past 10 years and created a unique compilation of cases and court decisions from domestic courts and the European Court of Human Rights. The work is essential reading to understand the situation in Chechnya. OHCHR would include such an NGO report on its UN global website as part of the background materials for a treaty body's review of Russia,[26] yet it is apparently unthinkable for the Moscow UN office to publish such a report on its site. UN offices in other regions of the world, and even this region, commonly include at least news reports about such human rights work on their websites.[27] If this report addresses issues on OHCHR's agenda, couldn't this publication and its authors be mentioned? Such mention would likely not endanger the ability of the UN office to continue under its limited mandate, but would empower significant NGO initiatives.

Another way of validating the concerns of human rights advocates in Russia and having more influence for the Office of the High Commissioner, even within the 'educational' mandate, would be to bring together representatives of the government with active figures from civil society movements and human rights organizations. These representatives need to be authentic activists and decision-makers. A true debate can only take place if both sides are fairly represented. Evidently, no high-caliber

---

24 Ibid.

25 Stanislav Mikhailovich Dmitrievskiy, Bogdan Isayevich Gvareli, and Oksana Anatol'yevna Chelysheva, *Mezhdunarodnyĭ tribunal dlia Chechni* (An International Tribunal for Chechnya) (Nizhniy Novgorod: Obshchestvo Rossiĭsko-Chechenskoĭ druzhby (The Russian-Chechen Friendship Society), 2009), http://www.scribd.com/doc/17647465/-1.

26 For example, OHCHR publishes NGO reports on Russia submitted to treaty bodies such as the Committee Against Torture on its website. See UN Committee Against Torture, "49th session (29 October to 23 November 2012)," http://www2.ohchr.org/english/bodies/cat/cats49.htm.

27 See, for example, United Nations in Moldova, "News Room," http://www.un.md/news_room/pr/2012/index.shtml.

meetings of this kind have ever taken place, even on the approved subjects, which is another lost opportunity.

Thus, while we recognize that OHCHR does not have the appropriate mandate to explicitly monitor and work on human rights cases, and only has a mandate for education, we believe that more meaningful and effective activities can be developed even under this rubric, and sustained by better content on the UN websites. Each time UN officials fail to work more creatively with the mandate, they lose a chance to establish a strong position as a main player in the field of human rights in Russia and to gain the respect of those who will eventually bring about real change in the area of human rights.

We need to ask why OHCHR in Moscow has failed to interpret its mandate creatively or push for its expansion to date. It may be a reflection of the general approach of the Geneva headquarters to its field presences, or perhaps a problem particular to veto-wielding Russia. Certainly, the various diplomatic circumstances under which the High Commissioner works need to be taken into account. One also needs to take into account, however, that Russian civil society has become very active in recent years, and that it is particularly crucial at this time that international actors support local organizations involved in the promotion and protection of human rights. It cannot be that in other countries where human rights violations are much more severe, for example in Afghanistan, the local OHCHR presence is engaged meaningfully with credible local human rights groups on sensitive issues,[28] while in the Russian Federation, the High Commissioner accepts a problematic status quo with its engagement solely in 'education.' Today, when Russian human rights organizations have themselves become an integral part of the international human rights community and are visible on the world stage in the media, the UN's very quiet diplomacy seems to be the wrong approach. The High Commissioner can validate the work of human rights groups and engage with civic leaders without thereby sparking a revolution. We should be able to expect the local presence of OHCHR to be a destination for civil society in its quest for advancement of human rights.

---

[28] See, for example, United Nations Assistance Mission in Afghanistan and United Nations High Commissioner for Human Rights, "A Long Way to Go: Implementation of the Elimination of Violence against Women Law in Afghanistan," November 2011, http://www.ohchr.org/Documents/Countries/AF/UNAMA_Nov2011.pdf. UNAMA/OHCHR undertakes a range of activities aimed at promoting and protecting women's rights to live free from violence and discrimination in partnership with Government of Afghanistan, the Afghanistan Independent Human Rights Commission, and civil society organizations, in particular women's civil society groups.

It is unacceptable that the work of a field presence receiving financial support from OHCHR should be largely unnoticed and even irrelevant. The High Commissioner should put an evaluation mechanism in place in order to assess the effectiveness of the OHCHR field presence in Russia and ensure it is based on clear criteria. The most obvious criterion in our modern information society is the frequency of references made to OHCHR in the mainstream media. Next, given the increasing relevance of the internet, the Office's website should be re-assessed with regard to the usefulness of information presented, comprehensiveness of documents posted, frequency of updates, traffic statistics, and accessibility of information in a user-friendly format.

Similarly, other relevant questions should be asked of OHCHR. Are NGOs throughout Russia able to access the OHCHR field presence? Is OHCHR consulting civil society leaders and involving them in its programs? Are the persons trained in educational programs later finding their way into meaningful positions in government or human rights NGOs? Have the Russian authorities showed an increased willingness to invite UN special rapporteurs to visit the country, and have they been given free access once within it, or delayed and curtailed in their movements? Has Russia signed or ratified additional UN human rights treaties (such as, for example, the Second Optional Protocol to the ICCPR or the Rome Statute of the ICC)? Has the field presence assisted in the implementation of recommendations to Russia made by UN treaty bodies?

Answers to these and other questions would help the High Commissioner and outside observers understand the overall contribution of the OHCHR field presence to the protection of human rights in Russia. Such an evaluation would most probably reveal factors contributing to the progress or lack of progress on specific topics within OHCHR's admittedly restricted mandate. Increased transparency and accountability will certainly enhance the field presence's overall performance. Ultimately, though, we must ask whether an ineffective field presence should be maintained at any cost – even at the expense of OHCHR's and the UN's credibility.

Individual Petitions to the High Commissioner

When the UN was founded in 1945, it was meant to be a political tool for Member States, not for individuals. Thus, while human rights were proclaimed as universal values, there was no legal mechanism in place to implement them, and it took some time for such a system to develop.

The adoption of the International Covenant on Civil and Political Rights and the International Covenant on Economic, Social and Cultural Rights in 1966 was the first step towards a binding, practical application of human rights, and the UN would go on to adopt several additional human rights treaties in the following decades. Several of the expert committees created by the UN human rights treaties were vested with the authority to receive petitions from individuals alleging human rights violations by states parties to the treaty in question, provided that the state had consented to the 'individual complaints procedure.' The Centre for Human Rights, which later became the Office of the High Commissioner for Human Rights, provided secretariat support to the treaty bodies, and thus had responsibility for receiving and helping to process these individual complaints. Additionally, beginning in the 1980s, the Commission on Human Rights (which in 2006 was replaced by the Human Rights Council) began creating special procedures, including working groups and special rapporteurs on thematic issues and countries of concern, which also had authority to receive petitions from individuals alleging human rights violations and to raise their cases with governments. The UN Centre on Human Rights, now OHCHR, provides secretariat support to these mechanisms and assists them in the receipt and processing of individual claims of abuse.

When the post of the High Commissioner for Human Rights was established in 1993, the High Commissioner became an additional form of recourse to which people worldwide could turn with individual appeals on human right violations. Shortly after assuming the post, José Ayala Lasso established a 'human rights hotline,' a 24-hour fax line for victims of human rights violations, their relatives, and NGOs.[29] Thus, OHCHR itself became a channel through which information on human rights situations 'in the field' was fed back to Geneva and to the High Commissioner personally. In this way, OHCHR's role in facilitating the development of individual human rights complaint mechanisms allowed the concept of human rights to become more widely known and popular around the world.

Despite expressing rhetorical support for empowering individuals to raise human rights complaints at the UN, the High Commissioner and OHCHR have been reluctant to fully embrace this approach in practice. Indeed, the High Commissioners have generally seemed to prefer the UN's

---

[29] "24-hour "Hot Line" for Reporting Human Rights Violations," UN news release, August, 1998, http://www.un.org/rights/dpi1550e.htm.

traditional approach to addressing cases of abuse: raising them privately, in quiet diplomacy and communication with governments. OHCHR does not seem to have developed adequate procedures for handling complaints directed at the High Commissioner personally rather than those addressed to the special procedures or treaty bodies. Accordingly, victims find that while the OHCHR website lists email addresses for victims to contact, and while OHCHR endeavors to communicate with the public on social networks such as Twitter, it remains a black hole for individual petitioners. OHCHR has not published criteria setting out how the High Commissioner selects cases for action. Applicants submitting details of their cases to OHCHR do not even receive an automated reply confirming that OHCHR has received their application. In fact, applicants may never learn whether their request was processed at all and, if it was, what action OHCHR took and what resulted from that action. Applicants are not informed about any communication on their case between the High Commissioner and the government of their country. In most cases, the impact of the High Commissioner on these cases can only be inferred from the subsequent action or inaction of governments.

OHCHR needs to adopt modern working methods in this area. While 'quiet diplomacy' may have been an appropriate approach to raising human rights violations with governments twenty years ago, this is not the case today. International legal institutions have become increasingly transparent, a trend which is both very positive and seemingly irreversible. Modern technology should make it easier to inform applicants of the status of their communication, and at the very least, to explain that due to the large volume of communications OHCHR receives, petitioners cannot expect an individualized response. OHCHR should also more explicitly acknowledge its limited capacity to address individual cases and direct would-be petitioners to other mechanisms such as the treaty bodies and special procedures, or even to NGOs that take on individual cases. When OHCHR does decide to act on a case, it should inform the victims so that they or their representatives do not persist in 'banging on open doors,' and OHCHR should also ensure that their expectations of what the UN can do for them are realistic. Any communication from OHCHR will offer encouragement to applicants by letting them know that their plea has been heard, and even this simple acknowledgement may serve as a measure of deterrence against abuse by officials at a local level.

It is time that the High Commissioner's Office adopts the level of transparency expected of other human rights offices and procedures by publishing the aggregate numbers and types of requests and inquiries made to the High Commissioner and the responses of governments to action taken by the High Commissioner on those requests or inquiries whenever possible from a diplomatic standpoint, or at least notifying applicants of developments in their cases.

Implementation of Decisions of the UN Treaty Bodies

Russia is a party to a number of UN human rights treaties, and as such is periodically reviewed by the independent expert bodies that monitor states' compliance with their obligations under each treaty.[30] As discussed above, Russia has accepted the competence of several of these treaty bodies to receive complaints from individuals claiming to be victims of human rights abuses, and they have adopted well-reasoned and useful decisions on dozens of such cases on Russia alone. These decisions have the potential to greatly promote the advancement of human rights. However, to date they have not had such an effect because the governments concerned generally do not implement the decisions. Even more troublingly, sometimes the UN does not even publish treaty body decisions in the language spoken in the country concerned.[31]

The Russian Federation has ratified the Optional Protocol to the ICCPR,[32] thus recognizing the authority of the UN Human Rights Committee (HRC) to receive and issue decisions on petitions from individuals claiming violations of the ICCPR perpetrated by Russia. However, Russia consistently disregards the HRC's decisions. In some cases, the government seems to have confused the HRC with other UN bodies not empowered to make binding recommendations, such as UN working

[30] OHCHR, "Russian Federation Homepage," http://www.ohchr.org/en/countries/enacaregion/pages/ruindex.aspx. Russia was reviewed by the UN Committee against Torture in 2012, by the Committee on Economic Social, and Cultural Rights in 2011, by the Committee on the Elimination of Discrimination against Women in 2010, by the Human Rights Committee in 2009, by the Committee on the Elimination of Racial Discrimination in 2008, and the Committee on the Rights of the Child in 2005.

[31] For example, a 2008 decision by the Human Rights Committee finding a violation by the Russian Federation had not been translated into Russian by the UN as of April 30, 2013, though it has been translated into French and Spanish in addition to the original English. UN Human Rights Committee, Ninety-second session, "Views / Communication No. 1310/2004," (Mr. Konstantin Babkin v. Russian Federation), UN Doc. CCPR/C/92/D/1310/2004 (2008).

[32] UN General Assembly, Resolution 2200 (XXI), "Optional Protocol to the International Covenant on Civil and Political Rights," U.N. Doc. A/6316, December 16, 1966, entered into force March 23, 1976, article 1.

groups and special rapporteurs.[33] While Russia should implement all recommendations made to it by UN human rights bodies, it has an even greater level of legal responsibility to implement decisions of the HRC because it is a quasi-judicial mechanism, similar to an international court such as the European Court for Human Rights.

Examples of HRC decisions that Russia has failed to implement include *Smirnova v. Russian Federation*,[34] where the HRC found that Russia had denied the petitioner access to a court to challenge the lawfulness of her detention, in violation of ICCPR Article 9. They also include *Lantsova v. Russian Federation*,[35] where the HRC found that the petitioner's son had died in a pre-trial detention facility because medical treatment was refused, in violation of ICCPR Article 6 on the right to life. In that case, the Russian government even admitted that the applicant's son died due to poor detention conditions, but paid no compensation to his mother.[36] They also include *Gridin v. Russian Federation*,[37] where for the first time in its history, the HRC found that the Russian Federation had violated the presumption of innocence in the petitioner's case. Despite the fact that the HRC determined that Gridin should be released from prison and paid compensation, to this day he remains in detention, serving a life sentence. Indeed, the Russian government has implemented none of the HRC's decisions, and continues to interpret them as mere recommendations. Russia acts with impunity, as neither the treaty body nor the High Commissioner has required Russian authorities to submit a plan for implementation of the HRC's decisions, let alone to actually implement them.

The current state of affairs constitutes a serious abuse of the entire UN human rights system, and makes it appear as if Russia's ratification of international human rights instruments and its agreement to subject itself to scrutiny by the treaty bodies has led to no improvement in its domestic situation, and has even permitted Russia to perpetrate violations with impunity. The failure to ensure that Russia suffers negative consequences when it continuously fails to comply with the decisions of international

33 As revealed by statements from the government explaining that it appreciates the HRC's views but will defer to the opinion of the Russian judiciary.

34 UN Human Rights Committee, "Communication No. 712/1996," (Yelena Pavlovna Smirnova v. Russian Federation), UN Doc. CCPR/C/81/D/712/1996 (2004).

35 UN Human Rights Committee, "Ms. Yekaterina Pavlovna Lantsova v. The Russian Federation, Communication No. 763/1997," U.N. Doc. CCPR/C/74/D/763/1997 (2002).

36 Ibid.

37 UN Human Rights Committee, "Gridin v. Russian Federation, Communication No. 770/1997," U.N. Doc. CCPR/C/69/D/770/1997 (2000).

legal bodies also sets a bad example for other countries with similarly flawed post-Soviet legal cultures, such as Belarus and Kyrgyzstan. This impunity – with tacit international complicity – has become so acute that human right defenders from former Soviet republics are now thinking twice about submitting individual cases to UN human rights bodies, as they have come to expect non-implementation of decisions, and worse, are concerned about possible retaliation against their clients by the authorities.

The High Commissioner should work with the UN treaty bodies to establish an oversight mechanism to follow up on implementation of their decisions. Each of the UN treaty bodies already has a follow-up procedure;[38] these should monitor implementation of decisions and collect relevant information on specific cases. In cases where a Committee finds systematic non-implementation of its decisions by a state party, it needs to find political avenues to address this non-compliance. This could involve raising the situation of the state party with the UN General Assembly and asking it to take action.[39]

Similar steps have already been taken in the European human rights system. There, the Committee of Ministers of the Council of Europe, a political body, oversees the implementation of judgments of the European Court of Human Rights (ECtHR).[40] While this mechanism is still very new and it is too early to assess its effectiveness, the Russian government has already signaled that it takes these procedures rather seriously. For example, the Russian government provides an action plan on general measures and on measures of an individual nature which it plans to take in each case in which the ECtHR finds it in breach of its human rights obligations.[41] The Russian government submits these plans within established deadlines and provides a solid basis for follow-up activities. Russia has an incentive to comply with these decisions because the Committee of Ministers has the ability to exert political pressure on countries with high

[38] See OHCHR, "Human Rights Committee," http://www2.ohchr.org/english/bodies/hrc/sessions.htm. and OHCHR, "Interim follow-up reports," http://www2.ohchr.org/english/bodies/hrc/interim_follow-up_reports.htm.

[39] The fact that the General Assembly is a political organ of the UN rather than an independent one would not in any way compromise the independence of the treaty body's decision; rather, countries recognize that the GA has authority that treaty bodies do not.

[40] Council of Europe Committee of Ministers, "About the Committee of Ministers," http://www.coe.int/t/cm/aboutcm_en.asp.

[41] Council of Europe, "Execution of Judgments of the ECHR: Russian Federation," http://www.coe.int/t/dghl/monitoring/execution/Themes/Add_info/RUS-ai_en.asp.

non-compliance with ECtHR decisions, for example by politically isolating them on various issues.[42] The Russian Federation has been very aware of the potential consequences at stake and has taken careful measures to avoid them. It is extremely important that the UN establish similar procedures so that states must implement the decisions of human rights treaty bodies or suffer consequences to their diplomatic relations and reputation.

Conclusion

The High Commissioner for Human Rights is an extremely powerful force for the advancement of human rights internationally. While the High Commissioner has already had a significant influence over the past 20 years, some suggestions can be made to enhance the work of OHCHR and the work of the field presence in Russia specifically. First of all, an important general recommendation is that the High Commissioner should strive for greater transparency when dealing with individual complaints, despite the challenges involved in doing so in the face of a high volume of complaints. Second, the High Commissioner should place greater emphasis on the implementation of the decisions of the Human Rights Committee and other treaty bodies, which in turn will help to decrease the number of incoming complaints of rights abuse. Third, the High Commissioner should negotiate and carry out visits to Russia at the highest level of government, in order to raise awareness of human rights issues, and should conduct those visits with a balanced attitude. Finally, the High Commissioner should negotiate a stronger mandate for the OHCHR field presence in Russia so that it can become a stronger partner to Russian civil society; failing that, OHCHR staff should work harder to use the existing mandate more creatively so as to better support the work of Russian human rights advocates.

[42] See Council of Europe, *Supervision of the Execution of Judgments of the European Court of Human Rights: Annual Report 2010* (Strasbourg: 2011).

THE HIGH COMMISSIONER AND HUMAN RIGHTS IN BURMA[1] (MYANMAR)

Jared Genser

Introduction

On November 7, 2010, Burma held its first election in 20 years. Though the election was far from free and fair and opposition leader Aung San Suu Kyi was only released from house arrest six days following the elections, reforms instituted following President Thein Sein's inauguration in March 2011 have given the international community reason to increase engagement with and ease economic sanctions against the country. Much of the reaction to these reforms reflects optimism that the country can break free from an authoritarian past rife with human rights abuses. Signs of change within Burma are encouraging. However, optimism must be tempered with the reality that only modest steps towards reform have been taken and each is readily reversible.

Further, there are significant and systemic obstacles to genuine reform in Burma that could easily prevent the country's continued progress towards respect for the human rights of its people. The military remains the driving force behind the government, both constitutionally and in reality; rule of law does not exist; and the economic and infrastructure development of the country is near non-existent. Yet, despite these obstacles, the international community's increased engagement with Burma allows for a unique moment to ensure that respect for human rights is a genuine priority of President Thein Sein's government.

Given the important shift in trajectory by Burma's leadership, it is an opportune occasion to reflect on the impact that the High Commissioner for Human Rights has had on the country and the impact it could have going forward. While the High Commissioner, the Office of the High Commissioner (OHCHR), and particularly the UN Special Rapporteur on

[1] In this article, the country examined is referred to as Burma rather than Myanmar. This is the form preferred by the leaders of Burma's democracy movement, which won the 1990 parliamentary elections. They do not accept that the government has the right to change the official name of the country to suit its own ends.

the Situation of Human Rights in Myanmar, which OHCHR supports, made sustained efforts over many years, this engagement had little practical effect. Nevertheless, the Special Rapporteur has played an important role in gathering information, highlighting particular areas of concern, and mobilizing greater international pressure. There is reason to be optimistic that the High Commissioner, independently and as the manager of OHCHR, can have a significant effect on improving the Burmese government's respect for human rights in the future, but this will require the High Commissioner to chart a new strategic direction to increase her personal engagement, attract further resources to support these efforts, and make the situation in Burma a higher priority.

UN Engagement on Human Rights in Burma, 1994–2009

Burma's recent history of widespread and systemic human rights abuses, rising to the level of crimes against humanity and war crimes, is well documented. The country experienced decades of political repression and human rights abuses following a 1962 military coup by General Ne Win in 1962. Student-led uprisings precipitated his resignation and forced the regime to hold democratic elections in 1990. Although Aung San Suu Kyi, daughter of independence-era leader General Aung San, and her allies won the vast majority of parliament seats, the military did not permit them to assume power.

General Than Shwe assumed control of the military and the country in 1992 and ruled Burma with an iron fist until early 2011. The horrors of life in the country during his rule included "[E]pidemic levels of forced labor... the recruitment of tens of thousands of child soldiers, widespread sexual violence, extrajudicial killings and torture, [ ] more than a million displaced persons...[and] the destruction, displacement, or damage of over 3,000 ethnic minority villages ...."[2] Arbitrary detentions, particularly targeted at the political opposition, were common.[3]

[2] International Human Rights Clinic at Harvard Law School, *Crimes in Burma*, report, May 2009, iii-iv, http://www.law.harvard.edu/programs/hrp/documents/Crimes-in-Burma.pdf.

[3] DLA Piper Rudnick Gray Cary US LLP, *Threat to the Peace: A Call for the UN Security Council to Act in Burma*, report, September 20, 2005, 8, http://www.dlapiper.com/files/News/8bcac83e-c5b9-4a8b-924e-a72ca16d5c1c/Presentation/NewsAttachment/39f15335-da9d-40f3-af49-ac9ff2c98c1e/BurmaReport.pdf.

The UN Special Rapporteur on the Situation of Human Rights in Myanmar

The primary means through which the UN engaged with the Burmese government on human rights from 1994–2009 was through the appointment of a UN Special Rapporteur on the Situation of Human Rights in Myanmar.[4] The Special Rapporteur position was originally created by the Commission on Human Rights in 1992 and was mandated to "establish direct contacts with the Government and with the people of Myanmar, including political leaders deprived of their liberty, their families and lawyers, with a view to examining the situation of human rights in Myanmar and following any progress made....[5] The Commission adopted annual resolutions, each of which synthesized key developments in the country in the prior year, between 1992 and 2005.[6] Since 2005, the Human Rights Council, which replaced the Commission, has also adopted annual resolutions to renew the mandate of the Special Rapporteur.[7]

Since the creation of the position in 1992, there have been four individuals who have served as Special Rapporteur: Tomás Ojea Quintana, from Argentina, who has served from 2008 to the present; Paulo Sergio Pinheiro, from Brazil, who served from December 2000 to 2008; Rajsoomer Lallah, from Mauritius, who served from 1996 to 2000; and Yozo Yokota, from Japan, who served from 1992 to 1996.

The Special Rapporteurs have played an important role in gathering information, highlighting areas of concern, and in mobilizing greater international pressure to address the situation in Burma, primarily through the use of reports. OHCHR has played a role in these efforts insofar as it provides all of the (unpaid) special rapporteurs created by the Council with staff support.

The Special Rapporteurs have published 36 reports to the General Assembly, Commission on Human Rights, and the Human Rights Council. They make for depressing reading – the same human rights violations are

[4] There are a range of other special procedures and thematic rapporteurs that have been engaged on Burma, including the UN Working Group on Arbitrary Detention. Since 1992, it has issued 28 opinions regarding wrongly detained Burmese, including six opinions regarding Aung San Suu Kyi's house arrest.

[5] UN Commission on Human Rights. Resolution 1992/58, "Situation of Human Rights in Myanmar," March 3, 1992.

[6] OHCHR, "Myanmar Resolutions of the Commission on Human Rights," http://ap.ohchr.org/documents/sdpage_e.aspx?b=1&c=125&t=11.

[7] See, e.g. UN Human Rights Council, Resolution 19.21, "Situation of Human Rights in Myanmar," U.N. Doc. A/HRC/RES/19/21, April 26, 2012.

highlighted every year.[8] These include summary or arbitrary execution in armed conflict; use of child soldiers; rape of ethnic minority women by soldiers; forced labor; extrajudicial killing; torture; cruel, inhumane, or degrading treatment or punishment; disappearance; and arbitrary detention. Over time and until the recent change in government, the reports' description of offenses increased in severity and their tone and approach grew more pointed and critical. Indeed, as the violence escalated, particularly in Eastern Burma, the Special Rapporteurs characterized these violations as being "widespread" and "systematic," suggesting that they could constitute crimes against humanity.

The role of the Special Rapporteur on Human Rights in Myanmar has become increasingly important in the last dozen years because of the talent and persistence of Paulo Sérgio Pinheiro and Tomás Ojea Quintana and their OHCHR staff. Their reports were closely read by governments, embraced by NGOs, and reported on by the media to highlight the ongoing and severe violations of human rights in Burma.

Despite the attention the Special Rapporteurs' reports received, they did not achieve many tangible changes within Burma. This failure led Special Rapporteur Quintana in March 2010 to call for the United Nations to consider the establishment of a commission of inquiry into international crimes in Burma.[9] The Special Rapporteur's endorsement reinforced a global campaign by NGOs to persuade governments to adopt this approach.[10] Sixteen governments publicly supported a commission of inquiry, including EU member states and the United States. However, High Commissioner Navi Pillay did not publicly lend support for the proposal. Given the recent developments within Burma and Aung San Suu Kyi's focus on reconciliation rather than prosecution, these efforts have stalled.

---

[8] In addition, from 2001–2009, the General Assembly requested and received additional annual reports by the Secretary-General addressing the broader political and human rights situation in the country. UN General Assembly, "Situation of Human Rights in Myanmar," UN Doc. A/RES/56/231, December 24, 2001; UN General Assembly, "Situation of Human Rights in Myanmar," UN Doc. A/RES/63/245, December 24, 2008.

[9] UN Human Rights Council, *Progress Report of the Special Rapporteur on Human Rights in Myanmar*, U.N. Doc. A/HRC/13/48, March 10, 2010, para. 122.

[10] Burma Lawyers' Council, *Revealing Burma's System of Impunity: A Briefer for the Commission of Inquiry Campaign*, report, September 9, 2011, http://www.burmacampaign.org.uk/images/uploads/Revealing_Burmas_System_of_Impunity_-_BLC_Briefer.pdf.

The High Commissioner and OHCHR

The direct personal role of the High Commissioner in addressing human rights violations in Burma following the appointment of the first High Commissioner in 1994 has been limited. No High Commissioner visited Burma from 1994 to 2009.[11] Instead, the High Commissioners issued public statements of approbation at particularly concerning moments in the country's history.[12] Mary Robinson issued several statements on Burma over the course of her tenure, including one in 1998 expressing concern about intensified repression of the political opposition, deaths in custody, forced labor, and forced displacement of ethnic minorities.[13] She also expressed concern that Special Rapporteur Rajsoomer Lallah had not been allowed to visit the country. Louise Arbour also released multiple statements of concern, in one example, condemning the "excessive force" deployed against unarmed protestors during the 2007 Saffron Revolution.[14] She also made statements about Burma to the Human Rights Council, urging member states at a 2007 special session on Burma to "impress upon the Government of Myanmar the urgent need to implement its international human rights obligations and to account publicly for past and on-going violations."[15] Current High Commissioner Navi Pillay also spoke out strongly in 2009 after Aung San Suu Kyi was convicted of violating the terms of her house arrest.[16]

While it is unlikely that additional actions by the High Commissioners would have yielded substantially different results for the country, it is unfortunate that each appears to have not expended much personal effort in trying. Direct diplomatic efforts by the High Commissioner, in addition to the efforts of the Special Rapporteur, might have had a bigger impact on the margins.

---

[11] Sergio Vieira de Mello was invited to travel to Myanmar shortly after being appointed High Commissioner, but he was appointed Special Representative of the UN Secretary-General to Iraq before he could make the visit.

[12] "Myanmar: UN Official Concerned About Rights Violations in Rakhine State," *UN News Centre*, July 27, 2012.

[13] "High Commissioner for Human Rights Concerned Over Intensification of Repression in Myanmar," U.N. Press Release HR/98/73, October 6, 1998.

[14] "Ban Ki-moon dispatches Myanmar envoy to region as situation worsens," *UN News Centre*, September 26, 2007.

[15] Louise Arbour, "Statement on the occasion of the 5th Special Session of the Human Rights Council," OHCHR news release, October 2, 2007.

[16] "UN Rights Chief Calls for Aung San Suu Kyi's Immediate Release," *UN News Centre*, May 15, 2009.

Until 2009, OHCHR's engagement on human rights in Burma was similarly limited. Indeed, despite the fact that OHCHR carried out 'technical cooperation' initiatives with several of its neighbors, including China, during this time, it did not do so in Burma. OHCHR merely provided staff and logistical support to the independent Special Rapporteur. However, over the course of 2009, the Burmese government began to express interest in entering into a dialogue with OHCHR on technical cooperation. To that end, OHCHR staff met with Burmese authorities during missions to the country in April and December.[17]

Other UN Entities

Since 1991, the General Assembly has adopted 20 annual resolutions on the situation in Burma.[18] These resolutions have welcomed the work of the Special Rapporteur and urged adoption of his recommendations since 1992.[19] Additionally, after the 2005 publication by former Czech Republic President Vaclav Havel and Archbishop Desmond M. Tutu of a report advocating for Burma to be voted on to the permanent agenda of the UN Security Council, and an intensive global campaign by NGOs, the Security Council complied, placing Burma on its agenda over the objections of China and the Russian Federation in 2006.[20] In January 2007, despite nine votes in favor, China and the Russian Federation vetoed a proposed Security Council resolution addressing issues in Burma including human rights abuses.[21] Nevertheless, the situation in Burma has been discussed in the Security Council on numerous occasions since it was placed on the permanent agenda.

Importantly, in the wake of the so-called Saffron Revolution and the gunning down of peaceful protesters in the fall of 2007, the Human Rights Council convened a special session on the situation. Both High Commissioner Louise Arbour and Special Rapporteur Pinhiero were

---

17 OHCHR, *2009 OHCHR Annual Report*, 133.

18 See e.g. UN General Assembly, Resolution 66/230, "Situation of human rights in Myanmar," U.N. Doc. A/RES/66/230, December 24, 2011.

19 UN General Assembly, Resolution 47/144, "Situation in Myanmar," U.N. Doc. A/RES/47/144, March 1, 1993.

20 "Myanmar Put on Security Council Agenda," *Chicago Tribune*, September 16, 2006. The author of this article led the team at DLA Piper Rudnick Gray Cary LLP in representing President Havel and Archbishop Tutu in connection with their report, entitled *A Threat to the Peace*. Jared Genser, "Myanmar: A Job for the Security Council," *International Herald Tribune*, September 19, 2005.

21 Colum Lynch, "Russia, China Veto Resolution on Burma," *Washington Post*, January 13, 2007.

invited to make statements, and the Council adopted a resolution[22] calling for the government to investigate human rights violations perpetrated during the demonstrations, release several political prisoners and detainees, engage in dialogue with OHCHR, and permit the Special Rapporteur to visit. The government thereafter entered into dialogue with OHCHR for the first time, and also invited Special Rapporteur Pinheiro to undertake a mission to Burma.[23] Shortly thereafter, the Security Council unanimously adopted a presidential statement that drew heavily on the recommendations in the draft resolution that had been vetoed earlier that year.[24]

Engagement by the UN on Human Rights in Burma, 2010–2012

Until 2010, the human rights situation in Burma was without a doubt one of the worst in the world. Since 2010, the situation has only marginally improved. Public perception of reform in Burma has led to a reduction in media coverage about the human rights abuses in the country, particularly following the April 2012 parliamentary by-elections when Aung San Suu Kyi secured a seat in Parliament. However, the reality on the ground has yet to shift fundamentally. There have only been very limited changes to restrictive laws that historically have been used against political activists, journalists, lawyers, and civil society groups; though use of these laws does appear to be on the decline. Most of the 2,100 political prisoners detained in the country in 2010[25] have been released since President Thein Sein's inauguration, but it is estimated that there are hundreds likely still in prison today,[26] and under Section 401 of Burma's Code of Criminal Procedure, many of those released can be re-arrested without a warrant and required to serve the remainder of their original sentence at the discretion of the President.

Ethnic and religious minorities in Burma continue to be subject to grave human rights abuses. The military continues its attacks on people in Kachin and Northern Shan state in what it claims are anti-insurgency

---

[22] UN Human Rights Council, Resolution S-5/1, "Situation of Human Rights in Myanmar," UN GAOR, 63d Sess., Supp. No. 53 A/63/53, October 2, 2007.

[23] OHCHR, *2008 OHCHR Annual Report*, 30, 99.

[24] UN Security Council, "Security Council Deplores Violence Used Against Myanmar Demonstrators, Stresses Importance of Early Release for All Political Prisoners," PRST/SC/9139, October 11, 2007.

[25] UN Human Rights Council, *Progress Report of the Special Rapporteur on Human Rights in Myanmar*, U.N. Doc. A/HRC/13/48, para. 15, March 10, 2010.

[26] "Burma Releases 500 Prisoners in Amnesty" *BBC*, September 17, 2012.

actions but may be motivated by economic concerns related to the oil and natural gas pipeline that will run from Rakhine state to China, as well as the suspended Myitsone dam project. It has been estimated that more than 80,000 ethnic Kachin live in internally-displaced persons camps across the state,[27] and it has been reported that more than 100 Kachin have been detained illegally and face possible torture.[28] Ethnic violence is also ongoing in Rakhine state in Western Burma, which has led to at least 80 deaths and the internal displacement of 70,000 people. The Burmese military reportedly killed, raped, and carried out mass arrests of Rohingya Muslims after deadly sectarian riots there in June 2012, and the government has refused to grant citizenship to many members of that community.[29]

Despite these enduring challenges, in the last few years, the opportunities for the High Commissioner, OHCHR, and the Special Rapporteur to engage the Burmese government on human rights have increased dramatically. In 2012, the UN and the government signed a plan to end the recruitment of child soldiers into the military and secure their reintegration into society, which arose out of years of engagement by the Secretary-General's Special Representative on Children and Armed Conflict, Radhika Coomaraswamy, and the International Labour Organization (ILO).[30] The Burmese parliament also adopted laws to allow labor unions and to criminalize forced labor and pledged to end forced labor by 2015, leading the ILO to lift punitive restrictions that had been in place for more than a decade.[31] A number of areas of ongoing legal reform could improve the human rights situation, including the adoption of the Peaceful Demonstration and Gathering Law and amendment of the Political Party Registration Law, as well as the planned revision of laws on prisons, media, and social security.[32] The government has also acceded to the Convention on the Rights of Persons with Disabilities and the Optional Protocol to the Convention on the Rights of the Child on the Sale of Children, Child Prostitution and Child Pornography,[33] and President Thein Sein has

---

27 UN High Commissioner for Refugees, "Thousands flee homes in northern Myanmar as fighting intensifies," September 28, 2012, news release.

28 "Illegal Detentions Soar in Kachin State," *The Irrawaddy*, July 31, 2012.

29 Martin Petty, "Rohingya Muslims 'Persecuted' After Myanmar Crackdown: Report," *Reuters*, July 31, 2012.

30 "Press Conference on Action Plan to End Recruitment of Child Soldiers in Myanmar," UN news release, July 5, 2012.

31 "Burma Hopes for End of EU Tariffs," *Mizzima News*, July 17, 2012.

32 UN Human Rights Council, *Progress Report of the Special Rapporteur on Human Rights in Myanmar*, U.N. Doc. A/HRC/19/67, paras. 8–10, March 7, 2012.

33 Ibid., para. 2.

established a National Human Rights Commission, though its independence and competence have been questioned.[34] The government has also reduced censorship of newspapers and magazines and restrictions on tens of thousands of internet sites, allowing users access to some political content for the first time.[35] While the changes so far remain opaque, and it is unclear whether they are sufficiently robust to satisfy Burma's international legal obligations, they are nevertheless encouraging.

The High Commissioner

As of January 2013, the Office of the High Commissioner had yet to have a significant impact on the human rights situation in Burma. However, even as the country began to engage in greater cooperation with OHCHR, High Commissioner Pillay demonstrated her willingness to speak out on human rights abuses there. In July 2012, she issued a press release citing reports that the security forces in Rakhine state were engaged in a "crackdown targeting Muslims," and called on the Burmese authorities to carry out an investigation into the violations and to allow the Special Rapporteur to speak to members of all affected communities during a planned visit to the area in the coming days.[36]

OHCHR

The opening by the Burmese government in 2010 provided an opportunity for OHCHR to undertake technical cooperation activities in the country for the first time. These activities include assisting with a Universal Periodic Review workshop in 2010, training government officials in 2011, and undertaking a capacity-building project on human rights targeting the Myanmar National Human Rights Commission and related stakeholders such as judges and law enforcement officials. These activities have been directed from the OHCHR Regional Office in Bangkok, Thailand.

In addition, OHCHR has advised on the draft law establishing the National Human Rights Institution and has worked in cooperation with United Nations Office on Drugs and Crimes with Burma's Home Affairs Ministry's Prison Department on its draft prisons law. OHCHR is also involved in a number of joint activities with other partners, including a series of planned trainings for the Burmese government on the rule of law

---

34 Ibid., paras. 17–20.

35 "Burma Abolishes Media Censorship," *BBC*, August 20, 2012.

36 "Myanmar: Pillay concerned about human rights situation in Rakhine state," OHCHR news release, July 27, 2012.

and legislative reforms with UN Women and the United Nations Population Fund. OHCHR is exploring the potential for joint activities with the Resident Coordinator's office on business and human rights matters.[37]

In 2012, as this cooperation deepened, OHCHR entered into discussions with the Burmese government regarding the possibility of establishing a field presence in the country.

The Special Rapporteur

As Burma has opened, Special Rapporteur Quintana has highlighted the necessity for law reform in addition to describing incidents of human rights abuse.[38] He has particularly noted that the country still lacks an independent, impartial, and effective judiciary capable of upholding the rule of law and protecting human rights[39] and has cautioned that while the government's reforms to date have improved the human rights situation, much more remains to be done, and the risk remains that the country will backtrack on the progress it has achieved.[40]

Following a visit to Burma from July 30 through August 4, 2012, Quintana issued a detailed statement that identified a range of positive steps taken by the government and a host of ongoing challenges.[41] Echoing Navi Pillay's call for an independent investigation into the authorities' conduct in Rakhine state,[42] Quintana also urged the release of six UN staff detained in connection with the events there, calling the charges against them "unfounded."[43] Most significantly, following his visit, the Special Rapporteur called for the creation of a "truth commission," which he described as "crucial for democratic transition and national reconciliation" to "address [ ] grievances from decades of human rights violations,"[44] including the treatment of ethnic and religious minorities such as the Muslim Rohingyas.

---

37 Examples of recent activities were provided by OHCHR staff.

38 *Progress Report of the Special Rapporteur on Human Rights in Myanmar* (2012), para. 10.

39 Ibid., paras. 12–13.

40 Ibid., para. 84.

41 "Statement of the Special Rapporteur on the Situation of Human Rights in Myanmar," OHCHR news release, August 4, 2012.

42 "Myanmar: UN Official Concerned About Rights Violations in Rakhine State," *UN News Centre*, July 27, 2012.

43 Kocha Olarn, "UN Envoy Warns of 'Serious' Rights Situation in Myanmar," *CNN*, August 5, 2012.

44 "UN Envoy Calls for Myanmar Truth Commission," *Agence France-Presse*, August 4, 2012.

Special Rapporteur Quintana has worked aggressively to engage with the government, while staying true to his obligation to provide an independent and impartial assessment of the human rights situation in the country.[45] This is particularly impressive in a context in which a wave of public praise for President Thein Sein's stated commitment to reform and the suspension or lifting of economic sanctions against Burma has created immense public pressure on officials wanting to present an objective assessment of both meaningful progress and the challenges ahead.

Major Challenges in Engagement on Burma

The High Commissioner has faced three primary challenges in attempting to engage with Burma, and these remain today: government impunity, a lack of in-country access, and a lack of financial and administrative resources.

Government Impunity

The biggest obstacle to the High Commissioner having an impact in any country-specific situation is not having a serious governmental partner that is concerned about human rights. Historically, the Burmese government has been unwilling to take the concerns of the United Nations seriously. It not only ensured a lack of accountability for perpetrators but in fact orchestrated most of the abuses itself.

Part of this culture of impunity has been the Burmese government's denial that abuses identified even exist. For example, in response to the 2008 UN General Assembly resolution on Burma, the Government insisted that the resolution was based on "unsubstantiated accounts by those who oppose the Government" and denied well-documented accounts of thousands of child soldiers and rape of ethnic minority women.[46] When Burma's human rights record was examined in January 2011 as part of the Universal Periodic Review process, its report ignored virtually every major human rights problem facing the country[47] and its delegation rejected numerous concerns

---

[45] UN Human Rights Council, Resolution 5/2, "Code of Conduct for Special Procedures Mandate-holders of the Human Rights Council," UN Doc. A/HRC/RES/5/2, June 18, 2007.

[46] Permanent Rep. of Myanmar to the U.N., Annex to Letter Dated 23 October 2009 from the Permanent Rep. of Myanmar to the U.N. Addressed to the Secretary-General, U.N. Doc. A/C.3/64/2, October 26, 2009, para. 3.

[47] UN Human Rights Council, *National Report Submitted in Accordance With Paragraph 15(a) of the Annex of Human Rights Council Resolution 5/1: Myanmar*, U.N. Doc. A/HRC/WG.6/10/MMR/1, November 10, 2010.

wholesale, making comments that were patently false.[48] President Thein Sein extended this pattern of denial, rejecting the use of the term 'prisoner of conscience' to describe any imprisoned persons in the country.[49]

In July 2012, the Burmese Foreign Ministry "strongly reject[ed]" concerns raised by the High Commissioner and Special Rapporteur that security forces had engaged in excessive force in Rakhine state,[50] and President Thein Sein proposed that UNHCR take responsibility for the 800,000 Rohingyas residing in the country. The President's proposal, if actually implemented, would amount to the crimes against humanity of deportation or forcible transfer of a population and persecution against an identifiable group on racial, ethnic, and religious grounds.

As a prerequisite to ending impunity, the government must acknowledge that abuses have been committed in the first place.

Lack of In-Country Access

All UN officials face a serious challenge in working to promote and protect human rights. On the one hand, doing their job well requires access to the county in question. But on the other, it is critically important that they truthfully address the severity of the human rights situation. Often the most repressive regimes refuse to cooperate with OHCHR field staff and special rapporteurs and deny them access if they criticize the situation in the country.

The Special Rapporteurs on the human rights situation in Myanmar, as a result of their public reports, have found themselves denied access for extended periods and subjected to lengthy delays in obtaining visas to visit the country. Even when they have been able to visit, they have reported difficulties obtaining requested meetings and access to certain parts of the country. In one case, then-Special Rapporteur Paulo Sergio Pinheiro cut short his visit to Burma after discovering a bugging device the size of a packet of cigarettes taped under a table in Insein Prison where he was meeting with political prisoners.[51]

---

48 UN Human Rights Council, *Report of the Working Group on Universal Periodic Review: Myanmar*, U.N. Doc. A/HRC/17/9, March 24, 2011.

49 Nay Thwin, "Thein Sein Says No Political Prisoners," *Democratic Voice of Burma*, November 21, 2011. More recently, however, President Thein Sein said there would be no prisoners of conscience by the end of the year. Time will tell if this commitment will come to fruition.

50 "Burma Rejects Criticism of Response to Buddhist-Muslim Riots," *Voice of America*, July 30, 2012.

51 Dominic Whiting, "Bugged UN Envoy Urges Myanmar to Free Political Prisoners," *Reuters*, March 26, 2003.

Although UN officials generally have access to Burma now, access to conflict zones such as Kachin and Rakhine states, each of which contains some 75,000 internally displaced persons, is severely restricted and must be negotiated on a case-by-case basis.[52] Special Rapporteur Quintana was able to travel to Rakhine state during his July-August 2012 visit to the country, but it will be critical for him to obtain unrestricted access to other conflict zones, and to meet with ethnic minorities and the political opposition.

In the coming years, the High Commissioner will also be faced with the challenge of balancing the need to gain the Burmese government's assent for access against the need to speak out against human rights abuses. Should the government agree to allow the High Commissioner to establish an OHCHR field presence, the High Commissioner must ensure that it has guaranteed unrestricted access to the entire territory, and both a mandate and a willingness to monitor human rights conditions and comment publicly on incidents of abuse.

Lack of Financial and Administrative Support for the Special Rapporteur

All the special procedures are unpaid experts who rely on administrative and financial support from OHCHR. Given the challenging situation in Burma, there have never been remotely sufficient resources allocated to assisting the Special Rapporteur on the human rights situation in Myanmar in gathering information, addressing specific complaints, traveling to the country, and reporting on the situation. Indeed, the Special Rapporteur has had only between one-third and one-half of a full-time staff person (OHCHR country desk officers often cover two to three countries) and the periodic support of UN officials inside the country and in Thailand when the Rapporteur visited the country and region.

The first two Special Rapporteurs on human rights in Myanmar complained about this issue publically. Yozo Yokota resigned both because of personal career changes but also what he cited as his frustration with a "lack of logistical support from human rights staff in Geneva."[53] Rajsoomer Lallah also resigned from his post citing "resource difficulties" and stating, "If I don't have the support, I don't feel I can contribute what I usually can....Maybe there are some resource difficulties ...maybe states of the UN should do more about financing."[54]

---

52 Seamus Martov, "UN Cannot Reach 25,000 Kachin Refugees," *The Irrawaddy*, August 17, 2012.

53 "UN Rights Monitor for Burma Resigns," *Reuters*, June 28, 1996.

54 "UN Rapporteur on Burma Resigns," *BBC*, November 4, 2000.

To be fair, OHCHR depends on the General Assembly for the allocation of regular budget resources. These funds provide minimal assistance to each special procedure mandate, and the budget for many mandates does not allow even for a full-time staff member. In such cases, OHCHR does its best to make up for this lack of resources with extra-budgetary funds. Further, OHCHR has had to cope with many additional unfunded mandates including the productions of reports/studies and hosting of major meetings. Nevertheless, the High Commissioner should continue to urge Member States to allocate more resources for special procedure mandates in general and Burma in particular. As the situation in Burma continues to evolve rapidly, providing additional staff support to the Special Rapporteur, perhaps located at an in-country office of OHCHR, could be invaluable.

Ultimately, these three primary challenges, among many others, have made it virtually impossible for OHCHR and the Special Rapporteur to have any meaningful and sustainable impact on Burma's record on human rights. These challenges will also continue to limit the effectiveness in Burma of OHCHR and the Special Rapporteur going forward.

The Way Forward for Future Engagement on Human Rights with Burma

If I had been asked immediately after the inauguration of President Thein Sein to write about the future of human rights in Burma, I would have painted a bleak picture. However, his approach thus far has been a dramatic change in tone for the leadership of the country. While many observers have concluded this means a clear course towards democratization and respect for human rights in the country, Aung San Suu Kyi's 'cautious optimism' seems to be the appropriate response at present.[55]

It is impossible to understate the size, scale, and scope of the challenges facing today's Burma. On the one hand, nothing irreversible has changed in the country: the 2008 Constitution enshrining permanent control of the military remains unchanged, and human rights abuses abound. It is unclear if the military, judiciary, and parliament, let alone the government agencies of the executive branch, share President Thein Sein's spoken commitments or will implement his reforms. Yet on the other hand, the President's openness and approach to governing and engaging with the

[55] "Aung San Suu Kyi: Should Be Cautiously Optimistic About Future of Myanmar," *Dow Jones*, May 31, 2012.

international community has marked a major break from Burma's authoritarian and isolationist past.

Given this potentially profoundly different approach, the High Commissioner and Special Rapporteur are uniquely positioned to support the government's stated commitment to reform and ensure genuine advancement of the promotion and protection of human rights in Burma. I make the following recommendations as to how the High Commissioner can help achieve this critical goal.

Establish an OHCHR Field Presence in Burma

Given the changes underway and the potential for further change, a key goal for the High Commissioner should be opening an office in Rangoon with appropriate staff support. Such an office should have a mandate to engage in activities such as monitoring, public reporting, provision of technical assistance, and the development of long-term capacities to address human rights issues in the country. This office could also provide in-country assistance to the High Commissioner and special rapporteur. The Burmese government previously committed to allowing such an office to be opened on the eve of President Obama's visit to the country in November 2012,[56] but there have been delays in reaching an agreement.

Alternatively, the Office of the High Commissioner could deploy a Human Rights Adviser to Burma. Such individuals, typically requested by UN Resident Coordinators, advise the UN Country Teams as a whole on strategies to build and strengthen the capacity of countries and their institutions in promoting and protecting human rights. They also engage with government and civil society on how best to promote and implement human rights standards.[57]

Secure Appropriate Resources for Work on Burma

I also recommend the High Commissioner seek and secure substantial additional budgetary support for OHCHR's work on Burma. As has been noted previously, the lack of resources allocated to staff support for the Special Rapporteur is a major obstacle to anyone in the position,

---

56 "Press Gaggle by Press Secretary Jay Carney and Deputy National Security Advisor Ben Rhodes," http://www.whitehouse.gov/the-press-office/2012/11/19/press-gaggle-press-secretary-jay-carney-and-deputy-national-security-adv.

57 OHCHR, "OHCHR in the World: Making Human Rights a Reality on the Ground," http://www.ohchr.org/EN/Countries/Pages/WorkInField.aspx.

particularly one who serves as a volunteer, having a demonstrable impact on the situation.

While resources are scarce at the UN and especially in the High Commissioner's Office, this moment of change in Burma must be taken advantage of, and only a properly resourced Office can ensure that human rights reforms are not forgotten as economic reforms in Burma advance. It will be particularly important for governments that wish to encourage reform in Burma to support the High Commissioner's efforts to secure the additional resources required, including considering earmarked country donations.

Defend the Mandate of the Special Rapporteur

There will undoubtedly be a number of governments, and perhaps the Burmese government itself, which will advocate for the abolition of the Special Rapporteur position or the watering down of the mandate when it comes up for its annual renewal by the Human Rights Council. Those so arguing may claim the position has been punitive and is no longer necessary given the change in approach of the Burmese government. It must be made clear that the work of the Special Rapporteur is intended to help the country achieve the goals that President Thein Sein has articulated and offers constructive advice about how to improve the country's adherence to international human rights standards. It is essential that this position be maintained and that it not be discontinued until the situation itself is substantially and irreversibly changed.

Engage Personally on Human Rights in Burma

Given the change in circumstances in Burma, which now provide significant opportunities to engage with the government, I recommend the High Commissioner take a much more public and active personal role in promoting and protecting human rights in the country. It is especially important that she visit Burma as soon as possible. While such a visit will provide opportunities to engage with government officials in Naypyidaw, she should push to visit areas currently inaccessible to the United Nations in Kachin and Rakhine states. While the more limited engagement of High Commissioners in the past could be explained by the lower opportunity for impact, there is now no substitute for the highest level engagement with the Burmese government to help advance human rights in the country.

Focus on Rule of Law and Law Reform

I recommend the High Commissioner and Special Rapporteur continue to prioritize and expand their efforts focused on advancing of the rule of law and law reform efforts. It is important that an appropriate balance be struck between monitoring and reporting on the human rights situation in Burma and assisting the reform process through the provision of training and technical support. Regular reporting on positive developments with respect to rule of law and ongoing challenges could be a major source of information in a system that remains opaque and would help focus international attention to top-priority issues of concern. The Special Rapporteur could also play a crucial role in ensuring appropriate training and technical support is provided. He is uniquely positioned to identify major legal reform needs and to mobilize and connect stakeholders in activities such as building an independent judiciary; drafting and amending legislation that is consistent with Burma's international legal obligations and best practices; and building capacity across all sectors to advance the rule of law.

With respect to rule of law and law reform, there are specific areas that should be priorities for the High Commissioner and Special Rapporteur: constitutional reform, creating an independent judiciary, and prioritizing legislative reform for those laws that lead to the most significant abuses of human rights. Without constitutional reform, major policy changes ensuring human rights are likely to be limited, ignored, or reversed. The current Constitution was adopted in 2008 in a constitutional referendum process which independent observers do not consider credible.[58] Moreover, the Constitution provides for military veto of decisions of the executive, legislative, and judicial branches of government; affords permanent immunity to the military for prior and future acts; and reserves 25 percent of the seats in the Parliament for the military, but requires an 80 percent vote to amend. It is therefore impossible for Parliament to adopt or change laws, let alone amend the Constitution, without the military's support. Moreover, the political opposition in Parliament, composed of Aung San Suu Kyi's National League for Democracy and its allies, currently holds less than 10 percent of seats.

Further, regardless other reforms, Burma needs an independent, impartial, and effective judiciary to uphold the rule of law, to act as a last

[58] "Myanmar Declares Victory for the Constitution – State Media," *Agence France-Presse*, May 26, 2008.

guarantor for safeguarding fundamental freedoms and human rights, and to ensure checks and balances on the legislative and executive branches, as well as the military. Legislative reform is also needed, particularly with respect to the State Protection Law, Electronic Transactions Law, Unlawful Associations Act, Criminal Law, and Criminal Procedure Law. Collectively, these laws allowed the regime to perpetuate some of its most dramatic human rights abuses. These laws must be significantly amended and then adhered to in order for human rights to be protected in Burma.

Focus on Foreign Investment and Human Rights

As the Special Rapporteur has noted, a "flood of foreign investment" could have a profoundly positive effect on Burma, particularly if it is conducted with a "human rights-based approach," which would ensure "the principles of participation, non-discrimination, transparency, accountability and the rule of law guide [the] process."[59] Former High Commissioner for Human Rights Mary Robinson similarly noted in a 2012 letter to EU foreign ministers that they should "make clear that respect for international human rights standards is integral to future trade with and investment in Myanmar."[60] However, a human rights based approach to investment will not be welcomed easily by the Burmese government or foreign investors.

The Special Rapporteur, in cooperation with the UN Working Group on the Issue of Human Rights and Transnational Corporations and Other Business Enterprises and with the support of the UN Country Team, is uniquely positioned to monitor foreign investment with a human rights-based approach. For example, the Special Rapporteur could lead a joint effort to produce a major report in six months and then perhaps at regular intervals report both on positive developments in this area and areas of substantial concern. The High Commissioner should encourage both the Special Rapporteur and the Working Group to pursue this approach.

Support the Establishment of a Truth and Reconciliation Commission

The High Commissioner should support Special Rapporteur Quintana's call for the establishment of a truth commission for Burma. Although at

---

59 *Constitution of the Republic of the Union of Myanmar* (Government of Myanmar, 2008).

60 "Open Letter from Mary Robinson and John Ruggie to EU Foreign Ministers and EU High Representative," April 19, 2012, http://www.ihrb.org/news/2012/open-letter-from-mary-robinson-and-john-ruggie-to-eu-foreign-ministers-and-eu-high-representative.html.

this point is it unlikely that the international community will create a commission of inquiry on Burma, a truth commission to support investigations into past abuses could aid Burma and its ethnically diverse population in moving forward towards democracy.

The Special Rapporteur has stated that Parliament should begin the process of creating such a truth commission by engaging in a process of consultation with all stakeholders on its shape.[61] The High Commissioner should offer public support for this proposal and should assist the Special Rapporteur in engaging the appropriate stakeholders to both provide for a truth commission and ensure its effectiveness. Only a truth commission that includes the diverse range of Burmese stakeholders, is properly resourced, and has an appropriate mandate of restorative justice can move Burma forward.

Conclusion

One cannot be especially critical of the High Commissioner for failing to achieve meaningful progress on respect for human rights in Burma over the past 20 years when the international community as a whole also failed until recently to achieve substantial improvements in any area. It has been particularly difficult for the High Commissioner to achieve results because neither she nor the independent human rights mechanisms staffed by OHCHR have enforcement power beyond moral suasion. Yet despite this modest record, if properly positioned, the High Commissioner, alone and with the support of the Special Rapporteur, could play a crucial role in ensuring change in Burma in the years to come.

The international community must not be content with Potemkin changes in Burma. It must remain vigilant in ensuring that all people of Burma have the human rights promised in the Universal Declaration of Human Rights and range of treaties to which the government is a party. This will remain an extraordinary challenge in the years to come, but this should not deter the High Commissioner or the world from their moral and legal obligation to do so.

61 "UN Envoy Calls for Myanmar Truth Commission," *Agence France-Presse*, August 4, 2012.

THE IMPACT OF THE HIGH COMMISSIONER ON HUMAN RIGHTS PROTECTION IN COLOMBIA[1]

Victor Rodriguez-Rescia

Background

Large, systematic violations of human rights in the context of historical structural violence – an armed conflict that has been raging for over 50 years – justified the establishment of a field presence of the Office of the UN High Commissioner for Human Rights (hereinafter "OHCHR") in Colombia in 1997. Since that time, significant changes have occurred in the country. Meaningful progress has been made in human rights protection and strengthening democratic institutions and the rule of law. The government has taken steps in the right direction to establish a transitional justice process through the adoption of laws relating to compensation to victims of armed conflict. Nevertheless, Colombia remains 'two different countries': Bogota, the capital, and other main cities where the rule of law and functioning democratic institutions exist; and the rest of the country, especially those departments where the state's institutional presence is weak and it lacks exclusive control over the territory.

To argue that levels of violence in Colombia have declined solely because of the presence of the OHCHR in the country would be pretentious. However, there is no doubt that the Office has provided great support for a significant increase in the promotion and protection of human rights in Colombia. Indeed, the on-the-ground activities of the Office, as well as its annual reports and its press releases, have provided added value. In sum, these efforts have increased the visibility of human rights in Colombia and improved Colombians' understanding of their rights and how to claim them; encouraged the government to more vigorously pursue implementation of human rights treaties; and contributed to the strengthening of the country's democratic institutions.

[1] Based on remarks delivered at "The UN High Commissioner for Human Rights: Conscience for the World," (conference convened by the Jacob Blaustein Institute for the Advancement of Human Rights, New York, NY, February 7–8, 2012).

The Context of Violence

Colombia is a country with human rights problems shared by many Latin American countries, but with the addition of international humanitarian law violations stemming from the internal armed conflict. This is the most important difference between Colombia and other Latin American countries.

Colombia is facing a long-standing internal armed conflict which began in the 1950s and which has intensified during the past 20 years.[2] Today, following a restructuring of the parties to the conflict, the main actors are, first, two groups of 'guerrillas,' the Revolutionary Armed Forces of Colombia (FARC in Spanish)[3] and the National Liberation Army (ELN in Spanish); paramilitary groups united under the umbrella of the United Self-Defense Forces of Colombia (AUC in Spanish); and the state, represented by the Armed Forces of Colombia.

After years of traditional military engagement, the nature of the conflict in Colombia changed, as irregular groups became involved in the production and trafficking of drugs. As a result, they have become known as 'narco-guerrillas' and 'narco-paramilitaries.' The armed conflict has thus 'mutated' from an ideological revolutionary struggle to an illegal effort to control territory and overseas production and distribution channels for cocaine.

In the coming years, a number of very complex issues and challenges must be addressed to ensure a successful transition away from conflict. These include ensuring demobilization, including by increasing the dismantling of armed groups and the gradual reintegration of their members into society to ensure that the events that led to previous gross violations of human rights will not be repeated.

The OHCHR Field Presence in Colombia

Background to the Establishment of the Office

In 1996, the Colombian government and the United Nations signed an agreement in Geneva establishing a field office of the High Commissioner

---

[2] Office of the High Commissioner for Human Rights in Colombia, "Pronouncement on the Recognition of Internal Armed Conflict in Colombia," [in Spanish] press release, May 10, 2011, http://www.hchr.org.co/publico/comunicados/2011/comunicados2011.php3?cod=9&cat=86.

[3] The FARC is the largest and most belligerent group.

for Human Rights in Colombia. This agreement has been extended periodically, most recently through 2013. In addition to an office in Bogota, the capital, OHCHR has established offices in the cities of Bucaramanga, Cali, and Medellin.

The impetus for the establishment of the OHCHR office in Colombia came from the first High Commissioner, José Ayala Lasso of Ecuador, who suggested to Colombian President Ernesto Samper at a meeting on December 13, 1994 that the President of the Republic might wish to consider the appointment of an expert, based in Colombia, who could provide technical assistance in the areas of legislative reform and the administration of justice.[4] Following this meeting, the High Commissioner sent an evaluation mission to visit Colombia in 1995 to ascertain the country's technical cooperation needs. The report of this mission recommended in part that the High Commissioner establish an office in Colombia to advise the government and relevant institutions on human rights. Samper officially expressed his support for the establishment of an office of the High Commissioner in Colombia in writing on April 2, 1996,[5] and on November 29, 1996, High Commissioner Ayala Lasso and the Colombian Minister for Foreign Affirms signed an official Agreement on the Establishment of an Office of the United Nations High Commissioner for Human Rights in Colombia.[6]

OHCHR's Mandate in Colombia

The OHCHR Colombia field presence was mandated to perform four main tasks: (1) to observe, systematically and analytically, the situation of human rights and international humanitarian law throughout the country; (2) to advise authorities (national, regional, and local) and civil society organizations on these issues and ensure that any proposed draft laws touching on human rights respect Colombia's international human rights obligations; (3) to provide technical cooperation to the state authorities and civil society organizations working to promote respect for human rights and observance of international humanitarian law; and (4) to

---

[4] UN Commission on Human Rights, *Report of the United Nations High Commissioner for Human Rights on Colombia*, UN Doc. E/CN.4/1997/11, January 24, 1997, para. 4.

[5] OHCHR, "Agreement for the Establishment of an Office of the UN High Commissioner for Human Rights in Colombia" [in Spanish] November 29, 1996, http://www.hchr.org.co/sobrenosotros/mandato.php3.

[6] *Report of the United Nations High Commissioner for Human Rights on Colombia*, UN Doc. E/CN.4/1997/11, para. 12.

inform, disseminate, and promote human rights and international humanitarian law among the Colombian population. The most recent extension of the Office's mandate specifically tasks the Office with a cooperative project: to advise to the government in creating a 'National Human Rights Center' that will develop, coordinate, and implement a comprehensive public policy on human rights.[7] OHCHR's work in Colombia must also comply with an agenda, focus, and priorities defined by the High Commissioner for Human Rights.

Representatives of the High Commissioner for Human Rights in Colombia

The first Representative of the High Commissioner in Colombia, Ms. Almudena Mazarrasa (1997–1998), a Spanish diplomat, focused her efforts on establishing the Office and providing the basis for it to fulfill its mandate. On 25 April 1997, the Colombian government issued Presidential Directive No. 05, in which all executive agencies, including the armed forces and the national police, were informed of the Office's establishment and functions and were advised to cooperate with it.[8] Most of the public statements issued by the Office during Mazarrasa's tenure denounced acts of human rights violations. However, Mazarrasa also recommended against the appointment of a special rapporteur of the Commission of Human Rights on Colombia, saying in a 1998 interview that "Colombia's human rights problems will not be resolved by international denunciations, but with international support."[9] She added that her view was that international delegates should play a completely neutral role in politically polarized environments like that prevailing in Colombia.

Mazarrasa left Colombia at the end of 1998, and her successors, the second and third Representatives of the High Commissioner in Colombia, Anders Kompass (1999–2002) and Michael Frühling (2002–2006), both from Sweden, were significantly more visible in their presence and impact on human rights in Colombia. The activities of the Office under both Kompass and Frühling consisted largely of carrying out observation

---

[7] Office of the High Commissioner for Human Rights in Colombia, "Government of Colombia and UN High Commissioner for Human Rights Extend Presence of UN Office in the Country for Three Years," [in Spanish] press release, November 23, 2010, http://www.hchr.org.co/publico/comunicados/2010/comunicados2010.php3?cod=36&cat=81.

[8] UN Commission on Human Rights, *Report by the United Nations High Commissioner for Human Rights*, UN Doc. E/CN.4/1998/16, March 9, 1998.

[9] Maria Isabel Garcia, "Conflict-Colombia: Fear, Mistrust Hamper Peace Process," *Inter Press Service*, December 16, 1998.

missions in the field and developing projects consistent with the findings obtained in these observations.

Kompass' tenure was characterized by direct and clear criticism of the country's human rights violations and structural conditions that allowed these to persist. For example, Kompass sharply criticized the failure of the Colombian judicial system to provide accountability for human rights violations.[10] He also issued damning reports on specific incidents of violations, including one in 2002 which found the Colombian Army responsible by omission for the massacre of 117 people inside a church at Bellavista-Bojayá by paramilitary fighters. The report was rejected by the Attorney General and the Army.[11]

Frühling's exposure in the media was particularly significant. For example, he openly challenged the approach to the conflict championed by President Uribe and some of his ministers, particularly with regards to the President's denial that the situation in Colombia constituted an internal armed conflict to which international humanitarian law was applicable.[12] Frühling also challenged the relationship of the Colombian government to paramilitary groups, arguing publicly that "the paramilitaries' self-assumed and illegal role in the internal armed conflict has led in a number of cases to collusion between paramilitary groups and individual public officials, both civilian and military. ... Some progress has been made, but much, much more needs to be done: the links with paramilitary groups still exist."[13] As a result of Frühling's critical posture, the relationship between OHCHR and the Colombian government grew increasingly strained over the course of his tenure. Near the end of Frühling's mandate, the Colombian government refused to extend the mandate of the Colombia office for a four-year term as requested by OHCHR, and instead

---

[10] Anders Kompass, interview by Javier Arboleda García and Carlos Alberto Giraldo, *Grandes Entrevistas*, El Colombiano, June 10, 2002, http://www.elcolombiano.com/proyectos/grandes_entrevistas/2002/junio/10/kompas.htm.

[11] Ibid.

[12] Arlene B. Tickner and Rodrigo Pardo, "In Search of Allies for 'Democratic Security': The Foreign Policy of the First Year of the Uribe Administration," [in Spanish] *Colombia International*, no. 56–57, (September 2002 – June 2003): 64–81, http://colombiainternacional.uniandes.edu.co/view.php/461/index.php?id=461; Michael Frühling, interview by Carlos Fernando Galán and Jorge Enrique Meléndez, "Frühling Bids Farewell to Colombia" [in Spanish] *El Tiempo*, February 22, 2006, http://www.eltiempo.com/archivo/documento/MAM-1925716.

[13] Michael Frühling in "The Peace Process in Colombia with the *Autodefensas Unidas de Colombia*-AUC," *Woodrow Wilson Center Report on the Americas #13*, ed. Cynthia J. Arnson (2005), 71.

authorized only one additional year of operation.[14] After Frühling's departure was announced, the Colombian government reportedly rejected the High Commissioner's first-choice successor,[15] and also threatened to eliminate the Office's mandate to publicly criticize human rights abuses in Colombia and to publish an annual report on the country, preferring instead to restrict its activities to the provision of technical assistance to the government.[16]

Juan Pablo Corlazzoli, a Uruguayan sociologist with over 30 years' experience working in Latin American and African countries, ultimately succeeded Michael Frühling as Representative of the High Commissioner in Colombia following Frühling's departure in 2006. He focused much of his efforts on reducing the stress between the Office and the government.

In part, Corlazzoli sought to accomplish this by increasingly recognizing the government's efforts to address human rights challenges and softening the tone of OHCHR reports highlighting human rights violations in the country. The effort was largely successful in dampening the Colombian government's hostility to OHCHR: in 2007, unlike in previous years, the Colombian government received the Office's annual report on the country "with satisfaction," and agreed to extend the Office's mandate thereafter.

Christian Salazar Volkmann of Germany succeeded Corlazzoli as Representative of the High Commissioner in Colombia on March 2, 2009. Under his leadership, OHCHR sought to recover the visibility and the impact it had had before 2006, and particularly to implement projects in cooperation with the government and to create openings with the Army and the Ministry of Defense. During his tenure, OHCHR Colombia supported the development of the military judicial system in Colombia to make it more professional, independent, and impartial.

The current Representative of the High Commissioner, Todd Howland, an American citizen, assumed the post of Director of the OHCHR Colombia office on January 30, 2012. Howland has more than 25 years' experience working on human rights and international humanitarian law and previously represented OHCHR in the Democratic Republic of Congo and

---

[14] Joshua Goodman, "Extrajudicial Killings by Colombia's Security Forces Rose Last Year, UN Reports Says," *Associated Press*, March 16, 2007.

[15] This was reportedly Scott Campbell, deputy director of the advocacy group Global Rights, based in Washington, DC, which had criticized the Colombian government's human rights practices. See "Colombia: President Alvaro Uribe Seeks to Restrict UN Human Rights Group, Say Diplomats," *NotiSur – South American Political and Economic Affairs*, September 8, 2006.

[16] Ibid.

Angola. In his first months in the post, Howland displayed an interest in maintaining the Office's tradition of condemnation of violations combined with support to the government on technical issues. For example, he publicly condemned cases of terrorism, kidnapping, and threats and attacks against human rights defenders, and also commented on transitional justice initiatives.[17]

The Work of the OHCHR Field Presence in Colombia

Press Releases

An analysis of OHCHR's press releases issued since 1997 on Colombia reveals that most of these, especially during the first years of operation of the Colombia Office, refer to alleged violations of human rights. The primary subject is acts of violence committed by state officials or guerrilla or paramilitary groups. Most public condemnations relate to crimes against humanity; massacres; assassinations; torture; forced disappearances; abductions; and threats against human rights defenders, union activists, judicial personnel, politicians, and relatives of victims of human rights violations. Of these victims, OHCHR's press releases most frequently highlight human rights defenders – indeed, the Office has issued such press releases every year since its establishment.[18] Additionally, several press releases call on the parties to the conflict to try to find a negotiated solution that respects human rights and international humanitarian law standards.

Some events on which the Office has reported since its installation in Colombia include the retention of OAS observers in 1997; attacks against members of the police and the army by irregular armed groups; massacres of peasants; murder, kidnapping and threats to union leaders, activists and human rights defenders; terrorist attacks against facilities and buildings perceived as having a military objective; acts of terrorism committed

---

[17] cf. "Press Releases of 2012," [in Spanish] Office of the High Commissioner for Human Rights in Colombia, accessed January 13, 2013, http://www.hchr.org.co/publico/comunicados/2012/comunicados2012.php3?cat=88.

[18] See, e.g., Office of the High Commissioner for Human Rights in Colombia, "Office of the United Nations for Human Rights Condemns Threats Against Defenders of Human Rights,"[in Spanish] press release, July 5, 2012, http://www.hchr.org.co/publico/comunicados/2012/cp1210.pdf; Office of the High Commissioner for Human Rights in Colombia, "High Commissioner Calls for Intensification of Efforts to protect Defenders of Human Rights in Colombia," [in Spanish] press release, June 24, 2002, http://www.hchr.org.co/publico/comunicados/2002/comunicados2002.php3?cod=19&cat=17.

against the civilian population; the kidnapping and holding in the jungle for years of public officials and politicians by irregular armed groups (especially FARC); and the commission of extrajudicial killings known as 'false positives' by the authorities.[19]

OHCHR also issued press releases confirming the facts of particularly notorious violations of human rights. For example, in 2011, OHCHR issued a press release supporting a 2005 decision by the Inter-American Court of Human Rights finding paramilitaries responsible for a massacre at Mapiripán in 1997 (and the state responsibility for supporting, acquiescing, and tolerating the group's activities) when that decision came under challenge.[20]

In one key battle, OHCHR also engaged in a dispute with the Colombian government under the administration of President Uribe over whether the situation in Colombia could be considered as constituting an 'armed conflict.' President Uribe's denial that the situation rose to the level of an armed conflict implied that international humanitarian law did not apply to the situation in Colombia, and therefore that victims of the violence were entitled to less protection. OHCHR disagreed, noting that Colombia should apply best practices to the situation to ensure the most robust protection for victims, and that the application of international humanitarian law would persist only so long as an internal armed conflict existed. OHCHR's position likely paved the way for Uribe's successor, President Juan Manuel Santos, to officially admit the existence of internal armed conflict in Colombia and to acknowledge that solutions to the conflict would have to be proposed within the framework of international humanitarian law.

Annual Reports

OHCHR prepares and publishes annual reports of the High Commissioner for Human Rights on the situation of human rights in Colombia, drawing heavily from input from the Colombia Office; these reports make recom-

---

[19] Office of the High Commissioner for Human Rights in Colombia, "United Nations Office of the High Commissioner for Human Rights in Colombia Urges Coordinated Efforts and Leadership to Clarify and Put an End the Practice of Alleged Extrajudicial Executions," [in Spanish] press release, September 26, 2008, http://www.hchr.org.co/publico/comunicados/2008/comunicados2008.php3?cod=21&cat=73.

[20] Office of the High Commissioner for Human Rights in Colombia, "United Nations Office of the High Commissioner for Human Rights Statement about the Mapiripán Case," [in Spanish] press release, November 1, 2011, http://www.hchr.org.co/publico/comunicados/2011/comunicados2011.php3?cod=19&cat=86.

mendations for future courses of action and are read by a wide group of key actors. The annual reports of the High Commissioner on Colombia are the clearest reference of the impact of that office in Colombia, as they recount the events and situations that have affected significant numbers of people but also recognize positive developments that have occurred. The recommendations made in the annual reports provide clear guidelines for both the state and irregular armed groups and are grounded in international human rights and international humanitarian law.

One of the main concerns of the Office has been pushing for an end to the internal armed conflict by means of a negotiated, sustainable peace. This is reflected, for example, in the recommendations of the High Commissioner's annual report on Colombia for 2010.[21] The High Commissioner's annual reports also take care to consistently reference the binding application of international humanitarian law in Colombia not only to the actions of the government but also to those of irregular armed groups. In this regard, the High Commissioner's February 2011 report "reiterates once again the call on all armed actors to fully accept and abide by international humanitarian law; and firmly insists that illegal armed groups release all kidnapped persons immediately and unconditionally, stop child recruitment and use, release all children in their ranks, and desist from using anti-personnel mines…."[22]

These annual reports are intended to influence public policies and actions of the government and to motivate officials to improve the human rights situation in the country. For example, the Foreign Affairs Ministry includes information from the OHCHR reports in its reports to the various human rights committees of the United Nations and the Inter-American Commission of Human Rights. The OHCHR reports are also used by nongovernmental organizations in preparing 'shadow' reports to international human rights bodies considering the situation in Colombia. OHCHR reports also serve as a source of documentation of cases and situations of human rights violations that can complement evidence in cases pending before national or international judicial mechanisms. OHCHR's reports are also incorporated into other UN reports on Colombia, such as the UN Development Programme (UNDP) Human Development Report on Colombia.

---

21 UN Human Rights Council, *Report of the United Nations High Commissioner for Human Rights on the situation of human rights in Colombia*, UN Doc. A/HRC/16/22, February 3, 2011, para. 107.

22 Ibid, para. 109.

Thematic Reports

To date, OHCHR has issued five thematic reports: a 2001 report on the situation of prisons in Colombia;[23] a 2002 report containing guidelines for the reorientation of the work of the public defender;[24] a 2002 report on an observation mission to the Middle Atrato–Bojaya, in which the Office investigated the killings of over 110 civilians by armed groups;[25] a 2003 follow-up report on that mission;[26] and a 2010 report on the Cemetery of La Macarena, Meta Department, at which the Office had found evidence of a large number of unidentified bodies buried in individual graves.[27] The impact of these reports depends on the time and circumstances in which they are issued. One of the most controversial reports was the Bojaya report, in which OHCHR supported the version of events put forward by FARC about the circumstances surrounding the civilian deaths it investigated and criticized the Colombian government for failing to take necessary steps to protect civilians despite advance warning of the harm they faced, and for collaborating with paramilitaries who used civilians as human shields.

Field Missions

OHCHR periodically carries out field missions, either on its own or together with state institutions like the Ombudsman. Some examples are a joint visit undertaken by OHCHR with the Ombudsman's Office to the Community of Caldono in 2001 and to the Department of Arauca and to the Municipality of San Carlos (East of Antioquia) in 2003, and visits to Cali and Medellin. Apart from these joint visits, OHCHR also conducts

---

[23] Federico Marcos Martínez, Morris Tidball-Binz, and Raquel Z. Yrigoyen Fajardo, *Report on Prisons in Colombia: An Unconstitutional State and the Flagrant Violation of Human Rights* [in Spanish] (Bogotá: OHCHR, October 31, 2001), http://www.hchr.org.co/documentoseinformes/informes/tematicos/informes.php3?cod=3&cat=13.

[24] Office of the High Commissioner for Human Rights in Colombia, Assessment of the Ordinary Penal Program of the Public Defender, [in Spanish] April 15, 2002.

[25] Office of the High Commissioner of Human Rights in Colombia, *Report on the Observation Mission in Medio Atrato*, [in Spanish] (Bogotá: OHCHR, May 20, 2002), http://www.hchr.org.co/documentoseinformes/informes/tematicos/bojaya.pdf.

[26] Office of the High Commissioner for Human Rights in Colombia, *Monitoring Report on the Situation in Medio Atrato*, [in Spanish] (Bogotá: OHCHR, June 2003), http://www.hchr.org.co/documentoseinformes/informes/tematicos/seguimientobojaya0703.pdf.

[27] Office of the High Commissioner for Human Rights in Colombia, *Report on the Cemetery of La Macarena, Meta Department*, [in Spanish] (Bogotá: OHCHR, September 7, 2010), http://www.hchr.org.co/documentoseinformes/informes/tematicos/cp1029.pdf.

independent field visits in which it has documented cases and situations of human rights violations. The findings of OHCHR field visits are then used as the basis for its press releases, thematic reporting, and annual reports. The effectiveness of OHCHR field visits has been enhanced through the establishment of branches of the Colombia field presence outside Bogota, such as in Bucaramanga, Cali, and Medellin.

However, while OHCHR's field missions in Colombia have been useful, the visits of UN special rapporteurs and independent experts to Colombia can be said to have had even more visibility and perhaps a greater immediate impact on human rights protection, as discussed later in this paper.

Prevention of Human Rights Violations

One of the most successful overarching initiatives undertaken by the OHCHR office in Colombia is its effort to support the implementation of an 'Early Warning System' (SAT in Spanish) within the Office of the Ombudsman. This protection mechanism is intended to provide reliable documentation on imminent threats to civilian populations in the course of the armed conflict. The 2008 OHCHR annual report on Colombia recommended that the Government of Colombia strengthen the SAT. Thereafter, in 2009, Christian Salazar, the Representative of the High Commissioner in Colombia at the time, explicitly and publicly urged the Colombian government to allocate sufficient resources to strengthen the SAT, particularly through the development of new risk assessment measures, expressing the view that early warning was one of the best mechanisms to reduce massive displacement and protect the population from serious rights violations in the context of internal armed conflict.[28]

The OHCHR Colombia Office has also had a role in specific cases of prevention of human rights violations. One example of such a case is the urgent appeal made by the OHCHR office to the Colombian government, urging it to take measures to protect civilians in the department of Nariño. The Office urged the state to immediately take urgent measures to protect the life and integrity of the people in the area and their leaders.[29]

---

[28] Office of the High Commissioner for Human Rights in Colombia, "UN Office for the High Commissioner for Human Rights Recommends Strengthening of Early Warning System of the Ombudsman," [in Spanish] press release, June 17, 2009, http://www.hchr.org.co/publico/comunicados/2009/comunicados2009.php3?cod=16&cat=74.

[29] Office of the High Commissioner for Human Rights in Colombia, "UN Office of the High Commissioner for Human Rights Asks for Urgent Protection of the Cumitara

Support for the Universality of Human Rights

Rights of Vulnerable and Marginalized Communities

Colombia is a multicultural and multiethnic country experiencing a variety of human rights challenges. Over time, the OHCHR field office in Colombia has stressed to the Colombian government the need for it to ensure universal enjoyment of human rights, particularly in the time surrounding the UN General Assembly's adoption of the Declaration on the Rights of Indigenous Peoples in 2007, which former High Commissioner Louise Arbour called "a triumph for justice and human dignity."[30] OHCHR has also issued press releases commemorating the International Day of Indigenous People,[31] the World Conference against Racism, Racial Discrimination, Xenophobia and related Intolerance,[32] and the International Day for the Elimination of Racial Discrimination.[33]

Since 2005, the OHCHR Office in Colombia has commented on the impact of violence on indigenous people and has recommended that the government adopt measures to protect indigenous communities at risk of extinction. In response, the Presidential Human Rights Program engaged in greater interagency coordination at the national and territorial levels to protect indigenous communities at risk of extinction.

Promoting Ratification and Implementation by Colombia of UN Human Rights Treaties

The OHCHR office in Colombia also promotes universality of rights through its mandate to ensure that the country's laws and policies respect

Population in Nariño," [in Spanish] press release, September 16, 2011, http://www.hchr.org.co/publico/comunicados/2011/comunicados2011.php3?cod=17&cat=86.

30 Office of the High Commissioner for Human Rights in Colombia, "High Commissioner for Human Rights Louise Arbour hails adoption of Declaration of Indigenous Rights," [in Spanish], press release, September 13, 2007, http://www.hchr.org.co/publico/comunicados/2007/comunicados2007.php3?cod=32&cat=68.

31 Office of the High Commissioner for Human Rights in Colombia, "Communication for the Occasion of the Celebration of the International Day of Indigenous People," [in Spanish], press release, August 6, 1999, http://www.hchr.org.co/publico/comunicados/1999/comunicados1999.php3?cod=19&cat=20.

32 Office of the High Commissioner for Human Rights in Colombia, "Start of the World Conference Against Racism, Racial Discrimination, Xenophobia and Related Intolerance," [in Spanish] press release, August 31, 2001, http://www.hchr.org.co/publico/comunicados/2001/comunicados2001.php3?cod=13&cat=18.

33 Office of the High Commissioner for Human Rights in Colombia, "Message of the Managing Representative of the OHCHR on the International Day for the Elimination of

Colombia's international human rights obligations. The primary tactic that OHCHR has employed in this regard has been to promote popular awareness throughout the country of the human rights treaties to which Colombia is a party. For example, in 2010, to commemorate the adoption by the UN of the international treaty on disappearances, OHCHR issued a press release that emphasized the relevance of the convention to Colombia, both for victims and for the state, and encouraged Colombia's Congress to conclude its efforts to ratify the convention as quickly as possible in order to strengthen the state's efforts to combat the crime and enhance its capacity to prevent, investigate, and punish enforced disappearances.[34] Similarly, OHCHR called on the government of Colombia to ratify human rights treaties that it considers necessary to improve the protection of human rights domestically, such as in the 2011 annual report on Colombia by the High Commissioner for Human Rights, which recommended that the government "ratify pending international instruments, in particular the Optional Protocol to the Convention against Torture and Other Cruel, Inhuman or Degrading Treatment or Punishment, the Optional Protocol to the Convention on the Rights of Persons with Disabilities and the Optional Protocol to the International Covenant on Economic, Social and Cultural Rights...."[35]

Cooperation between the OHCHR and Other Entities

Colombian Government Agencies

The presence of OHCHR on the ground in Colombia has allowed it to establish strong working relationships with and contacts within key Colombian agencies. For example, since 2003, the Presidential Human Rights and International Humanitarian Law Program, a governmental advisory agency headed by the Vice President of Colombia, has been the key point of contact for OHCHR in the preparation of the High

---

Racial Discrimination," [in Spanish] press release, March 19, 2008, http://www.hchr.org.co/publico/comunicados/2008/comunicados2008.php3?cod=9&cat=73.

[34] Office of the High Commissioner for Human Rights in Colombia, "New Treaty on Forced Disappearances Ratified, but More Remains to Be Done: UN Experts Committee," [in Spanish] press release, December 23, 2010, http://www.hchr.org.co/publico/comunicados/2010/comunicados2010.php3?cod=40&cat=81.

[35] UN Human Rights Council, *Report of the United Nations High Commissioner for Human Rights on the situation of human rights in Colombia*, UN Doc. A/HRC/19/21/Add.3, January 31, 2012, para. 118.

Commissioner's Annual Report. This Program sends information to OHCHR on the activities undertaken by government agencies to advance the recommendations contained in those annual reports on at least a biannual basis.[36] Additionally, in 2009, OHCHR entered into a strategic cooperation agreement with the Ministry of Foreign Affairs of Colombia, key areas of which include the promotion of social dialogue on human rights to increase public awareness of the need for protection of human rights and prevention of violations and the implementation of public policies that encourage the state to comply with its obligations under international human rights and international humanitarian law.[37]

Coordination between OHCHR and Other UN Agencies

The OHCHR Office in Colombia has also carried out important coordination efforts with other UN actors, which has helped to leverage the Office's influence and to mainstream concern for human rights protection throughout all aspects of the UN's work in Colombia. For example, the Office was heavily involved in carrying out a Common Country Assessment of Colombia, and also participated actively in drawing up of the UN Development Assistance Framework for Colombia (2008–2012), which the Colombian government signed with representatives of all UN agencies and programs operating in Colombia in July 2007.[38] This Framework is a programming exercise intended to define the main areas on which the United Nations would focus its assistance to the country in the coming years; as a result of the Office's involvement, these main areas of focus include "the upholding of human rights, the strengthening of citizens' participation, the culture of rule of law and the strengthening of public management," with the goal of these efforts being for "State institutions at the national and territorial levels [to] denote an improvement in their effective and democratic functioning, in accordance with human rights norms

[36] República de Colombia, Derechos Humanos y DIH, "Presidential Human Rights and International Humanitarian Law Program," [in Spanish] http://www.derechoshumanos.gov.co/Programa/Paginas/AreasFuncionesEquipo.aspx.

[37] Office of the High Commissioner for Human Rights in Colombia, "Strategic Lines of Cooperation of the Colombia Office of the OHCHR," [in Spanish] press release, November 18, 2009, http://www.hchr.org.co/publico/comunicados/2009/comunicados2009.php3?cod=24&cat=74.

[38] UN Human Rights Council, *Report of the United Nations High Commissioner for Human rights on the situation of human rights in Colombia*, UN Doc. A/HRC/7/39, February 29, 2008, para. 89.

and principles with a vulnerable group and gender focus."[39] This Framework was agreed to not only by the Colombian Minister for Foreign Affairs and OHCHR, but also by diverse UN agencies including the High Commissioner for Refugees, the UN Development Programme, the World Food Programme, and the UN Population Fund.

OHCHR has also cooperated with other UN entities through the "UN House in Soacha" and "House of Rights in Soacha," established in 2005 and principally coordinated by UNDP. The UN House is an inter-agency field office designed to improve coordination between the many UN agencies carrying out projects in the area, which has one of the highest concentrations of internally displaced persons in the country.

OHCHR's Support for Other UN Human Rights Bodies and Mechanisms

One key way in which OHCHR has assisted other UN human rights mechanisms investigating Colombia is to support the visits of special procedure mandate-holders to Colombia, including the visit of the UN Working Group on Enforced Disappearances in 2005, the visit of the UN Expert on the Independence of Judges and Lawyers in 2009, the visit of the UN Expert on Minority Issues in 2010, the visit of the Special Rapporteur on the rights of indigenous peoples in 2010, and the visit of the UN Special Rapporteur on extrajudicial executions in 2010. The main role of OHCHR in these visits has been to provide information on the situation of human rights in advance of the visit and to prepare a schedule of interviews in the field, including by securing facilities for meetings, communications, and transportation.

The existence of the OHCHR office in Colombia has also allowed the High Commissioners for Human Rights to call for greater attention by the Colombian government to the implementation of recommendations made to it by UN human rights treaty bodies and special procedures.

OHCHR's Provision of Technical Assistance

OHCHR signed a cooperation agreement with the Colombian Senate on December 18, 2002 allowing it to advise Congress on the protection and

---

39 UN System in Colombia, *United Nations Development Assistance Framework 2008–2012*, July 23, 2007, 5, http://nacionesunidas.org.co/wp-content/uploads/2012/03/Marco-Asistencia-Ingles-17-VII.pdf.

defense of human rights and international humanitarian law. Pursuant to this agreement, in 2003 OHCHR made comments and suggestions on draft constitutional amendments to combat terrorism, opposing language that would increase the risk that human rights defenders and trade unionists would be subject to arbitrary investigation and arrest on the grounds that they had engaged in 'subversive' activities. OHCHR also provided observations on the draft law on the reintegration of members of armed groups in 2003, noting the risk that the law would provide impunity for serious violations of human rights and international humanitarian law committed by former combatants. OHCHR also commented on the Justice and Peace Law in 2005 and criticized a draft law on restitution for victims in 2008 on the grounds that it discriminated between groups of victims.[40]

Protecting Human Rights Defenders

Defenders of human rights, including activists, trade unionists, and lawyers have been particularly affected by the structural violence and armed conflict in Colombia, and since its establishment, the OHCHR field presence in Colombia has placed particular emphasis on issuing public statements denouncing violations of the rights of human rights defenders. For example, in 1999, OHCHR condemned the brutal murder of three human rights activists,[41] and it has issued similar condemnations of abuses against human rights defenders almost every year since. In 2008, OHCHR also condemned attacks on the offices of human rights defenders and trade unionists in Arauca.[42] In doing so, OHCHR called on the

---

[40] The text stipulates additional requirements in order for the victims of human rights violations to have access to administrative reparation. Office of the High Commissioner for Human Rights in Colombia, "The Office of the High Commissioner for Human Rights Deplores a Discrimination in 'Victims' Law'," [in Spanish] press release, November 14, 2008, http://www.hchr.org.co/publico/comunicados/2008/comunicados2008.php3?cod=26&cat=73.

[41] The victims were Ingrid Washinawatok, a member of the Menominee Nation of Wisconsin, Lahe'ene'e Gay, a native of Hawaii and Director of International Culture Pacifica Conservatory, and Terence Freitas, from the Defense Working Group Uw'a. Their bodies were found on March 4, 1999, blindfolded and handcuffed with several shots to their heads. The victims were kidnapped on February 25 during a visit to Colombia supporting the Uw'a's indigenous population fighting against oil exploration in its territories. Office of the High Commissioner for Human Rights in Colombia, "Condemnation for the Brutal Assassination of Three Activists in Colombia," [in Spanish] press release, March 9, 1999, http://www.hchr.org.co/publico/comunicados/1999/comunicados1999.php3?cod=5&cat=20.

[42] Office of the High Commissioner for Human Rights in Colombia, "Condemnation for the Attack on Headquarters of Human Rights Defenders and Trade unionists in Arauca,"

Colombian government to ensure the effective operation of a Ministry of Interior and Justice program to protect human rights defenders and to require to the General Attorney to investigate and apply disciplinary sanctions to agents who jeopardize the work of human rights defenders and lawyers; and urged the Attorney General's Office to verify the accuracy and objectivity of the information contained in military intelligence files on human rights defenders and to publish the result of that verification exercise.[43] OHCHR also called on the Attorney General's office to ensure that all allegations of human rights violations were independently, effectively, and impartially investigated.

The Role and Impact of the High Commissioners for Human Rights on Human Rights in Colombia

The personal visits of the UN High Commissioners for Human Rights to Colombia have had an impact on the protection of human rights in the country. Several of the individuals to hold the post of High Commissioner have visited Colombia.[44] During these visits, the High Commissioners have had meetings to discuss a range of human rights concerns with highest civilian and military authorities in the country, including the president, senior ministers, members of the judiciary, and other national and local authorities in Bogota and elsewhere. The High Commissioners have also met with civil society representatives (members of vulnerable groups, victims' associations and trade unions; human rights defenders; and other groups).

On these visits, the High Commissioners regularly identify human rights situations of concern, but they also refer to progress made to promote accountability and respect for human rights by government agencies and the armed forces. For example, the current High Commissioner, Ms. Navi Pillay, visited Colombia in 2008 and during that visit, she expressed concern that while Colombia had made progress in

[in Spanish] press release, November 21, 2008, http://www.hchr.org.co/publico/comunicados/2008/comunicados2008.php3?cod=28&cat=73.

43 Office of the High Commissioner for Human Rights in Colombia, "Importance of Protection of Human Rights Defenders," [in Spanish] press release, September 17, 2003, http://www.hchr.org.co/publico/comunicados/2003/comunicados2003.php3?cod=27&cat=16.

44 Mary Robinson visited Colombia from October 20–22, 1998 and December 3–4, 2000; Louise Arbour visited from September 7–9, 2007; and Navi Pillay visted from October 27-November 1, 2008.

implementing human rights policies, grave human rights challenges remained. In this regard, she made recommendations to the government that were explicit and vehement, in diplomatic language, but without euphemisms. However, she also acknowledged the efforts made by the Government to protect vulnerable groups in a country facing such a complex and multifaceted conflict.

One aspect of the High Commissioners' practice when visiting Colombia has been to hold press conferences. At a press conference held during her visit, High Commissioner Pillay made several critical statements about the serious human rights situation, including characterizing the "systematic, protracted and widespread taking of hostages" as a possible crime against humanity; urging the Ministry of Defense to move away from 'counting bodies' as criteria of success in their operations and expressing support for the recent dismissal of Army Officers, including three Generals, for failure to exercise proper control over those under their command; calling for the expedited implementation of the Justice and Peace Law to ensure justice for all victims; and for the government to avoid *de facto* amnesties for past and current serious human rights abuses and to ensure that respect for the rights of victims remain at the core of any demobilization policy. The High Commissioner also suggested that victims should be able to benefit from a land restitution program and that victims of illegal groups as well as state agents should benefit equally from such a program, specifically noting the draft law on reparation for victims being debated in the Colombian Congress as an opportunity for progress.[45]

Analysis of the Impact of OHCHR and the UN High Commissioner for Human Rights on Human Rights in Colombia

Over the course of the past 14 years, in part due to the efforts of the OHCHR field presence in Colombia, the Colombian government has adopted important political and legislative measures to address human rights violations. These include the ongoing creation of a public policy consistent with international human rights and humanitarian law, including through the adoption and implementation of the Victims and Land Restitution

[45] Office of the High Commissioner for Human Rights in Colombia, "UN High Commissioner for Human Rights concludes visit to Colombia," press release, November 1, 2008.

Act, which does not exclude victims of violations perpetrated by agents of the state; the creation of a new National Protection Agency to replace the Administrative Security Department; and the initiation of a process of dialogue between the government and civil society on protection guarantees for human rights defenders.[46] As a result, the relationship between the government – particularly the executive and judicial branches – and NGOs has significantly improved, as have the government's efforts to combat impunity.

However, many serious problems remain: gross human rights violations remain persistent; both FARC and ELP continue to take hostages; new, extremely violent illegal armed groups have emerged, despite efforts to demobilize paramilitary organizations, and they too are engaging in organized crime; thirteen Congressmen have been investigated for alleged links to paramilitary groups; the government, and specifically the Administrative Security Department, has carried out illegal communications surveillance; the number of individuals making applications under the Justice and Peace Law has diminished; and although a National Commission for Reparation and Reconciliation has been established pursuant to the Justice and Peace Law, it is not fully consistent with the Chicago Principles on Transitional Justice, as it purports to apply only mild sanctions for very serious violations of human rights.

In the coming years, a particular challenge to the High Commissioner for Human Rights and the OHCHR field presence in Colombia will be pressing for the effective, fair, and sustainable implementation of the Victims and Land Restitution Act by the government. This will involve preventing and combating threats and attacks against claimants and/or government officials involved in the process; providing technical assistance to the government so that it can build a comprehensive national policy to protect the land restitution process and technical training of agrarian judges on international human rights standards; and the carrying out of a planned national campaign on the rights to protection and restitution as a joint endeavor of OHCHR, UNHCR, and the Catholic Church.

The work of OHCHR has been most visible to the Colombian public in the media. Press releases of the Office have been particularly valuable in this regard, but the Annual Reports of the High Commissioner for Human Rights have also had an impact on public policy in the country and have

---

[46] The new office has a mandate to improve the investigation of crimes within a framework of increased vigilance and respect for human rights of persons under investigation.

pressed successive governments to take action to resolve structural human rights problems.

OHCHR has made use of its presence in Colombia to promote the protection human rights in Colombia, including by carrying out its own investigations of alleged human rights violations. While these have been valuable, OHCHR has recognized that it cannot serve as a substitute for or replace national institutions. Thus, OHCHR has most frequently sought to serve as an independent voice on the human rights situation in Colombia, attempting to affect the policies and practices of the government through public denunciation of violations, based on its observations through its presence on the ground, and through the documentation of human rights violations in press releases and reports. OHCHR has also proposed prevention initiatives and worked with a variety of stakeholders on issues such as justice, security, and the rights of vulnerable groups. In the future, OHCHR's contributions to the development of Colombian public policy on human rights, and its work to facilitate social dialogue on these important issues, will be of particular importance.

SELECTED BIBLIOGRAPHY

OHCHR Documents

Reports of the High Commissioner to the General Assembly

2012: A/67/36
2011: A/66/36
2010: A/65/36
2009: A/64/36
2008: A/63/36
2007: A/62/36
2006: A/61/36
2005: A/60/36
2004: A/59/36
2003: A/58/36
2002: A/57/36
2001: A/56/36
2000: A/55/36
1999: A/54/36
1998: A/53/36
1997: A/52/36
1996: A/51/36
1995: A/50/36
1994: A/49/36

Annual Reports of the Office of the High Commissioner for Human Rights (2000–2011)

All available at http://www.ohchr.org/EN/PUBLICATIONSRESOURCES/Pages/AnnualReportAppeal.aspx.

Plan of Action by the United Nations High Commissioner for Human Rights

UN General Assembly, *In larger freedom: towards development, security and human rights for all,"* Report of the Secretary-General, Addendum 3, UN Doc. A/59/2005/Add.3, May 26 2005.

Management Plans of the Office of the High Commissioner for Human Rights (2006–2007, 2008–2009, 2010–2011, 2012–2013)

All available at http://www.ohchr.org/EN/PUBLICATIONSRESOURCES/Pages/AnnualReportAppeal.aspx.

Remarks of the High Commissioners

Statement by the High Commissioner of Human Rights delivered by José Ayala-Lasso at the Plenary of the Fourth World Conference on Women, Beijing, China, September 4–15, 1995, http://www.un.org/esa/gopher-data/conf/fwcw/conf/una/950906124120.txt.

Statement by UN High Commissioner for Human Rights Navi Pillay at the Human Rights Council 18th Special Session to Examine the Situation of Human Rights in the Syrian Arab Republic," Office of the High Commissioner for Human Rights, December 2, 2011.

Other OHCHR Documents

Louise Arbour, *Concept Paper on the High Commissioner's Proposal for a Unified Standing Treaty Body*, UN Doc. HRI/MC/2006/CRP.1, March 14, 2006.

Navi Pillay, *Strengthening the United Nations human Rights Treaty Body System: A Report by the United Nations High Commissioner for Human Rights*, June 2012, http://www2.ohchr.org/english/bodies/HRTD/docs/HCreportonTBstrengthening210612.doc.

Office of the High Commissioner for Human Rights, *Nepal Conflict Report 2012*, http://www.ohchr.org/Documents/Countries/NP/OHCHR_Nepal_Conflict_Report2012.pdf.

Office of the High Commissioner for Human Rights, "Pillay presents groundbreaking UN study on violence, discrimination against people because of their sexual orientation," March 7, 2012.

Other Documents

UN General Assembly, Resolution 48/141, *High Commissioner for the Promotion and Protection of All Human Rights*, UN Doc. A/RES/48/141, December 20, 1993.

Report of the Secretary-General, *Strengthening of the United Nations: an agenda for further change*, UN Doc. A/57/387, September 9, 2002.

World Conference on Human Rights, *Vienna Declaration and Programme of Action*, UN Doc. A/CONF.157/22, July 12, 1993, Part I, para. 5.

Afghanistan Independent Human Rights Commission, *A Call for Justice*, January 25, 2005 http://www.aihrc.org.af/en/research-reports/752/a-call-for-justice.html.

Fourth World Conference on Women, *Beijing Declaration and Platform for Action*, Annex I, UN Doc. A/CONF.177/20 (1995) and A/CONF.177/20/Add.1 (1995), September 15, 1995.

UN Commission on Human Rights, *Situation of human rights in the Darfur region of the Sudan*, UN Doc. E/CN.4/2005/3, May 7, 2004.

UN Commission on Human Rights, *Study of the High Commissioner for Human Rights on procedures for ensuring implementation of, and follow-up to recommendations of special rapporteurs/representatives, experts and working groups*, UN Doc. E/CN.4/1999/3/Add.1, July 31, 1998.

UN Human Rights Council, *Report of the United Nations High Commissioner for Human Rights on the Human Rights Situation in Afghanistan and Technical Assistance Achievements in the Field of Human Rights*, UN Doc. A/HRC/19/47, January 18, 2012.

UN Human Rights Council, *Report of the United Nations High Commissioner for Human Rights on the situation of human rights in Colombia*, UN Doc. A/HRC/19/21/Add.3, January 31, 2012.

UN Human Rights Council, *Report of the United Nations High Commissioner for Human Rights on the Situation of Human Rights in the Syrian Arab Republic*, UN Doc. A/HRC/18/53, September 15, 2011.

Report of the Secretary-General, *Cooperation with the United Nations, Its Representatives and Mechanisms in the Field of Human Rights*, UN Doc. A/HRC/21/18, August 13, 2012.

Books and Articles

Alston, Philip. "Hobbling the Monitors: Should U.N. Human Rights Monitors be Accountable?" *Harvard International Law Journal* 52 (2011).

Alston, Philip. "Neither Fish nor Fowl: The Quest to Define the Role of the UN High Commissioner for Human Rights." *European Journal of International Law* 8.2 (1997).

Aspen Institute. *Honoring Human Rights*. Edited by Alice H. Henkin. 3 vols. The Hague: Kluwer Law International, 2000.

Ayala-Lasso, José. "Defining the Mandate: New UN Efforts to Protect Human Rights." *Harvard International Review* Winter (1994–95).

Bassiouni, M.C., and W.A. Schabas, eds. *New Challenges for the Human Rights Machinery.* Portland: Intersentia, 2011.

Bayefsky, Anne. *The UN Human Rights Treaty System: Universality at the Crossroads*. The Hague: Kluwer Academic Publishers, 2001.

Blaustein, Jacob. "Human Rights: A Challenge to the United Nations and to Our Generation, Dag Hammarskjold Memorial Lecture," (lecture, Columbia University, New York City, NY, December 4, 1963). Reprinted in *The Quest for Peace: The Dag Hammarskjold Memorial Lectures,* edited by A. Cordier and W. Foote, 315, 318–319. 1965.

Clapham, Andrew. "Creating the High Commissioner for Human Rights: The Outside Story." *European Journal of International Law* 5 (1994).

Clapham, Andrew. "UN High Commissioner for Human Rights: Achievements and Frustrations." Paper presented at the Symposium on the United Nations High Commissioner for Human Rights: The First Ten Years of Office and the Next, Columbia Law School, NY (February 17–18, 2003). http://www2.law.columbia.edu/hri/symposium/ClaphamPaper.htm.

Clark, Roger Stenson. *A United Nations High Commissioner for Human Rights.* The Hague: Martinus Nijhoff, 1972.

Gaer, Felice. "A New UN High Commissioner for Human Rights: Meeting the Challenge," JBI Human Rights Information Paper, March 2008.

Gaer, Felice. "The United Nations High Commissioner for Human Rights: The Challenges of International Protection." *The American Journal of International Law* 98 (2004).

Gaer, Felice. "NGOs and the UN High Commissioner for Human Rights." In *Human Rights, The United Nations and Nongovernmental Organizations*. The Carter Center, 1997.

Goodman, Ryan and Thomas Pegram, eds. *Human Rights, State Compliance, and Social Change: Assessing National Human Rights Institutions*. New York: Cambridge University Press, 2012.

Howland, Todd. "Mirage Magic, or Mixed Bag?: The United Nations High Commissioner for Human Rights' Field Operation in Rwanda." *Human Rights Quarterly* 21, no. 1 (1999).

Human Rights Watch, *Protectors or Pretenders? Government Human Rights Commissions in Africa.* New York: Human Rights Watch, 2001.

Koh, Harold Hongju. "A Job Description for the U.N. High Commissioner for Human Rights." *Columbia Human Rights Law Review* 35 (2004).

Korey, William. "The 'Diplomatic Approach' vs. the 'Human Rights Approach': The High Commissioner for Human Rights, and the Blaustein Institute." In *NGOs and the Universal Declaration of Human Rights, 'A Curious Grapevine,'* by William Korey. New York: Palgrave, 1998.

Lynch, Colum, "U.N. Human Rights Chief to Leave Post," *Washington Post*, March 3, 2008.

Nossel, Suzanne. "Advancing Human Rights in the UN System." *Council on Foreign Relations International Institutions and Global Governance Program Working Paper*, (2012).

O'Flaherty, Michael. "Human Rights Field Operations: An Introductory Analysis." In *The Human Rights Field Operation: Law, Theory and Practice*, edited by Michael O'Flaherty, 30. London: Ashgate Publishing, Ltd., 2007.

O'Flaherty, Michael. "Reform of the UN Human Rights Treaty Body System: Locating the Dublin Statement." *Human Rights Law Review* 10.2 (2010): 319–335.

O'Flaherty, Michael and George Ulrich. "The Professionalization of Human Rights Field Work." *Journal of Human Rights Practice* 2, no. 1 (2010).

O'Neill, William. *Guiding Principles for Human Rights Field Officers Working in Conflict and Post-conflict Environments.* Nottingham: Human Rights Law Centre, University of Nottingham, 2009.

Piccone, Ted. *Catalysts for Change: How the UN's Independent Experts Promote Human Rights*. Washington, DC: Brookings Institution Press, 2012.

Pinheiro, Paulo Sergio. "Being a Special Rapporteur: a delicate balancing act." *International Journal of Human Rights* 15, no. 2, (2011).

Power, Samantha. *Chasing the Flame: Sergio Vieira de Mello and the Fight to Save the World*. New York: Penguin Press, 2008.

Price, Megan, Jeff Klingner, and Patrick Ball. "Preliminary Statistical Analysis of Documentation of Killings in the Syrian Arab Republic," *The Benetech Human Rights Program*, (2013).

Ramcharan, B.G. *The United Nations High Commissioner for Human Rights: The Challenges of International Protection*. The Hague: Martinus Nijhoff, 2002.

Ramcharan, B.G. *A UN High Commissioner in Defence of Human Rights*. Leiden: Brill, 2004.

Ramcharan, B.G. *Preventive Human Rights Strategies*. Oxon: Taylor & Francis, 2010.

Robinson, Mary and Kevin Boyle, eds. *A Voice for Human Rights*. Philadelphia: University of Pennsylvania Press, 2006.

Robinson, Mary. *Everybody Matters: A Memoir*. London: Hodder & Stoughton, 2012.

"The Promise of the United Nations High Commissioner for Human Rights," outcome document from *The UN and Human Rights*, convened by the Human Rights Program of the Carter Center and the Jacob Blaustein Institute for the Advancement of Human Rights, June 4–6, 1995.

INDEX

www.ingramcontent.com/pod-product-compliance
Lightning Source LLC
LaVergne TN
LVHW020650300926
849161LV00004B/881